INTERNATIONAL BUSINESS
STRATEGY IN COMPLEX MARKETS

INTERNATIONAL BUSINESS STRATEGY IN COMPLEX MARKETS

HANS JANSSON

Linnaeus University, Sweden

Edward Elgar
PUBLISHING

Cheltenham, UK · Northampton, MA, USA

Published by
Edward Elgar Publishing Limited
The Lypiatts
15 Lansdown Road
Cheltenham
Glos GL50 2JA
UK

Edward Elgar Publishing, Inc.
William Pratt House
9 Dewey Court
Northampton
Massachusetts 01060
USA

A catalogue record for this book
is available from the British Library

Library of Congress Control Number: 2020932139

ISBN 978 1 83910 181 6 (cased)
ISBN 978 1 83910 183 0 (paperback)
ISBN 978 1 83910 182 3 (eBook)

Printed and bound in Great Britain by TJ International Ltd, Padstow, Cornwall

CONTENTS

FIGURES

TABLES

PREFACE

This book is about how multinational corporations (MNCs) from mature European markets solve the different strategic business problems encountered in complex emerging markets during the Third wave of internationalization of firms. These have been key markets for MNCs since the 1990s. Moreover, a greater number of new MNCs have emerged from these countries and intensified competition in the global market. There are still few books about international strategic business problems grounded directly in the specific business conditions prevailing in such multifaceted and turbulent markets. Almost all books are largely based on the notion that business across the world is done in a similar way as in mature Western markets. A narrow view is taken by concentrating on traditional market actors such as customers and competitors. The major distinction between mature Western markets and emerging markets lies in their very different business environments. A typical textbook, for example in international business and marketing, international management or strategic management, under-estimates this problem and devotes only one or a few chapters to the macro environment of the firm. These chapters are also highly descriptive and not founded in any theory about the various types of international environments. Another aspect of this myopic view is that most literature is based on a shareholder view of international strategy, where profitability is the dominant goal of the MNC. This book is instead based on a stakeholder perspective, where the MNC is part of society. The purpose is to have a sustainable business, not only creating economic values but also social and ecological values. The dramatically increasing importance of natural environmental issues is considered by integrating them into the strategy models as a natural part of the international business strategy. New strategic tools are developed, for example the sustainable business triangle.

The book integrates the shareholder and stakeholder perspectives into a holistic perspective on international business strategy based on a broader societal approach. A comprehensive, integrated and pragmatic analytical framework to international business strategy is outlined and defined as the network institutional approach. The framework has been developed to be valid for complex international business environments in general, and not only for a particular country or region. Since MNCs today are active in many markets, frameworks are needed that make it possible for them to compare and learn from the strategies performed under the different conditions prevailing in various country markets around the world. This is also a basic requirement for a book intended for graduate courses in international business, strategic management and marketing. The book has been written for those who want to learn about business strategies in socially complex and dynamic foreign business environments such as emerging markets and developing countries. But the book is also quickly becoming more relevant for mature Western markets that are now under-going large changes due to increasing conflicts within and between them. The flattening of the world economy is reversing, the economy heading back to its previous, more spikey world. The Coronavirus 2019 pandemic seems to be the tipping point to considerably intensify this 'avalanche' of disintegrating economies. Above all, it demonstrates the paramount importance of studying the social and ecological issues of international business, especially as the pandemic has spread from the natural environment through the wildlife markets of the economic environment to the social environment.

This advanced textbook differs from textbooks at the undergraduate level by being more research oriented. To update the reader about theoretical developments over time, historical reviews are made of the research areas of relevance to the subject of the book. Such international business research is summarized in Chapter 4, general strategy research in Chapter 5, and the network view and business marketing in Chapter 7. A review is also given in the appendix of the evolvement of institutional theory since the beginning of the 20th century.

The purpose is to provide perspectives, backgrounds, insights and outlooks on a broad academic audience, including students, lecturers and researchers. Practicians such as managers and consultants will also find much to interest them, especially since there are few books that take a comparative holistic approach to international business strategy in complex global markets. Since readers are assumed to vary in their interest and background, a suggested reading route is proposed below for each of four major groups of readers: the master's student, the teacher, the researcher/doctoral student, and the management consultant/general manager.

TO THE MASTER'S STUDENT

If you are a graduate student who has experience of practical life, most probably a major reason for you to take a master's course is that you have realized that you need to develop your understanding of strategic issues in international business and to improve your analytical skills. Today's hectic business life in dynamic and complicated markets provides few opportunities to develop skills in dealing with long-term strategic issues, but rich opportunities to deal with the short-term tactical issues continuously emerging.

If you are a master's student with limited practical experience, you will benefit from the book in a different way. In particular, it will provide you with insights into the peculiarities of today's complex and turbulent global business world and enhance your understanding of how business is done there from a strategic perspective. Besides providing you with models for your studies and research on such markets, you will learn more about how to apply theories to real-life situations.

As a master's student you are already familiar with many business subjects. But to remind and update you on more recent developments, overviews are provided of relevant theoretical fields. Since the book is mainly written for the master's student, you are supposed to read the chapters in the order they appear. The Appendix is meant for those who want to gain further insight into the institutional theories on which many frameworks developed in the book are built.

TO THE TEACHER

This book is intended to be used in graduate-level courses in international business, international strategy and strategic international business marketing. It is based on the premise that students already have basic knowledge in these fields, normally acquired from undergraduate courses on these and related subjects. The book has therefore been written for the more advanced master's students and for the learning situations they face. It is mainly aimed at seminar-type courses, where students work more independently on their own or in a small group and where facilitation of the learning process is more important than lecturing. The focus is on interactive dialogue between students and teacher. The book is therefore best used in application-based courses, where learning from doing live cases or analysing ready-made cases are preferred to traditional root-learning and formal written examinations. The purpose is to develop the master's student's understanding of the particular circumstances in which business is done in the long term in complicated and irregular international business environments. The purpose is also to develop the analytical skills of the student. Describing, understanding, analysing and recommending are the key processes in developing analytical capacity. The simple short-lived solutions presented in many textbooks at undergraduate level are not so relevant for the very complex strategic environments of most international markets. The book contains a research-based framework meant for understanding and analysing business problems in such markets. The chapters are summarized at the end of Chapter 1, this outline being depicted in Figure 1.2.

Teachers at undergraduate level should mainly benefit from the book as a major source for their own teaching, providing models and examples that make them better equipped to teach these subjects at this more basic level. The layout of the chapters is mainly built on the major pedagogical ideas behind it, as referred to above.

TO THE RESEARCHER/DOCTORAL STUDENT

This book will give you knowledge of international business strategy in highly uncertain foreign markets and insights into the specific conditions under which strategy is conducted under such circumstances. It will provide you with a new approach to international business and international business strategy, an integrated theoretical framework based on a societal perspective containing a number of ideas and theories to base research on. You will also benefit from the summaries of the theoretical developments in social science fields of increasing relevance for business research in general such as network theory and institutional theory. For the strategy researcher in general, the book should be of special relevance if you are interested in the social side of strategy, for example legitimacy and corporate social responsibility issues and how the resource-based view of strategy can be developed to consider social issues and institutional change.

TO THE MANAGEMENT CONSULTANT/MANAGER

If you have business experience from complex and turbulent business environments such as emerging markets, you know very well that a broader approach is required to business in these markets, which demands improved social skills. As a manager, you have also most probably found that you have even less time to think about why this is so and to ponder about the long-term implications for the company. You have also probably realized the strategic importance of social and ecological issues in these countries, for example that natural environmental issues, social responsibility and good relations with governments are critical for achieving competitive advantages. This book will provide you with frameworks and strategic tools for being able to reflect on and increase your understanding of strategic issues like these. It is especially relevant if you have experience from more than one country market and want to compare these experiences. However, you should not be hesitant to read this more demanding and abstract text that distinguishes itself from the easily digestible text of many management books found in airports and mainly meant for jet-lagged managers.

MERGER OF TWO PREVIOUS BOOKS

This book is the second edition of two previous textbooks by this author, which were first published by Edward Elgar in 2007, namely *International Business Strategy in Emerging Country Markets: The Institutional Network Approach* (the IBS book) and *International Business Marketing in Emerging Country Markets: The Third Wave of Internationalization of Firms* (the IBM book). These two books have been consolidated into this new book *International Business Strategy in Complex Markets* as follows. Chapters 1–4, 7 and 16 are new. Chapters 5–6 are reworked versions of Chapter 3 in the IBS book, while Chapters 8–10 are new versions of Chapters 3, 4 and 6 in the IBM book. Chapters 11–15 build on the following chapters in the IBS book: 11 on 2, 12 on 5, 13 on 4, 14 on 6, and 15 on 7.

THE IMAGES

The photographs of the book are taken by the author. More wildlife photos from various parts of the world are found on my website: https://globalwingsphoto.com.

ACKNOWLEDGEMENTS

I want to express my deep gratitude to all my students of the master's programmes in international business strategy and international marketing who have contributed a lot to this book and helped me with it in many ways over the years, especially the students at Linnaeus University and Gothenburg University. This book builds on my two previous books *International Business Strategy in Emerging Country Markets: The Institutional Network Approach* and *International Business Marketing in Emerging Country Markets: The Third Wave of Internationalization of Firms*, both first published by Edward Elgar Publishing in 2007, which I started to write during my time as Professor of International Business at Gothenburg University.

In particular, I want to thank my present and previous colleagues at the School of Business and Economics, Linnaeus University for their continuous assistance in suggesting new literature, reading and discussing various versions of the book, namely Richard Owusu, Susanne Sandberg, Per Servais and Bertil Hultén. I also want to thank Mikael Hilmersson, now at the School of Business, Economics and Law, Gothenburg University, for his valuable advice and comments on the drafts. A great deal of thanks goes to my 'senior' colleague Sten Söderman at the School of Business, Stockholm University. The many discussions during our joint research projects on international business in China and on the strategic behaviour of football clubs have contributed a lot to the book. Many thanks and appreciation also go to my son Erick Löfdahl for his highly professional editing of the figures and tables of the book.

Of course, the rest of my family also deserves a special mention. I extend my warmest thanks to my wife Carina, and daughter Emma. As in the past, they were again very understanding of the demands of a scholary pursuit of this nature, and were a constant source of support and encouragement.

PART I

THE SOCIETAL PERSPECTIVE

Do storks supply babies?

Yes! This was confirmed in research done on statistics from Germany and the Netherlands, by correlating the number of babies being born in houses with storks on the roof in one study with the development of the stork population in another. This demonstrates that correlation is not causation, providing an example of spurious correlation. This association between storks and fertility is an old myth that goes back to the 18th century in Germany. Storks come back from Africa in spring just in time to deliver babies roughly nine months after the main baby-making time around midsummer. So even if this local myth is false, the international lifestyle of the white stork, as a long-distance migrating bird wintering in Sub-Saharan Africa, is true. The European stork population is divided into two groups, easterly and westerly, reflecting the two migration routes they take. These storks were once very abundant in southernmost Sweden. The decline of the species started in the middle of the 19th century, coinciding with the onset of the dramatic change in the agricultural landscape. The reconstruction of the 'landscape of the stork' to bring them back is a significant driving force in many ongoing restoration projects.

1
The network institutional approach to international business strategy

The international business context is organized in different ways, for example as markets, various private, public and political organizations, associations, states, federations, free-trade areas, and similar types of economic and political cooperation. This book is mainly about firms organized as multinational corporations (MNCs) doing international business with other firms and consumers in a foreign national market. This market context is defined as the economic environment of the firm, since the goals of the actors are mainly economical such as profitability and efficiency. But firms also depend on organizations outside the market, for example the government and other non-profit organizations. This part of the foreign context is defined as the social environment, since the goals of such organizations are oriented towards the social needs of the citizens.

The complexity of the international business environment has increased more lately, because the bio-physical limits of planet Earth are now being exceeded, as shown by climate change, mass extinction of species, considerably more disastrous pandemics, deforestation and pollution of the oceans. Historically, nature has been viewed as a threat by man. But the tables have turned and man has become a threat to nature. The increasing natural destruction is hitting back, however, threatening to considerably lower the living standards of future generations and even make Earth uninhabitable. The strategic importance of the natural–societal environment linkage has, there-fore, increased greatly during the 2000s.

The foreign country context is described by dividing it into three levels. The immediate envi-ronment of the MNC consists of groups of firms organized at the meso level, for example a part of the market such as a specific product market or in a national province. The organization of all firms in a country, on the other hand, takes place at the macro level. The internal organization of the in-dividual MNC takes place at the micro level. MNCs also need to relate themselves to organizations outside the foreign national market, for example organizations in the supranational environment such as the European Union (EU).

The multifaceted and diverse international business context does not stay constant but involves a lot of sudden changes, that is, it is turbulent. For example, a foreign market is often perceived as a kind of organized chaos. It works despite the fact that there seems to be a lot of confusion and no organization. This environmental complexity then concerns the state of things at a certain point in time. It also concerns erratic changes or turbulence, which relates to flows or processes over time. The supranational environment is even more complex. At present, for example, we could be in the midst of turbulent times of changing network structures implying a great environmental shift from a long period of globalization of continuously increasing world trade and foreign direct investment (FDI) to a period of decline and deglobalization. This major cataclysm may end the latest major growth period that began at the beginning of the 1990s, when the former centrally planned and other heavily regulated economies, such as China, India, Mexico, Brazil and most Central and Eastern European (CEE) countries, started to become liberalized and integrated into the global capitalistic market economy.

This complex contemporary dynamic international external set-up of the MNC encompasses a multitude of changing economic and non-economic actors. All activities undertaken by the MNC are related to this local and global environment, within which the enterprise finds its profit-generating market opportunities. The international competitiveness of MNCs depends on their skills and competences to relate these activities to foreign environments, that is, how well they relate to and learn from their environment. The internal environment of the MNC has also become more complex with the increasing globalization of the firms, making it harder to effectively execute international business strategy (IBS).

To cope with the uncertainty caused by this complex global environment, it is necessary to have a broad societal perspective on international business strategy. It is specified further to consist of a network view and an institutional view, which are combined into the network institutional approach (NIA). Based on the NIA, this chapter introduces the major strategic business problems discussed in the book, followed by the international business strategy and its substrategies: the international network strategy (INS) and international matching strategy (IMS). The IBS is based on the demands of stakeholders representing the three types of environments: economic, social and natural. To achieve a sustainable business, MNCs need to create an effective mix of economic values with stakeholders in the economic environment, social values in the social environment and ecological values in the natural environment. An outline of the book completes the chapter.

THE SOCIETAL PERSPECTIVE

International business research shows that the external international business context has become much more complex during the latest growth and liberalization period referred to above, stressing even more the high dependency of firms upon their environment (Jansson, 2007a, b; Meyer and Peng, 2016; Kostova and Hult, 2016). For example, the complexity of economic and institutional conditions remains high in CEE due to the fact that the market reforms have succeeded differently (Berry et al., 2014). Only those countries that have joined the EU have transformed themselves into full market economies. This book therefore addresses an issue of high current interest in international business research, namely the need for an integrated theoretical perspective on the external environment itself. In developing this perspective, the book analyses the diversity and turbulence of the external environment. It also looks at how the environment impacts firms and firms the environment from a strategic point of view. This context aspect is underdeveloped due to the fact that most research treats the external environment in a superficial way, with many parts of it even being ignored. As will be examined further in Chapter 4, the major reason for this is that traditional international business research has been on the mature market economies in Western Europe and North America, where the focus is on the most immediate economic environment, mainly the industry, where the firm operates. The firms in such economies can concentrate on the economic side of business, since the wider societal environment beyond the economic environment is quite alike between these countries. For example, governments normally take a back seat and control the economy indirectly through similar regulations and standards. The strong influence from economics also explains the focus on narrow and specific questions. Therefore, it is no surprise that international business research during the latest growth period has been increasingly focused on studying the wider societal environment and its impact on firms, involving broader societal issues of the social environment. Due to the high strategic importance of the natural environment, it is added to the economic and social environments as a key strategic context for the firm.

The societal perspective puts the MNC in its international context. As introduced above, this local and global international business environment is divided into the economic, social and natural environment. And as illustrated in Figure 1.1, the three environments are analysed at the supranational level (e.g. as groups of emerging and mature markets) and three levels of national context: macro (e.g. political system), meso (e.g. product/service market) and micro (mainly the MNC). The network institutional approach is applied to these environments, for example as a global industrial network (GIN) at the supranational level, a government network at the national level, an industrial business network at the meso level and an international network strategy at the micro level.

The organization of units at one national level is then dependent upon how a larger number of units are organized at the next level and the organization at the highest national level. This

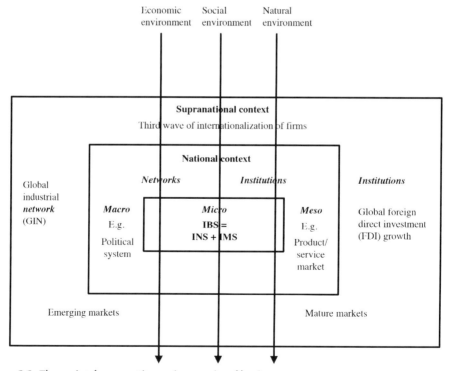

Figure 1.1 The societal perspective on international business strategy

means that the organization of society at one level is embedded into its organization at higher levels as well as into the supranational context. This perspective on international business strategy is defined as societal, since it is based on all three types of environment, not only the economic environment as is the case for most international strategy research. To cope with the uncertainty caused by this complex global environment, it is necessary to have a broad societal approach to international business strategy. It is specified further to consist of a network view and an institutional view, which are combined into the network institutional approach (NIA).

The globalization of firms has contributed a great deal to the increasing diversity and turbulence of the world economy. This evolution of the supranational context is elaborated on below and in Part II (Chapters 2 and 3). The long-term development is described in terms of three historical waves of internationalization of firms. This book is mainly about the current Third wave of internationalization of firms, which has been underway since the 1990s. It is considered a Golden era of international business due to the large and rapid growth of major international business activities – such as trade and FDI – during this period. International production has also been considerably more specialized and spread over the world as well as being been more integrated through the global value chain (GVC). This international production system is defined as the global industrial network (GIN).

MAJOR STRATEGIC BUSINESS PROBLEMS

The emerging markets have become critical markets for Western firms during the Third wave, and firms from emerging markets have internationalized to become major global competitors. These developments have made it necessary to rethink traditional perspectives on international business operations. Environmental differences between emerging markets and traditional Western market economies are still large and have changed character. This book is about the strategic implications of the Third wave for the MNC, especially about how MNCs and multinational exporters (see Chapter 10) from mature European markets have coped with these strategic challenges.

For the Western MNCs, the Third wave has resulted in a drastic and rapid change of the international business environment and new conditions for their global strategies and organization. They have changed their priorities, investing heavily in these emerging countries by setting up new businesses or expanding existing businesses, increasing their engagement in these emerging markets considerably. From their main activities being mainly concentrated in their 'home bases' in Western Europe, Japan and North America, they have now become much more global and spread throughout the world. Although many MNCs had previous experience of doing business in emerging markets, the magnitude of the shift meant this was a new strategic situation for them. They were now operating on a much larger scale in countries that were different from a business point of view compared to what they were used to in the mature market economies. They were competing head on, both locally and globally, with new and fairly unknown competitors, such as Korean and Chinese firms or newly restructured and privatized domestic companies in the CEE countries. Thus, they were now operating in another and more uncertain business environment of which they had less experience, learning that business systems in emerging markets work in a different way. Today, these companies are more experienced in how to operate in such complex environments.

Firms have realized that the market system of emerging markets is growth oriented, and that it is characterized by strong but unevenly distributed local demand. It is also uncertain, turbulent and messy. This business environment is relationship oriented, embedded, holistic, social, reforming and institution-building. Relationships are always important in business, but they are even more so in emerging markets, which therefore can be characterized as 'network societies'. The more holistic situation of 'everything influences everything else' is of particular importance in international business, being a major distinction between emerging markets and mature markets in the EU or in North America. In the latter markets, societal institutions are more established and specialized, meaning that there is a clearer borderline between different parts of the society.

How different parts of the society are related to each other is defined in this book as 'embed-dedness', meaning that the various sections of society illustrated in Figure 1.1 are embedded into each other. The MNC at the micro level executing the IBS is embedded into the market, which in turn is embedded into society as a whole. The borderline between different parts of society is more opaque than in the West. Another distinction is the faster pace of change, which makes the business environment more complex and uncertain compared to the that of mature Western markets.

This book is about how MNCs from Europe solve major business problems encountered in complicated and volatile markets. It looks at how business is done under the special circumstances discussed above, to what extent MNCs' experience from Western markets is relevant in these environments, and whether hitherto used global strategies are applicable.

Major strategic business problems faced in emerging markets include:
- how to untangle the embedded markets by analysing the different, varying, and changing markets, for example the product/service market, the financial market and the labour market;
- how to relate to the emerging and reformed formal systems (e.g. judicial system) influencing business;
- how to relate to the influences from changing informal societal systems such as different mixtures of local cultures;
- how to deal with the grave social and natural environmental problems in these countries that are represented by emerging social groups (stakeholders), for example various non-governmental organizations (NGOs);
- what strategy to apply in different sections of the transforming society;
- how to deal with governments that play such an important role for business in these markets, and where the role is changing throughout the reform process.

HANDLING ENVIRONMENTAL COMPLEXITY

An MNC's ability to handle such strategic business problems is critical in successfully managing business operations in these markets. According to Child (2001), uncertainty can be coped with by reducing complexity or absorbing it. On the one hand, the MNC may try to reduce complexity to known proportions and routines, which is defined as complexity reduction. This is the classic way of reducing complexity and improving decision-making by collecting information about the environment, and includes keeping complexity at bay by following well-known routines. For example, if the MNC's entry into a market usually takes place through wholly owned subsidiaries, this procedure is also followed in a new market. Another way to handle environmental complexity is to accept it as it is and try to live with it. This is referred to as complexity absorption, which is described as 'the attempt to ride with complexity' (ibid., p. 704). So instead of reducing complexity, the MNC tries to penetrate it, for example by networking with persons or organizations that have special knowledge or connections. If this latter strategy for handling environmental complexity is to be followed, joint ventures and other types of alliances are preferred entry modes to wholly owned subsidiaries. In emerging markets, MNCs usually follow a mixture of these two strategies. Since it is only possible to reduce the high complexity of these markets to some extent, the firm needs to join forces with local partners, in order, for example, to increase flexibility by receiving early warning signals.

The ability to cope with environmental complexity when internationalizing in the 'new' Europe (CEE), for example, mainly varies with how much experience firms have in operating in foreign markets, that is, how far they have come in the global internationalization process. Internationally experienced firms are in a better position to cope with complexity and take advantage of business opportunities in this new Europe and in Asia, both to sell more and to relocate production and shift the supplier base eastwards.

MNCs have gained experience from operating in emerging markets and solving problems of this type. However, research mostly indicates that MNCs still base their business in emerging markets too much on their experience from Western markets, one reason for this being a lack of business models that consider the large differences between emerging markets and traditional Western market economies. So there is a lack of literature providing firms with strategic business models for international business in emerging markets, both on initial establishment problems and on the problems and strategies of already established firms. There is a lot of literature about how to do business in specific emerging markets, from simple business guides to international management books, but there have been few attempts to develop general models that can be used in most of these markets, making it hard to compare the markets in various ways.

Thus, the basic tenet of this book is that traditional ideas and frameworks used for analysing, forming and implementing international business strategy in mature markets are less applicable, and in need of adjustment, in emerging markets. Due to the ongoing environmental shift in European and North American markets, the broad societal perspective of this book could also be useful for analysing this changing environment and the implications for IBS in these mature markets. For example, many of the policies implemented during the Trump presidency can be seen as representing a major attack on the traditional organization of the US federal state, namely the checks and balances founded on the power sharing between the executive, the legislative and the judiciary. Such a big political change could affect both local business and global business to a significant degree.

THE NETWORK INSTITUTIONAL APPROACH

The appearance of the emerging markets on the world scene mainly since the 1990s and the on-going transition in mature markets imply that the traditional approach in international business research of focusing almost entirely on strategic economic issues and less on social and ecological is-sues needs to change. In this book this approach is turned around by subordinating economic issues to social and natural environmental issues. The societal perspective illustrated in Figure 1.1 is speci-fied as a network institutional approach (NIA) to IBS, where the market economy is embedded into society as a whole. Of the various ways of theorizing about context reviewed by Redding (2005), this approach belongs within the socio-economic one, since it develops methods for understanding the environmental support of firms and markets and dealing with the limits of rational choice analysis. It is a high-context approach, since it is founded on social theories such as those related to networks, institutions and culture (Child, 2001). In accordance with the societal perspective, society is divided into different parts which provide different contexts for actions, resulting in various logics.

However, the various ways of theorizing about context that are reviewed by Redding, including his own work, do not include considering the firm itself. Instead, they concern business systems (e.g. Redding, 2005; Whitley, 1992a, b), clusters (e.g. Porter, 1990, 2000), and how they relate to their ex-ternal context, that is, how the meso level is linked to the macro level. This also goes for the research performed on CEE since the end of the 1980s which was reviewed by Meyer and Peng (2016). They show that certain theories are used to theorize about the environment, and certain others about the firm. The MNC itself is not linked to the environment using the same coherent theoretical base, for example to explain firm strategy under different environmental circumstances. Typically, one theory is used for environment, for example institutional theory, and another for how the firm acts, for ex-ample a strategy theory such as the resource-based view. The risk with such an eclectic approach is combining incoherent theories. A major contribution of this book is therefore the NIA to IBS, where coherent theories are used on the internal environment of the MNC and how it strategically con-nects to various levels of the external environment, that is, to the meso level, the macro level and the supranational level. For example, Redding's work and the work reviewed by him provide a number of useful models for classifying the external environment of the MNC. This is facilitated by the fact that most of these works have the same theoretical foundation as this book, namely societal theories such as institutional theory. The major ingredients of the socio-economic approach of this book are then the network view and the institutional view, which are integrated into one approach: the NIA to IBS.

The network view

As found in Figure 1.1, MNCs are linked to each other at the supranational level through the global industrial network and at the company level through the industrial network. Since emerging mar-kets are relationship oriented, firms are part of elaborate and complex local networks. However, business networks are not unique to these markets, since firms all over the world are connected through networks. But business networks in emerging markets differ organizationally, economi-cally and culturally from those in the West at the same time as they undergo strong changes. This means that inter-firm network relationships are more personal and embedded, that is, overlapping with other networks in society, while they are more impersonal and confined to the business sector in the Western markets. Actually, on a very general basis, and discussed in more detail later in this book, inter-firm relationships in emerging markets tend to transform from the former state to the latter state. Changes and relationship processes are important. The network view is therefore useful for describing an emerging market system and how to perform strategy there. Relationships are not only built with economic stakeholders but also with other stakeholders in society, for example government, local communities and interest organizations. One consequence of this inter-relatedness is that strategic action is interactive, where firms respond to the various activities of other firms as well as of other organizations of the external framework.

Thus, the network view is not only well suited for describing and explaining international business strategy in the complex local markets, but also as regards the IBS concerning how these markets are globally integrated. Additionally, a network view is taken on intra-organizational matters. The theoretical background of this view is examined in Chapter 7.

The institutional view

From a contextual point of view, the term 'institutional' is the other specification of the book of the international dimension of business, expressing that the different international contexts of Figure 1.1 are seen to consist of institutions. MNCs need to cope with differences in diverse political, regulatory and cultural prescriptions across country markets, resulting in institutional complexity (Kostova et al., 2008). Meyer and Peng (2016) also refer to an institution-based view, since they have found it to be the most frequently referenced theoretical basis regarding emerging economies. They note that it brings together several lines of research that have a shared interest in the interaction between economic actors and institutional environments at different levels of analysis. Two major fields of institutional theories are used by them to explain how the environment affects economic behaviour: 'new institutional economics' and 'institutions as pressures for legitimacy', a group of sociological theories (please see the Appendix). A focus is shared on institutions as rules under which economic and social actions take place. This institution-based view is therefore seen as an emerging paradigm in international business research. However, from a strategic perspective, these institutional theories are about the external environment of firms, one mainly about economic governance forms and the other about organizational fields. A major part of the external environment is then missing, namely the natural environment. This environment is organized nationally and internationally in different ways by society, meaning that nature becomes institutionalized into society to become part of it, resulting in certain rules about how society is related to nature, for example rules about how a national wildlife park should be organized and managed.

The institutional view of this book is therefore broader, since it is extended to include the MNC as an institutional set-up. Moreover, the institutional view is supplemented by cultural aspects and integrated with the network view to have a more complete societal perspective on IBS and the environments where it is played out. This is necessary for international business research so that, by leveraging the specific characteristics of the context and the firms in different countries to develop and modify existing theories and generate new theoretical ideas, insights and propositions, the research can be more impactful, as discussed by Bello and Kostova (2014) and Kostova and Hult (2016).

According to the sociological institutional theories referred to above, and the perspective on institutional theory taken, institutions consist of rules, rules, more rules, and even more rules. As developed in Chapter 11 and the Appendix, human behaviour is assumed to be rule-like, since it follows certain patterns that repeat themselves over time. We behave the same way today as we did yesterday, and we will do it the same way tomorrow. Like a computer, we are programmed to behave in a certain way – not entirely, but basically and generally. This programming or setting of rules takes place in the social groupings to which we belong. People interact thus influencing each other, and shared beliefs and values evolve, leading to the development of a common regular social behaviour which is maintained for a certain period and then changed. Human life is organized in certain ways. It is as if we follow certain paths through our lives; that is, behaviour is predictable.

Institutions are either described in the literature as such regular behaviour or as the social structure where such behaviour takes place. In the former case, words like habits, routines and procedures are often used to describe the regular and stable behaviour, while rules characterize the social structures. Examples of such structures that house the behaviour and which differ on rules are family, clan, organization, government, judiciary, nation, market, game or ceremony. In this book we combine these notions and define institutions as *habits and routines shaped by the rules typical of a legitimized social grouping of some kind, either explicit formal rules such as laws or implicit informal rules such as beliefs, values and norms*. Basically, institutional theory therefore deals with how society is organized. Within a grouping such as a firm are found rules (e.g. a formal hierarchy and a specific belief system) typical of this specific group, which result in a certain habitual and routinized behaviour.

This definition implies that when organizational behaviour is described and explained using institutional theory, all organizations are viewed as institutions. This gives the term 'institution' another meaning to that used in everyday language, where it normally signifies a certain type of organization, usually a public organization of some kind, for example a hospital, a government authority, a court or the whole legal system. Thus, a firm can be an institution in the former case but not in the latter. Unfortunately, these two connotations are often mixed up in international business research, confusing theoretical constructs with empirical terms. A good example is 'institutional void', which is a contradictory construct since it would mean that there is a black hole in the societal fabric sucking up all rules, making it impossible to apply institutional theory. Rather, 'institutional deficiency' is a better concept, since it would mean that a certain institution, such as the rules on competition of the Western legal system, is missing and needs to be introduced by replacing the existing rules.

Institutions, then, standardize behaviour and transfer rules, such as norms and ways of thinking, between individuals in groups and between groups. Behaviour following from them is repeated over time, meaning that behavioural regularities are also valid for future situations. Uncertainty is reduced by anticipation of repeated behaviour. Since institutions result in established patterns of behaviour, they are also stable. This makes institutional theory an excellent instrument for describing, explaining and predicting the actual strategic behaviour of firms, thus reducing uncertainty and ambiguity in international business. The theoretical background to the institutional view is taken up in the Appendix.

Cultural influence

Redding (2008) argues that while institutions are related to and informed by culture, the two are distinct, while Hofstede (2001) asserts that institutions and culture are two sides of the same coin.

Moreover, explicit institutional arrangements are not aspects of culture (Peterson, 2016). Based on this literature, cultural theory is separated from institutional theory at the same time as how they are related to each other is studied. In the main, culture is seen to infuse an institutional arrangement, chiefly the informal rules of a societal grouping, its world views, norms, values and regulations. Theories used to relate culture to organizations are, then, included in the book, as well as anthropology theory about the ideational and social systems of society.

The network institutional approach specified

The network and institutional views are combined into a common societal approach by looking at how international business strategy and organization depend on network, institutional and cultural factors inside and outside the firm. This network institutional approach is comprehensive, since it incorporates the role of networks, institutions and culture in designing and executing effective MNC strategies for international operations. It is also an integrated approach, since it highlights the continuous interplay between these factors. And it is a pragmatic approach, since it provides the analytical tools to assist in arriving at practically relevant decisions on how to undertake effective and profitable MNC operations in such environments.

The NIA is founded on the following premises:

- It is impossible to separate the world of business from non-economic realms, such as the worlds of politics or ethics. Since business action is a social activity, it implies that social, ethical and ecological issues are essential strategic issues in international business. The societal aspect of the strategy framework is therefore emphasized, that is, that the MNC is embedded into society. IBS is primarily developed to consider social and ecological aspects, where relationships, norms, values and beliefs are essential characteristics of the strategy framework. A main strategic purpose of the MNC is, then, to create societal values by addressing the needs and requirements of various social groupings. A basic objective of the MNC is therefore to create a sustainable business by promoting three major types of values based on such needs and requirements: economic value, social value and ecological value.
- The NIA to international business strategy concerns the consistency between strategy and the external sources of competitive advantage prevailing in the local country market. These include factors related to demand, such as industry, customers and competitors in the economic environment, as well as factors in the social and natural environments influencing these. This leads the MNC to take advantage of the opportunities prevailing in the local market. Contrary to most strategy theory, the NIA extends beyond the industry environment of the firm and considers the national context of the company. International business strategy literature mostly considers differences between national markets and industries, but not so much the national context outside this environment. This means that international business strategy usually takes place within the economic organization of society, and the impact from the social organization at the meso and macro levels is neglected.
- The MNC is connected with the local market environment through relationships. Networking becomes a critical strategic issue, since a major part of the business activities in these

markets concerns building and maintaining networks of relationships with major commercial parties and other actors of interest to the MNC in ensuring its success. Relationships are not only built with economic stakeholders, but also with other stakeholders in society, such as government, local communities and associations. One consequence of this inter-relatedness is that strategy is interactive, where the firm responds to various activities of other organizations in the external framework. This means that the network strategy becomes a critical part of the societal approach and the 'network' part of the NIA.

- The consistency between strategy and the external sources of competitive advantage, on the one hand, and the consistency between the strategy pursued in the local market environment and the resources and capabilities available for that environment, on the other, is achieved through matching. This involves linking the resources and capabilities of the internal environment with the various stakeholders in the external environment by making them compatible with each other. Together with networking, matching focuses on the social aspect of society: MNCs relate their own values, norms and beliefs to the values, norms and beliefs prevailing in the local market.

- The IBS process is not separated into two stages, namely formulation and implement/execution, as is common for strategic processes in general. Many activities take place without being formulated first. They are organized first and become strategy next. This means that international strategy and organization are two sides of the same coin. This process view to international business strategy is elaborated on in this book by going into how strategy changes with variation of the context of the local market, and with the various environments met along the internationalization process.

- The IBS on the local national market is mainly connected to the supranational environment through the transnational global industrial network.

A major conclusion from the points above is that the key aspect of international business strategy is the relation between strategy and organization of the MNC, as well as the organization of the societies where the MNC is active. The larger the differences are in the organization of societies, the more the MNCs need to consider this in their strategic operations.

MAJOR PARTS OF THE INTERNATIONAL BUSINESS STRATEGY FRAMEWORK

The fundamental international strategic dilemma of local adaptation versus global integration (Bartlett and Ghoshal, 1989, 1992) has become different and more serious during the Third wave: how should the company act locally and think globally in market situations that are so different from each other and when situations are rapidly changing? The issue of local adaptation concerns matters such as how much the MNC should adapt operations to the different international environments or build global competitiveness from local sources. This is particularly true for the business environment in emerging markets, since the differences from Western economies are of such a magnitude as to constitute very different business situations. The need for national responsiveness or local adaptation due to variation in global environments is thus a basic characteristic of the IBS. This is also true for the need to integrate various strategic activities globally, for example through standardization. This most basic of all international business strategic issues will be developed further in this book by looking at what is behind these forces of differentiation and standardization.

Business operations are viewed from a societal perspective, where the great variation of international environments at the global and local levels is described in terms of societal variation and explained by network, institutional, cultural and economic factors. This societal perspective on international business strategy specified as the network institutional approach is summarized as consisting of the following main parts:

- The incorporation of strategy and organization into the NIA, creating an integrated societal focus on international business strategy. The NIA is given concrete form through three major models developed in this book: the basic networks model, the basic institutions model and the basic rules model. Based on the fact that culture infuses institutions, cultural aspects are integrated into the two institutional models.
- The international network strategy (INS), which concerns how to connect the MNC to parties in both economic and social environments.
- The international matching strategy (IMS), which mainly deals with how the MNC relates to its social environments in foreign markets by matching the beliefs, values, norms and enforcement mechanisms of the external environments to its own beliefs, values, norms and enforcement mechanisms.
- Establishing a mix between the international network and matching strategies that creates sustainable competitive advantages.
- Making the international business sustainable by creating three major types of values according to the following formula:

  Sustainable business = economic value + social value + ecological value.

  Economic value is achieved within the economic context by creating customer value in a profitable way. But this cannot be done without considering how the social and ecological values are influenced. Social and ecological values are created through being socially responsible. Ecological value is separated from social value as the specific value inherent in protecting the natural environment and conserving resources so that nature is not destroyed, thus considering the needs of future generations. These values may also add to customer value by creating more satisfied customers.
- A methodology for analysing the external environment of foreign local markets. It is important for the MNC to have analytical tools for analysing and predicting developments in the broader and embedded market systems.
- A methodology for evaluating the effectiveness of the IBS through making an organizational life cycle sustainability assessment of various mixes of the ecological, economic and social values. Based on this assessment, how sustainable competitive advantages are achieved by making trade-offs between legitimacy and efficiency as well as transforming societal advantage into competitive advantage is analysed. Evaluating performance is part of a strategic change process analysed as institutional change taking place within the hierarchical network organization of the MNC.

THE THIRD WAVE OF INTERNATIONALIZATION OF FIRMS

As discussed above, the supranational environment has become more and more important with the increased globalization of firms and the growth of bilateral and multilateral trade and investment treaties together with the rise of intergovernmental organizations such as the World Trade Organization (WTO), the United Nations Conference on Trade and Development (UNCTAD) and the World bank. Global agreements on climate change and biotope destruction are becoming more inclusive. There are also more all-inclusive international organizations, such as the European Union (EU) and the United Nations (UN), where countries cooperate on vital economic as well as ecological and social issues. This has made the supranational context more complex and dynamic. To bring some order into the evolvement of this global environment over time, it is split into and described as three periods of geographic spread of international business activities throughout the world, focusing on the MNC. The main driver of this internationalization of the MNC is the growth of foreign direct investments. Each period is described as a wave of FDI growth from home countries to host countries. The outward and inward FDI in various host countries by the home countries are related to each other through the trade of the products and services produced. This integration of FDI on a global basis mainly takes place through the flow of inputs and outputs between the production units. This supplier chain is usually defined as the global value chain, or the GVC. Based on the network view of this book, it is here called the global industrial network, abbreviated as GIN.

The current growth period of FDI and foreign trade is defined as the Third wave of internationalization of firms. It began at the beginning of the 1990s and seems to be nearing its end, and possibly transitioning into a new period of either continued FDI growth or decline. The First wave of internationalization of firms began during the first half of the 19th century and lasted until 1973. Since it mainly involved companies from Europe and the US, the Western multinational corporation was formed during this period. As will be developed more in Chapter 2, the First wave is divided into two major periods, namely the British epoch and the American epoch. During the 1960s the market economies destroyed during World War II had been rebuilt and new institutions of the world economy were put in place, for example the world bank system and the General Agreement on Tariffs and Trade (GATT). This paved the way for the Second wave of internationalization of firms as more and more countries mainly from East Asia became incorporated into the global market. This Second wave favoured the big Japanese conglomerates reorganized after the war, and later took South Korean and South East Asian firms out into the world market and saw an expansion of Western MNCs to East Asia. This added the Japanese keiretsu and Korean chaebols as well as the overseas Chinese business system to the group of MNCs. Integration of product markets, in particular, but also service markets, was greatly boosted during the Second wave and at the beginning of the Third wave as various associations of economic cooperation came about all over the world, most notably the integration of the European Economic Community (EEC) and the European Free Trade Association (EFTA) into the EU in 1993. This increased international business within Western Europe considerably.

The Third wave of internationalization of firms started when MNCs originating from mature

Western markets began to establish themselves on a big scale in the third world of China and India and the second world of Russia and Central and Eastern Europe, while firms from these countries started to internationalize. With the disappearance of the iron curtain and the dissolution of the Soviet Union, the second world of centrally planned economies collapsed at the beginning of the 1990s. At about this time the Chinese economy also began to be liberalized and privatized into a market economy, and India started to further liberalize its economy as well, much more so than earlier. The growing importance of such emerging markets during the Third wave has resulted in internationally experienced firms increasing their business in such markets and many internationally inexperienced firms from these markets entering the global market. Another development is that home-market-oriented small and medium-sized enterprises (SMEs) from mature markets have increasingly internationalized their business operations, especially to proximate new market economies. This Third wave of cross-hauling of foreign direct investments (FDIs) also includes some African countries. This wave of internationalization of firms is described in detail in Chapter 2 and evaluated in Chapter 3. The latter chapter also looks into whether there are any new emerging markets emerging.

It was thought by many that the speeding up of the globalization process would eventually turn the world into one big market economy. The world was said to be becoming flat instead of spikey. This idea was also based on the international spread of the Western democratic system, making political systems more and more similar. Thus, the 'End of History' as proposed by Francis Fukuyama in 1989 seemed to come true with the spreading of the Western market-economic and political system to most corners of the world. However, this epoch of unifying world markets and countries may have come to a halt in 2016–17, mainly indicated by two critical events: Brexit and the election of Donald Trump as the president of the US. With increasing cracks in the global economic and political systems, global markets started to disconnect and move backwards to an earlier spikier stage. The mature markets are now undergoing strong changes as the remaining large economic and political disparities between nations are strengthening and earlier ones re-emerging, leading, for example, to increasing trade and non-trade barriers.

Emerging markets

The emerging markets are undergoing a transformation from a non-market or highly imperfect market system to a more developed market economy. The pace of liberalization and privatization of the economy has been very high and has turned China, in a rather short time, into the 'factory of the world' and India into its 'software centre'. Chinese firms in particular expanded internationally on a big scale, beyond Asia to the EU, the Americas, and to Africa. This global effect was strengthened by the growth of the Brazilian and Russian economies during the end of the 1990s and beginning of the 2000s. As will be discussed further in Chapter 3, the major characteristics of the market systems of the emerging markets can be summarized as being growing economies with strong and unevenly distributed local demand, while also being uncertain, turbulent and messy. Also, the strategic environment of such markets is relationship oriented, embedded, holistic, social, reforming and institution-building. The emerging markets are divided into different groups based mainly on the industrial policy behind the reformation process.

The golden era of international business

A major conclusion from comparing the First and Second waves of internationalization of firms with the Third wave is that the latter can be seen as a kind of golden era of international business. The major reasons for this include the following:

- The supranational environment encompasses most of the globe and reflects the great diversity and dynamism of its many nations.
- International trade has increased a lot.
- International production has been considerably more specialized and spread over the world. It has also been more integrated through the GIN.
- With the increasing number of countries becoming market economies, the total stocks of both inward FDI and outward FDI have grown a great deal. These stocks have also been more integrated through the GIN.
- The international business during this era has become more challenging from a strategic point of view, since it now takes place in a much more complex and turbulent supranational environment.

CONCLUSIONS

Based on above, the purpose of this book can be summarized as to outline a comprehensive, integrated and pragmatic analytical approach towards undertaking effective MNC strategies in complex international business environments. This approach is based on a societal perspective on IBS, labelled the network institutional approach. It is comprehensive, since it is founded on the major characteristics of international environments and incorporates the role of networks, institutions and culture in designing and executing effective MNC strategies for international operations. It also includes the strategic aspects of the natural environment. It is a pragmatic approach since it provides the analytical tools for arriving at practically relevant decisions on how to undertake effective and legitimate MNC operations. It is mainly relevant for multifaceted and turbulent environments as in the complex emerging markets. But its relevance for traditional mature markets is increasing, as they are starting to undergo large environmental changes.

A point of departure is the fundamental strategic dilemma in international business of local adaptation versus global integration, where the former aspect is stressed in the way strategy is adapted to the particular circumstances of these markets.

The international network strategy emphasizes the importance of effective networking, by means of establishing relationships between decision takers in the MNC and those active in the country who are exponents of the specific network setting in that country's emerging market. The INS is not only executed on the complex local markets but also in globally integrating manufacturing and supplier activities through the global industrial networks at transnational and inter-firm levels.

As a consequence of the influence of institutions on international network strategy, the international business strategy is also defined by various rule systems of the institutional environment prevailing outside and inside the MNC. Such rule systems can be of a purely economic nature but may also be of a non-economic nature. Based on an understanding of the logic of the institutional setting in markets, and the institutional setting internal to the MNC, the MNC decides on its international matching strategy, that is, whether and to what extent its internal institutional setting has such characteristics as to be able to match effectively the requirements of the external institutional setting of the market in which the MNC operates or intends to operate.

The supranational environment is characterized as a Third wave of internationalization of firms, which has been underway since the 1990s. It is considered as a golden era of international business due to the large and rapid increases of major global business activities such as trade and FDI. That international production has been considerably more specialized and spread over the world, being more integrated through the global industrial network. MNCs originating from mature Western markets have established themselves on a big scale in emerging country markets, while firms from these markets are internationalizing and becoming new MNCs. The next two chapters are devoted to the three waves of internationalization of firms and the emerging markets, that is, to the major external environments of the MNC during this wave.

OUTLINE OF THE BOOK

The outline of the book is summarized in Figure 1.2.

Part I introduces **the societal perspective** on international business studies.

Chapter 1 on *the network institutional approach to international business strategy* presented the major strategic business problems of the book and the network institutional approach, which is the societal perspective valid for international business strategy in complex business contexts. The international business strategy was also introduced inclusive of its substrategies: the international network strategy and international matching strategy. The supranational business environment of the Third wave of internationalization of firms was advanced, inclusive of the emerging markets – the dominant national environment of this golden era of international business.

Part II describes **the external environment** of the MNC during the Third wave of internationalization of firms, first the supranational environment and then the major national environments during this period, namely emerging markets.

In *Chapter 2* the long-term evolution of the supranational environment is studied by mainly focusing on *the Third wave of internationalization of firms*, which is related to the First and Second waves. A closer look is taken at the development of the outward and inward FDI stocks of the major economies during the Third wave, starting with the BRICS (Brazil, Russia, India, China and South Africa), and followed by the new members of the EU. The effect of this wave on major Latin American countries is also analysed, as are Second wave emerging markets from East Asia and mature market economies. This is followed by a study of the integration of the FDI of emerging markets into the global industrial network (GIN), which is specified as the global value chain (GVC). It is also noted how the importance of natural environment as a strategic issue increased greatly during the Third wave.

In *Chapter 3* on *assessing emerging markets*, the major national business environment of the

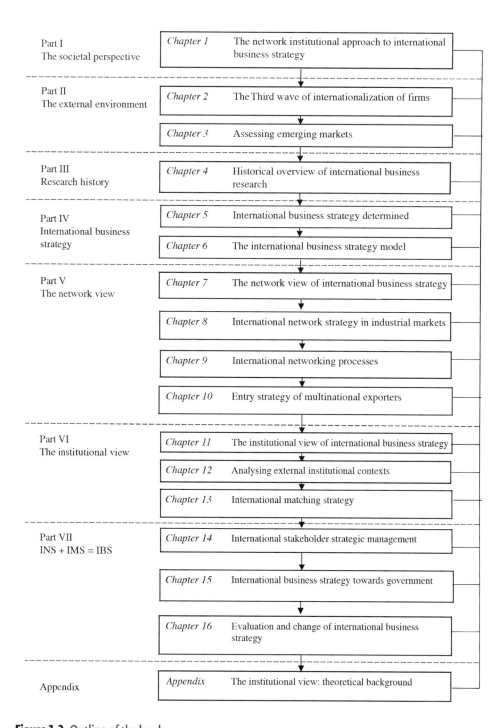

Part I
The societal perspective

| Chapter 1 | The network institutional approach to international business strategy |

Part II
The external environment

| Chapter 2 | The Third wave of internationalization of firms |

| Chapter 3 | Assessing emerging markets |

Part III
Research history

| Chapter 4 | Historical overview of international business research |

Part IV
International business
strategy

| Chapter 5 | International business strategy determined |

| Chapter 6 | The international business strategy model |

Part V
The network view

| Chapter 7 | The network view of international business strategy |

| Chapter 8 | International network strategy in industrial markets |

| Chapter 9 | International networking processes |

| Chapter 10 | Entry strategy of multinational exporters |

Part VI
The institutional view

| Chapter 11 | The institutional view of international business strategy |

| Chapter 12 | Analysing external institutional contexts |

| Chapter 13 | International matching strategy |

Part VII
INS + IMS = IBS

| Chapter 14 | International stakeholder strategic management |

| Chapter 15 | International business strategy towards government |

| Chapter 16 | Evaluation and change of international business strategy |

Appendix

| Appendix | The institutional view: theoretical background |

Figure 1.2 Outline of the book

Third wave is first defined and characterized. The emerging markets are then divided into major country groups, and an account given of theories on industrial policy reforms in these groups. Transition markets are transformed from a centrally planned economy, while progressing markets are transformed from a highly imperfect market stage. Next, this reformation process and how various groups of emerging markets have performed during the Third wave in comparison to mature markets is analysed as a Third wave scorecard. Finally, potential new emerging markets are identified and discussed.

In **Part III**, an odyssey is taken through the **research history** of international business, especially on MNCs and internationalization processes.

Chapter 4, on a *historical overview of international business research*, further describes and explains the development of FDI and MNCs during the three waves of internationalization of firms. It then lays the theoretical foundation for the 'IB' part of 'IBS', while the next chapter does that for the 'S' part. The development of major theories in international business, since such research started in 1950s, is outlined. First, various general theories about the MNC are examined to find out how it has been explained over the years. Next are found theories about how the global industrial network is established and organized at the MNC level, mainly theories on the global factory and two types of sustainable GINs. The 'markets and hierarchy' theory is also included. These theories represent a structural or spatial perspective on the MNC by describing where, why and how MNCs have operated internationally. The 'when' question is answered by examining the process of internationalization, or the time dimension, while the 'with whom' question is covered by considering the social dimension through the internationalization in networks theory. Finally, the structural and temporal dimensions are combined to develop a typology of international firms. Internationalization process theory is integrated with theories on ways to organize MNCs over time.

The **international business strategy** is established and described in **Part IV**.

In *Chapter 5*, *international business strategy* is *determined*. It is grounded in the international strategy literature and the basic strategic dilemma of local responsiveness versus global integration. Strategy theories antecedent to the IBS are covered next, before developing the societal perspective. The international business strategy is then formulated and implemented within the framework of networks and institutions. The outside-in perspective signifies that markets and the wider environment determine the rules of the game and constrain strategy. The inside-out perspective on IBS embraces how the value-creating internal network and institutional context is related to the external context. The international business strategy is next defined and described. To gain a sustainable competitive advantage in the economic environment the IBS also needs to be legitimate in the social environment by achieving a societal advantage. The separation of the IBS into two substrategies is based on different rationalities, namely efficiency and legitimacy.

In *Chapter 6*, *the international business strategy model* is outlined, covering its substrategies, namely the international network strategy and the international matching strategy, and establishing the basic strategy formula of the book: IBS = INS + IMS. The IBS is related to the external environment of Part II. The major factors of the internal environment included are the hierarchy of resources and capabilities, organizational learning capabilities, and institutional controls. The chapter ends with evaluation criteria of the IBS.

Part V is about **the network view** and the international network strategy.

Chapter 7 takes up *the network view of international business strategy* as one of two key dimensions of the NIA. This view is defined through four background models to the international business strategy. First, the three major aspects of the network view are specified as networks as relationships, networks as structures and networks as processes. The first aspect is about what relationships look like, how they are established, and whether they are direct or indirect. Network structure concerns the number of links and the degree to which the nodes as organizations or persons are linked to each other. Network processes relate to the sequence over time of the network activities, for example if they are stable or turbulent. Second, this general network view is developed into the basic networks model, which shows how markets and society are strategically related to each other. Third, certain major aspects of the general network view are combined into an outside-in perspective on international network strategy. Fourth, the intra-organizational network of the MNC is developed as an inside-out perspective on the INS.

Chapter 8 is about *international network strategy in industrial markets*, taking up networks as structures and relationships. The MNC, markets and society are described based on the network view, illustrating the relationships between the MNC and some of its major external parties in product/service markets. The INS then concerns the nodes of the network, that is, the actors or the stakeholders (e.g. customers, suppliers and competitors), and the linkages to them. The strategy utilizes a network map to decide which actors to include, which to focus on, and how to combine them. The linkage mix, the competitive mix and first-mover advantages are seen to be critical for achieving competitive advantages. The INS is conditioned by the capability profile of the internal environment, that is, the MNC needs to have certain resources or capabilities localized to the country to be able to effectuate the INS strategy there.

Chapter 9 extends the international network strategy to the industrial product/service market further by focusing on *international networking processes*, that is, how business relationships are initiated, developed, maintained and terminated during the different stages of marketing. The chapter delves deeper into networks as processes by distinguishing between three major networking processes: the marketing process, the relationship process and the product/service process. It focuses on the networking process in connection with marketing to large projects. This process is divided into four cycles of shifting marketing activity, namely the scanning cycle, the tendering cycle, the completion cycle and the follow-up cycle, which are further sub-divided into a number of phases. The marketing activities are handled by various project teams (action networks), which are organized differently depending on, for example, process stage and size of the project.

In *Chapter 10* on *entry strategy of multinational exporters*, the local INS in Chapters 8 and 9 is developed further by connecting it to the internationalization process. An extended internationalization in networks theory is combined with the exporting theory to explore the international network strategic process of multinational exporters (MNEXs) and their internationalization process, especially focusing on how they enter and establish network relations in emerging markets. This entry strategy takes place through the entry network, where network type, network position and entry node are key aspects. In the entering process, the MNEX exposes itself first to the foreign market through the exposure network, then builds local relationships through the formation network and finally maintains the relationships and establishes new ones in the sustenance network. Thereafter, the focus is shifted to MNEXs from emerging markets exiting their home market, which is defined as the take-off strategy. Before going into the entry and exit aspects of the inter-national network strategy, the chapter compares the entry modes of MNEXs and MNCs and their motives for investing in local emerging markets.

Part VI concerns **the institutional view**, inclusive of the international matching strategy.

In *Chapter 11, the institutional view of international business strategy* is examined, that is, the other key dimension of the NIA. More on the theoretical background of this view is found in the Appendix. The societal infrastructure is first specified as a basic institutions model, which consists of an embedded system of institutions at three analytical levels. At the centre of the model is the MNC – the key institution or micro institution of the book – which is surrounded by the two layers of meso and macro institutions. The 'basic rules' model is established next by delving deeper into the contents of the institutions. The organization of every society is viewed to be founded on basic rules, then also working as institutional controls of the IBS. These orders are thought styles, values, norms and enforcement mechanisms. Cultural aspects are integrated into the institutional view to further specify the informal rules.

Chapter 12 takes an institutional view on *analysing external institutional contexts* mainly rele-vant for complex business environments. The chapter develops a methodology to analyse past and present institutional structures of relevance to the IBS: how they have changed, and how they are predicted to change in the future. Unlocking information codes deeply embedded in institutions requires knowledge about the institutional and cultural origin of information. Cultural factors are then integrated into the institutional view to further specify the informal rules at the meso and macro levels. The analytical procedure is divided into three stages: identification of institutions, explanation of institutions and prediction of institutional developments. It is a qualitative meth-odology that focuses on the deeper parts of markets and society. Scenario planning is included as a method for predicting institutional developments.

Chapter 13 focuses directly on the second substrategy of the IBS – *international matching strat-egy*. The foundation of this strategy is that MNCs legitimize their operations in complex and dy-namic markets by matching the rules prevailing in society, these rules being housed in different organizational fields and societal sectors. Grounded in the logic of appropriateness, four strategic matching situations are detailed. The basic objective of the MNC is to create a sustainable busi-ness by creating economic, social and ecological values. Corporate social responsibility (CSR) is advanced as a critical management issue in IMS. MNCs justify their operations in the society to gain legitimacy, thereby becoming a source of societal advantage. Based on the definition of sus-tainability in Chapter 2, the sustainability business triangle is developed as a foundation for CSR. Finally, the development goals of the Sustainable Development Agenda 2030 are integrated into the international matching strategy as critical strategic issues.

Part VII is about the combined international business strategy (**INS + IMS = IBS**) as well as the assessment of strategic performance and possible ensuing change behaviour analysed as institutional change.

In *Chapter 14*, and building on Chapter 13, *international stakeholder strategic management* is taken up by integrating the international matching strategy and international network strategy. Primar-ily, the institutional view of the NIA is deepened by examining socially oriented matching strate-gies towards stakeholders. The international matching strategy model is established and applied to the case of an MNC in Malaysia. A network map is generated of the stakeholder network, and the external and internal institutional contexts are extracted through institutional analysis as a background to the CSR matrix. Societal values are created by considering long-term stakeholder interests regarding social responsibility issues such as health, infrastructure and pollution. Through matching the stakeholders' expectations, MNCs justify their operations to gain legitimacy, which then becomes a source of societal advantage.

Chapter 15 on *international business strategy towards government* builds directly on Chapter 14 by concentrating on the international stakeholder strategic management of the MNC towards one major stakeholder, namely the government. Since government is both a social and economic actor, the international network and matching strategies are more explicitly combined by analysing how they are integrated to achieve a sustainable competitive advantage for the international business strategy as a whole. The chapter is chiefly about the IBS towards the executive parts of government, that is, the authorities and other administrative bodies engaged in implementing government policy. The legitimacy-based strategic orientation is also developed further by adding three major types of legitimacy of special relevance to government. The IBS is executed through the MNC–government network (MGN), where MNCs both cooperate for common causes and compete with one another. An INS model towards government is presented, which focuses on how an individual firm maintains contacts and develops legitimacy towards the executive bodies.

In *Chapter 16* about *evaluation and change of international business strategy*, a broad view is taken towards the evaluation of the IBS, where not only strategic performance is evaluated but also how the MNC could act based on the result found. Strategic performance is analysed by making an organizational life cycle sustainability assessment of various mixes of the ecological, economic and social values created with the stakeholders. This is followed by an evaluation of the trade-off between legitimacy and efficiency for achieving sustainable competitive advantages, and how to transform societal advantage into competitive advantage. Assessing strategic performance is part of the strategic change process. Based on the network institutional approach, it is analysed as an institutional change process taking place within the hierarchical network organization of the MNC. How internal conflicts originating in the external institutional context are solved influences the change outcome, as does the dynamic interaction between the resources and capabilities. The basic rules work as dispositions by being stabilizers or facilitators of change, while the capacity to change is determined by the capability to learn.

In the **appendix** of *the institutional view*, an account is given describing its *theoretical background*. Major institutional theories of relevance to the institutional view of the international business strategy are taken up. The theories originate from different academic disciplines, mainly organization studies, sociology, economics, and economic history, and deal with institutional arrangements and change. The institutional theories examined are grouped as a multi-layer nested system. There are three levels of institutions: the micro-institutions level (e.g. the MNC), the meso-institutions level (e.g. industry markets, organizational fields) and the macro-institutions level (e.g. culture, political system). The institutional theories explored for each of the three levels are listed in Table A.1. A distinction is then made between institutional theories based on economics and institutional theories with a socio-economic disciplinary background. A section is devoted to the roots of institutional theory, going back to the end of the 19th century.

PART II
THE EXTERNAL ENVIRONMENT

Small waves but high ecological impact

Southern sea otters once ranged from Baja California to the Pacific Northwest. But by the 1920s they were almost extinct due to intensive hunting. Since then, they have slowly expanded their range and grown in number to nearly 3000. They were listed as threatened under the Endangered Species Act in 1977. Sea otters are a keystone species, determining the health of species in near-shore environments. Without them, urchins prevent kelp forests from forming important habitats for many animals. Similarly, their consumption of crabs in estuaries reduces predation on snails. Sea otters also provide good indicators of an ocean's health. Since they are a top predator of invertebrates, changes in their health can make scientists aware of variations in the ocean environment itself. They are also important to human health: as it was found that they are immune to cancer, they are being studied by researchers to find out why.

2
The Third wave of internationalization of firms

As noted in Chapter 1, the Third wave of internationalization of firms is seen as the golden age of international business. First, there was a steep rise of foreign direct investment (FDI) from already internationally active home countries and a broadening of FDI to and from new destinations. Second, the international trade between countries became more and more intertwined. Third, natural environmental issues emerged as being critical in international business during this period. In this chapter, a much more detailed story is told about this basic shift that has occurred in the Third wave. A closer look is taken at the fundamental economic realities of the international business world: FDI and international production and trade. The major outward and inward investor countries are taken up, focusing on the emerging markets. How different types of FDI are related to each other through the international trade of industrial goods, forming the global industrial network, is also examined. This network is specified as the global value chain (GVC), which is a global supplier network of industrial goods. Though the main focus is on economic issues, the chapter also develops further the strategic international business issues that are emerging in the natural environment. A historical background to the Third wave is given by taking up the development of multinational corporations (MNCs) until the beginning of the Third wave in 1990, that is, during the First and Second waves of internationalization of firms.

THE FIRST WAVE

The First wave of the internationalization of firms began during the first half of the 19th century and lasted until 1973. Since it mainly involved the internationalization of companies from Western Europe, Scandinavia and North America, the Western MNC was formed during this period. The choice of starting point is chiefly based on Chapter 6, but also Chapters 2 and 21, in Dunning and Lundan (2008). The First wave is divided into two major periods: the British epoch and the American epoch.

The British epoch

The British epoch is divided into stage 1 up to 1914 and stage 2 up to 1939. These stages also coincide with the periods of historical growth of international production found by Bénétrix et al. (2012), that is, the first wave of globalization between 1870 and 1913, and the disintegration during the interwar period. According to this study, new technologies spread with a short lag from Great Britain to western continental Europe, Scandinavia and North America, giving way to the Great Divergence of the 19th and 20th centuries. For example, as early as 1913 the incomes of western Europe and the British colonies in North America and Oceania were five and eight times higher, respectively, than those of the British colonies in Africa. This divide was manifested in international trade by exports of manufactured goods from this rich industrial core and imports of primary goods from the poor periphery consisting of southern and eastern Europe, Asia and Africa. Falling transport costs opened up opportunities for the poor countries to join the faster-growing industrial countries through developing their industry. But, on the other hand, their exposure to west-European competition could lead to deindustrialization. Rapid industrial growth began in Latin America and the European periphery in the 1870s, and became widespread before World War I (WWI). This growth spread to Asia after 1890, where it became widespread during the interwar period. It also spread to the Middle East and North Africa (MENA) as well as to sub-Saharan Africa in the interwar period. But it only became widespread in MENA during the Second wave and in Africa at the beginning of the Third wave.

The embryonic form of the modern MNC began to emerge during the first half of the 19th century, when mainly British but also other European firms started to set up subsidiaries in the US. Due to the colonial economies of this epoch, these international firms mainly acted as economic colonists on behalf of their home countries. The market economy created by the industrial revolution in the UK at the end of the 18th century had at that time spread to other parts of Europe and to North America. This new economic system started to replace the traditional subsistence economy in the major economies of the world. It was based on industrial capitalism characterized by a factory system of high specialization and division of labour. This new market system and major innovations in transport such as the steam engine resulted in a large reduction of inter-country locational barriers, which led firms to begin to replace trade with FDI. These were mostly free-standing investments coordinated by merchant houses, a kind of network-based trading house resembling those still found in most countries, including the Japanese sogo shosha. During this period the foreign-owned trading and sales ventures also continued to grow and the first foreign banking and insurance affiliates were established. The first foreign investments by US firms in the UK took place in the 1850s. At this time American technology had overtaken European technology in a wide range of metal-using industries and in those using mass production techniques, for example machine tools and sewing machines. Since exports were often uneconomical, foreign manufacturing affiliates were established.

With dramatic advances in transport, communication, storage techniques and organization (e.g. joint stock companies and trained managers), the modern MNC began to take form from 1870 onwards and developed into the managed multi-plant firm. This took place during the first globalization wave that ended in 1913. Due to more suitable institutional mechanisms and organizational structures many of these innovations, such as economies of scale in production and economies of scope in marketing, were created and taken advantage of in the US. The earlier inter-firm trade economy was gradually complemented by an intra-firm trade dominated market economic system. Firms started to create new assets of their own like machines and manufacturing know-how as well developing management knowledge on how to internalize international market transactions. FDI was almost entirely market-seeking and resource-seeking.

The British dominated the global economy until around the early 1930s, when the economy began to close in on itself with the disintegration of the existing international economy due to the collapse of the international capital markets and the ensuing Great Depression. New economic policies based on Keynes's macro-economic theory started to be used to lift the economies out of depression. During this interwar period, international business decelerated, therefore creating an interregnum between the growth period of international business before WWI and the one after World War II (WWII). This period was characterized by protectionism and economic independence along with monopoly tendencies such as international cartels, more than by FDI. Defensive market-seeking investments dominated, which resulted in MNCs taking more interest in their highly independent affiliates (working mostly as market outlets) and beginning to integrate them.

The American epoch

The American epoch started after WWII and lasted until 1973, when the famous oil crisis resulted in a period of lower industrial growth in the countries dominating industrial development during the First wave. This period is defined by Dunning and Lundan (2008) as stage 3 in the evolution of the global economy. The competitiveness of US MNCs grew more and more during the British epoch, helped by the fact that they remained intact during the war. This resulted in the dominance of these corporations as foreign investors after WWII. FDI increasingly grew at the expense of non-equity investments, which dominated the British epoch. The US creation of the modern multi-unit MNC managed through a hierarchy was completed during this epoch.

This was the period of reintegration of the Atlantic economy, which coincided with the spread of communism, decolonization and state-led import substitution industrialization (ISI) in most of the developing world (Bénétrix et al., 2012). The market economies were re-established and new international organizations built to facilitate international trade and investment, for example the World bank, the International Monetary Fund (IMF) and the General Agreement on Tariffs and Trade (GATT). The rapidly rising demand for raw materials and food stuffs increased FDI in Canada, Australia and some of the larger developing countries. Investments in the latter countries were also made in manufacturing to avoid the high import duties of the ISI policy now practised to promote industrialization. Governments then took a larger role in influencing FDI, mainly by continuing to use Keynesian economic policies. The factor endowments increasingly became created rather than just natural. Due to increasing international business, many companies reorganized by replacing the international division of an otherwise functional organization by a cross-border divisional structure based on product or region.

The American epoch coincided with the start of the Cold War and the division of the world economy into three major blocks. Many countries resented the capitalistic market system for ideological reasons, instead establishing a centrally planned economy based on the communist ideology and run by the state. The ISI policy was also based on a disbelief in the market as an industrial development mechanism. Many countries therefore had different types of mixed economies with varying proportions of public and private companies, where state control of the market was strong. At the end of the First wave, the world economy therefore consisted of three major economic blocks that were deeply divided economically, politically and culturally: the first world consisting of mature market economies that industrialized during the British epoch, the second world of central-ly planned economies, and the third world of developing economies at different levels of industrial and market development. Many of the centrally-planned economies were former colonies, for example Laos, Cambodia, Vietnam and Cuba. This transition period after WWII saw the beginning of an almost uninterrupted globalization with expansion of all kinds of trade and investment throughout the world. It lasted throughout the Second wave and continued into the Third wave until 2017.

THE SECOND WAVE

As a result of the oil crisis in 1973, industrial growth in the first world stagnated and was low in most of these countries until the end of the 1980s. By 1973, industrial diffusion was also almost complete, since industrial growth had by then been attained by countries accounting for most of the population of the three poor periphery regions of eastern Europe, Asia and Africa (Bénétrix et al., 2012). However, industrial growth continued in Asia, particularly East Asia. According to this source, industrial growth between 1973 and 1989 increased by 3.9 per cent in Japan, 11.8 per cent in Korea, 8.4 per cent in China, 8.7 per cent in Hong Kong, 9.0 per cent in Taiwan, 6.7 per cent in Singapore, 7.7 per cent in Thailand and 5.0 per cent in India (ibid.). But as seen in Table 2.1, this resulted in a large increase of inward FDI in these countries as well as a moderate increase in outward FDI, except for Japan, whose outward FDI increased by 18 times. This also increased both types of FDI for the developed economies, resulting in global FDI stock being much higher at the end of the period. The Second wave is also characterized by a number of ground-breaking technological discoveries in process technology (automation and computerization) and telecommunications.

Internationalization of Japanese firms

Japanese exports took off on a big scale. The internationalization of Japanese firms started as early as the 19th century with the industrialization of Japan primarily through importing raw materials from neighbouring countries to feed the growing Japanese manufacturing industry. A network of trading companies, the sogo shosha, was established to handle these imports as well as exports, the latter mainly to the US. As will be discussed below, the outward stock of FDI increased tenfold between 1980 and 1990, from US$20 billion to $201 billion, and increased to $278 billion in 2000. This expansion was very skewed, since no comparable FDI was taking place by foreign firms in Japan. The inward stock of FDI only increased from $3 billion in 1980 to $9 billion in 1990, and $50 billion in 2000. These figures show that the domestic market was almost closed for foreign investment until the 1990s, when it started to open up. This substantial global expansion during the Second wave was primarily export led and made possible by extensive reforms. The trust-like family-owned zaibatsu behind the war effort were outlawed and busted by the occupational power, the US. They were transformed into keiretsu. The companies of such a group own each other (cross-holdings), but still consists of both sogo shosha as the international business part and manufacturing firms, mostly located in Japan.

Internationalization of other firms from East Asia

The international business of firms from other East Asian countries also began to rise during the Second wave, but their FDI mainly took off at the beginning of the Third wave. A similar growth pattern to Japan of outward FDI in relation to inward FDI was followed by Taiwan. Its outward FDI rose from $13 billion in 1980 to $30 billion in 1990, while inward FDI rose from $2 billion to $10 billion during this period. Behind this rapid growth of international business was another and different Asian business system: the Chinese family firm. This reflects another industrial development strategy: export-led industrialization based on indigenous firms, and the establishment of free-trade zones (FTZ) to lure FDI into the country.

Since South Korea started to follow this industrialization policy later, while both types of Korean FDI increased somewhat, they were still small during this period. Similar to Japan, the large-firm economy of South Korea was the indigenous foundation of this policy. It was dominated by chaebols, which are family owned.

Export-led industrialization became the development strategy of choice instead of industrialization through import substitution, the former also being practised by Hong Kong and five countries in South East Asia (Singapore, Malaysia, Thailand, the Philippines and Indonesia). Market-seeking inward FDI therefore started to increase substantially. With the increase of FTZs in East Asia, the efficiency-seeking motive of FDI also became important, leading to a large increase in international subcontracting through outsourcing and offshoring. This led to the unbalanced FDI pattern typical for East Asia. For example, for Singapore, which developed into one big FTZ, inward FDI stock increased from $6 billion in 1980 to $30 billion in 1990 (see Table 2.2), while outward FDI stock rose from $0.6 billion to $8 billion during this period. This latter type of FDI was mainly undertaken by Western MNCs and a few indigenous large firms such as Singapore Airlines. Regarding the other four South East Asian countries, exports and FDI were carried out by a mixture of large state-owned enterprises (SOEs) and small Chinese firms, often in neighbouring markets.

The Second wave then began to take companies from these East Asian countries out into the world market and saw an expansion of Western MNCs mainly to South East Asia. This added the Japanese and Korean large firms to the group of global firms as well as the small-firm Chinese family business system. They were first very successful exporters and later foreign investors, which created a big interest in these new MNCs, especially in their different ownership and management systems. The high growth in East Asia during this and the following periods was built upon the liberalization and privatization of the economic sector which aimed to make these economies competitive in world markets. The economic success of these newly industrialized countries (NICs), or Asian 'tigers', made them role models. The three East Asian systems of business firms were organized very differently from the Western MNCs dominating the First wave (Whitley, 1990, 1992b; Chen, 1995; Luo, 2002). This showed that success in international markets could be achieved through different ways of organizing a country's business system, making the forms of organization MNCs more pluralistic and international business more complex and uncertain. This complexity increased even further during the Third wave.

Market integration

Global integration of product markets in particular, but also service markets, was greatly boosted during the Second wave as existing forms of economic cooperation were integrated further and new ones came about all over the world. As mentioned in Chapter 1, the European Economic Community (EEC) and European Free Trade Association (EFTA) were merged into the European Union (EU) in 1993. This increased international business within Western Europe considerably. The Association of Southeast Asian Nations (ASEAN) was formed by five countries in 1967 and gradually expanded during the Second wave to include all ten South East Asian countries from 1992. The Asia-Pacific Economic Cooperation (APEC) was initiated in 1989 between most countries of the Pacific Basin, and the agreement on the North American Free Trade Agreement (NAFTA) was signed in 1993 between the US, Canada and Mexico at the beginning of the Third wave. The regional integration of markets allowed the MNCs to increasingly centralize their international business by rationalizing their value-added activities through concentrating their sales and manufacturing companies in certain locations, and benefitting from increased product and plant specialization and intra-firm trade.

Most of the international business in the world now took place in the triad (East Asia, the EU and NAFTA) within and between economic blocs on three continents. The mutual cross-hauling of FDI was not limited to the Atlantic Ocean any longer but also included the Pacific Basin. For example, European FDI in the US increased a lot during the 1980s and 1990s, that is, in the years overlapping the Second and Third waves. With the break-up of the Western conglomerates during these decades, an international market was created for the buying and selling of firms, which also increased market integration. It was now much easier to acquire companies, which allowed international mergers and acquisitions (M&As) to grow. This represented a major shift from green-field investments to acquiring existing firms, which also introduced asset-seeking as a major FDI motive. However, Japanese and Korean firms were almost impossible to acquire by Western MNCs, since the ownership structures of these conglomerates hindered such a move. This made international trade and investment very lopsided, mainly favouring companies from these two countries. This started to change during the Third wave with the Asian financial crisis in 1997–98, which mainly involved South East Asia, Hong Kong and South Korea.

THE THIRD WAVE

Dunning and Lundan (2008) as well as Bénétrix et al. (2012) cover this period until about 2007. The former authors define it as stage 5 in the evolution of the global economy, while the latter authors call it the second wave of globalization. As stated previously, it is the golden age of international business or global business, since most countries have been linked together within one economic system based on market exchange. But this does not mean that international business is easier. On the contrary, the international business environment has become more diverse and turbulent.

FDI from East Asian countries started to grow during the Second wave but took off at the beginning of the Third wave and continued to grow further due to a series of major events.

With the disappearance of the iron curtain and the dissolution of the Soviet Union, the second world of centrally planned economies collapsed at the beginning of the 1990s. A little earlier, the Chinese economy also began to be liberalized and privatized into a market economy, and from 1991 India began to reform its economy as well, much more so than in previous periods. This encouraged MNCs internationalized during the previous two waves to expand to China, India, Russia and Central and Eastern Europe, while firms from these countries slowly started to internationalize. The Asian financial crisis in 1997–98 was also important, since it led to the disintegration of the conglomerate structures of the chaebols and the keiretsu. This did away with important non-tariff barriers, inter alia opening up these markets for international M&As. As seen in Tables 2.1–2.3, both inward and outward FDI increased the most during the Third wave in the now fully industrialized economies in Europe, North America, most of Asia, parts of Latin America, and some African countries. Compared to previous waves, FDI and MNCs now play a bigger role in global economic development and international business.

The rapid pace of scientific and technological development continued through a number of dramatic advances in information technology (IT) and organizational methods, which turned many countries into knowledge economies. This made it possible for the MNCs to invest heavily in better information systems and knowledge management, inter alia to control and integrate their international business activities much more throughout the globe. But due to the expansion to very different and diverse emerging markets, MNCs also became increasingly aware of the need to be responsive to the local market conditions. This created a dilemma of how to take advantage of economies of scale and scope through centralization and global integration and at the same time be locally responsive by giving enough independence to local units. In the early 2000s, the large MNCs increasingly, therefore, assumed the role of orchestrators of international business activities within a network of cross-border internal and external relationships. This was a major change compared to earlier, when capital, management and technology were mainly provided to the outlying affiliates, each operating rather independently. A new generation of entrepreneurial small and medium-sized enterprises (SMEs) internationalized rapidly throughout the globe, becoming known as international new ventures or 'born globals'. Artificial factor endowments created by governments became more and more common, for example in Singapore and especially in the Gulf countries, where modern cities and markets arose in the deserts, mainly providing international services such as travel and tourism.

Emerging markets

The scale of the transformation process of the emerging markets during the Third wave, where markets in the Western capitalist sense have emerged by developing from centrally planned economies and by reforming earlier highly regulated imperfect market economies, is unparalleled in history. The most important emerging markets are described below.

BRICS

A study by Goldman Sachs in 2003 (Wilson and Purushothaman, 2003) predicted that India and China plus Brazil and Russia (BRIC) would dominate the world economy in 2050 provided that

Table 2.1 Outward and inward FDI stocks: emerging markets I

Country/Group		FDI stocks (billions of US$)				
		1980	1990	2000	2010	2017
BRICS						
China	Out	–	4.5	27.8	317.2	1482.6
	In	6.3	20.7	193.3	587.8	1491.4
India	Out	0.1	0.1	1.9	96.9	155.3
	In	1.2	1.7	17.5	205.6	377.7
Brazil	Out	38.5	41.0	51.9	191.3	358.9
	In	17.5	37.2	103	682.3	778.3
South Africa	Out	5.5	15.0	32.3	83.2	270.3
	In	–	9.2	43.4	179.5	150.0
Russia	Out	–	–	19.2	336.4	382.3
	In	–	–	30	464.2	446.6
Vietnam	Out	–	–	–	2.2	10.5
	In	0	1.7	20.6	57.0	129.5
EU Enlargement Countries						
Czech Republic	Out	–	–	0.7	15.0	23.6
	In	–	–	21.6	128.5	153.4
Hungary	Out	–	–	1.2	22.3	28.6
	In	–	–	22.9	90.8	93.2
Poland	Out	–	–	0.2	16.4	31
	In	–	–	33.5	187.6	234.4
Slovakia	Out	–	–	0.5	3.5	3.4
	In	–	–	4.0	50.3	52.0
EU-4 [1]	Out	–	–	1	17	20
	In	–	–	9	51	74
EU-3 [2]	Out	–	–	–	8	11
	In	–	–	12	184	170
EU-2 [3]	Out	–	–	1	258	290
	In	–	–	5	328	430

Notes:
[1] EU-4 = Estonia, Latvia, Lithuania, Slovenia.
[2] EU-3 = Bulgaria, Croatia, Romania.
[3] EU-2 = Cyprus, Malta.
Sources: Dunning and Lundan (2008, chapter 2); UNCTAD (2018).

their fast growth persisted until then. Later South Africa was added to this group. These five econ-omies came to be known as the BRICS countries, or the R countries if the acronym is based on their currencies, that is, R as in rial, rubel, rupee, renmimbi, rand. There were also speculations of a 'Chindia effect', since China and India are large enough to be their own economic blocs. To-gether they were seen to possess the potential to transform the 21st-century global economy. They account for one-third of the world population, whose demand and supply became integrated into the world economy, a revolutionary change by itself.

However, due to the comparatively lower economic growth of India and the much lower growth of its FDI stock during this period, there is mostly a China effect. At the beginning of the 2000s, China, and to some extent India, started to act as the second engine of worldwide growth after the US (UNCTAD, 2005). For India, this was still a big change compared to the steady 'Hindu' growth of 3 per cent ever since its independence in 1947. It turned India into the world's 'software centre'. The transformation to a more efficient market economy from the earlier highly regulated market economy based on central planning started mainly in 1994.

The pace of institutional changes and industries being liberalized has been very high in China, and this turned the country, in a rather short time, into the 'factory of the world'. This was seen, for example, in the much higher productivity in the manufacturing sector in China, and in the services sector in India, compared to the overall productivity in each of these countries (UNCTAD, 2005). The internationalization of firms to most parts of the world, for example Asia, the EU, the Ameri-cas and Africa, increased significantly, especially from China, this being an important contributing factor to the higher growth of many African country markets in particular. China's outward FDI stock slowly increased from $4.5 billion in 1990 to $28 billion in 2000, after which it jumped to $317 billion in 2010 and $1482 billion in 2017 (see Table 2.1). That year it became almost as big as the inward FDI of $1491 billion, which had increased from $193 billion in 2000 and $588 billion in 2010. This growth of FDI becomes even more impressive when taking into account Hong Kong's FDI development. Here outward FDI increased from $12 billion to $1804 billion and inward FDI from $45 billion to $1969 billion during this period (Table 2.2). In 2017 Hong Kong had the second biggest FDI stock after the US. China's FDI stock is therefore bigger than the figures above suggest, since Chinese investment is also taking place through Hong Kong, and is registered there and not in China, the so-called round-tripping of Chinese FDI.

Indian FDI, on the other hand, took off later, and on a much smaller scale compared to China. Outward FDI was only $2 billion in 2000, and increased to $97 billion in 2010 and $155 billion in 2017. India is therefore still mainly a receiver of FDI, demonstrated by inward FDI being $18 billion in 2000, $206 billion in 2010 and $378 billion in 2017.

Outward FDI from Brazil was already $39 billion in 1980, and increased first slowly to $52 bil-lion in 2000, and then more rapidly to $191 billion in 2010 and $359 billion in 2017. Brazil started as outward investor but has become more and more a receiver of FDI. The inward stock was $17 billion in 1980, $103 billion in 2000 and $778 billion in 2017. Outward FDI from South Africa grew more slowly until 2010, when it increased from $83 billion to $270 billion in 2017. The inward FDI grew from $9 billion in 1990 to $180 billion in 2010 and diminished to $150 billion in 2017.

Russia has become the dominant country for FDI of the East European transition economies as inward FDI rose from $30 billion in 2000 to $464 billion in 2010 but diminished to $447 billion in 2017. Outward FDI increased from $19 billion in 2000 to $336 billion in 2010 and $382 billion in 2017.

Vietnam

The inward FDI of the former centrally planned economy Vietnam took off as late as the 2000s by increasing from $21 billion to $57 billion between 2000 and 2010 and to $130 billion in 2017. The outward FDI is still insignificant.

EU enlargement countries

The enlargement of the EU through the accession of 11 former centrally planned East European countries led to an increase in both outward and inward FDI in these economies. As can been seen in Table 2.1, the increase in the outward FDI stock is much less than the increase in the inward FDI for all of them. Of the four largest transition economies, the outward FDI of the Czech Republic, for example, increased from almost $1 billion in 2000 to $15 billion in 2000 and $24 billion in 2017, while its inward FDI increased from $22 billion to $129 billion, and then to $253 billion in these years. The increase in foreign investments between 2000 and 2010 was much bigger than between 2010 and 2017. The other three large transition economies – Hungary, Poland and Slovakia – showed a similar growth pattern, including the tapering off after 2010.

The smallest transition countries have been aggregated in EU-4, this group being made up of Estonia, Latvia, Lithuania and Slovenia. Their outward FDI increased from $1 billion to $20 billion and the inward FDI from $9 billion to $74 billion during this period. Those countries that joined the EU later are also treated as a group, since they represent a more recent enlargement effect. The combined outward FDI of Bulgaria, Croatia and Romania, defined as EU-3, increased from almost zero in 2000 to $11 billion in 2017, while the inward FDI increased from $12 billion to $184 billion in 2010, but decreased to $170 billion in 2017.

Finally, there is the EU-2 group, which consists of Cyprus and Malta. These countries are mainly financial hubs or tax havens, and this is reflected in their comparatively high FDI stocks. The combined outward FDI of the EU-2 increased from $1 billion in 2000 to $258 billion in 2010 and $290 billion in 2017, while the inward FDI changed from $5 billion to $328 billion, and then to $429 billion. In other words, there was larger slowdown in the growth of outward FDI than that of inward FDI.

Second wave emerging markets

The other Asian growth countries of the Second wave also benefitted from the growth of the new emerging markets of this Third wave. But they were also greatly affected by the Asian financial crisis in 1997–98, which made some ASEAN countries and South Korea more competitive. A major cause of this crisis was the rising integration of financial markets worldwide. It started as a currency crisis in Thailand and spread like wildfire to the other countries through the highly interdependent financial markets. It turned into an economic crisis and resulted in economic reforms, guided by the IMF. In Korea, for example, new policies resulted in the restructuring of the chaebols. The former very diversified conglomerates were broken down into smaller more homogeneous companies. The restrictions on foreign ownership were greatly reduced, which made it possible for foreign firms to acquire local firms. Western MNCs increasingly became engaged in M&A activities. This led to an increase in inter-firm market transactions at the expense of intra-firm hierarchical transactions. These companies became more embedded in a network of contractual and cooperative market relationships, where coordinating activities across borders mattered more than owning assets.

As noted in Table 2.2, Hong Kong's outward as well as inward FDI rose considerably between 2000 and 2017. This is also true for Taiwan, whose outward FDI increased to $191 billion in 2010 and $321 billion in 2017, while the inward FDI rose from $63 billion to $87 billion. The corresponding numbers for Korea's outward FDI was $144 billion in 2010 and $356 billion in 2017, and for inward FDI $136 billion and $231 billion, showing that these two countries are still mainly foreign investors. But the most remarkable increase in FDI activity was by Singapore. Its outward FDI increased eightfold between 2000 and 2010, to $466 billion, which almost doubled to $841 billion in 2017. Inward FDI increased sixfold to $633 billion in 2010, which also doubled to $1286 billion in 2017, further confirming its position as the leading Asian centre for FDI activity along with Hong Kong. A more economically and politically reformed Indonesia after the Asian financial crisis became another important host country for FDI, with inward FDI increasing more than before the crisis, to $161 billion in 2010 and $249 billion in 2017. Outward FDI was insignificant until 2017, when it was $66 billion. Thailand and the Philippines also continued to be host countries rather than home countries. For Malaysia, on the other hand, both types of FDI increased, making the economy more balanced.

Middle East and North Africa (MENA)

With the Third wave of globalization of firms, the cross-hauling of FDI came to encompass a greater part of the world economy. The global economy is now larger than the aforementioned triad and is more multipolar with the addition of the large emerging markets, including those from the Middle East. The inward FDI was $19 billion in Turkey, which increased to $188 billion in 2010 before declining slightly to $180 billion in 2017. The inward FDI of Saudi Arabia shows a similar pattern in that it was $18 billion in 2000 and increased to $176 billion in 2010. However, this increased to $232 billion in 2017. The outward FDI was low in both countries until 2010, growing from $4 billion in 2000 to $41 billion in 2017 for Turkey and from $5 billion to $80 billion in those years for Saudi Arabia. The United Arab Emirates (UAE) beats Turkey but not Saudi Arabia in outward FDI, increasing from $2 billion in 2000 to $125 billion in 2017. The UAE's FDI is balanced, since inward FDI was only a little larger during this period.

Other emerging markets in Latin America

Mexico had a low outward FDI but high inward FDI between 1990 and 2017. The latter increased from $22 billion in 1990 to $97 billion in 2000, $390 billion in 2010 and $489 billion in 2017. The outward FDI took off from a very low level in 2000 ($8 billion) to reach $117 billion in 2010 and $180 billion in 2017. This is mainly a NAFTA effect, inter alia involving US investments in Mexican labour-intensive industries. Similarly, Chile's, Colombia's and Argentina's growth in FDI stocks was unbalanced. Both types of FDI stocks in Chile were larger than that in Colombia and Argentina.

Table 2.2 Outward and inward FDI stocks: emerging markets II

Country/Group		FDI stocks (billions of US$)				
		1980	1990	2000	2010	2017
Second Wave Emerging Markets						
Hong Kong	Out	0.1	11.9	388.4	944.0	1804.0
	In	138.8	45.1	455.5	1067.5	1968.5
Taiwan	Out	13.0	30.4	66.7	190.8	321.4
	In	2.4	9.7	17.6	63.0	86.8
Korea, Republic of	Out	0.1	2.3	26.8	144.0	355.8
	In	1.1	5.2	37.5	135.5	230.6
Singapore	Out	0.6	7.8	56.8	466.1	841.4
	In	6.2	30.5	112.6	632.7	1285.5
Indonesia	Out	0.0	0.1	6.9	6.7	65.9
	In	10.3	8.9	24.8	160.7	248.5
Thailand	Out	–	–	–	21.4	107.3
	In	1.0	8.2	29.9	139.3	219.4
Malaysia	Out	0.2	2.7	22.9	96.9	128.5
	In	5.2	10.3	52.7	101.6	139.5
Philippines	Out	–	–	1.0	6.7	47.8
	In	–	–	13.8	25.9	78.8
Middle East and North Africa (MENA)						
Turkey	Out	–	1.2	3.7	22.5	41.4
	In	–	–	18.8	188.0	180.7
Saudi Arabia	Out	–	–	5.2	26.5	79.6
	In	–	–	17.6	176.4	232.2
UAE	Out	–	–	1.9	55.6	124.5
	In	–	–	1.0	63.9	130.0
Latin America						
Mexico	Out	1.6	2.7	8.3	116.9	180.1
	In	8.1	22.1	97.2	389.6	489.1
Chile	Out	0.1	0.2	11.1	62.3	124.3
	In	0.9	10.1	45.8	162.1	275.3
Colombia	Out	–	–	3.0	23.7	55.5
	In	5.3	8.8	11.0	83.0	180.0
Argentina	Out	–	–	21.1	30.2	40.9
	In	–	–	67.6	85.6	76.6

Sources: Dunning and Lundan (2008, chapter 2); UNCTAD (2018).

Mature markets

Thus, MNCs that internationalized during the Second wave took advantage of the newly opened emerging markets by investing there. This is also true for the developed economies that internationalized during the First wave. The US continued to be the largest investor, although its relative share of the world direct capital stock fell from 47 per cent in 1960 to 42 per cent in 1980, 24 per cent in 1990 and 19 per cent in 2005 (Dunning and Lundan, 2008). As observed in Table 2.3, it is still the world's leading economy regarding FDI. Outward FDI was $4810 billion in 2010 and $7799 billion in 2017, while inward FDI increased from $3422 billion to $7807 billion during this period, the latter being only 8 billion more than outward FDI in 2017. European investors also increased their share, as did Japan. The UK was the second largest EU investor after Germany. The UK's outward FDI was $1532 billion in 2017, an increase from $898 billion in 2000 and $1686 billion in 2010. Germany increased its FDI from $542 billion in 2000 to $1365 billion in 2010 and $1607 billion in 2017. Sweden's outward FDI stock increased from $123 billion in 2000 to $395 billion in 2010 and $401 billion in 2017. These numbers reflect the reinstatement of European countries as leading outward investors. Although being at a lower level, they were also host to considerable inward FDI. The UK leads Germany, where inward FDI rose from $439 billion in 2000 to $1564 billion in 2017 compared to $272 billion and $931 billion for Germany. Compared to outward FDI, Sweden's inward FDI was a little smaller in 2010 ($353 billion) and more so in 2017 ($335 billion). As is apparent from the table, FDI stocks increased much in more European economies during the Third wave (see, for example, the Netherlands, Belgium, Ireland, France and Switzerland). The overall growth pattern for these European economies is that outward FDI is significantly higher than inward FDI during this wave, the exceptions being the UK and Ireland in 2017. This makes them different from the US, where the two FDI flows are of equal size, thus growing in a similar way during this period. The Third wave also witnessed the maturing of Japan as a major global player, increasing its outward FDI further following the Second wave, to $831 billion in 2010 and $1520 billion in 2017, and now being at the same level as the large European economies. However, it was a much smaller FDI destination than many European countries. Although Japanese inward FDI grew to $215 billion in 2010, before falling somewhat to $208 billion in 2017, the country is still rather closed.

Financial hubs

Tax havens attract a lot of FDI activity, mainly financial investments. Inward FDI of the British Virgin Islands and the Cayman Islands in the Caribbean was $662 billion and $374 billion respectively in 2017, while outward FDI was $880 billion and $235 billion in these years (UNCTAD, 2018). Other similar transit countries mentioned above are Cyprus and Malta in the EU.

The global industrial network (GIN)

A key strategic issue is how related are the outward and inward FDI stocks found in Tables 2.1–2.3 to each other, and particularly how are inward and outward FDI in the production of one country

Table 2.3 Outward and inward FDI stocks: mature markets

Country/Group		FDI stocks (billions of US$)				
		1980	1990	2000	2010	2017
Mature Markets						
USA	Out	220.2	430.5	2694.0	4809.6	7799.0
	In	83.0	394.9	2783.2	3422.3	7807.0
Canada	Out	23.8	84.8	442.6	998.5	1487.1
	In	54.1	112.8	325.0	984.0	1084.0
UK	Out	80.4	229.3	897.8	1686.3	1531.7
	In	63.0	203.9	438.6	1068.2	1563.9
Germany	Out	43.1	151.6	541.9	1364.6	1607.4
	In	36.6	111.2	271.6	955.9	931.3
Sweden	Out	3.7	50.7	123.2	394.5	401.0
	In	–	–	93.8	352.6	335.0
Netherlands	Out	42.1	106.9	305.4	968.1	1604.9
	In	19.2	68.7	243.7	588.1	974.7
Belgium	Out	–	–	na	950.9	691.0
	In	–	–	na	873.3	566.9
Ireland	Out	–	–	28.0	340.1	899.5
	In	3.7	56.5	127.0	285.6	880.2
France	Out	23.6	110.1	365.9	1173.0	1451.7
	In	22.9	86.8	184.2	630.7	874.2
Switzerland	Out	21.5	66.1	232.2	1043.0	1271.7
	In	8.5	34.2	101.6	648.1	1060.0
Japan	Out	19.6	201.4	278.4	831.1	1520.0
	In	3.3	9.9	50.3	214.9	207.5

Sources: Dunning and Lundan (2008, chapter 2); UNCTAD (2018).

related to that of other countries. Together, these manufacturing units are viewed as a global in-dustrial system, the units being related to each other through the international trade of the inputs used and outputs produced. This global manufacturing system, which is intertwined through in-ternational trade, is defined in this book as the global industrial network, abbreviated as GIN. It is operationalized as the global value chain (GVC), which is illustrated in Figure 2.1. The more deeply embedded the GIN, and therefore the MNCs, is in the global economy, the more fragmented the network is. This global dispersal of production mainly began during the Second wave with the establishment of free-trade zones primarily in East Asia. The efficiency-seeking motive became important for MNCs, that is, to outsource products offshore to increase the efficiency of its pro-duction worldwide.

The GVC is a global input–output system or supplier chain of inputs (raw materials and inter-mediate products) traded between countries, where how much value is added by each country is studied. It consists of a material flow of products throughout the world, that is, the hardware part of the exchange. A FDI in local production adds value to the GVC in two ways, provided that its output is exported. It adds value either to imported products or to local products. The former value is defined as foreign value added (FVA) in exports, while the latter value is defined as domestic val-ue added (DVA) in exports. These values are also contributed by local firms that export. The FVA is, then, relevant for countries that both import and export, and the DVA when exported products are based on local rather than imported inputs. Only raw materials and intermediate products imported and re-exported by the next country along the GVC are included in the DVA, meaning that products consumed by the importing country are not inputs into the GVC. No value added is, therefore, contributed by the exporting country in this latter situation. Thus, the DVA is the first value of the GVC and arises in the exporting country when the exported output becomes an imported input that adds value to a product exported from the importing country. The FVA then represents the second, third, fourth values and so forth along the GVC.

Upstream and downstream positions

Participation in the GVC involves both upstream and downstream activities. The upstream suppli-er exports products that contain foreign inputs produced upstream in the GVC, that is, the FVA. The exports of the downstream supplier, on the other hand, do not contain any foreign input or upstream component. Participation in the GVC involves both upstream and downstream activi-ties. As illustrated in Figure 2.1, the upstream supplier of Country B is already part of the GVC by exporting products that contain foreign inputs produced upstream in Country A, that is, the FVA.

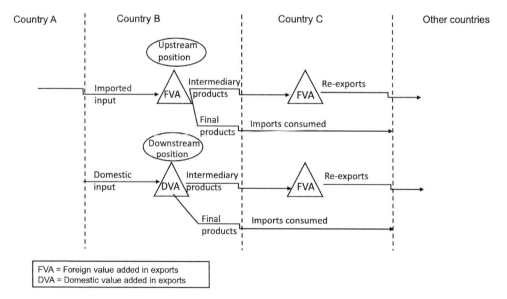

Figure 2.1 The global value chain

The exports of the downstream supplier, on the other hand, do not contain any foreign input from Country A or any upstream component, meaning that the GVC begins here. The raw materials and intermediate products exported by Country B are therefore first added value as a DVA in this country, and in a second cog of the GVC in Country C as FVA, third in another country as FVA, and so on. Thus, the DVA part represents the downstream factor.

A country's position in a supply chain can, then, be summarized by comparing its upstream and downstream activities. For example, in a study of the major trading partners of the euro area in 2009 (ECB, 2013), Russia had an extreme downstream position, since it mainly exported raw materials such as oil and gas, which were used up in the manufacturing of exports in the euro countries. Hungary and the Czech Republic, on the other hand, had extreme upstream positions as they mostly exported goods with a high import content such as intermediate products. This trade mainly consisted of imported intermediate goods re-exported to third countries. The Czech Republic moved up to 3rd position in 2009 as an exporter of such products, being at 7th position in 1995, and Hungary rose to 8th from 14th. China improved its position even more by moving up to the no. 1 position from 10th. Sweden, for its part, moved down from 3rd to 5th, and the UK from no. 1 to no. 2. These countries are also ranked high regarding intermediate goods imported from the euro area and then returned there. The Czech Republic moved up from 2nd to 1st position, while Hungary moved up from 7th to 5th. A third highly ranked new EU member in this category is Poland, which moved up to 2nd from 5th. China was no. 4, and earlier no. 13, while Sweden was no. 7, and earlier no. 3. The UK was no. 3 compared to no. 1 in 1995. These numbers show the change in the major outsourcing destinations of the euro countries between 1995 and 2009, that is, during the initial period of the Third wave. However, this trade flow was much less than the intermediate goods re-exported to third countries.

Two other groups of goods dominate exports from the euro area, but which are not re-exported from the importing country, namely final goods and intermediate goods that are absorbed in the importing country. Irrespective of how service provision and the ensuing knowledge flow is defined, it will be viewed as a final provision or an intermediate provision of services consumed in the importing country. Thus, no value is added downstream, since these products or services are not exported. They are therefore not included in the GVC. In 2009, eight countries were the main destinations of both these types of exported products: the US, the UK, China, Russia, Poland, Sweden, Turkey, and the Czech Republic. Their ranking order is about the same for both groups of goods. The rankings of China, Poland and the Czech Republic increased the most from 1995 for both groups, while that of Sweden decreased by several positions.

The shares of FVA (upstream) and DVA (downstream) are then key measures of how countries participate in GVCs. Those countries having an upstream position are more integrated than those with a downstream position. World production has been more fragmented and globalized during the Third wave. For example, between 1990 and 2010, the share of FVA in total world exports increased from 24 to 31 per cent, although it declined by 1 per cent in the period to 2017, the first decline after 20 years of steady growth (UNCTAD, 2018). In addition to those products included in the FVA and DVA, gross exports include final goods and intermediate goods absorbed in the importing country. This reversion in the trend of FVA share is consistent with the recent slowdown in economic globalization and with the trend in FDI. The FVA share of developing economies was 28 per cent of total exports, 6 per cent lower than that of the developed economies. East Asia and Central America stand out with shares of 34 per cent and 29 per cent respectively. The other developing economies have significantly lower FVA levels and are thus less integrated in GVCs.

The integration of emerging markets' FDI into the GIN

An interesting question is how these trade flows and positions relate to the inward and outward FDI patterns of the Third wave described above. This analysis is founded on the GVC participation rate of the top 25 gross exporters in 2017, which is presented in Figure 2.2, and taken from the 2018 *World*

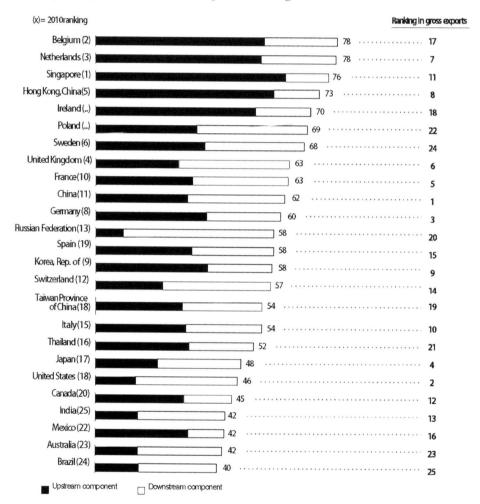

Figure 2.2 shows:

(x)= 2010 ranking — Ranking in gross exports

Country	GVC participation rate	Ranking in gross exports
Belgium (2)	78	17
Netherlands (3)	78	7
Singapore (1)	76	11
Hong Kong, China (5)	73	8
Ireland (..)	70	18
Poland (..)	69	22
Sweden (6)	68	24
United Kingdom (4)	63	6
France (10)	63	5
China (11)	62	1
Germany (8)	60	3
Russian Federation (13)	58	20
Spain (19)	58	15
Korea, Rep. of (9)	58	9
Switzerland (12)	57	14
Taiwan Province of China (18)	54	19
Italy (15)	54	10
Thailand (16)	52	21
Japan (17)	48	4
United States (18)	46	2
Canada (20)	45	12
India (25)	42	13
Mexico (22)	42	16
Australia (23)	42	23
Brazil (24)	40	25

■ Upstream component   □ Downstream component

Source: Figure 1.17 (WIR 2018); UNCTAD; based on data from UNCTAD-EORA GVC database.

Note: Ranking excludes predominantly oil-exporting countries. The symbol (..) identifies countries that were not in the list of top 25 exporters in 2010.

Figure 2.2 Top 25 exporting economies by GVC participation rate, 2017 (per cent)

Investment Report (UNCTAD, 2018). Complementary information to that on this figure, about the top three products exported in 2017 by these countries, has been collected from the web. Five countries found in Figure 2.2 followed an export-led industrialization policy, in order of ranking: Singapore, Hong Kong, Republic of Korea, Taiwan and Thailand. There are three countries that followed an import substitution industrialization policy: India, Mexico and Brazil. Three former centrally planned economies transformed during the Third wave are also included: Poland, China and Russia. The other countries in this figure are mature market economies: Belgium, the Netherlands, Ireland, Sweden, the UK, France, Germany, Spain, Switzerland, Italy, Japan, the US, Canada and Australia.

The emerging markets that are most integrated into the GVC are Singapore and Hong Kong. Their position is chiefly upstream (a large FVA), that is, this upstream part is larger than the downstream part (a small DVA). Their top three exports are mainly intermediary products. The magnitude of the contribution is considerable, which is indicated by the high rankings of the two countries in gross exports (no. 11 for Singapore and no. 8 for Hong Kong). These countries work as large free-trade zones. Their small domestic markets have led them to invest in providing high value-added services to global production by being global service, technological and financial hubs, for example by attracting regional headquarters and establishing logistical centres. The volume of re-exports, mainly through their very large commercial ports, contributes to the FVA. MNCs play a significant role in accomplishing the high participation rate in the GVC, which is indicated by the high inward FDI. The likewise high but lower outward investments indicate that foreign firms are also highly involved in exports, in many cases in the form of internal transactions to their own units in East Asia.

These exports are largely done by foreign firms in Singapore. Thus, Singapore is mainly integrated into the GVC through MNCs. Hong Kong has a more balanced FDI pattern, which is mostly due to the 'round-tripping' of Chinese FDI mentioned above. Although Belgium and the Netherlands are similar regional HQs of MNCs and logistical service centres in Europe, their FDI pattern differs to that of Singapore and Hong Kong because of the dominance of outward FDI, especially in the Netherlands. The major reason for this is that these countries host a larger number of MNCs of their own making that invest abroad. Another FDI hub in the EU specializing in administrative services, namely Ireland, has a more balanced pattern resembling Hong Kong's, indicating that more FDI is routed through the country. The upstream position of the Republic of Korea is largely due to the exports by domestic and foreign MNCs of products that have been refined further, often in the free-trade zones, from imported raw materials and intermediate products. This is indicated by outward FDI being much higher than inward FDI. The similar upstream position of Thailand and Mexico, on the other hand, is mainly due to foreign MNCs, as shown by the dominance of inward FDI over outward FDI, in Thailand by East Asian MNCs and in Mexico by US MNCs. Taiwan has an intermediate position between upward and downward, meaning that half the valued added of the products exported comes from imported inputs and half from domestic inputs. The very low inward FDI compared to outward FDI indicates that these exports are done by domestic MNCs.

The growing integration of two other emerging markets into the GVC, namely India and Brazil, is based upon a downstream position (DVA). They mainly export raw materials together with intermediate products and services based on local inputs, especially from the Indian 'software centre'. Typical of these countries is inward FDI stock being higher than outward FDI stock, indicating that foreign firms are important local producers and service providers. China, on the other hand, participates equally much from downstream as from upstream, by exporting various types of low- and high-value-added products and services. For example, China has received large inflows of FDI into manufacturing based on imported semi-finished products, which are processed further and then exported. A major part of the high outward FDI stock is domestic small and large firms investing abroad, for example in the processing of raw materials abroad, which are exported from a downstream position (e.g. in Indonesia – coal briquettes, palm oil, petroleum gas) to China, where value is added, and then the refined product re-exported from an upstream position. The magnitude of the GVC participation rate of such big economies is high due to their large gross exports, especially for China, which is ranked no. 1. This big contribution is made by both foreign and domestic MNCs, which is demonstrated by rapidly growing inward and outward FDI, the two being of equal size in 2017 and among the largest in the world. The relatively lower GVC rate is also explained by the large exports of final products (e.g. computers) and the big domestic market. A major part of the high inward FDI stock is MNCs investing in manufacturing and sales for the local market. The structure of the Chinese FDI is thus quite complex.

The rapid growth of emerging markets and their integration into the world economy has created a dual effect of a strong global pull from growing demand and a strong international push from growing competition. This dual effect involved market growth, relocation and outsourcing of production as well as shifting of supplier bases from mature market economies to new and emerging market economies. The economic integration between mature and emerging market economies was speeded up and was seen to have turned the world into one big market economy. With this globalization, the world was said to have become flat instead of spikey. The political and cultural systems of various country markets were also converging and becoming increasingly similar. With the enlargement of the EU eastwards, the former European communist countries were turned into democratic states. India and Hong Kong were already largely democratic, Taiwan democratized during the 1980s and 1990s, and there were tendencies towards the former communist countries of East Asia becoming less authoritarian.

NATURAL ENVIRONMENT AS A STRATEGIC ISSUE

As introduced in Chapter 1, issues concerning the natural environmental have become of increasingly high strategic importance in international business during the Third wave. These issues are organized by society by being institutionalized into the social and economic environments. For example, international organizations like the Intergovernmental Panel on Climate Change (IPCC) and the Intergovernmental Science-Policy Platform on Biodiversity and Ecosystem Services (IPBES) have been set up to deal with natural environmental problems from a scientific point of view. Many political parties and other non-profit organizations see themselves as representing various issues related to the natural ecosystem, with specific government bodies handling them.

The urgency of making the natural environment a key strategic issue for MNCs is made plain by some alarming recent reports. According to the *Global Assessment Report on Biodiversity and Ecosystem Services* produced by IPBES in 2019, one million species are threatened with extinction.

As summarized by the IPBES Chair, Sir Robert Watson:

> The overwhelming evidence of the IPBES Global Assessment, from a wide range of different fields of knowledge, presents an ominous picture. The health of ecosystems on which we and all other species depend is deteriorating more rapidly than ever. We are eroding the very foundations of our economies, livelihoods, food security, health and quality of life worldwide. The Report also tells us that it is not too late to make a difference, but only if we start now at every level from local to global. Through 'transformative change', nature can still be conserved, restored and used sustainably – this is also key to meeting most other global goals. By transformative change, we mean a fundamental, system-wide reorganization across technological, economic and social factors, including paradigms, goals and values. The member States of IPBES Plenary have now acknowledged that, by its very nature, transformative change can expect opposition from those with interests vested in the status quo, but also that such opposition can be overcome for the broader public good. (Ibid., p. 1)

The economic environment is influenced by increasing demand for renewable forms of energy, recycling and food and travel, which is beginning to make consumption more sustainable. An important example of how critical natural environmental issues can be solved within the economic environment is the EU emissions trading system, which has been set up as a market tool to reduce greenhouse gas emissions in a cost-efficient way (ec.europa.eu). It is the first and biggest carbon market, operating in 31 European countries. By setting a price on carbon, a financial value is given to each tonne of carbon saved. A cap is set on the total amount of certain greenhouse gases that can be emitted. Within this limit companies receive or buy emission allowances which are tradeable. They can also buy limited amounts of international credits from emission-saving projects, thereby promoting investments in low-carbon solutions globally. The limit on the total number of allowances available ensures that they have a value. When emissions are reduced, companies can keep the spare allowances for future needs or sell them to those firms that are short of allowances. This market mechanism is meant to bring flexibility that ensures emissions are cut where it costs least to do so. This system was established in 2005 and is now in its third phase; it has also been adapted to the 2015 Paris Agreement in a fourth phase. But it might also need to be adjusted by considering the IPCC's latest report *Global Warming of 1.5°C*. According to this report, human activities have so far been estimated to have caused approximately 1.0°C of global warming above pre-industrial levels. This is likely to reach 1.5°C between 2030 and 2052 if emissions continue to increase. Climate-related risks for natural and human systems are higher for global warming of 1.5°C than at present, but lower than at 2°C. Limiting global warming to 1.5°C compared to 2°C is projected to lower the impacts on terrestrial, freshwater and coastal ecosystems and to retain more of their services to humans.

However, the trading system is mainly limited to Europe and to industrial and energy production, and concerns greenhouse gas emissions that are possible to quantify and even monetize. Moreover, according to the World Bank, the carbon price is still too low to reduce emissions enough. It needs to be raised from €25 to €40–80 to be cost-efficient. Agriculture and transports are, then, excluded, and national emission goals often do not live up to the Paris Agreement. Another report, namely the Sustainable Development Agenda 2030 (United Nations, 2015), therefore becomes important, since it covers the most important environmental issues from a strategic point of view for MNCs. There are no market solutions for many of these issues; they are external effects outside the market, or externalities, for example other types of pollution than greenhouse gas emissions caused by market transactions. Rather, they are social issues that need to be solved within the social environment. The report specifies 17 sustainable development goals (SDGs), some of which are very general and valid for the whole society, for example sustainable cities and communities, and peace, justice and strong institutions, but most of which are more specific and makes it possible to refer to a specific environment, for example the natural environment, such as the goals of clean water and sanitation, climate action, and life below water and life on land. The SDGs on no poverty, zero hunger, good health and well-being, quality education, gender equality, and reduced inequalities mainly concern the social environment. Examples of SDGs for the economic environment are responsible consumption and production; decent work and economic growth; and industry, innovation and infrastructure. The report also contains a guide for business action on the SDGs – 'The SDG Compass'. The stakeholder approach of the guide fits well with the network institutional approach of this book, and will therefore be used here, mainly in Chapters 13–15 on international matching strategy towards stakeholders.

CONCLUSIONS

Information was given in this chapter about the major fundamental economic realities of the international business world, told as a story about three waves of internationalization of firms. The world has become much more integrated during the Third wave through the steep rise of FDI from mature markets that internationalized during the First and Second waves and a broadening of FDI to and from emerging markets. The major outward and inward investor countries were taken up, focusing on the emerging markets. It was also shown how FDI and the home and host countries have become more intertwined through international trade, which has mainly taken place through the global industrial network operationalized as the global value chain.

A historical background to the Third wave was provided, by illuminating the development of MNCs from the end of the 19th century until the beginning of the Third wave in 1990, being divided into the First and Second waves. This segmentation of the historical evolution of FDI into three periods corresponds well with the periods identified as reflecting the international growth and spread of manufacturing over time. Inter alia, a division is made between a first period of globalization between 1870 and 1913 and second period of globalization that mainly took off in 1990s, that is, coinciding with the Third wave.

The relations created during the Third wave between the emerging markets and the mature market economies, mainly Europe and North America, are now changing. They are becoming more conflict oriented. The maturing of the emerging markets has made them more competitive. For example, China has upgraded the competitive advantages of the firms in its industries, for instance the hi-tech industry, where MNCs from Western mature industrial countries have traditionally had competitive advantages. A major result is that the internationalization of its firms increasingly could take place at the expense of MNCs that internationalized earlier. In the telecommunications industry, for example, Huawei has become a main player on the world market, gaining market shares by outperforming Ericsson and other MNCs in certain markets. This creates a dual effect of a strong global pull from growing demand and a strong international push from growing competition that dramatizes the competitive situation, increasing the risk of mature market MNCs being outperformed by emerging market MNCs, both large and small. This conflict is now being played out fully in the ongoing trade war between the US and China.

Another conclusion is that the fruits of globalization have been distributed unequally. The winners of globalization are mainly the emerging markets of the Second and Third waves and the mature market economies of the First wave. This might have serious effects on international trade and investments, which spread rapidly during the Third wave in the global world of the highly inter-linked value chains of the global industrial network. The mature markets of the First wave have started to undergo strong institutional changes comparable to those of the emerging markets, but in the opposite direction. The long-term effect of this transformation could be that the already large institutional differences between nations widen more. The worlds of the First and Second waves have been replaced by a new divide within and between the already rich mature market economies of the first world, the new rich emerging market economies of the previous second and third worlds, and a still poor world consisting of least developed countries (LDCs) and land-locked developing countries (LLDCs) mainly in Africa and West and Central Asia.

3
Assessing emerging markets

As seen in Chapter 2, international business during the Third wave has been mainly centred on the emerging markets. The international activities of firms from these markets have grown substantially, and firms internationalizing in the previous two waves have spread their business further to these markets. The scale of the transformation process of these markets, where markets in the Western capitalist sense have emerged by developing from centrally planned economies and by reforming earlier highly regulated imperfect market economies, is unparalleled in history. Consistent with the societal perspective of this book, the focus is now shifted to the linkage between economics and politics by taking up international business research on the reformation process in major emerging markets. First, the main characteristics of these emerging markets are defined and described. Then, the markets are divided into various types based on how they are transformed to mature market economies. Transition markets are transformed from a centrally planned economy, while progressing markets are transformed from a highly imperfect market stage. Next, this reformation process and how various groups of emerging markets have performed during the Third wave in comparison to mature markets is analysed. Finally, potential new emerging markets are identified and discussed.

EMERGING MARKETS DEFINED

Some general traits of emerging market systems are economic growth, complexity and turbulence (Jansson, 2007a). They undergo liberalization and privatization of ownership as part of a general reformation of the whole society. The changing market structures are characterized by different degrees of imperfection. The early stage of transformation is normally characterized by rather homogeneous, rigid, closed and concentrated market structures consisting of a limited number of dominating big companies as well as relatively few modern small and medium-sized enterprises (SMEs), resulting in low levels of competition. This stage gradually transforms to form a more developed market structure, which becomes increasingly more heterogeneous, fluid, open and fragmented. Rivalry between firms is changed from being domestic to being global, as well as from being supply driven to being demand driven. The number of large and small companies increases gradually, which gives rise to more intense competition. The transition process in China, for example, consisted of three major stages (Jansson and Söderman, 2012). In the first stage, the market structure was highly concentrated, often being oligopolistic and dominated by state-owned firms.

With privatization and other market reforms, the number of firms expanded. The market structure became highly fragmented, with a very low concentration ratio. The low entry barriers of this second stage created a disorderly competition with variable quality, fierce price competition and low business morale, and where counterfeiting was common. In the third stage, the market was consolidated, resulting in a shake-up of firms. The wild and fragmented market of the second stage was turned into a more adolescent and 'tamed' Western-style market, changing rivalry from supply driven to demand driven. Competition on quality increased as companies relied more on the development of science and technology than on low prices for their competitiveness.

As new markets develop, business relationships change from being mainly personal to being impersonal. The unevenly distributed emerging demand is segmented into different mixes of traditional and modern consumption behaviours, which change over time. A major shift of demand takes place, moving from price orientation to quality orientation. Commercial practices change, consisting of a mix of old and modern ingredients which alters over time. In general, they are more personal and socially oriented, as well as more influenced by corruption.

With the rise of the service economy, transformation occurs, moving from a low level to a high level of service orientation. A major characteristic of emerging markets is their deficient financial markets, which gradually improve, normally lagging behind developments in product/service markets. Government plays a pivotal role in reforming the economy and other parts of society, such as the political system and the legal framework. This is a complicated and sluggish process. For this reason, the legal system, for example, is generally weak and 'people' oriented during most of the reform period, at least compared to the strong and formally developed system found in Western markets. This is often demonstrated by the lack of laws protecting property rights as well as by problems in enforcing laws through the judiciary system. The democratization of the political systems of these societies is another slow process, if it happens at all.

Market change is entangled with the evolvement of society. Markets do not develop by themselves but rather require basic support systems to be in place – for example, a legal system, a public support system, and suitable values and belief systems. This 'embeddedness' in institutions is a key characteristic of these markets, meaning that not only is the market emerging but also more or less the whole society. A democratic political system and other related Western systems, such as a legal system, are built, mostly from a system of absolute rule such as exists in a socialist/communist state (World Bank, 2002b). Serious social problems that create injustice need attention, such as corruption, criminality, poverty and malnutrition. Another downside is environmental degradation, such as depletion of rainforests, pollution of air and water, and soil erosion. Finally, the agricultural sector diminishes in importance, but still forms a critical part of the economy.

Based on the discussion above and economic theory, an emerging market can therefore be defined as *a growing market, which is being transformed from a pre-market economy stage (mainly a centrally planned economy) or a highly imperfect market (mainly in a developing country) to the market stage of the mature Western capitalistic economy, by way of integrated and successful structural reforms of companies, markets and society.* Depending on the speed of the transformation process, these emerging economies have been reaching the mature Western market stage at different times. The various country markets are therefore found at different stages of the transformation process, somewhere in between a non-market stage and a mature market stage, either being a mixture of both Western markets and centrally planned systems, or highly imperfect market economies. The first type of emerging market is defined as a transition market, while the second type is called a progressing market.

INDUSTRIALIZATION POLICIES

Depending upon the type of industrial policy practised, progressing markets are sub-divided into two groups: those countries having an export-led policy and those having an import substitution industrialization (ISI) policy. Progressing market economies practising an ISI policy as well as transition market economies are mainly reformed by government, while governments practising an export-led industrialization policy more support the market to make the changes.

Progressing market economies – export-led industrialization policy

Most of the East Asian progressing market countries referred to in Chapter 2 practised an export-led industrialization policy, which in most cases began in the 1970s. Singapore and Hong Kong opened up their markets to foreign direct investment (FDI) and trade by abolishing most tariffs and introduced a number of investment incentives to lure foreign companies into the country. Both countries then became free-trade zones (FTZs). South Korea also established FTZs, but only in certain areas, mostly in and around harbours and airports. But the policy almost failed towards the end of the 1990s, when these large Korean conglomerates (or chaebols) had become too inefficient as a result of being protected too long from foreign competition by a high wall of tariffs and far-reaching restrictions on foreign acquisitions. The Asian financial crisis in 1997 forced the government to change this policy by breaking up the monopolistic chaebols and allowing foreign acquisition of domestic firms. This change is reflected in the development of Korea's inward FDI, as illustrated in Chapter 2. This group of economies also includes Taiwan and the Association of Southeast Asian Nations (ASEAN) countries, and are often called newly industrialized countries (NICs). Their rapid growth during the Second wave has been sustained during the Third wave, mainly due to increasing FDI and trade. The United Arab Emirates (UAE) is a later addition to the group of emerging markets, since market reforms during the Third wave have resulted in the development of an internationally competitive service industry in this country.

Progressing market economies – import substitution industrialization policy

The progressing market economies also consist of former highly regulated market economies whose markets have been liberalized and privatized to form more efficient market economies. Most of these countries earlier practised an ISI policy, where the economy was tightly controlled by the state. India's earlier quasi-social economic system is a good example. The federal state played a decisive role in planning the economy and executing strict controls of FDI and trade. This strong control of the market made it highly imperfect and inefficient.

Five Latin American countries have also reformed their inward-looking economies and integrated them more into the global market: Brazil, Argentina, Chile, Colombia and Mexico. For the same reason, Turkey is also included in this group, as is South Africa. However, Venezuela is excluded, since earlier promising market reforms have been reversed through more regulations, ending the earlier high growth and throwing the country into economic chaos.

The Latin American countries implemented an ISI policy as early as the 1930s, mainly as a reaction to the Great Depression and the introduction of Keynesian economic policies. So did India after its independence in 1947. The aim was to replace foreign imports by local production through favouring local firms and making foreign firms invest in local production instead of exporting. The policy is based on the 'infant industry argument' of letting national industry develop behind high tariffs until it has become internationally competitive. Since the principal idea is to reduce foreign dependency, the policy is inward-looking and often hostile to FDI. It is based on beliefs about the strong state in contrast to the free-market ideology behind the export-led policy. Therefore, by implying that development should be government led and focused on imports rather than market led and focused on exports, the ISI policy heads in the opposite direction to the export-led policy.

The reform process in India started from a position where there was a mixture of a centrally planned economy and a highly imperfect market economy. During the centrally planned era, long before the tipping point in 1991, the Indian government realized that the economy needed to be liberalized. There was a lot of 'talk' about doing something, but only minor incremental changes were made to increase the traditionally slow 'Hindu' growth rate. But by 1991, internal pressures driven by increasing conflicts of interest due to the gradually deteriorating economy had built up to such a level that a major external push helped to bring about a drastic change in the process of reforming the economy. The major vested interests of the centrally planned period, represented by the 'iron triangle' of politicians, bureaucrats and domestic business people, was broken, and many liberalization policies were implemented in a rather short period of time (Jansson et al., 1995), leading to a deinstitutionalization of the central planning system and a more developed market.

Transition market economies

A major group of emerging markets are the transition market economies that have changed their economic system entirely, from a centrally planned economy to a market economy. The group consists of the former Soviet Union and its satellite states in Eastern Europe. It also includes China and Vietnam but not North Korea, which is still a centrally planned economy. Transition market economies are the major addition to new market economies during the Third wave. They have emerged in different ways. In all the countries of the former Soviet bloc, for example, total output fell between 1989 and 1999, capital stocks were reduced dramatically, trade was reoriented to industrial countries, and the share of value added by industry in gross domestic product (GDP) declined rapidly (Campos and Coricelli, 2002). The former institutions of the Soviet bloc collapsed with the fall of communism, creating an enormous institutional vacuum before new institutions evolved. There was a rise in unemployment, income inequality and mortality rates, while school enrolment rates declined. This slump, often called the 'valley of tears', was caused by the collapse of the previous economic system, and that change was hampered by the socialist traditions that existed. However, with the enlargement of the European Union (EU) eastwards in 2004, most of these countries recovered and started to grow. The new EU members underwent a strong transformation to a market economy and democratic society. Other former communist countries, for example in Belarus, and all former Soviet republics in Central Asia, are not included in this group, since they have been less reformed, and retain too much of the former political system. Even if they partly democratized, the authoritarian 'Homo sovieticus' is still very much alive in many of these countries.

In China, the old system was gradually replaced over a long period by the new system. China has reformed its centrally planned economy at a faster pace than India. The private sector in China expanded into a powerful growth engine between 1985 to 2005 through a drastic government-led marketization transformation (Shi et al., 2017). China has liberalized its economy but not democratized the political system. A strong government-led transformation took place to produce a highly developed market economy. Partly, it resembles South Korea's initial mix of inward and outward industrialization described earlier, which started after the Korean War and went on until the beginning of the 1980s. During this period, the country was a dictatorship under Park Chung-Hee. China has learned from Korea how to turn its large domestic firms into multinational corporations (MNCs), a lesson it also learned from Japan. Compared to these countries, China has better managed to internationalize its small-scale industry, by building on its own entrepreneurial tradition than learning from other countries. China's industrial policy is also inspired by Singapore's government-led industrialization. Through its successful internationalization, China has demonstrated that it is possible to modernize an economy without giving up too much of the authoritarian political system.

Reformation process

A major characteristic of government-led reformation processes of progressing markets with an ISI policy and transition markets is that institutions change in a contradictory way, changes being both sluggish and swift or incremental and discontinuous. Peng (2003) concludes that research on the transition process in Central and Eastern Europe (CEE) has found that long periods of relative stability involving incremental development are punctuated by discontinuous transformations from one stable stage to another. These discontinuities seem to result from an 'avalanche' of minor incremental changes, each of which is not strong enough to break the resistance from vested interests. But over time, the momentum of the 'avalanche' grows to such an extent that there is a swift and unexpected break in the inertia of the old institution, a kind of tipping point. This change pattern is also valid for India (Myrdal, 1968).

Even though the private sector in China expanded into a powerful growth engine between 1985 to 2005, the market reforms at the provincial level have been uneven. Not all provinces have advanced at the same pace, creating a misaligned change process (Shi et al., 2017). Guangdong and Shanghai have reformed the most, getting closest to a market-oriented economy. Some reforms have made progress, while others have been diluted and opposed by vested interests. Most notably, there has been a clampdown on civil society and the media, as well as on legal and non-governmental organizations (NGOs). Moreover, an increasingly strong central authority has stifled important reforms, removing authority and accountability from those agencies responsible for implementing them. This misaligned transformation process increases cognitive complexity by creating turbulence that disrupts the checks and balances of existing systems, weakening the external institutional environment and rendering it fragile, and thereby increasing the uncertainty perceived by firms. This misalignment causes friction and clashes that trigger strategic responses.

Peng (2003) divides his and others' research on institutional transformation of transition market economies into two major stages or modes of transacting in markets (e.g. see World Bank, 2002a, b). Business in the first stage is relationship based and characterized by an informal rule-based personalized exchange with the parties policing each other. Business takes place in a network society, where the penalty system is informal and mainly trust based. This earlier stage is gradually transformed into a second transaction mode that is a formal rule-based impersonal exchange with third-party enforcement founded on market-supporting formal institutions designed to facilitate this more impersonal economic exchange. Traditional institutions are gradually transformed into the new institutions of the market-based society. Even if informal business relations are basically changed into formal relations, it does not mean that informal relations disappear entirely. Rather, they take another form and meaning within the new market society, such as being more professionally based than family based. Since a market in transition is found along the road between a non-market economy and a fully developed Western market economy, it consists of a mix of characteristics from both these types of economies.

A study of the exchange between production units from a network perspective found that the Russian planned economy was characterized by fragmented relationships, which included either connections on the exchange level or use-level dependence related to resources (Hallén and Johanson, 2004b). Owing to shortages, production units were sometimes forced to solve their resource dependence by developing relationships with other units. These unofficial personal contacts were characterized by mutual trust. Personal favours played an important role in this social network, which is often called the 'blat' network (Ledeneva, 1998). These production units of a fully centralized political bureaucratic system were then transformed into the firms of a decentralized capitalistic market system through the transition process. According to Hallén and Johanson (2004a), the thin networks and fragmented relationships of the centrally planned economy were replaced by integrated relationships (Hallén and Johanson, 2004b). Per Jansson et al. (2007), the blat network was an informal barter system during the centrally planned era, where the exchange of favours was built on favours of access to goods and services. As a result of the transition towards a market economy, the blat network changed character from being based on friendship corruption to money corruption. Blat was transformed from being based on moral and ethical considerations to having an explicit financial expression. As blat is often illegal in character, it is kept hidden, and firms and the people involved try to keep it closed to outsiders.

There are striking similarities between this Russian nomenklatura network and the Chinese guanxi network (Jansson et al., 2007), as well as with other major East Asian business networks (Hamilton, 1996; Hamilton and Biggart, 1988). These are mainly social networks based on favours and gifts, as well as on strong personal emotional bonds, through which status is ascribed (ibid.).

THIRD WAVE SCORECARD

The contribution of the most influential individual countries' inward and outward FDI to the process of growth in global FDI during the Third wave is summarized in Table 3.1. It includes the top 25 exporting economies with the highest global value chain (GVC) participation rates, which are taken from Figure 2.2. The reason for choosing these countries is that they are also major home and host countries of FDI. The speed of growth of FDI is based on Tables 2.1–2.3. The factor by

Table 3.1 Third wave scorecard

Country	1980–1990 FDI In/Out	1990–2000 FDI In/Out	2000–2010 FDI In/Out	2010–2017 FDI In/Out	FDI IW rank	FDI OW rank	Club In	Club Out	GVC rank	Gross exports rank
Singapore	5/13	3.7/7.2	5.6/8	7/1.8	5	12	1977	2007	3	11
Hong Kong		10/32	2.3/2.4	1.8/2	2	2	1993	1993	4	8
Korea	5/23	7/11.6	3.6/5.4	1.7/2.5	22	20	1921	2007	14	9
Taiwan	4/2.3	1.8/2.2	3.6/3	1.4/1.7	25	21	1914	2007	16	19
Thailand		3.6/	4.6/	1.6/5	23	24	1979	2007	18	21
Mexico	2.7/1.6	4.4/3	4/14	1.3/1.5	16	22	1902	1983	23	16
Brazil	2/1	2/1.3	6.6/3.7	1.1/2	12	19	1884	1982	25	25
India	1/1	10/19	12/51	2/1.6	19	23	1929	2007	22	13
Poland			5.6/82	1.2/2	21	25	1928	2007	6	22
Russia			15/17.5	0.9/1.1	17	18	1880	2007	12	20
China	3/	9/6	3/11	2.5/5	4	8	1900	2007	10	1
USA	4.7/2.2	7/6	1.2/1.8	2.3/1.6	1	1	1886	2002	20	2
UK	3.2/3	2/4	2.4/2	1.5/0.9	3	5	1941	1962	8	6
Canada	2/3.6	3/5	3/2	1.2/1.5	6	7	1885	2002	21	12
Netherlands	3.6/2.5	3.5/3	2.4/3.2	1.6/1.7	8	4	1880	1975	2	7
Belgium				0.6/0.7	15	13	1928	1975	1	17
Ireland	15/	2.2/	2.2/12	3/2.6	10	11	1950	2007	5	18
Switzerland	4/3	3/3.5	6.4/4.5	1.6/1.2	7	10	1887	1932	15	14
Sweden	/14	/2.4	3.7/3	0.9/1	20	17	1896	2007	7	24
France	4/4.6	2/3.3	3.4/3.2	1.4/1.2	11	9	1927	1978	9	5
Germany	3/3.5	2.4/3.5	3.5/2.5	0.9/1.2	9	3	1939	1968	11	3
Japan	3/18	5/1.4	4/6	1/1.8	24	6	1899	1993	19	4
Spain			4/5	1/0.9	14	14	1884	1980	13	15
Italy			2.7/3	1.3/1	18	15	1911	1982	16	10
Australia			4.3/5	1.2/1	13	16	1886	1971	24	23

Sources: Bénétrix et al. (2012); Tables 2.1–2.3 (this volume).

which the stock of inward (IW) and outward (OW) FDI increased for each country in each decade between 1980 and 2017 is calculated. Similarly, the rankings of these two types of FDI are based on the FDI stock in 2017 given in these tables. Note that only the top 25 exporting economies are ranked, not any other economies. The years of entering (In) and exiting (Out) the 5 per cent growth club are based on Bénétrix et al. (2012). The table shows the first year that each country joined the 'modern industrial growth club', and when it left. 'In' is defined by Bénétrix et al. (2012) as the first year in which a country posted a cumulative ten-year growth rate superior to 5 per cent per year. 'Out', on the other hand, indicates the last year that a country experienced a ten-year average backward-looking growth rate greater than 5 per cent. The rankings of the top 25 exporting economies by GVC participation rate and by gross exports in 2017 come directly from Figure 2.2. The analysis below is also based on information collected from the web on the top three exports of the 25 countries in 2017.

Progressing market economies – export-led industrialization policy

Singapore and Hong Kong were found to be the emerging markets that were most integrated into the GVC, their GVC participation rate being ranked as no. 3 and no. 4 respectively of the top 25 exporting countries. Their position is very much upstream, since this component in Figure 2.2 is much larger than the downstream component. The volume of trade is considerable, since their rankings in gross exports are 11th and 8th respectively.

Singapore is mainly integrated into the GVC through MNCs, while Hong Kong has a more balanced FDI pattern, which is mainly due to the 'round-tripping' of Chinese FDI (see Chapter 2). Hong Kong's FDI numbers are, therefore, inflated, which makes it hard to determine its contribution to global FDI. But since based on the official number its ranking is no. 2 for outward FDI in 2017, it is most probably higher than Singapore's contribution, given the latter's ranking at no. 12. Inward FDI is higher than outward FDI for both countries (especially for Singapore), making them key nodes in the dispersed global industrial network (GIN) as well as global MNC hubs. As shown in Table 3.1, inward FDI contributed a lot to this. The growth of Hong Kong's inward and outward FDI accelerated substantially between 1980 and 2000, and doubled both in the decade to 2010 and in the seven years to 2017. Singapore's inward FDI grew rapidly at about the same pace between 1980 and 2017, while its outward FDI increased very rapidly between 1990 and 2010 as well as almost doubled between 2010 and 2017.

Korea and Taiwan are less integrated as shown by their GVC rankings (14th and 16th respectively). Korea participates from an upstream position, while Taiwan contributes equally much from both positions. They contributed much less to global FDI, since both countries' outward FDI was roughly 40 per cent of Singapore's in 2017, occupying the 20th and 21st positions respectively. While higher for Korea, the growth pattern of these two countries was similar, since the most rapid growth of outward FDI took place between 1980 and 2010 and, in absolute numbers, increased substantially to 2017. Although at less speed, the same goes for the inward FDI, which is smaller than outward FDI for Korea and much smaller for Taiwan.

Thailand contributes even less to global FDI, since its outward FDI was US$107 billion in 2017, or one-third of Taiwan's, corresponding to a position of 24th. It grew by a factor of five between

2010 and 2017, being negligible before this period. Inward FDI, on the other hand, grew most rapidly between 1990 and 2010, and almost doubled to $219 billion in 2017, now being twice as large as outward FDI, and thereby contributing to local economic growth. Thailand contributes a little less to the GVC (18th), mainly from an upstream position, ranking 21st in gross exports.

As seen in the table, these three countries, Hong Kong, Singapore and Thailand, are the latest members of the 'modern industrial growth club' of the top 25 exporting economies. Hong Kong was only a member during 1993, while Singapore and Thailand became members in 1977 and 1979 respectively and were still members in 2007, the last year of the period investigated by Bénétrix et al. (2012). The same goes for Korea and Taiwan, but they have been members of this club for a longer period, since 1921 and 1914 respectively, that is, since the First wave. The initial high industrial growth in those days took place in a colonial type of economy, where the countries mainly exported agricultural products to the Japanese Empire. This high dependence existed until World War II (WWII). After the war Taiwan was taken over by China, and became a nation in its own right when China was divided up into People's Republic of China (PRC) and the Republic of China as a consequence of the civil war. The latter country, or Taiwan, began its export-led industrialization policy in the 1960s. Korea, for its part, was divided up into two administrative zones after the war: South and North Korea. They became permanent nations in 1953 after the Korean civil war. South Korea started to develop its export-dominated economy in the 1960s, while North Korea is still a centrally planned economy. Thus, Taiwan and South Korea began their export-led policy at about the same time.

The numbers for the five progressing economies analysed above show that the export-led industrialization policy has been successful, especially since they were still members of the club in 2007. This is also mostly true for Hong Kong even if its political background is different. It had a free-market policy as a British colony until 1997, after which it became politically affiliated with the PRC. However, this industrial policy is still in place today.

Progressing market economies – import substitution industrialization policy

The Latin American progressing market economies had an import substitution industrialization (ISI) policy from the 1930s to the 1980s, as did India between 1947 and 1991. Mexico and Brazil are among the least integrated countries among the top 25 exporting economies, their GVC participation rate rankings being 23rd and 25th respectively. Mexico's position is upstream and Brazil's downstream, which reflects that Mexico is mainly an exporter of intermediate products, ranked 16th in gross exports, and Brazil of raw materials (being a net exporter of crude oil since 2011), ranked 25th in gross exports here. Brazil's much higher inward FDI (12th vs 16th) shows the considerable participation by MNCs in producing these exports. Regarding outward FDI, Brazil (19th) contributes equally as much to global FDI as Korea, while Mexico contributes less with its position at 22nd.

India lags behind China in infrastructure development and needs to reform its labour market and bureaucracy more. The much lower inward FDI at a quarter of China's has contributed less to India's economic development. Even though India has developed a highly competitive information technology (IT) industry (services), it has not been equally successful in developing its manufacturing industry. This is reflected in its far lower contribution to global FDI, the outward FDI in 2017 being one-tenth of China's and ranked at no. 23, in between Mexico and Thailand. Inward FDI grew most rapidly between 1990 and 2010. India is less integrated into the GVC, being ranked 22nd, up from 25th in 2010. Its upstream position is also less than China's, with India still mainly participating from downstream. The ranking in trade volume is higher than the GVC participation rate position, India being 13th in gross exports.

As 'the Jewel in the Crown' of the British Empire, India had a colonial economy in 1929, when it became a member of the growth club, which it still was in 2007. The lower growth during the period of the import substitution policy, which ran from independence in 1947 until 1991, has obviously been compensated for by higher growth in the liberalization period after 1991, allowing India to stay in the club.

Mexico was a member of the growth club between 1902 and 1983 and Brazil between 1884 and 1982. Compared to India, this early membership is partly explained by both countries having won their independence much earlier, Mexico in 1821 and Brazil in 1822. Brazil's peaceful transition from Portugal compared to Mexico's independence war with Spain might also be a major factor behind the earlier industrialization of Brazil. They were able to keep up their average 5 per cent industrial growth until 1982 (Brazil) and 1983 (Mexico), but, at least until 2007, have grown less during the Third wave and hence fallen out of the club. Their liberalization policies have therefore been less successful than India's.

Transition market economies

Poland is the most integrated country (6th GVC position) among the three countries belonging to the transition markets group (i.e. Poland, Russia and China), being ranked almost as high as the most integrated progressing market countries Singapore and Hong Kong. It is mostly integrated into the EU, being the only representative of the EU enlargement effect (see Chapter 2) in the top 25 exporting economies. The country is ranked 22nd in gross exports and participates from a position that is a little more downstream than upstream, its exports consisting of both traded and own-produced intermediate products as well as raw materials such as coal. But it is less integrated into the FDI flows. Inward FDI (21st) is considerably higher than outward FDI and therefore contributes to the economic development of the country, which is also reflected by its growth accelerating by roughly a factor of six between 2000 and 2010 before stabilizing between 2010 and 2017. The very low outward FDI (25th) makes an insignificant contribution to global FDI (the increase of 82 times between 2000 and 2010 is overblown, since its base is almost zero).

Russia's lower GVC ranking (12th) reflects its extreme downstream position, mostly exporting raw materials (20th in gross exports), with its offshore underwater natural gas pipelines (Nordstream I and II) being representative of its problematic relationship with the EU. Still, Russia's FDI picture is rather balanced as shown by its rankings of 17th in inward FDI and 18th in outward FDI, the two increasing at about the same pace between 2000 and 2010 before levelling out up to 2017. This means that the contributions by FDI to indigenous economic development and to global FDI have overall increased considerably during this period. However, compared to the size of the country, the contributions are not that impressive. The low contribution upstream also shows that Russia has not managed to develop an industry competitive enough to export intermediate products.

China continues to be by far the most successful transition market economy during the Third wave. It has transformed into a mature market economy with the help of inward FDI, which grew most rapidly between 1990 and 2000, but even more in absolute numbers to $1491 billion in 2017, ranking at no. 4. The somewhat lower outward FDI (8th) still makes a high contribution to global FDI. It has grown rapidly since 1990, accelerating the most between 2000 and 2010, that is, a decade later than inward FDI. If the round-tripping of FDI through Hong Kong is included, the growth of FDI becomes even more impressive. But as discussed above, it is hard to estimate how big this share is. It is therefore no surprise that the only progressing market economy with a higher FDI ranking is Hong Kong, which is a part of China. China's high inward FDI along with the development of many highly competitive domestic MNCs (both public and private) and SMEs has turned the country into a leading foreign investor and the world's no. 1 gross exporter. Being ranked as no. 10, it is well integrated into the GVC, in which it participates from a shared upstream and downstream position.

The three transition market economies also have a long history of industrial growth, Poland being a member of the club since 1928, Russia since 1880 and China since 1900. As was the case for India, but not Mexico and Brazil, they were still members in 2007. This means that the industrial growth of these countries has been high throughout the period they possessed a series of three types of economic systems, namely the market-oriented system before the centrally planned economy, and the market system that followed. While they all left the centrally planned economy almost simultaneously, they originally transformed into this system in different years: Poland at the end of WWII, China in 1947 and Russia in 1917. Poland's and China's much longer experience of a market economy before the centrally planned economy could explain why they have developed a more advanced industrial system than Russia after leaving the centrally planned economy. Still, Russia has kept up its high industrial growth during the period of possessing these three economic systems, by developing a domestic industry and by exporting raw materials, this latter aspect being reflected in its lower GVC rank.

Mature market economies

Of the mature market economies found in Table 3.1, the outward FDI of the US, the UK, Canada, the Netherlands, France and Germany grew the most between 1990 and 2000, while the FDI of the Ireland, Switzerland, Sweden and Japan grew most rapidly between 2000 and 2010. The growth pattern of inward FDI was different. The inward FDI of the US grew most rapidly between 1990 and 2000, while in the UK, Canada, Switzerland, Sweden, Germany and Japan it did so between 2000 and 2010. France's inward FDI increased the most between 1980 and 1990, and Ireland's between 2010 and 2017. Since these relative growth numbers are generally lower than those of the emerging market economies, it looks like they grew at a slower pace. However, as seen in Table 2.3, their FDI growth is mostly higher in absolute terms. The reason is that the relative number is based on the much bigger FDI stocks of the mature market economies at the beginning of the Third wave. Therefore, these relative numbers are not comparable between the two country groups.

The no. 1 country regarding both inward and outward FDI is still the US, contributing the most to global FDI, four times more that the second biggest outward investor, Hong Kong, and five times that of China. The US's inward FDI, on the other hand, is four times higher than Hong Kong's (2nd) and five times higher than the UK's (3rd) and China's (4th). The US is ranked no. 2 in gross exports, and 20th in GVC participation rate, which is about the same as that of Japan and Canada. The country is therefore among the least integrated into the GVC of the top 25 exporting economies, its participation mainly taking place from a downstream position.

The UK is ranked no. 5 and Canada no. 7 in outward FDI, the growth rate for both countries being stable between 2010 and 2017. Their positions mean that they made crucial contributions to global FDI. The UK's inward FDI (3rd) is higher than Canada's (6th). Canada (21st) is almost as equally integrated into the GVC as the US, while the UK is more integrated (8th), being 6th in gross exports compared to Canada's 12th position. The UK's contribution is from a slight downstream position and Canada's from a slight upstream position.

The smaller economies of the Netherlands, Belgium, Ireland, Switzerland and Sweden as well as the larger economy of France are well integrated into the GVC. The first three countries contribute from an upstream position, Switzerland from a downstream position, and Sweden and France equally much from both positions. Their rankings in gross exports vary quite a lot, from 5th (France) and 7th (the Netherlands) to 24th (Sweden). In absolute terms, the high outward FDIs are larger than the corresponding high inward FDIs for these countries. But the contribution to global FDI varies. The Netherlands contributes the most (4th) and Sweden the least (17th).

Germany's larger outward FDI and inward FDI tripled each decade between 1980 and 2010, stabilizing at $1607 billion and $931 billion respectively in 2017. This makes the country the third largest contributor to global FDI and the 9th largest receiver of FDI. It is also 3rd in gross exports and 11th in GVC participation rate, being well integrated and contributing from an upstream position. Japan's very much larger outward FDI compared to inward FDI stands out among the mature market economies. The former is the 6th largest, which makes a vital contribution to global FDI. The latter, at a meagre $207 billion, is the second lowest of the top 25 exporting economies by GVC participation, being a little higher than Taiwan's contribution and a little lower than Thailand's and Korea's. However, it is ranked as 4th in gross exports and 19th by GVC participation, mainly from a downstream position.

Almost all the 14 mature market economies joined the growth club very early, at the end of the 19th century. The Netherlands is (together with Russia) the earliest member, joining in 1880. Italy joined in 1911, Belgium in 1928 and Germany in 1939. The latecomers are the UK and Ireland, which joined in 1941 and 1950 respectively. Most of these countries exited the club long before the Third wave, while Germany exited in 1993, and the US and Canada in 2002. The only two members still in the club in 2007 were Ireland and Sweden, with Sweden being a member the longest time, having sustained high industrial growth from 1896 to 2007.

The mature market economies, then, mainly internationalized during the First and Second waves. The economic policies of these economies are similar in the sense that they are welfare oriented, but they differ in how to achieve welfare. After WWII the policies were based on Keynesian economics, where the government plays a central role in controlling the business cycle and in the redistribution of wealth. Keynesian economic policy was particularly practised by social democratic run governments in most of Western Europe, but not in the US. It included a key role for state monopolies, which in many countries remained from the war, when industrial production was centrally planned. A major economic problem of this policy was inflation. This situation changed in the 1980s with the new policy of British prime minister Margaret Thatcher, which was based on a belief in free markets. This policy stated that rather than planning and regulating people's lives, the role of the government should be restricted to the bare essentials, such as defence. This coincided with the supply-side economic policy of the Ronald Reagan presidency of tightening money supply in order to reduce inflation and deregulate the economy. These free-market policies were adopted by most governments in mature market economies, as well as in many emerging markets, and thus have been the major type of economic policy behind globalization since the 1990s, that is, during the Third wave.

POTENTIAL EMERGING MARKETS

As seen above and in Chapter 2, the emerging markets country group has grown as a consequence of the internationalization of firms during the Second and Third waves, and now includes a considerable number of economies of critical importance to world economic development. All originate from East and South Asia, Europe and Latin America except four: one from Africa (South Africa) and three from MENA (Turkey, Saudi Arabia and the UAE). Whether any other developing economy can be identified as becoming an emerging market will now be discussed. Since the integration of Africa into the global market has increased recently, more so than earlier during the Third wave, there might be new growth markets emerging from this continent. Or perhaps from the MENA, which is also under-represented among the emerging markets.

A number of candidates for becoming emerging markets have been selected among the developing countries. They are listed in Table 3.2 together with data on the key parameters according to which they have been chosen. These criteria concern FDI (outward and inward), international trade (gross exports and position in the GVC) and period of a domestic industrial growth rate of at least 5 per cent.

Six are ranked higher on international trade than the other candidates in Table 3.2 regarding both gross exports and GVC participation rate (Peru, Pakistan, Bangladesh, Egypt, Morocco and Ghana). They are seen as the primary candidates for the following reasons: all of them contribute to the GVC from an extreme downstream position except Morocco, which has a little more of an upstream position. Morocco, unlike the other candidates, also has an intermediate product among its top three exports, namely insulated wire. The other five mostly export raw materials and agricultural products. All six are important host countries to inward FDI, which has grown rather a lot during the Third wave (2000–2017). However, their outward FDI is very low, which indicates that these countries have not developed the competitiveness of their industries enough to be able to invest abroad. This is also indicated by their dominating downstream positions. They have an industrial base, since they have been members of the 'modern industrial growth club' for rather long periods. Peru left the club in 1971, Morocco in 1982 and Egypt in 2006, while Pakistan, Bangladesh and Ghana were still members in 2007, the final year of the study by Bénétrix et al. (2012).

The other five candidates differ from the six above by not being among the top 25 developing countries regarding either gross exports or GVC participation rate. They are therefore considered more as secondary candidates, mainly being interesting due to their relatively high inward FDI.

Table 3.2 Potential emerging markets

Continent/Country		FDI stocks (billions of US$)			GE rank	GVC rank	GC period
		2000	2010	2017			
South America							
Peru	Out	0.5	3.3	5.4	18	17	1907–1971
	In	11.0	43.0	99.2			
Asia							
Kazakhstan	Out	n//a	16.0	20.0	–	–	–
	In	10.0	82.7	147.1			
Pakistan	Out		1.3	1.9	24	20	1961–2007
	In	6.9	19.8	43.1			
Bangladesh	Out			0.3	20	25	1971–2007
	In	2.1	6.0	14.5			
Lebanon	Out	0.3	6.8	13.9	–	–	–
	In	14.2	44.3	63.7			
Africa	Out	39.8	134.3	365.7			
	In	152.8	598.2	866.8			
Egypt	Out	0.7	5.5	7.2	21	12	1962–2006
	In	20.0	73.0	110.0			
Morocco	Out	0.4	2.0	5.9	22	11	1949–1982
	In	9.0	45.1	62.7			
Ghana	Out	n/a	0.1	0.4	25	16	1961–2007
	In	1.6	10.1	33.1			
Nigeria	Out	4.1	5.0	14.2	–	–	n/a
	In	23.8	60.3	97.7			
Angola	Out	n/a	6.2	26.8	–	–	2003–2007
	In	8.0	16.1	12.1			
Mozambique	Out	n/a	n/a	0.1	–	–	–
	In	1.2	4.3	38.1			
LDCs	Out	2.7	6.2	26.8			
	In	35.8	144.8	312.1			
LLDCs	Out	1.1	29.3	41.7			
	In	33.8	180.8	369.6			

Notes:
GE rank = Top 25 gross exports of developing countries in 2017.
GVC rank = Top 25 exporting developing countries by GVC participation in 2017.
GC period = 'Growth club' membership period
Sources: UNCTAD (2018); Bénétrix et al. (2012).

Like the primary candidates, their outward FDI is low or even negligible. Two countries are Asian (Kazakhstan and Lebanon), while three are in sub-Saharan Africa (Nigeria, Angola and Mozambique). Kazakhstan is the largest recipient of foreign investments of the Central Asian countries. The inward FDI stock of this transition economy was $10 billion in 2000, $83 billion in 2010 and $147 billion in 2017. Lebanon's inward FDI increased from $14 billion to $64 billion between 2010 and 2017, while Nigeria's inward FDI increased from $24 billion in 2000, to $60 billion in 2010 and $98 billion in 2017. Angola had the lowest inward FDI among the secondary candidates but was the only country with a considerably higher outward than inward FDI.

Mozambique experienced an even more unbalanced FDI situation with negligible outward FDI as well as inward FDI, the latter only growing after 2010, reaching $38 billion in 2017. Four countries almost entirely export raw materials such as oil, gas and minerals, while Lebanon mainly exports gold but also scrap minerals.

Three of the primary candidates and three of the secondary candidates are African. As seen in Table 3.2, Africa as a whole benefitted from the increased FDI activity of the Third wave from 2000 and onwards. Inward FDI increased from $153 billion in 2000 to $598 billion in 2010, and to $867 billion in 2017, far exceeding outward FDI, which was $40 billion, $134 billion and $366 billion during these years. Africa is thus still mainly a destination for FDI, having developed few export industries beyond oil, gas, minerals and agricultural products. The total outward FDI stock in 2017, for example, is about half that of Singapore and a little less than Sweden's. The GVC participation rate is therefore low, and almost entirely originates from a downstream position. These FDI stocks were concentrated in a few countries, with South Africa being the leading destination and outward investor, as found in Table 2.1.

On the whole, few candidates could be found in Africa, Central Asia and West Asia. This is no surprise, since these regions are dominated by least developed countries (LDCs) and land-locked developing countries (LLDCs) with even lower GVC participation rates, and where there is even less FDI. Two such countries were included above, namely Mozambique as a LDC and Kazakhstan as a LLDC. The total outward FDI stock of an aggregate of the LDCs and LLDCs in these regions was a low $69 billion in 2017. The inward FDI stock was much bigger in this year, 312 for LDCs and 370 for LLDCs, being about the size as India's FDI stock. These groups of economies are thus loosely coupled to the GVC, mainly being the first leg of the GVC as illustrated in Figure 2.1.

The little higher share of the upstream component of Morocco implies that this country is more integrated into the GVC, and is therefore a more promising candidate for becoming an emerging market than the others. A major reason for finding so few candidates is that the liberalization and privatization of these candidate markets lag behind the emerging markets discussed earlier. This applies to the African countries noted above as well as Kazakhstan, Saudi Arabia and Lebanon. Kazakhstan seems to have got stuck somewhere between the old centrally planned economy and a more developed market economy, the main reason being the still very authoritarian political system and the lack of judicial reform.

Since 2017, the chances that the candidates above will grow fast enough through reforming and upgrading their industries to classify as emerging markets have reduced considerably. The Third wave has started to undergo a major shift, following crucial signs that the flattening of the world came to a halt in 2016–17. This could mean that the candidate countries will become even more disconnected from the GVC. Even the mature and emerging markets are becoming more divergent. If markets continue to disintegrate, there could be a transition into a new period, which could then be defined as the 'divergence period' in contrast to the previous 'convergence period'.

CONCLUSIONS

During the Third wave of the golden age of international business, the world has become much more integrated. First, the traditional exchange of FDI across the Atlantic Ocean during the First and Second waves increased substantially with the addition of the rising emerging market economies along the Pacific rim and the steep increase of outward FDI from Japan. Second, the increased FDI of the home and host countries have been more intertwined through international trade, mainly expressed through a country's participation in the GVC. From the growth patterns of outward FDI of the top 25 exporting economies analysed above, it can be deduced that the Third wave emerged in the form of rapidly growing global FDI between 1990 and 2010, which continued to grow up to 2017, but at a slower pace. The FDI of most emerging markets grew most rapidly between 2000 and 2010. The deep roots of this industrial growth during the Third wave is demonstrated by how long the countries have been members of the 5 per cent growth club. As expected, the industrialization of the mature market economies took place earlier than most emerging markets. Likewise, their industrial growth rate peaked earlier, often long before the Third wave. The membership period of the progressing market economies with an export-led policy started later than the ISI countries and the transition market economies. All emerging markets were members in 2007 except Mexico and Brazil, which left in 1983 and 1982, that is, during the Second wave. Hong Kong is a special case since it was only a member during 1993.

The fastest growth period for the transition market countries and the ISI countries India and Mexico took place between 2000 and 2010. The same applies for the progressing market economies Taiwan and Singapore. Thailand's outward FDI, however, rose most rapidly between 2010 and 2017. And the other two progressing market economies, Hong Kong and Korea, grew the most one decade earlier, that is, 1990–2000. The growth of these emerging markets was also impressive between 2010 and 2017, when the figures for both types of FDI mostly doubled, and for some countries even increased more: China's outward FDI (5 times) and Singapore's inward FDI (7 times).

Few countries among the LDCs and LLDCs were found to be candidates to become the next emerging markets during the Third wave. The main losers of this wave are therefore most of the LDCs and the LLDCs, which are still loosely coupled to the global industrial network and have benefitted from only a trickle of the global FDI flows. Some of these countries are even considered to be failed states, which have been torn apart by war. Examples include Somalia, Southern Sudan, Yemen, Syria and Afghanistan. This disparity between these countries and the rest of the world now risks widening even further in the future due to the increasing divergences that have occurred in recent years.

PART III
RESEARCH HISTORY

Bumblebee economics

The question is whether economic man disguised as a bumblebee can help to save the bees from becoming extinct. According to the sociobiology approach established by Bernd Heinrich in his book *Bumblebee Economics* published in 1979, an energy economics framework explains how bumblebees provide ecology services to society. They are produced in a hive economy likened to small-scale cottage industry, which differs from the large-scale industry of big corporations of honeybees. Resources (pollen and sugar) produce the machinery (combs and new workers) of the factory, which in their turn produce drones and new queens for the survival of the colony. Foraging strategy in terms of individual initiative and competition is founded on optimizing energy returns per units of time and energy spent in foraging for the sugar. As illustrated in the photo, the bees (e.g. the garden bumblebee) and the flowers (e.g. the foxglove) have coevolved according to the bees' goal of reaping maximum rewards and the flowers' goal of supplying the least amount of food necessary to attract pollinators.

4
Historical overview of international business research

In this chapter an odyssey is taken through the history of international business research on multinational corporations (MNCs) and internationalization processes to systematize and explain the fundamental economic realities of the international business world described in Chapter 2, namely foreign direct investment (FDI) growth, international production and international trade, as three waves of the internationalization of firms. The focus is still on the Third wave, and the emerging markets characterizing this period.

A major conclusion from Chapters 2 and 3 is that the business opportunities created by the growth of the emerging markets during the Third wave have mainly been taken advantage of by the already established MNCs from the First and Second waves, that is, MNCs from the US, Europe and East Asia. This is indicated by the dominance of inward FDI over outward FDI throughout the emerging markets. Even though this book is mainly about the experience of how European MNCs compete on these markets through their international business strategies, most theories referred to in this chapter are also relevant for US MNCs.

Another major conclusion from these chapters is that it takes time for firms from emerging markets to become competitive on international markets. The domestic market economy normally needs to be developed first to make it possible for its firms to develop competitive strength at home before being able to compete on foreign markets. So far, only China, as the major beneficiary of the Third wave, has managed to establish a sufficient number of internationally competitive indigenous MNCs that a balance between inward and outward FDI has been achieved, namely in 2017. Another contributing factor is that foreign investors have started to export from China.

The three waves are analysed in this chapter by looking closer at how the internationalization of firms can be assessed and explained with the help of international business research. A historical account is not only given of theories about the emergence and evolution of the international firm during the three waves, but also of the evolvement of international business as an academic discipline. The development of major theories in international business, since such research started in 1950s, is outlined.

These theories are arranged so that they answer five major questions in international business research: Where to do international business? Why? How? When? With whom?

To start with, the first three questions are answered by examining various general theories about MNCs to see how the internationalization of such firms has been described and explained over the years since their emergence in the 19th century. Next are found theories that describe and explain how the global industrial network (GIN) at the supranational level, discussed in Chapter 2, has been established and organized as an industrial network at the MNC level. A vital economic explanation is provided by the theory on the global factory, using transaction cost theory to explain the configuration of the global vertical production system. However, it is too limited to explain the sustainability aspect of the GIN. This is a cyclical and broader value chain that not only adds economic value but also ecological and social values. Still, a broader transaction cost theory, namely the markets and hierarchy theory, is presented that gives more insights into the economic organization of the value chain and the MNC in general. After this, the structural and spatial perspective on the MNC and its internationalization represented by these economic theories is contrasted with the dynamic dimension of internationalization, that is, the 'when' question. The major internationalization process theories are taken up to systematize and explain the internationalization of firms over time, covering MNCs, multinational exporters (MNEXs) and international new ventures (INVs). One theory, namely the internationalization in networks theory, mainly focuses on the 'with whom' question. These internationalization process theories are followed by theories on the international organization of MNCs which explore how they have been organized over time. A typology of international firms is finally developed by integrating internationalization process theory with typical ways of organizing MNCs worldwide.

INTERNATIONAL BUSINESS RESEARCH AS ACADEMIC DISCIPLINE

International business as an academic discipline is relatively young. Research started towards the end of the First wave, during the 1950s, and took off in the 1960s and 1970s (Wright and David, 1994). During this period, the focus was almost entirely on business operations in the first world of today's mature market economies, that is, on the international business between Western firms. International business research grew even more during the Second wave and came to include studies of primarily Japanese firms and management but also South Korean and overseas Chinese firms. Asian researchers mostly from these countries and India now also joined the international business community, often studying and working in universities in the US, the UK and Australia. In the Third wave, the international business community has become more global, with new researchers joining from the former centrally planned economies, demonstrating a 'Chindia' effect and an EU enlargement effect also in research. Many researchers from Africa, Latin America and the Middle East have also joined the international business community, making global business research truly global. Moreover, the many firms that have internationalized from and to emerging markets have provided international business scholars with more subjects to study, which has hugely increased the research output and publications in the field.

International business is an inter-disciplinary field of research. The origin of the field is mainly in economics, particularly international trade. More and more business subjects have been added such as finance, organization, marketing and strategy, and many issues are now studied using a mixture of theoretical frameworks originating in economics, psychology, sociology, culture, political science and law. This evolvement of the international business field is analysed here in more detail from a theoretical perspective by looking closer at the major theories on the MNC and the internationalization of firms.

THEORIES ON THE MNC

Based on Casson (1987), one can conclude that the theory on the multinational corporation evolved over three steps, where each step represents a solution to the first three of the major research questions raised above.

Where to invest abroad?

The first question answered is about where the international business takes place, that is, the location issue. This is mainly explained using international trade theory and location theory. However, these neoclassical economic theories are very general and do not go into the firm itself. An early example of this is the product cycle theory (Vernon, 1966). It combines the product cycle concept from micro-economic theory with trade theory to explain all the foreign activities of US MNCs during the post-war period, that is, during the American epoch of the First wave of the internationalization of firms. It explains the change of the location of production based on varying international factor endowments and national demand. Initially, production is for the home market due to its favourable production environment (e.g. innovative technology) and large market with demand for sophisticated products. At a later stage of the product cycle, the product is exported to countries that are similar to the home market in terms of demand patterns and supply capabilities. Next production is moved to foreign locations due to the higher importance of low labour costs and rising foreign demand. The product has now lost its uniqueness by being mature, which makes cost-efficiency important, increases competition and heightens the risk that the product is copied. This internationalization of production is hastened by differences in trade barriers, for example high import duties. This theory has not withstood the test of time, the main reason being that the major empirical base was US FDI during the American epoch when there were relatively high trade barriers, which could not be generalized to later periods. Moreover, the theoretical development went more and more into the international firm, which reduced the interest in such macro-oriented theories.

Why invest abroad?

Trade and location theories explain where to locate foreign production, but not why a foreign firm takes advantage of such locations and not local firms. Rather, a foreign firm should have a disadvantage due to being unfamiliar with the local market. It became possible to answer this 'why' question with the emergence of a new field in economics in the 1950s, namely industrial economics theory or 'market imperfections theory' (Bain, 1956, and summarized in Scherer, 1971). Firms now emerged from the shadows of neoclassical economics as economic units thriving in this new economic world of market imperfections, inter alia by having resources of their own. This theory was introduced into the field of international business to explain why foreign firms invest abroad despite their locational disadvantage (such as a liability of foreignness, usually defined as the extra costs of entering a foreign market above those of local firms) relative to local firms in the foreign markets. Foreign firms were now seen to have strategic advantages based on their assets, which enable them to out-compete local rivals in advantageous locations. These strategic advantages were defined as firm-specific or ownership advantages by Hymer in his PhD thesis from 1960, which was published in 1976 (see Hymer, 1976). Examples of intangible assets found to result in strategic advantages include technology, human capital, brands and organizational capabilities. Another closely related development during the 1970s was the research into the inverse relationship between the why and where questions, that is, that the strategic response to the location variables also influences the spatial distribution of the economic activity of firms. Oligopoly theory was used by Knickerbocker (1973) and others to explain why firms tend to cluster their investments in certain locations at a specific time. Oligopoly is a market imperfection, where the market consists of a few large firms that influence each other's strategic behaviour, leading to price rigidity among other things. These firms have heterogeneous products and face entry barriers. In such a market structure, strategic behaviour is interactive in that firms tend to follow each other into foreign markets, for example by imitating each other. Such crowding of FDI was found to take place among US firms in manufacturing during the American epoch, and also among US, European and Japanese MNCs in certain industries during the Second wave of internationalization of firms. The linkage between industrial organization theory and corporate strategy is thoroughly investigated in Caves (1979). Through the work of Caves and Porter, this market imperfections theory made a huge impact on another nascent research field, namely business strategy. As an industrial economist and student of Caves, Porter studied strategic behaviour in imperfect markets. For example, he derived five market forces of strategic importance to the firm: threats of new entrants, threats of substitutes, bargaining power of customers, bargaining power of suppliers, and industry rivalry (Porter, 1980, 1985). This theory inspired international business research, leading to further development in the why issue in FDI theory and strengthening the rather new research on international strategy. This theoretical background, as an antecedent to the international business strategy (IBS), is developed more in Chapter 5.

How to invest abroad?

Another major question about FDI remained unanswered: how does the firm invest abroad? For example, does it do so by establishing a firm of its own rather than selling the asset in the market through licensing it to a firm in the foreign market? With the wakening-up in the 1970s of a dormant economic theory from the 1930s (Coase, 1937), namely transaction cost theory, it was possible to answer this question. This theory is about how firms organize their business activities, externally through the market or internally through the hierarchy. This issue was developed in international business as internalization theory, mainly by Buckley and Casson (1976) but also by Rugman (1980, 1986) and Hennart (1982). It explains how firms organize their international activities in advantageous locations in which they possess firm-specific advantages. It is founded on four major assumptions taken from transaction cost theory:

- Firms can fail to allocate factor services and goods efficiently due to high transaction costs. This is called a market failure rather than a market imperfection. Normally a distinction is made between costs for information, bargaining (e.g. negotiating) and enforcement.

- Markets and firms are alternative ways of organizing factor services and goods. Licensing and outsourcing are examples of ways of organizing transactions via the market, while FDI is a hierarchical way, that is, a market failure.
- Exchange is internalized within the firm when its costs are less than market exchange.
- The MNC is, then, an institution that internalizes cross-national exchanges through FDI in international production.

The OLI paradigm

The major building blocks for a general theory on the multinational firm were now in place, and these were put together by Dunning (1981) in the eclectic paradigm to international production. It is also called the OLI paradigm, where O stands for ownership-specific advantages (the why question), L for location-specific advantages (the where question) and I for internalization advantages (the how question). Its theoretical bases are illustrated in Figure 4.1, while the OLI parts are detailed in Box 4.1, which is an excerpt from Dunning and Lundan (2008, pp. 101–2).

This is the most general economic international business theory developed so far. Still, it is limited to explaining FDI in international production at a high level of abstraction, saying very little about the MNC as an organization. This is the main limitation of economic theory in general, and why organization theory is mostly based on social disciplines, mainly psychology, sociology and culture. One can also doubt its applicability to today's global world of more complex international business, where non-economic factors need to be considered much more. But it is still very important as a theoretical framework from which to select suitable constructs for more specific theories.

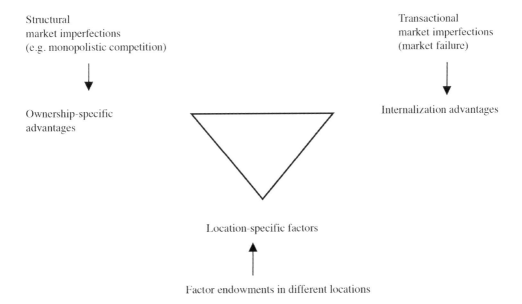

Figure 4.1 Theoretical bases of the OLI paradigm

BOX 4.1

THE ECLECTIC (OLI) PARADIGM OF INTERNATIONAL PRODUCTION

OWNERSHIP-SPECIFIC ADVANTAGES (O) OF AN ENTERPRISE OF ONE NATIONALITY (OR AFFILIATES OF SAME) OVER THOSE OF ANOTHER

(a) Property rights and/or intangible asset advantages (Oa)

The resource (asset) structure of the firm. Product innovations, production management, organizational and marketing systems, innovatory capacity, non-codifiable knowledge; accumulated experience in marketing, finance, etc. Ability to reduce costs of intra- and/or inter-firm transactions (also influenced by Oi).

(b) Advantages of common governance, that is, of organizing Oa with complementary assets (Ot)

1. Those that branch plants of established enterprises may enjoy over de novo firms. Those resulting mainly from size, product diversity and learning experiences of the enterprise (e.g. economies of scope and specialization). Exclusive or favoured access to inputs (e.g. labour, natural resources, finance, information). Ability to obtain inputs on favoured terms (e.g., as a result of size or monopsonistic influence). Ability of parent company to conclude productive and cooperative interfirm relationships. Exclusive or favoured access to product markets. Access to resources of parent company at marginal cost. Synergistic economies (not only in production, but in purchasing, marketing, finance, etc. arrangements).

2. Those that specifically arise because of multinationality. Multinationality enhances operational flexibility by offering wider opportunities for arbitraging, production shifting and global sourcing of inputs. More favoured access to and/or better knowledge about international markets (e.g. for information, finance, labour, etc.). Ability to take advantage of geographic differences in factor endowments, government regulation, markets, etc. Ability to diversify or reduce risks. Ability to learn from societal differences in organizational and managerial processes and systems (also influenced by Oi).

(c) Institutional assets (Oi)

The formal and informal institutions that govern the value-added processes within the firm, and between the firm and its stakeholders. Codes of conduct, norms and corporate culture; incentive systems and appraisal; leadership and management of diversity.

LOCATION-SPECIFIC FACTORS (L) (THESE MAY FAVOUR HOME OR HOST COUNTRIES)

1. Spatial distribution of natural and created resource endowments and markets.
2. Input prices, quality and productivity (e.g. labour, energy, materials, components, semi-finished goods).
3. International transport and communication costs.

4. Investment incentives and disincentives (including performance requirements, etc.).
5. Artificial barriers (e.g. import controls) to trade in goods and services. Infrastructure provisions (educational, transport and communication).
6. Cross-country ideological, language, cultural, business, political differences.
7. Economies of agglomeration and spillovers.
8. Economic system and strategies of government; the institutional framework for resource allocation.
9. Legal and regulatory system (e.g. protection of propriety rights, credible enforcement).

INTERNALIZATION ADVANTAGES (I) (I.E. TO CIRCUMVENT OR EXPLOIT MARKET FAILURE)

1. To avoid search and negotiating costs.
2. To avoid costs of moral hazard and adverse selection, and to protect the reputation of the internalizing firm.
3. To avoid cost of broken contracts and ensuing litigation.
4. Buyer uncertainty about nature and value of inputs (e.g. of technology being sold).
5. When market does not permit price discrimination.
6. Need of seller to protect the quality of intermediate or final products.
7. To capture economies of interdependent activities (influenced by Ot).
8. To compensate for the absence of future markets.
9. To avoid or exploit government intervention (quotas, tariffs, price controls, tax differences, etc.).
10. To control supplies and conditions of sale of inputs (including technology).
11. To control market outlets (including those which might be used by competitors).
12. To be able to engage in practices such as cross-subsidization, predatory pricing, leads and lags, and transfer pricing as a competitive (or anti-competitive) strategy.

Sources: Dunning and Lundan (2008, pp. 101–2). These variables are culled from a variety of sources, but see especially Dunning (1981, 1988a) and Ghoshal (1987).

The global industrial network

The global industrial network (GIN) consisting of material flows between countries at the supranational level was explored in Chapter 2. This network is now viewed from the perspective of the MNC by exploring how firms act along the value chain. Regarding production, it has been internationalized by firms through five phases (Farrell, 2004). First, when being less global and entering markets, the firm's domestic production is 'cloned' abroad. Next, whole production processes are relocated to take advantage of worldwide cost differentials. Third, the global industrial network emerges by virtue of the fact that the value chain of the MNC is disaggregated globally, and individual product components manufactured in different locations. Fourth, companies re-engineer the now global value chain by redesigning their production processes to maximize efficiencies and cost savings. According to Dunning and Lundan (2008), a deepening and widening of the value-added network takes place during the third phase, while the MNC becomes an integrated network multinational during the fourth phase. The third phase deals with how to integrate the various parts of the value chain already established, perhaps also adding new local activities. The fourth phase deals with how to coordinate this local organization within the international organization of the MNC, that is, the common governance issue. Farrell (2004) adds a fifth stage: that at a highly global stage new markets are created due to the lower costs resulting from globalization. Here, production is wholly integrated globally, both geographically and with the other activities in the value chain. Companies can offer new products at lower prices and can penetrate new market segments or geographies, or both.

The global factory

These theories provide insights into how MNCs organize production along the global value chain (GVC). A more developed economic explanation of this global production system at the MNC level is provided by Buckley (2009) and Buckley and Ghauri (2004). They see it as the global factory of the MNC, through which the world economy has been reconfigured by 'fine slicing' the vertical production system into more and more specialized and small parts. The idea with the global factory is to take a systemic economic approach to this highly disaggregated system by looking at the entire input system of the products produced by the MNC. This production system is, then, about the upstream activities of the firm. The analysis of this global factory is mainly based on Coase's (1937) theory of the firm, which stresses information costs. The reconfiguration of the global production system is explained by the fact that firms minimize such costs occurring in producing and transacting raw materials and intermediary products along their global value-added chain. The theory of the global factory is thus closely related to the internalization theory discussed above. However, it excludes other major transaction costs such as bargaining costs and enforcement costs (Jansson, 1994a, b).

Still, this theory does not say much about various activities along the value chain and how they are organized. Porter (1985, 1986) elaborates on the company activities along the value chain considerably. He distinguishes between primary management activities directly related to the value chain (e.g. production operations and inbound logistics) and secondary activities indirectly related to the value chain (e.g. procurement and firm infrastructure). Since this value chain is part of his strategy theory, it is taken up more in Chapter 5.

The sustainable global industrial network

It was increasingly realized from the 1960s onwards that mass production in industry led to high consumption of resources and excessive pollution. The first legislation on industry introduced demanded pollution control. It resulted in environmentally friendly technologies being developed for the end of the production line, involving mainly specialized equipment as well as materials and energy. Eventually, industry realized that it was better to prevent pollution than fight it, especially in the manufacturing phase and through the reduction of raw materials. As noted above, the global society underwent a paradigm shift during the Third wave from environmental protection towards sustainability (Finkbeiner et al., 2010). Sustainable development was first defined in 1987 by the Brundtland Commission. Such development should cover the current needs for an intact environment, social justice and economic prosperity without limiting the ability of future generations to meet their needs (United Nations, 1987). Thus, sustainability rests on the three pillars of natural environment, economy and social well-being. It does not focus entirely on ecological impact, but also on economy and social well-being. Society needs to find a balance between these three, both nationally and internationally.

The sustainable global industrial network, abbreviated as SGIN, further demonstrates that the world's industry has been highly intertwined during the Third wave, not only economically as in the GIN but also ecologically and socially. Problem-solving along this global value chain therefore demands close cooperation within and between MNCs, as well as with governments, non-governmental organizations (NGOs), international organizations and so on. A distinction is made between two types of SGINs, namely the 'cradle-to-grave' industrial network and the 'cradle-to-cradle' industrial network.

The 'cradle-to-grave' industrial network. The idea of sustainability as a basis for industrial strategy was expanded and developed not only for the manufacturing phase, but also to cover all stages of the life cycle, from the extraction of materials to the end of the product's life. Based on Peralta-Álvarez et al. (2015), this type of global value chain is defined as the 'cradle-to-grave' industrial network, which is different from the 'cradle-to-cradle' industrial network. The global industrial network at the country level is enlarged to include more activities, mainly product use, disposal and recycling. These two types of networks are also cyclical (i.e. processual) rather than structural and exist at the firm level. Last but not the least, such sustainable production networks are broader value chains, since they not only add economic value but also ecological and social values.

The 'cradle-to-cradle' industrial network. This is a fully circular system, where products are reused or recycled without reducing quality. This network is seen to represent a new paradigm for the ecological reformation of the industry and as a start of the next industrial revolution. While the focus in the 'cradle-to-grave' industrial network is on increasing the proportion of materials recycled, the focus in the 'cradle-to-cradle' industrial network is on reducing waste as well as increasing both the quantity and the quality of the materials recycled. This is necessary to avoid future shortages of many materials and to considerably reduce greenhouse gas emissions. The products and associated systems (manufacturing processes, use and disposal) are seamlessly integrated with the flows of matter and energy of the natural ecosystem. Products are regenerated by nature in that materials are returned to the biosphere as organic material, that is, being neither synthetic nor toxic. Eighty per cent of a product's ecological impact is decided at the design phase. Products and infrastructure should therefore be designed for circularity, that is, with renewable, reusable and recycled materials, to prolong life spans as well as to reduce the waste of materials, water, energy and chemicals. For example, products should be designed so that components and materials can be separated to facilitate sorting, reuse and recycling.

How these global industrial networks and activities along the global value chain in general are organized is developed as an inter-organizational industrial network in Chapter 7, thereby establishing the foundation for the international network strategy in ensuing chapters.

The markets and hierarchies theory

The internalization theory behind the global factory can be used to explain how firms solve the classic 'make or buy' issue in supply chain management, that is, whether to outsource an activity or keep it in house. A fuller economic explanation is provided by the markets and hierarchies theory. This is a more ambitious attempt to develop the MNC as an economic organization by building on another transaction cost theory, namely the markets and hierarchy theory developed by Williamson (1975). As with economic theories in general, this theory takes the individual as the starting point. Hierarchies or organizations are often more efficient than markets in effectuating transactions, for example by keeping production in house rather than externalizing it to the market. The reason is that they place a more effective check on opportunism as well as on market situations involving a small number of parties exchanging goods. This control is executed through a more formalized authority structure. Information impactedness is also less due to the information and control systems of the hierarchy. This organizational economics theory distinguishes between six ways of organizing transactions or governance forms. The three market institutions are market governance, bilateral governance and trilateral governance (see Appendix for more details). The first approximates the perfect market of neoclassical economics, while the last two are more imperfect, sharing characteristics of both the market and the hierarchy. There are three market failures or types of hierarchies: the U-form, the M-form and the H form. The first represents the classic unitary one-business organization consisting of departments, the second the multi-business firm organized in divisions, and the third the diversified multi-business firm or conglomerate consisting of businesses with different technologies and a holding company at the top, running the hierarchy through financial measures.

This theory was used to study the international business of Swedish MNCs in South East Asia between 1984 and 1991 (Jansson, 1994b). The hierarchical governance forms were developed into types of international organization to study how these MNCs organized their subsidiaries in the area. The M-form was developed into the transnational M-form, the major reason being that most firms had a multi-divisional organization. The governance forms of the market, inter alia the entry forms, were included to study the external business-to-business transactions of the Swedish firms in the area, resulting in the development of the marketing economics approach (Jansson, 1994a).

A major conclusion from the discussion above of the theories on the MNC is that all of them originate from economics. The extent of such economic analysis of the MNC is well summarized in Caves (1982). As stressed throughout this book, these theories have their limitations in describing and explaining the international business of Western MNCs in emerging markets. Unlike mature markets, business is much more integrated into society, making it necessary to include non-economic factors to a larger extent. With the spread of international business to many more emerging markets during the Third wave, the social impact on the MNC has increased. Even if a business firm is mainly driven by economic considerations, there are now more social restrictions on the business operations.

INTERNATIONALIZATION PROCESS THEORIES

Three basic questions in international business research about MNCs were raised and answered above: where to invest abroad, why firms do so, and how this is done. By combining these three key questions in the eclectic paradigm, a basic explanation is given about the existence of the MNC and its major international business activities. But these questions and the theories examined to answer them are static and therefore say very little about when to export or invest abroad, or how to internationalize over time.

When to do international business?

The 'when' question considers the time dimension by describing and explaining international business operations over time. To know when to do international business, one needs to know about the internationalization process, for example what happens when leaving home, when entering the foreign market and when expanding further abroad. The theories on the MNC referred to above, with the exception of the product cycle theory, are not very useful, since they are static. The latter theory, on the other hand, being based on economics, is too general, since it does not go into the organization of the international firm, for example how decisions are made about international business matters. Several internationalization process theories are now explored in relation to the internationalization process of different types of firms, namely MNCs, multinational exporters (MNEXs) and international new ventures (INVs). More knowledge is then provided about the three waves of the internationalization of firms. Some of the internationalization process theories have been major international business theories since the early days of international business research. Most of them originate in the social sciences, even if there are some economic theories on topics related to this process. This latter research mainly explains the choice of entry mode based on transaction cost analysis (see, for example, Anderson and Gatignon, 1986; Brouthers, 2002; and Brouthers and Nakos, 2004). But they do not go much into the process itself, looking rather at only one aspect of it, namely entry. Moreover, they are not very useful for studying the socially oriented internationalization processes of emerging markets.

The Uppsala internationalization process theory

A major internationalization process theory was developed at Uppsala University in the 1970s based on the early internationalization of large Swedish MNCs (Johanson and Wiedersheim-Paul, 1975; Johanson and Vahlne, 1977). This Uppsala model is grounded in the theory on the growth of the firm (Penrose, 1959) and organizational behavioural theory founded on cognitive decision theory (Cyert and March, 1963). According to this 'Uppsala chool', the internationalization process takes place in a stepwise manner. Companies commit themselves through a gradual learning process, which is incremental and occurs when business is practised abroad, that is, knowledge is experiential. The internationalization process is divided into different stages or degrees of internationalization. According to Johanson and Mattsson (1991), the internationalization process of inexperienced firms such as the 'late starter' is slow and gradual, while it is less so for a more experienced company, for example the 'international among others'. According to the establishment chain of this theory, companies tend first to establish themselves in geographically and culturally proximate markets and increase their commitment more and more, starting with agents, and passing through sales companies to manufacturing companies. Internationalization then starts as sales or purchasing activities and production is moved abroad later. In today's global world this establishment process might still be true for the internationalizing firm, especially when entering the first foreign countries, for example emerging markets. But this might not be relevant for the already internationalized firm, which can better take advantage of the greater possibilities of economies of scale and scope as well as low labour costs at the global level. According to the OLI paradigm, for example, the internationally experienced MNC can take advantage of common governance, especially that which arises because of multinationality, for example production shifting and global sourcing of inputs in its 'global factory' (see Table 4.1 above).

A basic characteristic of the Uppsala internationalization process theory is that knowledge accumulation is continuous and depends on the duration of foreign operations (Forsgren, 2002; Sharma and Blomstermo, 2003a). The longer the firm has been involved in foreign operations, the more knowledge is accumulated and the less uncertain the foreign market is perceived to be. Firms that lack knowledge about foreign markets therefore tend to overestimate risks. This corresponds to what Jansson (1989a, 1994b) found about establishment processes in the regional emerging market context of South East Asia. The pace of investments between countries accelerated the more experienced the firms became, at the same time as the mode of establishment became slightly more direct for the later establishments.

This internationalization process theory has mainly been used to study MNCs, but it has also been applied to studies of SMEs (Hohenthal, 2001). Research on the exporting activities of mainly North American small and large companies has reached similar conclusions as the Uppsala internationalization process theory (Bilkey, 1978; Reid, 1981, Czinkota, 1982).

The exporting theory

Another internationalization process theory focuses on the export development process. There are many such studies (Leonidou and Katsikeas, 1996), among which Cavusgil's (1980) theory for exporting firms is one of the most well known. This theory is less general than the Uppsala model, since it mainly focuses on those parts of the process that concern exporting rather than FDI. This exporting model was originally developed to study US SMEs exporting to Canada, but has also been found to be relevant for European exporting SMEs (Gankema et al., 2000). It is used by Jansson and Sandberg (2008) and Hilmersson and Jansson (2012a, b) to study Swedish MNEXs and by Jansson and Söderman (2012) to study Chinese ones. The theory is illustrated in Figure 4.2. The five stages of the model are now presented in more detail.

Domestic market focus. The SME is operating in the domestic market and has no international business, and consequently no internationalization or foreign market knowledge. Still, this stage is important from the internationalization point of view, since the potential for being able to internationalize is developed here. This is especially relevant for firms from emerging country markets, where markets are in a process of transition from an immature to a mature stage. Most firms need to first develop their sources of competitive advantage at home to be able to compete in foreign markets, especially in the more advanced mature markets.

Pre-export stage. At this stage, awareness is emerging within the firm about business opportunities in foreign markets or about threats from imports on the competitiveness of the firm in the home market, for instance due to offshoring. 'Wake-up signals' could include that such international issues are becoming 'hot' in the trade, press and politics, or that customers and competitors are internationalizing. During this stage, the firm also starts to passively react to unsolicited orders. Since the focus is still on the domestic market, the firm perceives export markets as very troublesome and risky. The firm might start to investigate foreign markets, but it does not usually invest in export promotion campaigns and has little contact with foreign companies. The firm feels little real need to export and has no plans to do so in the future. There is no internationalization or foreign market knowledge.

Experimental export stage. The company is now actively reacting to the internationalization challenge through a trial and error process. It begins to develop a commitment to foreign customers and markets, first temporarily and irregularly on a small scale, and then more permanently on a larger scale, by:

- carrying out marketing research about foreign markets;
- participating in export promotion campaigns;
- feeling the need to export, and indeed planning to export;
- actively reacting to unsolicited orders;
- entering the foreign relationship process by developing relationships with firms abroad, normally as three-party relationships using agents or distributors;
- forming regular contacts with key customers as well as developing alliances with export partners;
- being prepared to make adaptations, for example of products;
- starting to build up an export organization by appointing dedicated staff for this type of business.

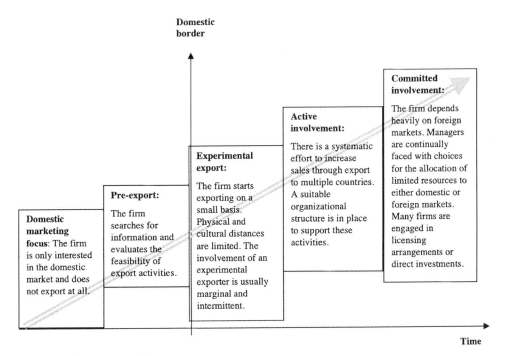

Figure 4.2 The exporting theory

At this stage the firm has low internationalization knowledge and highly focused market knowledge (network experiential and institutional knowledge).

Active involvement. International business is a regular feature. The company is focusing on key export markets and devotes substantial amounts of time and resources to entering and developing new markets. There are regular assessments of foreign markets, and marketing is adapted to them, for example promotional material is produced in foreign languages. International business has been integrated into the organization of the firm, for instance senior management regularly visits key partners to maintain relationships with them. Since exporting may account for up to 50 per cent of the turnover, opportunities on foreign markets are welcomed and seen as crucial to the business.

Committed involvement. The majority of the turnover is generated through exports and significant amounts of time are spent on this activity, with senior and middle managers frequently visiting customers and foreign business partners. Exporting now accounts for more than 50 per cent of turnover, and the domestic market is viewed as just another market.

The theory on international new ventures

In the 1990s new hi-tech industries emerged and grew rapidly, for example in information technology (IT) and biotechnology. Due to the now highly globalized world, these industries spread quickly throughout the globe. They were found to have started internationalizing earlier in their life than firms of the 'old' industries, many becoming international from inception, and therefore being called 'international new ventures' (INVs). They are defined by Oviatt and McDougall (1994) as firms that coordinate multiple value chain activities across borders. They also go by the name of 'born globals', since the firms of these industries are seen to be 'born' into the global market (Knight and Cavusgil, 1996; Sharma and Blomstermo, 2003b). Since they are defined more narrowly as young firms that are active through early export sales, they can be seen as a certain type of INV. Both types have been found to internationalize in a different way to earlier firms (see, for example, Cavusgil et al., 2002 and Zahra, 2005). The traditional stage models discussed above have been found to be invalid for these new mostly small hi-tech firms. The internationalization process was much faster and less incremental as they were 'leap-frogging' the stages. They were also found to be operating in networks through establishing and maintaining business relationships in these industries (Bell, 1995; Madsen and Servais, 1997; Coviello and McAuley, 1999). It therefore became more difficult to capture internationalization by using only extant theoretical frameworks (Coviello and Munro, 1997; Björkman and Forsgren, 2000; Meyer and Skak, 2002; Bell et al., 2003).

INV research belongs to the larger research field of international entrepreneurship (IE), which originally was defined by McDougall and Oviatt (2000, p. 903) as 'a combination of innovative, proactive and risk-seeking behaviour that crosses national borders and is intended to create value in organizations'. A review of 323 articles in the IE field classified the articles into three types (Jones et al., 2011). One type is studies on entrepreneurial internationalization, where research on INVs and born globals belongs. A second type is international comparisons of entrepreneurship. Another literature review of this topic found that this subfield is highly fragmented with substantial knowledge gaps related to content, theory and methodology (Terjesen et al., 2013). A detailed future research agenda is therefore outlined. While the former type focuses on internationalization, that is, entrepreneurship crossing borders, the latter type of research examines if and how entrepreneurial behaviour differs by country and/or culture. The third type identified is comparative entrepreneurial internationalization. It is a combination of the first two, where cross-border entrepreneurship is compared across countries or cultures.

More recently, INV research has been moving into the general entrepreneurship field, for example by focusing on the individual rather than on the organizational level of INVs in studying entrepreneurs (Cavusgil and Knight, 2015; Coviello, 2015).

Whom to do international business with?

Even if some of the theories above take up how individuals do international business, they do not say much about how they do that with one another, that is, the social aspect. This 'with whom' question is a rather recent addition to international business research and has been developed mainly in relation to internationalization processes. As understood from previous chapters, this social aspect is vital in this book, and its societal perspective on IBS, especially the network view of the network institutional approach (NIA).

Internationalization in networks theory

As discussed above, emerging markets are characterized as networking societies. For SMEs entering Eastern European markets, for example, business networks were shown to be of extra high importance, since relationships are considered to be developed to build bridges into foreign markets (Meyer and Skak, 2002; Meyer and Gelbuda, 2006; Jansson, 2007b; Jansson and Sandberg, 2008).

Network theory started to be integrated into traditional internationalization process theory by these authors and others. For example, Johanson and Vahlne (2009) extends the Uppsala internationalization process theory with the network aspect. This integration was facilitated by the fact that traditional internationalization process theory mainly focuses on international business activities in markets, that is, marketing and purchasing. The network view on business marketing in international markets could therefore be directly combined with internationalization process theory to give a theory on internationalization in networks. This business marketing theory was originally developed by another branch of the Uppsala school, where relationships are viewed as constituting the core of the international marketing process (Axelsson and Johanson, 1992; Hammarkvist et al., 1982; Jansson, 1989b, 1994a; Håkansson, 1982; Håkansson and Snehota, 1995; Johanson and Vahlne, 2003; Majkgård and Sharma, 1998). Since this inter-organizational network theory on international business marketing is a critical part of this book, it is presented in more detail in Chapter 7.

A network view on the internationalization process means that network relationships are established and operated in foreign environments. For instance, an exporter/importer network is viewed as a temporary set of units which has been formed out of different units in the organizations of the buyer and the seller. It is a value constellation established for the task of marketing/purchasing a product/service package involving a certain combination of competences. A value constellation is a group of actors representing different units at the buyer and the seller that work together to create value for the customer (Normann and Ramirez, 1993). This international marketing and purchasing of products and know-how through this direct exporter/importer network means that a vertical network in the exporting region (e.g. a supplier's supplier network) is indirectly connected to another vertical network in the importing region (e.g. a buyer's buyer network). This larger vertical network, in its turn, is embedded in other regional and national networks, for example a financial network. The exporter/importer network is then part of a larger value constellation consisting of a supplying export network connected to a buying network in the emerging market. Such value constellations and international business marketing situations can be analysed using network maps similar to those described in Chapter 8.

Internationalization through networks is the outcome of firms' actions to establish relationships by strengthening network positions (Jansson and Sandberg, 2008; Johanson and Vahlne, 2009; Hilmersson and Jansson, 2012a). Firms establish new positions, develop old positions or increase the coordination between positions in different country-based networks. Firms are grouped into different categories depending on their degree of internationalization and the market's degree of internationalization (Johanson and Mattsson, 1988). According to Chetty and Blankenburg Holm (2000), SMEs move between these categories by extending their networks, a strategic change which is influenced by the SMEs' business relationships (Agndal and Chetty, 2007).

In this book, the network view is one part of the network institutional approach, that is, the broad societal perspective on international business strategy. This view is accounted for in Chapter 7. The network view includes the physical and information relationships and adds social relationships. This means that the material and information relationships of the vertical network delimiting the global factory above are extended further by also including social relationships. Moreover, by also being embedded into the social relationships, the economic explanation based on transaction cost theory of the configuration of the global industrial network is subordinated to explanations based on social network theory. The international network strategy in the internationalization process is covered in Chapter 10.

INTERNATIONALIZATION OF THE ORGANIZATION

To delve deeper into the international firm than the theories referred to so far, other theories from the business field are explored, especially organization theory based on sociology, psychology and culture. Such theory on the internationalization of the MNC's organization mainly relates to the how and when questions above.

MNCs have been found to change organizational form as the number of foreign operations increases. The interwar period during the First wave of internationalization favoured a multi-domestic pattern of competition developed on a country-by-country basis, where little coordination and multinational control was required (Dunning, 1993). Western MNCs were not very diverse and were functionally organized. Subsidiaries were loosely coupled and controlled more through informal means. This early type of worldwide organization of the MNC is defined as the multinational organization (Bartlett and Ghoshal, 1989) or the multi-domestic organization (Doz, 1985). This type of organization promotes local responsiveness and there is little global integration between various units throughout the world.

The change to more global competition from multi-domestic competition during the American epoch and at the beginning of the Second wave affected the long-term competitive positions of MNCs and, as a consequence of that, their goals. The global integration of local market activities became more essential for international competitiveness. With a rising international commitment and a growing interest in increasing the control of international operations, an international division was sometimes created within the group, especially in MNCs from the US. Later, during the Second wave, when international business had outgrown domestic business, the whole organizational infrastructure of the group changed to be based on the international operations, and a global divisional structure took form (Stopford and Wells, 1972; Bartlett, 1986). This later form of worldwide organizational structure is defined as a multi-divisional organization (Doz, 1985) or international organization (Bartlett and Ghoshal, 1989). Based on the network view (see Chapter 7), the international organization is defined as a specific type of hierarchical intra-organizational network: the clustered group network (Jansson, 2007b).

With the rapid internationalization of Japanese firms during the Second wave, another way of organizing international business activities appeared on the world scene, namely the keiretsu. This is a highly centralized form, where the international production system is highly controlled from Japan, where key production, research and development (R&D) and the top of the pyramid are located. The value chain was increasingly internationalized during the Second wave to South East Asia and during the Third wave to chiefly China, forming a primarily East Asian global industrial network. The internal sogo shoshas work as an international sales and marketing organization that includes both internal and external marketing units. The organization structure of a keiretsu is defined as global organization (Bartlett and Ghoshal, 1989), and is based on functions and not divisions. At that time, the world had become more globalized, which also made it possible to integrate on a world scale from Japan.

From the 1980s onwards, and especially during the Third wave, global competitiveness has increasingly come to originate from coordination of inter-related activities worldwide. With an established market position in most local markets of interest to the MNC and rising global competition, growth increasingly came from a greater international involvement of the whole MNC than from initial entries into new geographic markets. It became vital, for instance, to utilize synergistic advantages and to rationalize production and marketing. The competitive advantage achieved from integration through this organization is more sophisticated than that which could be achieved through the earlier types of global organization. Coordination is based on both the global interest and the local interest and not just on one of these. This has resulted in many MNCs changing their organization into a 'glocalized' transnational or differentiated organization that is both global and local at the same time (Bartlett and Ghoshal, 1989; Jansson, 1994b), also being defined as the differentiated group network (Jansson, 2007b).

A key aspect of the internationalization of the organization is the ownership structure. Due to the globalization of financial markets and the mergers and acquisitions (M&A) wave of the 1980s and 1990s, the ownership structure of the MNCs has been internationalized. Together with the increasing 'cross-hauling' of FDIs between countries, this has resulted in most economies today containing a mix of companies from many countries, representing different types of international firms and ways of organizing international activities.

A TYPOLOGY OF INTERNATIONAL FIRMS

The theories above on the evolution of the worldwide organization structure of the MNC and internationalization processes are now combined to develop a typology of international firms. The foundational premise of research on internationalization processes is that internationalization is defined as the crossing of national borders, that is, the geographic spread of the firm takes place from the home country to foreign country markets. This spreading over the world is defined as the global internationalization process. Based on the work of Cyert and March (1963), it is usually looked upon as a cognitive process, that is, how international business decisions are perceived. For example, psychic distance plays a key role in the Uppsala model, where distance is perceived based on the international experiential knowledge of the firm. It is assumed that the more such knowledge the firm possesses of a foreign market, the shorter the psychic distance is perceived to be. Such cognitive aspects of internationalization are closely related to the mind-set – the world view – of the firm. One of the major cultural theories on the organization of the MNC, namely Hofstede's famous five dimensions (Hofstede, 1980, 2001), is about its cognitive structure. These five dimensions of national culture are based on a number of aspects of a national cognitive system that are reflected within the firm, mainly assumptions, views, preferences, themes, meanings, beliefs, attitudes, frames of reference, knowledge and skills. This structure is developed into a major institutional theoretical dimension in Chapter 11, where it is defined as one of four basic rules of the society: the thought style.

The world view is now assumed to become increasingly global the more national borders that are crossed. It is specified by Heenan and Perlmutter (1979) as a management philosophy, being about the orientation towards foreign people, ideas and resources in headquarters and subsidiaries, and in host and home countries. Similar to Hofstede's five dimensions (1980, 2001), it mainly reflects specific country or national mind-sets found within the MNC. Based on the stage models and how the world view changes as the international experience develops, companies are grouped into five major categories:

1   *The domestic firm.* This company operates in the home market and has not yet started to internationalize and therefore has insignificant international experience. The management philosophy is entirely oriented towards doing business at home.
2   *The internationalizing firm.* This firm is internationalizing its activities in the value chain and is found somewhere in between a fully domestic firm and a globally experienced internationalized firm, being an immature MNC. Cavusgil's (1980) exporting model is mostly relevant for this type of firm, as the firm passes through its various stages. In Sweden today, these firms are mostly SMEs, either of the traditional type or new international venture type, that either have the potential to internationalize further or have recently started to internationalize. Despite the fact that new mind-sets might enter the firm, the dominating one mainly stays home-market oriented throughout this process.
3   *The internationalized firm.* This MNC has a large geographic spread and has reached the final phase of the global internationalization process and is therefore considered to be an internationalized firm. Most activities of the value chain have been internationalized, and the firm has developed an organization suitable for its geographic spread of activities across

the many international markets. Depending upon type(s) of mind-set(s) existing within its global organization, three major types of internationalized firms are distinguished, namely the ethnocentric MNC, the polycentric MNC and the geocentric MNC. These types of firms are normally large MNCs, except for the ethnocentric MNC that is often an SME. This internationalized SME is defined as a multinational exporter, or MNEX.

The ethnocentric MNC

The cognitive structure or the mind-set of the ethnocentric MNC is still dominated by that of the home market, which is also its major strategic base. Since most of its key activities are located at home, there is a strong national bias within the MNC. As found above, the organizational infrastructure of large MNCs belonging to this category is characterized as being either global or multinational (Bartlett and Ghoshal, 1989). Japanese MNCs often have a global organization, while European MNCs had a multinational organization during the First wave, up to the American epoch, when it changed into an international organization, before then becoming a polycentric MNC.

The multinational exporter

The multinational exporter (MNEX) is a smaller MNC that differs from the large ethnocentric MNCs by chiefly doing international business through the market, that is, direct with customers abroad or through intermediaries like agents and distributors. International transactions are not internalized into a hierarchy. MNEXs might own a few subsidiaries in key markets, but the major part of the international business is done by external parties such as agents and distributors. The world organization of the MNEX is mainly based on flexibility. To spread the business risks, the MNE is normally active on a small scale in many foreign markets at the same time as it is flexible enough to be able to increase or reduce market presence in line with the business cycle of the various markets. Chapter 10 is entirely devoted to the entry strategy of multinational exporters into emerging markets.

The polycentric MNC

The polycentric MNC is epitomized by the multi-divisional organization or international organization, since it is based on the organization being centred on these product/business divisions. This means that various mind-sets coexist within the MNC, in the separate divisions and their local subsidiaries. The cognitive structure of the home market still remains but does not dominate as in the ethnocentric MNC. So even if the strategic bases of the polycentric MNC are spread over the globe, one major centre remains in the home country. The firm may still have many activities in the home country: production, R&D activities, group HQ. But most business areas are located to other parts of the world. In this international organization, the value chain is often disaggregated and reengineered on a global basis. Usually the home market is still important, but there are also other strategic centres located in host countries.

Big MNCs in the vehicle industry, such as Volvo or Scania, are good examples of this kind of firm. The Volvo Group has its HQ and most business areas located in Sweden, but there are also vital centres in other European countries, in the Americas (the US and Brazil) and in Asia, for example in South Korea, Japan, China and India.

The geocentric MNC

An MNC with a transnational organization or being a heterarchy (Hedlund, 1986), or a metanational corporation (Doz et al., 1996), is closest to the geocentric firm. It is a kind of uninational firm, where the world is seen as one entity in the same way as a nation is. The company meets different demands in the world market, even having global customers. It employs the best people for a certain job irrespective of their nationality. The best location is found for the different units depending upon actual worldwide needs and not because of the origin of the company. For instance, where a product company that is responsible for the entire global business of a certain business area within the group is located depends on the worldwide interests of the company. However, few MNCs have reached this state of the true transnational firm. They are still bound by historically and geographically based institutional ties. The main point is that the MNC's organization is globally based and it does not have one dominating regional strategic base, for example in Europe, Asia or North America. Rather, it is more or less the same small size in each of these continents, having a multi-centred organization based on all three continents.

The geocentric MNC is global in the true meaning of the word. It has opened up to the world. It takes advantage of outside opportunities no matter where they arise, uses the cheapest resources no matter where they are produced, hires the best people no matter where they were born, and faces any competitor no matter where it comes from. There might not be any strategic base left in the home country. It is not traditionally bound to any particular place, rather looking at the world as one big market, and therefore being located in the most suitable place in relation to its activities. This includes its headquarters. This type of firm can be said to represent the end of the globalization process according to traditional internationalization process theory. Viewing the firm from a global strategic perspective, it has left its original home base and is a fully global firm. Home is everywhere or in no particular place.

The geocentric MNC is founded on an ideal of a highly globalized world, where national barriers have been reduced to such a degree that a unified world has been created. One example would be if the European Union expanded into a World Union, that is, a political union not only encompassing Europe but most of the world. This dream is becoming increasingly difficult to achieve in the current multinational and multicultural world, where divergences are increasing rather than decreasing. However, this does not mean that there are no characteristics of the geocentric MNC in the current organization of the MNCs. Many operate on a global basis for all business activities and have a global firm infrastructure. It is best characterized as following the principles of the transnational organization, sometimes operating a 'region-centric' organization. There is either a continentally based headquarters or one virtual global headquarters for the worldwide operations. This type of organization structure approximates to the geocentric MNC due to the mind-set being mainly globally oriented, for example being expressed as 'think and act globally and locally'. However, whether this cognitive structure manages to replace the polycentric structure of many MNCs is questionable, especially today where there is decreasing global FDI and the disintegration of global industrial networks.

CONCLUSIONS

The emergence and evolvement of international firms is assessed and explained in this chapter by answering five research questions based on theories in international business research. First, various general economic theories about the MNC are examined, covering the period from the 19th century when this type of international firm emerged. The OLI paradigm is found to be the most general theory as it integrates other vital economic theories such as internalization theory to answer the where, why and how questions on FDI and the MNC. Second, internationalization theory is taken up as an international business theory to explain the configuration of an MNC's global value chain. This whole vertical production system is likened to a global factory. Third, since this economic theory is too limited to cover the sustainability aspect of the global industrial network, two types of sustainable global industrial networks are developed, attaching social and ecological values as two additional values. By including more activities, mainly product use, disposal and recycling, these networks are more extensive. Fourth, the transaction cost theory behind the global factory is broadened by going more into the economic organization of the MNC with the help of the markets and hierarchy theory. Fifth, major internationalization process theories are taken up to systematize and explain the when and with whom questions about the internationalization of the firm over time. Sixth, the black box is further opened to find out how the MNC has been organized over time, the chapter covering MNCs, MNEXs and INVs. This international organization research mainly concerns four major organization structures: the multinational, the international, the global and the transnational organization. Seventh, a typology of international firms based on their world views and degree of international knowledge is developed by integrating internationalization process theory with typical ways of organizing MNCs worldwide.

Through these theories the historical development of major parts of the international business field has been accounted for up until the beginning of this century. Other and later theoretical developments in international business research will be introduced in the subsequent chapters if found to be relevant for international business strategy in emerging markets.

PART IV
INTERNATIONAL BUSINESS STRATEGY

The international migratory strategy of the hummingbird in your garden

The hummingbird hawk-moth has an extended proboscis used for feeding and sucking when hovering, causing a buzzing sound like a hummingbird. It is a migrant from Southern Europe to the North, its migration mainly occurring from May to July. So, just like birds, many populations of moths and butterflies (or Lepidoptera – the scientific name of this order of insects) operate internationally, having some kind of global migrating strategy. By migrating they can avoid unfavourable local conditions, such as adverse weather, food shortage or over-population. The best-known such migration is that of the monarch butterfly, which migrates from southern Canada to wintering sites in central Mexico. In early spring, the adults leave Mexico for a more northern climate. Mating occurs and the females begin laying eggs, usually first in northern Mexico. The offspring migrate to southern Texas, where a new generation of butterflies is born. Many of them migrate further north to breed, often as far as Canada. Finally, this last generation completes the international migratory cycle by flying to the Mexican wintering grounds. A similar international migratory strategy is found with the painted lady in Europe. This tiny butterfly has been recorded flying an incredible 2500 miles at a time. Some years it appears in very large numbers, such as in Sweden in 2019.

5
International business strategy determined

This chapter is about defining and developing international business strategy (IBS) in emerging markets. Initially, it is grounded in the international strategy literature, from which the basic international strategic dilemma of the book is derived, namely local responsiveness versus global integration. General strategic theories on which it is based are then probed, namely strategic planning, competitive strategy, strategy as process, the resource-based view and systemic theory. A closely related international strategy theory is also included among the antecedents, namely the tripod theory. The societal perspective on international strategy is developed next by integrating the strategy into the network institutional approach (NIA). This means that the international business strategy is formulated and implemented within the framework of networks and institutions. The outside-in perspective signifies that markets and the wider environment influencing strategy are defined from a network institutional perspective. Institutional factors determine the rules of the game and constrain network strategy. The inside-out perspective embraces how the value-creating internal network and institutional context is related to the external context. The international business strategy is next defined and described. To gain a sustainable competitive advantage in the economic environment the IBS also needs to be legitimate in the social environment by achieving a societal advantage. This occurs when the multinational corporation's (MNC's) business is sufficiently effective in its creation of economic value and social value together with ecological value. The separation of the IBS into international network strategy (INS) and international matching strategy (IMS) is seen to be based on two major rationalities. The main motive behind the international network strategy in industrial markets is to earn profits, which is an efficiency rationale derived from the economic environment of the MNC. Differently, the main motive behind IBS towards government and other non-profit actors outside the market is to achieve legitimacy. The latter is especially true for the international matching strategy, which is oriented towards the social needs in society.

MAJOR STRATEGIC ISSUES

Fundamental business problems of high strategic importance facing MNCs in emerging markets were discussed in Chapter 1. Three major strategic issues for MNCs are identified by Tallman and Yip (2001):

- *Geographic spread.* This aspect has to do with the spread of business beyond the borders of the home country – the original issue in international business. It concerns strategic issues related to the internationalization process of the firm such as entry strategy and take-off strategy.
- *Local adaptation.* This aspect is about the degree to which business is adapted to the specific circumstances of the foreign markets entered.
- *Global integration.* This third international strategic issue is about the extent to which the MNC integrates its business operations in different national markets to better leverage the locally based resources. Examples of such strategic issues are how much standardization of products and other marketing variables can be achieved; the location of various business activities; and how competitive moves are integrated between different country markets (Tallman and Yip, 2001; Yip, 1992; Zou and Cavusgil, 1996, 2002). The global integration problem concerns the MNC as a whole, and is about how the company takes advantage of its geographic spread (Ghosal, 1987).

Most literature on international business strategy is about these three issues. Geographic spread was covered in Chapters 2 and 3 and will be so even more in Chapters 8 and 9 on local international network strategy. The local adaptation issue is also taken up in this chapter and other chapters throughout the book. The present chapter is mainly about the classic international strategic dilemma of local adaptation versus global integration. For example, Bartlett and Ghoshal's (1989, 1992) well-established typology concerns this dilemma. The multinational strategy focuses on local adaptation, and the global strategy on global integration, while the international strategy and the transnational strategy are about finding the right mix between local adaptation and global integration. Porter (1986), Doz (1985) and Prahalad and Doz (1987) have developed typologies along similar lines.

This strategic dilemma is highly relevant when doing business in emerging markets. Business is mostly adapted to the greatly varying conditions in emerging markets, involving most operations such as marketing, production, purchasing and financing. The high importance of local adaptation in emerging markets makes it the key focus of this book, meaning that global integration is viewed from the perspective of local responsiveness. This local/global approach to the dilemma reverses the classic 'glocal' order, which is based on the major sources of competitive advantage of the MNC being found at its home base. These sources have traditionally been developed in mature markets in Europe or America. The responsiveness issue is then about leveraging this competitive advantage developed 'at home' over the various markets of the world where the MNC operates. The local/global approach, on the other hand, is based on variety rather than similarity, being a question of harnessing diversity globally. Each local site is required to achieve global standards on local terms, that is, to think and act locally and globally.

As noted by Kotabe (2001), management and strategy research are in the main not integrated with marketing research, implying that marketing's role in international strategy is largely ignored:

> Management and strategy researchers tend to focus on the supply side of the dyadic relationships between firms and customers, while marketing researchers tend to focus on the demand side of the relationship. In a positive light, international marketing researchers

complement management and strategy researchers in subjecting supply-side theories to demand-side considerations. (Ibid., p. 486)

However, strategy issues are also under-represented in international marketing. This book will provide such demand-side considerations to supply-side theories, bridging the gap between the strategy literature and the international marketing literature. It then develops the international strategy subject, which is done by anchoring the strategy topic firmly in the international business field.

ANTECEDENTS

The NIA to IBS is grounded in five major strategy theories, mainly developed after World War II (WWII). These are depicted in Figure 5.1. The two earliest theories – on strategic planning and competitive strategy – appeared during the First wave of internationalization of firms and mainly concern Western MNCs, especially US firms. The following theories on strategy as process and the resource-based view emerged during the more globalized world of the Second wave of internationalization of firms and therefore also relate to firms internationalizing during this wave, in particular Japanese MNCs. The systemic theory mainly derives from this wave, since it is founded on major business market systems in East and South East Asia, as well as Western business systems. But it is also relevant for the Third wave of internationalization of firms, since it compares emerging and mature markets.

Strategic planning

Early business research on strategy dealt with corporate strategy in general, specifically strategic planning. It mainly started after WWII and was based on the experience of the strategic

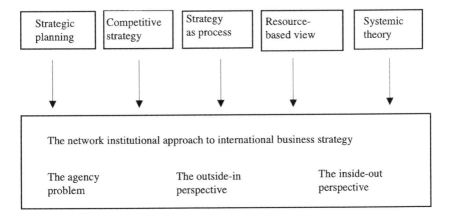

Figure 5.1 Antecedents of international business strategy

management of large US MNCs during the American epoch of the First wave of internationalization of firms. Strategy is viewed mainly as being formal and based on a profit-maximizing rationale, making the strategic process analytical. Strategy focuses on internal plans, and the key influences come from economics and the military. Chandler, in his famous book *Strategy and Structure: Chapters in the History of the American Industrial Enterprise* from 1962, defines corporate strategy as the determination of long-term goals and objectives, the adoption of courses of action and the associated allocation of resources required to achieve goals (Chandler, 1962). Strategy is viewed as a general plan of action for achieving the firm's goals and objectives. Strategic management provides overall direction to the enterprise in performing these tasks as well as implementing the plans. It is separated from operational management, which is concerned primarily with improving efficiency and controlling costs within the boundaries set by the organization's strategy. His research on strategic planning was mainly about large corporations, namely Du Pont, General Motors and Sears, Roebuck and Company, that had a dominant market position and could therefore control the market to a high degree between 1850 and 1920. The plans were decided by top management and implemented by lower management. A large planning bureaucracy was established within the MNCs, which can be seen as a company version of a centrally planned market economy as previously discussed in Chapter 3. There were long-term plans of up to ten years, medium-term plans of two to five years, and one-year plans (budgets). Another well-known strategic marketing planning tool from those days is Ansoff's (1957) strategy matrix that distinguishes between market penetration, market development, product development, and diversification (developing new products for new markets).

The introduction of the mainframe business computer in the 1950s and the coming of the information age greatly facilitated strategic planning, for example in building large databases, developing advanced methods for forecasting and future studies, and creating decision models in operation research. Numerous strategic management models and frameworks were developed by academics and consultancy firms to assist in strategic decision-making, for example the growth–share matrix introduced by the Boston Consulting Group (BCG) in 1970. The product portfolio of a company is broken down into four categories: 'dogs', 'cash cows', 'stars' and 'question marks'. 'Cash cows' should be milked as long as possible, since they are products in low-growth areas, but where the market share is high. However, 'dogs' should be sold due to the low market share in such a low-growth area. 'Stars' should be invested in, since this category has a high market share in a high-growth market, while 'question marks' should be investigated more due to low market share in such a market.

Competitive strategy

During the 1970s and the beginning of the Second wave of internationalization of firms, strategy research increasingly became focused on competitive strategy. Porter (1980, 1985, 1986, 1991, 1996) is the most well-known proponent of this new direction. Strategy is mainly determined by external factors, since generic competitive strategies are carried out within the framework of the market structure. Porter's version of strategic management partly builds on previous research on strategy as plan. While he focuses on competitive strategy, older classical research is broader and deals with corporate strategy in general. As discussed in Chapter 4, his conception is based on the market imperfections theory or the structure–conduct–performance paradigm; that is, he interprets strategic choice from an economic perspective. The strengths and weaknesses of firms are interpreted in terms of the five forces, for example mobility barriers, the number of competitors and degree of rivalry between them, the relative power of suppliers and buyers, and the potential of substitute products. The firm's purpose is to manipulate these factors within the market structure of an industry, through either modifying or activating them, in order to earn higher than normal economic returns on investment. The proper formulation of strategy is seen as being based on knowing what structural elements to change, for example in its organizational capabilities or routines. It is suggested that the five forces model should be used to analyse this market structure. Another key structural element concerns the firm's position in the value chain. The management activities affecting this competitive position which are directly related to the internal value chain are inbound logistics, operations, outbound logistics, marketing and sales, and finally services. Indirect activities supporting and influencing the primary ones are procurement, technology development, human resource management and how the company is organized, that is, the firm infrastructure. This value-chain model considerably develops the global industrial network taken up in Chapter 2, especially as a strategic tool.

Strategy as process

The dominant view on strategy as plan, in particular, but also as competitive strategy, was questioned by Mintzberg in two seminal articles published in 1987 (a, b). His main argument is that strategy is a very complex subject that has several meanings. It is not only a consciously intended course of action like a plan or a guideline as in the earlier approach, but also a ploy, a pattern, a position and a perspective. The intended course of action could be a ploy, that is, a manoeuvre, often dishonest, to outwit an opponent, for example a threat in a bargaining situation. Since the intention is mostly the threat, not the act, strategy as ploy is very similar to 'talk', that is, promising to do things but then not acting. Since an intended plan may not be realized, it is also vital to look at the behaviour following from the plan, that is, to define strategy as a pattern in a stream of actions. It is no coincidence that planning was disputed at this time, since the international business world had become more complex and dynamic during the Second wave. It is also typical that this new idea was largely based on a study of Honda's entry strategy into California, that is, on a Japanese MNC.

The ground for this shift to strategic processes and behavioural organization theories had earlier been laid by March and Simon (1958) and Cyert and March (1963). It is not based on economics as the other two theories are, but on social sciences, mainly psychology but also sociology. It is founded on the satisfying and imperfect decision-making characterized by bounded rationality and uncertainty. This imperfect decision-making makes it impossible to make optimal choices between known alternatives. Instead, routines and standard operating procedures are followed, and these are adapted to an imperfectly known dynamic environment. The implications of these cognitive limits to rational decision-making for strategic management were developed by Mintzberg and Waters (1985), resulting, inter alia, in the continuum of strategies mentioned below and the idea that strategy evolves through a gradual, incremental process.

As will be found below, strategy is defined in this book as a process (Mintzberg et al., 1995). Strategy as position was discussed above, especially as competitive position based on Porter. While strategy as position looks out and tries to locate the organization in the external environment, strategy as perspective looks inside the organization at the 'ingrained way to perceive the world' (Mintzberg, 1987a, p. 16). Such a world view of the organization is a key aspect in analysing the internal strategic environment of the organization and is discussed and defined below. A more thorough inquiry into the arguments against the classical strategy school is found in Mintzberg's book from 1994, titled *The Rise and Fall of Strategic Planning* (Mintzberg, 1994).

The resource-based view

Competitive strategy is too much pre-occupied with strategy in the market, and therefore neglects the resource side of strategy, for example if the firm has enough resources to implement the strategy in the market. The major new direction of strategy research based on this idea is the resource-based view (RBV), which appeared in the 1980s (Wernerfelt, 1984; Barney, 1991). It stresses internal factors behind strategy rather than external factors, for example the core competence of the firm (Prahalad and Hamel, 1990, 1994). Moreover, it challenges the focus on competitive strategy rather than strategy as plan, that is, strategy as position. As competitive strategy, the RBV is based on economic theory, namely Chamberlainian competition instead of industrial organization competition (Barney and Ouchi, 1986, pp. 372–80). Some fundamental rules in monopolistic competition are that firms are heterogeneous and have unique assets. This means that strategy exploits not only external market factors but also the unique internal skills, resources and distinctive competencies of firms. RBV is, then, based on an efficiency orientation to strategy. Following Grant (1998, p. 111), a distinction is made between resources and capabilities:

> Resource analysis takes place at two levels of aggregation. The basic units of analysis are the individual resources of the firm: items of capital equipment, the skills of individual employees, patents, brands, and so on. But to examine how the firm can create competitive advantage we must look at how resources work together to create capabilities: this is our second level of analysis.

Barney (1991) classifies resources into four categories: financial resources, physical resources, human resources and organizational resources. Financial resources include debt, equity and retained earnings, while physical resources include such things as the technology used by the firm, its plant and equipment, and its geographical location and access to raw material. Human resources consist of, inter alia, all the experience, knowledge, judgement, risk-taking propensity, wisdom, intelligence, relationships and insight of all the individuals within the firm. Company resources can also be divided into tangible (physical and financial) resources, intangible resources (technology, reputation and culture), and human resources (specialized skills and knowledge, communication and interactive abilities, and motivation) (Grant, 2002).

Dynamic capabilities
A competitive advantage based on a specific combination of resources and capability only lasts for a certain period of time. The more durable the resources and capabilities are, the more valuable they are to the firm, since the longer it takes before they depreciate or become obsolete (Collis

and Montgomery, 1995). The durability varies with type of resource or capability. While the rapid technological change shortens the life span of, for example, capital equipment and technological resources, other resources like, for example, reputation and brands, as well as higher-order capabilities such as organizational capabilities, depreciate relatively more slowly. The durability of an asset can be related to Schumpeter's waves of innovation. From time to time waves of innovation wash over the market and allow early movers to dominate the market and earn substantial profits. Eventually, this domination erodes as the valuable resources of the early movers are imitated or surpassed by the next great innovation. Thus, most resources and capabilities only last for a limited time and therefore only earn temporary profits.

This aspect is closely related to the dynamic capabilities of the MNC. In the strategy literature is found a number of management processes regarding how to evaluate product strategies in order to see how they need to be changed. These are meant to create dynamic capabilities, since they concern the MNC's 'ability to integrate, build, and reconfigure internal and external competences to address rapidly changing environments, viz. the business market environment' (Teece et al., 1997). Dynamic capabilities thus reflect an organization's ability to achieve new and innovative forms of competitive advantage given path dependencies and market positions (Leonard-Barton, 1992). Three main types of general dynamic organizational processes are identified and classified as dynamic capabilities by these researchers: coordination or integration, learning, and reconfiguration or transformation.

Systemic theory

The systemic theory (Whittington, 2001) develops the institutional aspect of strategy based on the business systems theory (Whitley, 1992a, b). The three books cited here are mainly a child of the Second and Third wave of internationalization of firms, since they analyse the corporate systems of major emerging markets in Asia and Europe. The business systems theory originates from sociology. Due to this systems approach, it is called the systemic strategy theory. As with strategic planning and competitive strategy, it deals with deliberate strategy, which distinguishes it from strategy as process. The idea is to 'play by the local rules' rather than 'analyse, plan and command' or to 'stay close to the ground and go with the flow'.

According to Whittington (2001, p. 26):

A central tenet of Systemic theory is that decision-makers are not simply detached calculating individuals interacting in purely economic transactions, but people rooted deeply in densely interwoven social systems. Granovetter's (1985) notion of social 'embeddedness' captures the sense that economic activity cannot be placed in a separate ratified sphere of impersonal financial calculation. In reality, people's economic behaviour is embedded in a network of social relations that may involve their families, the state, their professional and educational backgrounds, even their religion and ethnicity (Whittington 2001). These networks influence both the means and ends of action, defining what is appropriate and reasonable behaviour for their members. Behaviour that may look irrational or inefficient to the Classical theorist may be perfectly rational and efficient according to the local criteria and modus operandi of the particular social context.

THE TRIPOD THEORY

The tripod strategy theory (Peng, 2009; Peng et al., 2008, 2009) integrates three of the strategy theories above with the purpose of developing a more suitable strategy theory for the emerging markets, especially the transition market economies. One leg of this metaphor represents competitive strategy or the industry-based view, another leg the resource-based view, while the third leg concerns the institutional-based view on the macro environment beyond the industry. While the first two are market-based economic theories, the third leg is a non-market-based social theory mainly dealing with the influence on strategy of factors such as culture, corruption and government. Institutions are defined as the formal and informal rules of this social environment. The major contribution of the tripod theory is this institutional part and its integration with the other two theories. The major argument for adding this third leg was the discovery that the two major theories were less useful in emerging markets, since the market situations there differ very much from those of the mature market economies. Thus, the purpose behind this strategy theory is the same as in this book: to develop a more relevant strategy theory for emerging markets. However, the social theory is rather loosely coupled to the two economic theories. This is developed more below.

THE NETWORK INSTITUTIONAL APPROACH TO IBS

The societal perspective on IBS is now developed further, beyond the limits of the tripod theory and the systemic theory. The quote above from Whittington clearly demonstrates that the systemic perspective is based on the same idea as the network institutional approach, namely that strategic behaviour is embedded in a particular societal context. This aspect is particularly underdeveloped in international strategy, despite the fact it unfolds in many and highly different contexts. The relationships part of the systemic theory is developed more with the help of network theory, while the institutional part of this theory and the tripod theory is broadened to include more institutional theories. These two theories lean too heavily on deterministic institutional theories. They deal with the environment of the firm as a factor influencing strategy but do not treat the MNC as an institution. So the institutional theories used are limited to describing the external environment of the MNC and understanding how the MNC is influenced by this environment. Actually, the business systems theory is included in the IBS but only as a framework valid mainly for the external environment. The institutional view on IBS, then, builds on the integration of a wider base of institutional frameworks (see the Appendix for further information on the institutional background of this book).

The network view

As will be developed in Chapter 7, the MNC is embedded in a great number of market-related relationships – for example, business relationships, buyer–supplier relationships, supplier–buyer relationships, supplier–distributor relationships, seller–competitor relationships, buyer–bank relationships, inter-organizational relationships, intra-organizational relationships and personal relationships. One consequence of this relatedness is that strategy is interactive, and the MNC responds to various activities of other organizations found in the external framework.

Even though relationships and networking behaviour are connected to strategy theory by some authors, for example Axelsson (1992), Håkansson and Snehota (1995), Snehota (1990) and Morgan (2000), they mainly deal with strategic issues in a general way. For example, resources, together with the activities and actors, are the basic elements of the network as specified in the actors–resources–activities (ARA) model. But a resource here is mainly seen to constitute a power base rather than being an economic asset. Since this is not so useful when dealing with business strategy, the resource-based view needs to be incorporated into the inter-organizational approach. This elaboration extends further the industrial network models found in Axelsson and Easton (1992), Håkansson and Johanson (1992), Håkansson and Snehota (1995) and Ford (1997, 2002). A major problem with the network view on strategy is that, by mostly focusing on the ego network, that is, the direct relationships of a particular actor, and thus excluding the indirect relationships of the larger environment, it is too myopic.

The institutional view

The problem with many institutional theories from a strategy perspective is the opposite, that is, they focus too much on the environment. Even worse, they are deterministic, leaving no room for organizational discretion. For example, in systemic theory and neo-institutional theory, the organization is completely in the hands of the environment, only reacting to environmental pressures towards conformity. This does not fit well with most strategy theories above that have the opposite approach, namely seeing the organization as an agent with its own intentions. This is particularly true for large corporations like MNCs, which mostly can influence their environment. Despite being a major theme in the literature on institutional theory (see the Appendix), this agency problem has only recently been realized in institutional analysis of MNCs (Kostova et al., 2008; Saka-Helmhout and Geppert, 2011). But how MNCs act in various institutional environments, for example how to comply with institutional pressures and how to influence external institutions, is still poorly developed. Based on Oliver (1991), Regnér and Edman (2014) identify different types of strategic responses and the enablers and mechanisms of agency behind the responses. However, since strategy theory is not used to describe and explain these responses, the study becomes too general and of little practical value. As shown in Chapter 13, much more can be gained from Oliver's (1991) responses if they are looked at through a strategy theory lens. She loosens the deterministic role of the environment, including in her typology strategic responses such as defying and manipulating the environments in addition to the more common and passive actions such as acquiescence and compromise. Tsai and Child (1997) give the MNC a more active and freer role vis-à-vis its environment by introducing a strategic choice perspective into institutional theory, thereby including a range of proactive strategies missing in Oliver (1991). However, they do not fully solve the agency problem from a strategic perspective. The reason for this is that they do not go enough into the organization as an institution. When the role of the organization in strategy increases, it becomes necessary to penetrate it more deeply and study the circumstances under which a certain passive or proactive strategy is formed. The focus is shifted from the environment towards the MNC itself. Thus, a logical consequence of having an institutional approach to business strategy is to view the MNC as an institution in its own right, that is, to open up the black box and look closer at its contents. By integrating such an institutional view with the network view, the agency aspect is developed further. The best of two worlds is then achieved by giving equal importance to external and internal factors. The former perspective is defined as the outside-in perspective and the latter as the inside-out perspective on IBS.

The outside-in perspective

Applying the institutional view to Porter's theory means that this theory is seen to be about rules of competition in one of the main organizational fields: product/service markets. It is further concerned with how strategy is influenced by the rules of the economic game within industries. The theory asserts that to make good profits, a company not only actively competes with its competitors but also with its suppliers, customers, regulators and employees. Profits are maximized by restricting or distorting competition in a specific industry, from which it follows that this is one of the most important tasks that managers are paid to do. Such profit-maximizing economic goals imply that strategy is oriented towards efficiency, which is mainly decided by market forces. This approach is defined as the outside-in perspective on strategy: from the external environment (in this case the market) to the MNC.

This book also develops the institutional-based view of the tripod theory by going deeper into the wider environment of social rules within and outside markets. In that way, Porter's emphasis on the interdependence between market structure and strategy, for example, is transformed by instead stressing the interdependence between institutions. Whereas Porter builds on economic theory such as industrial organization theory, the strategic approach of this book is also based on social and cultural theories. This means that international business strategy is formulated and implemented within the framework of networks and institutions. Markets and the wider environment are defined from a network institutional perspective, where institutional factors determine the rules of the game and constrain network strategy, for example.

The inside-out perspective

The definition of strategy as perspective by Mintzberg implies that there is also an inside-out perspective on international business strategy. While strategy as position through Porter's theory is helpful in relating the external environment to strategy, it does not help much when trying to understand what this value-creating internal context of the MNC looks like. One major aspect of this internal context is the world view of the organization, that is, how strategists perceive and think about strategy. Another major aspect concerns the resources and capabilities of the organization, on which the strategy is based. Both these aspects are defined as organizational routines based on institutional theory.

According to Kogut and Zander (1995, p. 420):

Strategy is much more than the selection of product markets and technologies of production. Above all, it is the creation and maintenance of superior organizational routines that reproduce and develop the strategy and the organization over time. In the struggle to improve and innovate, firms grope towards better methods with only partial understanding of their own capabilities and of technologies' opportunities.

International business strategy is therefore also about creating such superior organizational routines regarding how actions and decisions to act are formed (planned) as well as how these acts and decisions are executed. These organizational routines mainly concern the management of the internal resources and capabilities of the MNC, which is done with the purpose of creating competitive advantages in the environment of the MNC. This focus on the internal environment of the firm represents an inside-out perspective on strategy: from the MNC to the external environment. The network institutional approach is also applied here.

As mentioned above, one main foundation of the internal conditions for strategic action is the resource-based view. It is used as a base to develop the strategic analysis of the internal environment, assuming that the resources and capabilities are the basis of competitiveness and, in the end, profitability. To achieve this, this resource base mostly needs to be adapted to the varying international context, in particular to the quite different external environments of emerging markets. The internal resource setting therefore plays an important role when the MNC adapts and takes advantage of resources found in various national environments. However, even though the RBV has been considered in research on international strategy (e.g. Collis, 1991; Zou and Cavusgil, 1996), the international aspect is still poorly developed. According to the institutional view, the profit orientation of the RBV implies that it is based on an efficiency-oriented rationale. For the details of this economic logic, the reader is referred to the economic theory about monopolistic competition, mainly developed by Chamberlain in the 1930s.

INTERNATIONAL BUSINESS STRATEGY SPECIFIED

Through the NIA, the inside-out and outside-in perspectives are combined into one common approach to international business strategy. The resource-based view is integrated into the societal context of the network institutional framework. International business strategy is then influenced by the rule system within the MNC, at the same time as it is influenced by the outside rule systems in organizational fields and societal sectors. This makes it possible to compare the environments of different countries and companies with each other using institutional dimensions. So a theory highlighting different external and internal environments around the world based on networks and institutions provides the major route towards an analysis of both the external and the internal dimensions of business strategy.

The MNC is then defined as *an international actor involved in a conscious internal strategic management process that transforms, through organizational rules and regulative mechanisms, external influences into reactive or proactive actions towards the environment, based on the resources and capabilities.*

Thus, the definition of strategy used in this book is based on strategy as process: strategy formation takes place as 'a pattern in a stream of actions' (Mintzberg, 1978, p. 935). This definition covers a broad range of strategic behaviours and allows international business strategy to be viewed in a non-prescriptive way: how MNCs actually decide and act, not how they should decide and act. Moreover, this definition lays the foundation for the development of the network institutional approach to IBS. For example, when a product development process is interpreted as a stream of actions, it becomes a routine, since behaviour is repeated in a rule-like fashion.

A continuum of strategies

The definition of strategy as a pattern of actions makes it possible to distinguish between deliberate strategies that are carried out as intended and emergent strategies that are patterns of action carried out despite, or in the absence of, intentions:

> It is difficult to imagine action in the total absence of intention – in some pocket of the organization if not from the leadership itself – such that we would expect the purely emergent strategy to be as rare as the purely deliberate one. But again, our research suggests that some patterns come rather close, as when an environment directly imposes a pattern of action on an organization. (Mintzberg and Waters, 1985, p. 258)

Such a deliberate strategy is either the same as a plan resulting from strategic planning or a position as in competitive strategy. Such a strategy presupposes an environment that is perfectly predictable and under the full control of the organization. However, this book focuses on strategies that fall between this type of strategy and the pure emergent strategy. Mintzberg and Waters (1985) present a continuum of strategies, with these pure strategies as end points. A planned strategy is, in their terms, the most deliberate one, whereas an imposed strategy is the least deliberate but also the most emergent one. This means that both strategy formulation and implementation of strategy are considered. Sometimes the classical sequence of formulation first, then implementation is followed; sometimes this process is reversed, when strategy is discovered in action (March, 1976); and sometimes there is a mixed process, for example when there is a strategic intent that gives direction for implementation as well as providing flexibility for discovering new strategy in action along the way.

This processual approach is a gradual adaptive approach to strategy, being called 'logical incrementalism' by Quinn (1980). Another aspect found in Cyert and March (1963) of importance as a basis for the institutional approach to strategy is the micro-political view of organizations (Whittington, 2001), or the social side of the organization as this aspect is described in this book. It concerns the internal political side of an organization, and has its origin in the personal objectives and cognitive biases that individuals bring to the organization. The organization is seen as a coalition of interests, where bargaining is important. As stressed by Whittington (2001, p. 22):

> … the combination of political bargaining and bounded rationality strongly favours strategic conservatism. … Strategic behaviour therefore tends to become entrenched in the 'routines' and 'standard operating procedures' imposed by political exigency and cognitive limits. Rather than perfectly rational strategies, organizations opt simply for 'adaptive rationality', the gradual adjusting of routines as awkward messages from a dynamic environment eventually force themselves on managers' attention.

It can now be concluded that the approach to international business strategy developed in this book is based on strategy as process, specified as a continuum of strategies.

Sustainable competitive advantage

The major purpose of the IBS is to gain a competitive advantage, which is defined as follows:

> When two firms compete (i.e. when they locate within the same market and are capable of supplying the same customers), one firm possesses a competitive advantage over the other when it earns a higher rate of profit or has the potential to earn a higher rate of profit. (Grant, 1995, p. 151)

According to this definition, profitability is the primary target of the MNC. The MNC therefore has a competitive advantage if it possesses the ability to outperform its competitors with reference to profitability. This also implies that at the same moment as a competitor successfully implements the same value-creating strategy as the MNC and thereby obtains the same profitability, the MNC ceases to have a competitive advantage.

If the competitive advantage is to be retained, it also needs to be sustainable: 'A firm is said to have a sustained competitive advantage when it is implementing a value creating strategy not simultaneously being implemented by any current or potential competitors and when these other firms are unable to duplicate the benefits of this strategy' (Barney, 1991, p. 102). A competitive advantage is, then, considered to be sustained if the advantage still exists after any attempts to duplicate it have come to an end. If the MNC manages to create a sustainable competitive advantage, it increases its discretion and control over the environment. But sustained competitive advantage does not last forever. A change in the prerequisites within an industry might result in a resource that earlier was considered to be an asset becoming a liability, or vice versa. The MNC's source of sustained competitive advantage is then nullified and instead a competitor achieves the competitive advantage.

Societal advantage and sustainable business

A major conclusion from the definition of competitive advantage as profit driven is that IBS is efficiency based and takes place in the economic environment. But, as found above, IBS is embedded into the social environment, which means that profitable MNCs also need to be legitimate. Competitive advantage is, then, affected by how successful the MNC is in the social context. The outcome of IBS is therefore not only efficiency based but also legitimacy based. MNCs legitimize their operations by adapting to the social values, norms and beliefs prevailing in the national market. Since these institutional elements are housed in different organizational fields and societal sectors, a vital part of strategy analysis is to identify and analyse these institutional factors according to the methodology developed in Chapter 12. This strategy analysis sets the background for how to match such social characteristics. In matching, the MNC aims to add value to society so that a societal advantage is achieved (see Chapters 13–15). The latter takes place when the business of the MNC is sustainable for society, that is, when the MNC does business so that the possibilities for future generations to enjoy similar standards of living to the present generation are not compromised. Sustainable business concerns the way economic value relates not only to social but also ecological value. The MNC therefore achieves sustainable business by creating three major types of values according to the following formula:

Sustainable business = economic value + social value + ecological value

Economic value is created within the economic context by creating customer value in a profitable way. But this cannot be done without considering how the social and ecological values are influenced. This link between these triple values is developed further in Chapter 13 by introducing the sustainable business triangle. Social values as well as ecological values are created through being socially responsible. Ecological value is separated from social value as the specific value inherent in protecting the natural environment and conserving resources so that nature is not destroyed, hence considering the needs of future generations. Social value and ecological value may also add to economic value by creating more satisfied customers. These three values of sustainable business constitute a 'triple bottom line' for the performance or effectiveness of the MNC in IBS, which are defined as competitive and societal advantages.

The benefits experienced by society from international business operations create social and ecological values. For example, the more the MNC is seen to be responsible in this way by different stakeholders, the higher the values created for these constituents, and the higher the legitimacy achieved. So the more the MNC creates such values, the more sustainable the MNC's business is from a societal point of view. Finally, this also means that the societal advantage of the MNC increases. Societal advantages are then achieved by enhancing long-term stakeholder value through addressing the needs of relevant constituents and adding ecological and social value to the economic value.

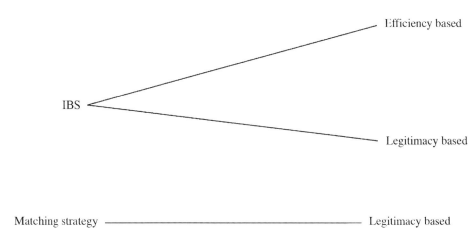

Figure 5.2 Major rationalities of international business strategy

MAJOR STRATEGIES AND RATIONALITIES

As illustrated in Figure 5.2, a distinction is made between two major international business strategies, namely international network strategy (INS) and international matching strategy (IMS). INS is directed at stakeholders in both economic and social environments, while IMS is only practised in social environments. The logical basis for the course of action or strategy varies with the type of environment. Depending upon the economic or social consequences of changes in the natural environment, it is institutionalized into either the economic or the social environment. The set of reasons for strategic action in the economic environment relates to efficiency, while the reasons for action in the social environment concern legitimacy.

A divide, then, runs through the international business strategy framework founded on the rationality of strategy, meaning that behind a certain type of activity pattern is found a basic reason according to which strategy is rationalized. Two main ways of rationalizing activity patterns or logics are then distinguished: one based on the economic context and one based on the social context (Jansson, 1994a, b; Jansson et al., 1995; Oliver, 1997; Redding, 2005).

Efficiency-based IBS

The efficiency rationale of the international network strategy in industrial markets is inferred from the economic environment of this market. In accordance with March and Olsen (1989) the praxis of decision-making following from the efficiency-based logic is defined as the *logic of consequentiality*. To be able to survive in an efficiency-oriented market environment, the MNC needs to be cost-efficient or profit 'maximizing'. This implies that decision-making is done according to some formal rational logic based on individual utilities. The most extreme form of this type of rationality is represented by 'economic man'. This is a perfectly rational and emotion-free individual, who has complete information about all decision alternatives and who has the capacity to calculate and select the optimal alternative (see Chapter 11 for further details). This represents a kind of 'either–or' thinking, where it is a question of always finding one best alternative.

Legitimacy-based IBS

The definition of international network strategy as being grounded in an efficiency rationale can be subsumed under a more general definition of strategy given by Johnson and Scholes (1999, p. 10): 'Strategy is the direction and scope of an organization over the long run, which achieves advantage for the organization through its configuration of resources within a changing environment, to meet the needs of markets and fulfill stakeholder expectations.' This general definition of strategy also covers the IBS based on the legitimacy-based rationality, if the term 'markets' is replaced by 'society' and if the term 'stakeholders' is defined in a broad way to include their social behaviour in addition to the economic behaviour. The major strategic orientation in social environments in and outside markets is legitimacy, where the MNC adheres to a number of rules, regulations, values and norms in order to gain, or maintain, environmental support. As will be discussed in Chapter 7, the inter-organizational industrial network is embedded in the social relationships. The major strategic orientation in the market environment, however, is to be efficient and competitive with regard to marketing, distribution and production. This logic of consequentiality does not consider:

> … the social context within which resource selection decisions are embedded (e.g., firm traditions, network ties, regulatory pressure) and how this context might affect sustainable firm differences (Ginsberg, 1994). Nor has the resource-based view addressed the process of resource selection, that is, how firms actually make, and fail to make, rational resource choices in pursuit of economic rents. (Oliver, 1997, pp. 697–8)

Thus, it is vital to include social aspects in the IBS, since MNCs in emerging markets normally need to prove that high efficiency in the market does not contradict basic social needs. In organizational fields outside markets such social aspects are usually more pronounced. With governments, for example, MNCs often need to acquire political acceptance by showing respect for national laws and being a good citizen, contributing to national development and economic welfare.

The praxis of decision-making following from the legitimacy-based rationality is defined as *the logic of appropriateness* (March and Olsen, 1989). According to this logic, organizational members create order by matching rules and situations. It is a way of establishing which rules are appropriate for solving a certain problem by using criteria of similarity or difference. This is not a simple and straightforward process as in the economic environment. Rather, it is open to various interpretations by the individual, making sense-making and other cognitive aspects important as well as norms and values behind the decision-making.

EFFECTIVENESS OF THE IBS

To know if strategy has to be changed, it needs to be evaluated, that is, assessed as to whether it is effective and sustainable. As elaborated on above, the MNC achieves sustainable business by creating a mix of economic, social and ecological values. These major values constitute a 'triple bottom line' for the performance of the MNC in IBS, which concerns either competitive advantage or societal advantage. The benefits and costs experienced by various stakeholders from international business operations create this combination of values. The more the MNC is seen to be efficient and responsible in this way, the higher the values created for these stakeholders. The more the MNC creates such values, the more sustainable the MNC's business is, provided that the societal advantage of the MNC increases.

Strategic performance is defined as effectiveness or doing the right things. Since this has to do with the objectives, performance concerns the degree to which the objectives are fulfilled. The higher the combined value of the mix of the triple values created, the higher the degree to which the objectives are fulfilled and the more effective the strategy. The more exactly the objectives can be formulated, the easier it is to assess the performance. For example, the sustainable development goals taken up in Chapter 2 can be an initial aid in formulating goals for which economic, social and ecological values to create with the stakeholders and how to mix them. Most of them are specific enough to be able to refer to a certain type of environment. But they are too general to help in operationalizing company goals, especially for quantifying them. An organizational life cycle sustainability assessment is a better tool to evaluate the impact the MNC has on the natural environment, and the costs and social consequences of this impact over time. The better the mix of economic, social and ecological values created with the stakeholders, the higher the degree to which the objectives are fulfilled. This first assessment of strategic performance is finalized by analysing how sustainable competitive advantages are influenced through the trade-off between legitimacy and efficiency. A vital part of this analysis is to study how the societal advantage influences competitive advantage. Based on such further strategic analysis, more exact goals can be formulated. Assessing strategic performance is then a continuous process of strategic evaluation regarding when and how to change strategy, this being a critical part of the strategic change process. These aspects regarding the effectiveness of the IBS will be advanced in Chapter 16.

CONCLUSIONS

The IBS is based on the network institutional approach. The agency problem, as a major aspect of the NIA, is solved through having a conscious internal strategic process, which exploits not only external market factors but also the unique internal skills, resources and distinctive competencies of firms. It is not a question of stressing either the external or the internal aspects of strategy, but of combining these aspects, that is, through the outside-in and the inside-out perspectives on IBS.

The NIA is rooted in five major strategy theories. Two of them originate from the First wave of internationalization of firms and mainly concern Western MNCs. Three others were developed for the more complex and dynamic business environment of the Second wave, also including new MNCs from this wave, foremost Japanese MNCs.

The IBS is defined and described based on a number of potential international business strategies available to the decision-maker, ranging from proactive intended strategies to passive imposed emergent strategies. A major objective in the economic environment is to gain a sustainable competitive advantage. But to succeed with that, the IBS also needs to be legitimate in the social environment by achieving a societal advantage. This occurs when the MNC's business is sustainable, that is, if the IBS is effective enough in its creation of the triple values.

The separation of the IBS into the INS and IMS is, then, based on two major rationalities. The main motive behind the international network strategy in product/service markets is to earn profits, which is an efficiency rationale derived from the economic environment of the MNC. Strategic decision-making to achieve goals by competing in economic environments is assumed to follow the logic of consequentiality. Differently, the main motive behind the INS towards the social environment of the market, the government and other non-profit stakeholders outside the market is to achieve legitimacy. The latter is especially true for the international matching strategy, which is also oriented towards social needs but focuses on the rules behind the strategic social behaviour. Legitimacy is, then, the major strategic orientation in social environments, and where the praxis of decision-making follows the logic of appropriateness.

Strategic performance is defined as effectiveness, that is, doing the right things. Since this has to do with the objectives, performance concerns the degree to which the objectives are achieved. The more exact the goals can be formulated by operationalizing and even quantifying them, the easier it is to assess the performance. A critical issue is how to make a strategic assessment by carrying out an environmental analysis to learn as much as possible about which parts of the environment influence the MNC and how the MNC can influence the environment. A second critical strategic issue concerns how to make an effective trade-off between legitimacy and efficiency, and a third is how the societal advantage influences competitive advantage. These strategic issues concerning effectiveness are developed more in Chapter 16.

6
The international business strategy model

The international business strategy (IBS) formulated and implemented within the framework of networks and institutions is developed further in this chapter. The international network strategy (INS) and international matching strategy (IMS) are described in more detail, and the outside-in and inside-out perspectives are integrated into an overall international business model. An internal strategic fit is achieved for the mix between INS and IMS if the MNC has the management capability to exploit its resources in order to have relationships with various actors at the same time as it fully matches the external institutional set-up by having an external strategic fit. Sustainable business is achieved by addressing the needs and interests of relevant stakeholders, adding ecological and social values to the economic value. A sustainable competitive advantage is in turn accomplished through having an effective mix of competitive and societal advantages. The focus is on the hierarchy of resources and capabilities of the value-creating internal context. To find out about the potential to achieve a sustainable competitive advantage, the resources and capabilities are evaluated based on four major criteria.

THE INTERNATIONAL BUSINESS STRATEGY MODEL

The international business strategy model is outlined in Figure 6.1. To achieve an internal strategic fit for the mix between international network strategy and international matching strategy, the execution of the IBS needs to be based on an appropriate combination of resources and capabilities. Still, it is not enough to have an efficient link between strategy and the internal environment; IBS also needs to be effective, that is, valuable to customers and other stakeholders in the external environment. So, to achieve sustainable business, competitive advantage and societal advantage, there must be an external strategic fit between the international business strategy and the external environment of the MNC.

The IBS is founded on the fact that the MNC is not alone in the world but highly dependent on the environment in which it operates. Because of this leading role of the external environment in governing international business strategy, an approach is required that gives a rich description of the environment as well as of how strategy and environment are related. This is not achieved with the one-sidedness of most of the present literature, which looks at the MNC either from an institutional perspective or from a network perspective. In this book, both these views are combined to form the

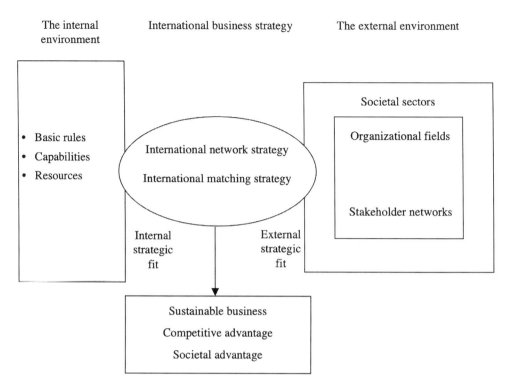

Figure 6.1 The international business strategy model

network institutional approach, stressing that the MNC is embedded within an environment consisting of networks and institutions. When there is a network view on the environment, the proximate external network environment consists of stakeholder networks, for example customers, suppliers and competitors in the product/service market network; workers in the labour market network; and units in the government network. The wider external environment affecting the MNC consists of the more distant factors in the macro environment, with which the MNC has no direct relationships, such as the political system and the legal system. When this external environment is viewed to consist of rules or institutions constraining network behaviour, it is defined as the external institutional setting. This setting is divided into two major parts: organizational fields and societal sectors.

Sustainable business is achieved by enhancing long-term stakeholder value through addressing the needs and interests of relevant stakeholders and adding ecological and social values to the economic value. The strategies and operations employed are then effective when goals are achieved in creating this triplet of values in society. If this creates an advantage over the competitors in the market, a competitive advantage is achieved. Competitive advantage is, then, achieved through efficiency-based strategy in economic environments. The advantage gained over competitors in social environments, on the other hand, is defined as societal advantage. The higher the legitimacy gained with stakeholders in relation to competitors, the greater the advantage. Additionally, sustainable competitive advantage is achieved through accomplishing an effective combination of societal and competitive advantages.

To be able to undertake various operations, such as marketing, purchasing and production, to arrive at efficient and legitimate international operations, the MNC performs environmental analysis. Chapter 12 is devoted to this issue of how to analyse and interpret external institutional contexts. The internal institutional setting is also analysed and defined as suggested in this chapter to establish whether the MNC has the capacity to respond effectively to the requirements of the external environmental setting.

An organizational field like the product/service market consists of both an economic environment and a social environment, since many stakeholders have both economic needs and social interests. As noted in Chapter 5, the economic or social consequences of changes in the natural environment are manifested in the economic environment as sacrifices and benefits and in the social environment as increased or reduced legitimacy. The set of reasons for effective strategic action towards such stakeholders then becomes a mix between the efficiency and legitimacy logical bases.

As set out in Chapter 5 and developed in Chapter 16, strategic performance is defined as effectiveness. The more exact the goals can be formulated by operationalizing and even quantifying them, the easier it is to assess the performance.

International network strategy

International network strategy in local product/service markets deals with relationships towards market actors that have both economic needs and social interests. Even if it is primarily a question of satisfying economic goals by promoting efficient relationships, it is also important to satisfy social goals by being legitimate in the eyes of the stakeholders. With stakeholders outside the markets, for example with governments, non-governmental organizations (NGOs) and local communities, it is normally the other way around: relationships are dominated by social goals, while economic goals are of secondary importance.

International network strategy in a dominating economic environment is taken up in Part V and in a dominant social environment in Part VII, where it is combined with international matching strategy. The major aspects of the INS are taken up in the following chapters:

- The network view – the theoretical foundation of the INS – is established. (Chapter 7)
- The international network strategy in the dominating economic context of the product/service market as an inter-organizational industrial network. The INS model developed consists of the network map, linkage mix and competitive mix. Moreover, first-mover advantages and the capability profile of the MNC play critical roles in achieving competitive advantages. (Chapter 8)
- The strategic international networking process, that is, how relationships are initiated, developed, maintained and terminated in marketing large industrial projects. The chapter deals mainly with the networking marketing process but also with the product/service process. (Chapter 9)
- The adaptation of the INS of multinational exporters to local market networks. Relationships constitute the core of the strategic internationalization process, where internationalization

takes place through exiting the home market (the take-off strategy) and entering the foreign market (entry strategy) by establishing and maintaining network relationships. (Chapter 10)

- The international network strategy in the social environment of emerging markets as part of international stakeholder strategic management. It is combined with a dominating international matching strategy as the international business strategy towards stakeholders. (Chapter 14).
- The international network strategy as the dominating part of the mix with IMS as the IBS towards governments in emerging markets. (Chapter 15)

International matching strategy

While the international network strategy is valid for both economic and social environments, the international matching strategy is only valid for the social environment. The logical basis for IMS is legitimacy, where the MNC adheres to a number of rules such as regulations, values and norms in order to gain, or maintain, environmental support. One specific feature of an emerging market is the critical importance of non-economic aspects for MNC strategy, both regarding the social environment as such and the problem of separating economic and social environments. Stakeholders in economic environments, for example customers, also have social goals. In some environments, such as markets, economic aspects predominate, while social aspects are dominant in other environments. In non-economic environments, IMS is oriented towards satisfying non-economic goals, for example related to corporate social responsibility. IMS is, then, based on the institutional view, which is developed further in Part VI (Chapters 11–13). As stated above, IMS is combined with INS in Chapter 14 as being part of the IBS in international stakeholder strategic management and in Chapter 15 in IBS towards government. While it dominates the mix in Chapter 14, it plays a minor role in Chapter 15.

According to the institutional view, the external environment is seen in terms of an institutional set-up within which the enterprise conducts its business. It is critical for the MNC to have skills and competencies to exploit the resources of the internal set-up within which the enterprise conducts its business operations. To be successful in this respect presupposes management capabilities that make it possible for the MNC to fully match the external institutional set-up of the enterprise. That MNC, which then – *ceteris paribus* – has the best ability to design its internal institutional set-up in such a way that it permits the enterprise to act effectively through the matching and network strategies towards its external institutional set-up, will be the most competitive enterprise in its industry, and thus will be in the best position to exploit market opportunities.

The external environment

The external environment consists of stakeholder networks and organizational fields, which are embedded in societal sectors. Stakeholder networks are grounded in the basic networks model, organizational fields in the basic institutions model, while the societal sectors are founded on both these models. The various institutions found are penetrated further with the help of the basic rules model. The basic network model is introduced in Chapter 7, while the other two models are developed in Chapter 11. Two major IBS processes are found within the MNC:

- *Management of the external context in relation to resource decisions.* It concerns the management of the external framework within the constraints formed by the internal MNC framework. This was defined as an outside-in perspective on IBS in Chapter 5. It starts with the external environment, which is related to the resources and capabilities of the internal environment.
- *Management of the internal resources and capabilities.* By explicitly stressing the influence on resources from different national frameworks, resource-based strategy is turned into international resource-based strategy. Since the strategic analysis starts with resources and then relates these to the external environment, this was defined in Chapter 5 as an inside-out perspective.

The internal environment

Through the creation and maintenance of superior organizational routines in accordance with the definition of IBS above, the strategy is reproduced or changed. To be able to gain competitive advantages in emerging markets, the MNC needs to possess specific resources and capabilities relevant to these markets. Successful IBS is therefore assumed to be based on the capability to exploit unique resources and internal skills. This ability to organize, or the organizational capability, is then the key factor behind successful IBS. This inside-out perspective on IBS is now developed by exploring further the resources and organizational capabilities of the internal environment.

The hierarchy of resources and capabilities

Resources are individual inputs into organizational processes, for example items like capital equipment and the skills of individual employees. Few resources are productive in their own right. Rather, they need to be bundled together and coordinated, that is, organized. The capacity of a collective entity to perform some task or activity is then defined as an organizational capability, for example the capability of a team of humans to handle a bundle of resources to do certain things. The capabilities possessed by organizations to utilize resources can be classified according to the different activities in the value chain, or according to activities performed within the different functional units. Such organizational processes or routines are defined as capabilities, for example the formal reporting structure, the formal and informal planning systems, the controlling and coordinating systems and the governing management style. This means that informal relations built up by groups of individuals within the firm are included. Organizational capabilities therefore represent collective entities and processes within the MNC, or the entire MNC as a collective unit. They represent broad capacities for combining and utilizing groups of resources, thereby being capacities for collectively performing strategic action. The organization as a collective entity consists of a number of resources and capabilities that work together to create stakeholder values. The competitiveness of the MNC is therefore determined by how the resources and capabilities are integrated with one another into a system.

The internal resources and capabilities are arranged in a hierarchy showing the architecture of the resources and capabilities of the MNC. Differences between types of resources and capabilities are illustrated in Figure 6.2, where they are ordered from simple or low-order types of capabilities to complex and high-order types of capabilities. The hierarchy includes different aggregates of capabilities and resources that are organized in a specific order. At the lower levels, simple capabilities handle simple resources. At the higher levels, complex combinations of capabilities handle complex combinations of resources. High-order capabilities are aggregates of low-order capabilities.

The hierarchy of resources and capabilities can be further exemplified with the help of a typology developed by Leonard-Barton (1992) as well as Day (1994). It illustrates the relation between advanced skills in the form of organizational routines and other capabilities, as well as the difference between collective and individual knowledge. The components are:

- Accumulated individual employee knowledge and skills on how to decide and act, being general and not specified according to function or activity. This is a low-order capability.

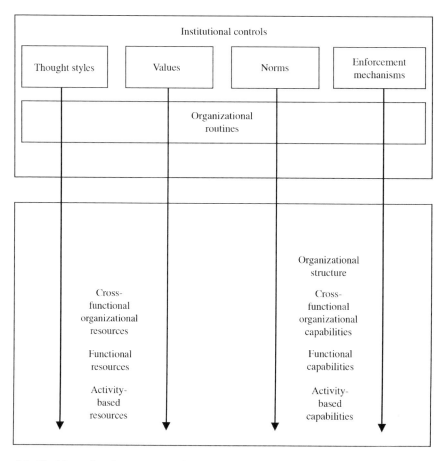

Figure 6.2 The hierarchy of resources and capabilities

- Technical systems, which are another resource of the MNC, for example information in linked databases and computer systems.
- Management systems, defined as formal and informal rules of creating and enforcing knowledge, for example product development systems, management information systems and marketing research procedures. These are higher-order capabilities, since they integrate various resources and capabilities into a whole. Such a system can either be defined as an organizational structure or as an organizational process.

Organizational learning capabilities

There is then a certain stock of organizational capabilities within an MNC, not only a capability to reproduce this stock but also to change it. This is a dynamic capability based on an organizational learning process. Learning capabilities are therefore critical for making the capabilities of the MNC dynamic, that is, to be able to continuously adjust the stock of organizational capabilities to different local markets and create new knowledge about the changing external environments. An organizational routine is a capability to act in a coordinated way, to manage internal activities appropriate for a certain local market framework based on a combination of low-order resources and other capabilities. One such process concerns a heuristic like a capacity to make certain joint decisions. This is an organizational process about how knowledge is created and used by the MNC's employees.

A distinction is made between four types of organizational learning capabilities grouped into three orders of learning, namely the first order (or proto) of single- and double-loop learning (Argyris and Schon, 1978, 1996), the second order of deutero-learning, and the third order of tri-to-learning (Visser, 2003, 2007). Single- and double-loop learning both concern problem-solving, where the former has to do with learning from mistakes. This is a capability to create new knowledge from correcting mistakes by asking the question: are we solving problems in the right way? This is operational learning, where knowledge is created about how to perform a process in the best possible way, that is, a know-how process. The latter is a more advanced learning capability that goes beyond the mistakes to know why they take place, asking the question: are we solving the right problems? To answer this question one can look into the goals or strategy pursued or the assumptions on which problem-solving are based. This double-loop learning, then, concerns an ability to learn more about the circumstances behind the single-loop learning, for example know more about why mistakes are done and if the heuristics of problem-solving need to change, that is, a know-why process. This is a kind of conceptual learning involving a more elaborate cognitive process that focuses on looking into the causes and effects of certain actions.

However, it does not make learning continuous or self-perpetual, since it does not include reflections on the learning process itself. It is not about the learning itself or about learning as a process, that is, about how firms learn in general, not only from mistakes when solving problems. It is a question of reflecting on this routine to understand the assumptions and values behind it. In this even more advanced learning capability, firms learn about how to learn. This is a second-order learning capability that is called deutero-learning. It is a kind of triple-loop learning that goes deeper into the learning process. The overall learning process of the firm is questioned by asking: how do we decide what problems are right? A firm needs to have this learning capability to be a unified learning organization where employees have learned how to learn. The organization has then created an ability to carry out single- and double-loop learning in an effective way. While these two loops concern learning by individuals, deutero-learning is collective, since it links together organizational units in one overall learning infrastructure. It is dynamic, since it develops the competences and skills to use this infrastructure in order to produce new strategies and structures for learning. The prevalence of such a more elaborate kind of learning capability provides the ground for having continuous sustainable competitive advantages. These organizational learning capabilities and organizational learning in general are elaborated on more in Chapter 16 as part of developing a strategic institutional change process.

In deutero-learning, it is a matter of questioning how an organizational process works by considering the basic rules behind what problems are right or wrong, that is, whether strategy takes place in accordance with these rules. They are then given and not questioned further. To learn more about the basic rules of the organization by questioning them, for example about how and why they influence organizational learning, is an even more complex procedure of conceptual learning. It would involve questioning the basic organization of the whole society by looking into how it influences organizational strategy. Such learning about the societal context of the contexts of organizational fields and organizations is defined as trito-learning (Visser, 2003), that is, a third-order learning capability. At the individual level, it regards the profound redefinition of a person's character or self, the aggregate of the past deutero-learning. It would be a result from an important reconstruction of life like religious conversion or thorough change of lifestyle to adapt to preventing a severe climate change. A corresponding situation for a firm would be replacing its organizational learning style completely, for example for a traditional Chinese firm if it were to be acquired by a Western firm and turned entirely into a Western-style firm. The challenges in trito-learning are elaborated on in Chapter 16 about how change in the organizational context is affected over time by change in the macro context, in particular the country culture.

Institutional controls – an illustration

To be able to deutero-learn by reflecting on a decision routine, one has to understand the assumptions and values behind the routine, for example the world view of the organization such as how strategists perceive and think about strategy, or strategy as perspective. Such a world view is defined in this book as a thought style based on institutional theory, being one of four basic rules (see Chapter 11). These basic rules are related to the assets of the firm, not only to the organizational learning capabilities but also to the organizational capabilities and resources in general. The basic rules are then assumed to act as a major control of how the low-order assets are integrated into high-order composite capabilities. How the basic rules work as institutional controls of the hierarchy of resources and capabilities is also illustrated in Figure 6.2. For example, certain resources and capabilities are bundled together through an organizational process for a specific purpose, such as developing new products. When basic rules are institutionalized into an organizational process, this process is turned into an organizational routine.

Values then constitute a basic rule controlling strategic behaviour. For example, most firms base their business on core values, where a common value is high quality. The institutionalization of this value into the product development process means that it is ingrained in the minds of the product developers as a high-quality focus to be followed. Trustworthiness is another basic rule working as an institutional control. It is formed out of the resource base of relationships as well as gives a capacity to form new relationships. This norm is institutionalized into the network behaviour as a routine, so that, for example, promises made by sales representatives can be trusted by the customers. Otherwise the offer may not be competitive. How trustworthiness is established through relationships and used in developing, establishing and maintaining new relationships is taken up as a critical factor throughout the book.

The basic rules as controls of the use of resources and capabilities are illustrated by the operations of a leading bearing MNC on the world market. This case is also used to illustrate international matching strategy towards stakeholders in Chapter 14. As will be noted there, this company is operating in a truly global industry, where the company is active all over the world, having its main markets in Western Europe and North America. Only the business of one of its many subsidiaries in Asia is exemplified, namely the one in Malaysia. Many of the capabilities reside at the group level of the MNC and are transferred to the local level. However, they are not useful and do not become an organizational capability at the local subsidiary level if they are not institutionalized there. The illustration mainly shows the consistency of the basic rules between the Malaysian subsidiary and the group. Inconsistencies are of two major kinds. First, the group might not have managed to carry over the major institutional contents from the centre to the subsidiary, for example due to insufficient institutionalization in the subsidiary. Second, the specific types of institutional controls of the group are unsuitable for the local emerging market and therefore replaced by other types of institutional controls. Some major basic values of the internal institutional setting of the Malaysian subsidiary are illustrated in Figure 6.3, namely a number of values and thought styles.

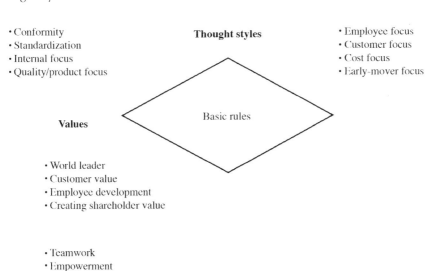

Figure 6.3 Basic rules as institutional controls in the bearings MNC

Values. Four key values of the MNC are expressed: to be the *world leader* in bearings through providing *customer value, developing the employees* and *creating shareholder value*. Even if these values are not formally emphasized at the subsidiary, they are still embedded in its organization. For example, all meetings start with a small talk about the customers and many activities increase the customer value such as product development, education of the customers, a superior distribution network and good after-sales services.

Four values are further articulated within the group: *teamwork, empowerment, openness* and *high ethics*. These values are long term, consistent and rather well institutionalized in the organization of the local subsidiary. They have a long history within the group and are well institutionalized throughout the group. The MNC has actually focused on these values since the beginning and most subsidiaries are in line with the mother company. The group has environmental policies, which are pursued actively. Production is certified and there is a 'zero-accident programme'. The company has also initiated various social activities and is a member of the Dow Jones Sustainability Group Indexes.

There is also some indication that the value of high ethics is not particularly emphasized and therefore not institutionalized enough to govern the company's actions. This is particularly true for external relations, where the group is not proactive. The rather new concept or programme of corporate social responsibility (CSR) is therefore mainly used internally towards the employees and does not work externally as an institutionalization mechanism. Another indication of this is that many employees view CSR mainly as a cost.

There are differences among the values at the subsidiary, which implies that not all of them are given the same attention and that the degree of their institutionalization varies. In general, the atmosphere at the company is open and the workers are never far from the managers. However, with a change to a more authoritarian managing director and the implementation of more hierarchical levels, the openness has been reduced. The employees are discouraged from participating in any labour union, which lessens the value of empowerment and results in an uneven institutionalization of the value throughout the organization. The empowerment of the local factory towards the group is also rather limited, due to a too centralized decision-making process within the group in this business area.

Thus, the stated values do not always equal the actual values permeating the company, meaning an uneven institutionalization of company values. The formal values cannot be considered as an organizational capability at the local subsidiary level if they have not been institutionalized there as real values. The same goes for the thought styles illustrated below.

Thought Styles. The main themes of the strategic thinking in the MNC are the following: *Quality and product focus*. Stressing quality has been a major ingredient of the thought style ever since the group's early days and is then based on a core value well institutionalized in the organization.

Customer focus. The key value of providing customer value is institutionalized as customer focus in the local organization, inter alia a worldwide customer coverage through the immense distribution system, and the appreciated after-sales service. It is manifested in organizational routines such as customer complaints being dealt with carefully and each meeting at the subsidiary being initiated with a talk about the customers. However, since the local subsidiary as a factory is not directly engaged in sales activities, customers become somewhat invisible, which might weaken the local institutionalization of this global thought style.

Cost focus. Being a large company with small margins, the focus in manufacturing is on costs and cost management. However, the risk is that this well-ingrained thought style conflicts with the customer focus, making it hard to reproduce the latter more long-term thinking. This also seems to have happened in the Malaysian company, which has become more short-sighted and does not stress business development to the same extent as before.

Early-mover focus. The focus on research and development (R&D), product quality and customers has enhanced a thought style of the group as being an early mover in their core operations.

Internal focus. Outside the specific industry and the closest customers, the bearing company is not well known and does not put much effort into marketing (partly because it is a production unit).

Employee focus. There is a large number of different education and training programmes. But nobody at the managerial level at the subsidiary mentioned the development of employees as an important goal, which shows that the local institutionalization of this aspect of the thought style can be improved at the local company.

Conformity of views. The subsidiary is so closely tied to one division within the group that there is not much room for own initiatives and innovations. Therefore, people within the subsidiary tend to think in the same way as is done within the group. A major part of this thought style is *standardization* through a routine of measuring 'everything'.

It is concluded that most institutional controls above in the form of values and thought styles concern how resources and capabilities should be bundled together through organizational routines to gain competitive advantages. If the mix of organizational capabilities and resources increase the economic value of the offers to customers so that higher profits are earned than competitors, then a competitive advantage is achieved. However, these resources and capabilities need to be integrated in another way to achieve societal advantages in social environments. For example, as illustrated above, ecological values are created with stakeholders by institutionalizing ethical core values into the asset base through the formation of a specific thought style about how to influence the natural environment. In performing the IBS, MNCs then utilize the resources and capabilities so that higher ecological values are created compared with competing alternatives. If this stakeholder value created benefits society in the long term, the MNC's business is sustainable. Where this sustainable business also results in an advantage over the competitors, there is a societal advantage. If the resources and capabilities behind this stakeholder value cannot be duplicated by competitors, the competitive advantage also becomes sustainable. Thus, competitive advantages and societal advantages might jointly lead to a sustainable competitive advantage.

EVALUATION CRITERIA

To find out if it is possible to gain a sustainable competitive advantage or staying power in the foreign market, the effectiveness of resources and capabilities need to be evaluated. For example, a change of the prerequisites within an industry might make it impossible to sustain a competitive advantage. The MNC's source of sustained competitive advantage could then be nullified and instead a competitor might achieve the competitive advantage. As demonstrated by the hierarchy of resources and capabilities, it is not one single superior resource or capability that will give the firm a sustained competitive advantage; rather it is the combination of them in the form of an integrated organizational capability, mainly an organizational routine. None of the capabilities alone is superior, but in combination they might give the MNC a competitive advantage and a societal advantage. This is a very complex configuration of organizational capabilities found at different levels in the hierarchy, which is complicated even more by being spread over several national contexts. Resources and capabilities only create value for the MNC when they are related to customers and other stakeholders as well as to the markets and market environments of these parties. Thus, the organization of the architecture of resources and capabilities is the basis of competitiveness and in the end profitability.

To evaluate whether an international hierarchy of resources and capabilities can create sustainable competitive and societal advantages, four major criteria are developed based on both economic and social aspects, namely if they are suitable, valuable, rare and non-reproducible (see Figure 6.4).

Suitable

A critical evaluation issue is whether the resources and capabilities fit the specific local environment/s where they are used. The local knowledge and skills together with their supporting resources and capabilities located outside the country need to be appropriate for the requirements of the local market and society. The ability to reproduce an organizational process is influenced by how specific the foreign market is, for example whether resources can be transferred there or need to be built up separately for that specific market. The suitability criterion is then critical, since it mainly defines the local responsiveness aspect of the major international strategic dilemma of the MNC. The resources and capabilities are adapted to or developed based on the particular conditions of the foreign market. Still, even if resources and capabilities are suitable to a certain market context, they might not create any competitive advantage. For that to happen they also need to be valuable and rare.

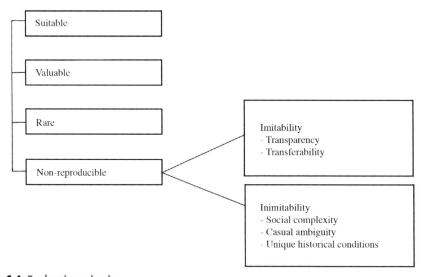

Figure 6.4 Evaluation criteria

Valuable and rare

Another condition for being a source of competitive advantage and societal advantage is that the resources and capabilities must be valuable to the firm. This happens when the offers are profitable and legitimate by creating economic, social and ecological values with the stakeholders.

Even if an asset is suitable to the foreign market and valuable to the MNC, it is not enough for the resource or capability to become a source of competitive advantage and societal advantage. For example, if a number of companies possess the same valuable and suitable organizational capability, they all have the possibility to implement the same value-creating strategy. The capability is therefore not a source of competitive advantage. The question is then how rare an asset must be to become such a source. If the assets fulfil these two criteria, the firm can achieve a temporary advantage over its competitors, at most.

Non-reproducible

To be sustainable, the resources and capabilities should be too expensive or impossible to imitate by the competitors, that is, be non-reproducible. For example, an organizational capability that can be imitated in a mature market might be new to an emerging country market and not possible to copy, therefore creating a sustainable competitive advantage in that market but not in another. If a resource is to be a source of sustained competitive advantage for the MNC, its competitors should face a cost disadvantage when they try to imitate the resource (Barney, 1991, 1994). For imitation to occur, the strategy and the means behind it should be possible to reproduce, and the competitors able to do it. Inimitability can be divided up in two sub-criteria, transparency and transferability (Grant, 1991).

Transparency is about how easy it is for the competitors to imitate the IBS. The easier it is to copy the resources behind it, the faster the competitive advantage is lost. They can either be imitated though duplication or substitution. When duplicated, a competitor creates the same kinds of resources and capabilities. When substituted, the imitating firm successfully replaces some resources that the original firm possesses with other resources that perform the same service. If the resource can be imitated in either of these two ways, the resource will not be considered as a source of sustained competitive advantage. Transferability relates to if the assets can be transferred to the competitors. In order to provide a sustained competitive advantage, the suitable, valuable and rare asset must then be impossible or too costly to obtain for firms that do not possess it.

Barney (1991, 1994) mentions three reasons for this inimitability: social complexity, causal ambiguity and unique historical conditions. Collis and Montgomery (1995) mention four reasons: physical uniqueness, path dependency (or unique historical conditions), causal ambiguity and economic deterrence.

Social complexity is according to Barney (1991) a major reason for sustained competitive advantage. The complexity increases because economic resources and capabilities are embedded in social structures such as the institutional controls. Examples of such assets include interpersonal network relations among managers and employees in a firm controlled by norms such as friendship and trustworthiness. In many cases socially complex assets are not unique to a company, only very costly to imitate. For example, if local conditions are socially complex, the local IBS process could become highly embedded and difficult to transfer to outside parties. The local organizational routines will be hard to integrate with outside organization structures, making the overall MNC organization structure loose. The NIA considerably develops social complexity as a factor behind inimitability.

Barney (1991) and Collis and Montgomery (1995) stress another factor related to social complexity, namely *causal ambiguity*. This is a consequence of organizational capabilities being often found in a complex web of social interactions. Causal ambiguity exists 'when the link between the resources controlled by a firm and a firm's sustained competitive advantage is not understood or understood only very imperfectly' (Barney, 1991, p. 109). If this link is not understood, it is very hard for an imitating firm to know what resource of the successful IBS it should try to duplicate or substitute. This can only be a source of sustained competitive advantage if neither the firm nor its potential imitators understand which particular resource or capability is providing the competitive advantage or how to re-create it. As soon as the successful MNC or its competitors find out about this link, the causal ambiguity as a source of sustained competitive advantage ceases to exist. In considering the complexity of the MNC and its environments, it is easy to understand that causal ambiguity is an important factor behind the sustainability of IBS. Collective combinations of resources and capabilities are hard to study by themselves. If organizational capabilities are included and arranged in a hierarchy and constrained by institutional controls, the causal ambiguity increases even more.

Unique historical conditions as a third major factor refer to what is also called path-dependent evolutionary historical change processes. While the previous two factors concern structural complexity, this factor is about environmental turbulence or change. The performance of a firm does not only depend on its position within the industrial structure at a certain point in time, but also on the path the firm followed through time to arrive at this point. If the MNC follows a unique path in the form of an institutionalized routine of organizing certain valuable and rare resources in a specific way, then the firm can use these resources to implement its strategy so that it cannot be duplicated by other companies, since they have not followed this particular path. This means that this organizational routine is costly or hard to imitate and would take a long time to obtain, if this is possible at all. A unique and valuable organizational process developed during earlier stages of an MNC's history is then an example of an inimitable organizational routine. Studying such path-dependent processes is useful to find out how such an organizational process evolved into an organizational routine through an institutionalization process. This dynamic or process aspect is studied in greater detail as institutional change in Chapter 16.

CONCLUSIONS

International business strategy is about finding a relevant mix between international network strategy and international matching strategy, that is, IBS = INS + IMS. An internal strategic fit is achieved for this mix through a suitable combination of the organization of the resources and capabilities. This strategic fit produces a specific solution to the fundamental international strategy dilemma of local adaptation versus global integration. However, there must also be an external strategic fit to achieve sustainable business in the external environment by addressing the needs and interests of relevant stakeholders, adding ecological and social values to the economic value. Competitive advantage can thereby be achieved in efficiency-based environments, while the advantage in legitimacy-based environments is defined as societal advantage. A sustainable competitive advantage in emerging markets is in turn accomplished through having an effective mix of competitive and societal advantages. A precondition is that the MNC has the management capability to exploit its resources in order to have relationships with various actors at the same time as it fully matches the external institutional set-up.

The strategic analysis of the internal environment is based on a hierarchy of resources and capabilities, which is governed by institutional controls in the form of four basic rules. To find out about the potential to achieve a sustainable competitive advantage, the resources and capabilities are evaluated based on four major criteria. They need to be suitable for the specific environment where the resources and capabilities are used. But to gain a sustainable competitive advantage, these assets must be valuable, rare and non-reproducible.

PART V
THE NETWORK VIEW

Local networking – embeddedness can be risky, especially for males

The cross orbweaver spider is known for its skilful network strategy. The female establishes webs by spinning them up to half a metre in diameter. The net is highly geometrical and symmetrical, and built across a single plane. It has between 25 and 30 radial lines of silk which extend from the web's hub to the perimeter. To ensure continued sustainability, the web is often consumed, recycled and rebuilt. The net is oriented so that insects are likely to fly into it. The spider operates in the network from a position at the centre of the sparkling, radial web in gardens across Europe and North America. The insects caught are paralysed with a venom, which is slightly toxic and harmless to humans. The prey is consumed directly or stored for later consumption. Female orbweavers often also consume their partners.

7

The network view of international business strategy

This chapter introduces Part V on the network view, which also includes Chapters 8–10. As found in Chapters 4 and 5, the production of the multinational corporation (MNC) is linked to other companies' production through the value chain of the global factory or the inter-firm global industrial network (GIN), for example the sustainable global industrial network (SGIN). As examined in Chapter 2, these inter-organizational value chains occur at the country level as aggregates, forming at the supranational level the transnational global value chain (GVC). The network view is therefore useful for describing and explaining these global industrial networks further. Moreover, as concluded from Chapter 3, this view is helpful in analysing the emerging market system and how to perform strategy there, that is, in explaining what market networks look like, how to establish and maintain relationships with various actors in local markets, how to organize international network strategies and how to compete in emerging markets. As noted there, emerging markets are relationship oriented, where firms are part of elaborate and complex local networks. Relationships are, then, not only built with economic stakeholders but also with other stakeholders in society, for example government, local communities and interest organizations. One consequence of this inter-relatedness is that strategic action is interactive, where firms respond to the various activities of other firms as well as to those of other organizations of the external framework. The network view is also good for describing and explaining the strategic internal organization of the MNC, especially the informal organization.

Thus, no international business firm is an island; rather, international strategy is interactive. A major argument for such a network view is that it focuses on how the MNC is related to its environment, or the contingency aspect. Another argument is that the MNC itself can be seen as an organizational network consisting of exchange relationships among organizational units, in accordance with works such as Jansson et al. (1995), Ghoshal and Bartlett (1990) and Rugman and D'Cruz (2000).

A network view is then well suited to describe and explain international business strategy in complex global markets. First, in accordance with Scott (1983), the environment of firms in emerging markets is organized as networks. Second, a network is loosely coupled and therefore allows flexibility. It contains interdependent actors that vary in the number and strength of their interdependencies at the same time as they are subject to spontaneous changes and have some degree of independence. A network is simultaneously open and closed, indeterminate and rational, spontaneous and deliberate (Orton and Weick, 1990). Contrary to organization theory, including inter-organizational theory, organizations are not taken for granted. Rather, a closer look is taken at international organizational boundaries and how they are organized.

Third, a network view provides a dualistic quality of combining the whole with the particular by giving a holistic view of entire organizational/social structures as well as illuminating particular elements within such structures (Knoke and Kuklinski, 1982; Jansson et al., 1995). The focus of the network view is then more extensive than the common type of network, being centred on the firm and the external network in its immediate environment. This latter type of network is defined as an organization set by Aldrich and Whetten (1981). Neither is the network seen as a whole, where the function of the individual components is to serve the interest of this totality. Rather, the networks have both these characteristics. Firms within the network both have their own interests and are part of a larger collective with a right to carry out work on behalf of the whole network.

Fourth, by using network theory, it is possible to gain an understanding of how firms and individuals coordinate activities to solve strategic problems and implement them at different organizational levels. A major question, then, is how various networks are related to each other (Uzzi, 1996; Van Wijk et al., 2004). In accordance with Brass et al. (2004), a multilevel view is taken of networks, where a distinction is made between two levels of network organization: interpersonal or social networks, and inter-organizational networks. These networks interact in the sense that activities at one level result in consequences, which become antecedents for the other level. For example, the formal organization structure of an MNC can be seen as a hierarchically determined network, which is seen as an antecedent for the social network, since it determines how individuals build networks among themselves, that is, it constrains the formation of informal relationships. Similarly, the resulting structure of the informal social network becomes an antecedent to the inter-organizational network, since it influences the pattern of cross-unit connections.

The network view mainly originates in sociology and is made concrete through specifying four background models to the international business strategy. First, a general network view is specified as consisting of three major aspects: networks as relationships, as structures, and as processes. Second, the basic networks model is developed based on this general network view. Third, certain major aspects of the general network view shown in Figure 7.1 are combined into an outside-in perspective on international network strategy (INS). This approach lays the ground for the internationalization in networks theory, which was introduced in Chapter 4 and is developed further in Chapter 10 on the local entry network strategy of multinational exporters (MNEXs). But first and foremost, the inter-organizational approach sets the stage for the international network strategy in Chapters 8 and 9. Fourth, and also founded on certain aspects of the network view, the intra-organizational network of the MNC is developed as an inside-out perspective on the INS.

THE NETWORK VIEW SPECIFIED

A distinction is made here between three aspects of networks, as relationships, as structures and as process (Easton, 1992). The relationships aspect focuses on what they look like, how they are established, and whether they are direct or indirect. Network structure concerns the number of links and the degree to which the nodes in the form of organizations or persons are linked to each other. Network processes concern the sequence over time of the activities going on within the network, for example if they are continuous or change. These parts are specified further in Figure 7.1.

Networks as relationships

The relationships part builds on Jansson et al. (1995), which is developed further by making a distinction between four major aspects of relationships: purposes, types, trustworthiness and directions. Of the two major purposes, instrumental factors concern the tasks or purposes of the network or of its environment. Communitarian factors express the relationship between the individual unit and the community. This social aspect may be instrumental but not necessarily so. A main communitarian factor is trustworthiness, which is taken up as a separate aspect of relationships and divided into two features (organizational and individual). There are two major types of relationship contents (resource exchange and social exchange), and three types of directions (vertical, horizontal and diagonal). Trustworthiness is also closely related to social exchange.

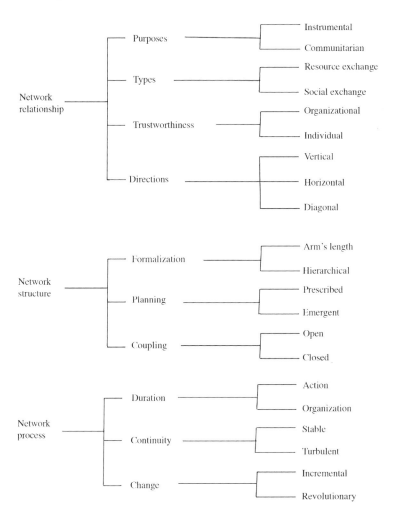

Figure 7.1 The network view

Purposes

Purposes, or reasons behind the collective orientation, or for establishing relationships, differ between organizational and social networks. Either organizations are connected for instrumental reasons, or they are connected for communitarian reasons. Instrumentality is defined as purposive action, that is, organizational units or persons are assumed to make conscious, intentional decisions to establish relationships. The network-like production structures of previous chapters, that is, the global value chain and the global factory, are instrumentality driven. The human side of relationships is missing. Social relationships take place for three reasons. First, persons could share a liking for each other due to individual attributes, for example 'kindness'. Second, because they belong to the same social group, kinship or occupation. Third, due to the fact that they come from the same cultural group, such as an ethnic or religious group.

Types of relationship contents

One distinguishes between two main types of relationship contents or flows: exchange of resources and social exchange. Products, gifts and money are common examples of resource exchange. The GVC is a typical example of a network only containing such material resources. Another type of resource flow is the communications network, where intelligence such as information and ideas as well as skills, knowledge and solutions are exchanged. As found in Chapter 4, the theory on the global factory builds its explanation of the configuration of a company's vertical production system on the information on which the decision-making is based.

Excluded from these theories, then, are affection and liking, which are the expressive, or emotional, factors of the exchange – both originating from the social element. Such social network relationships take place between individuals, and how they form networks influences the formation of inter-organizational networks. Such network ties are therefore socially embedded. Actually, major network theories concern social networks, for example 'social exchange theory' (Blau, 1964), 'weak/strong ties theory' (Granovetter, 1973, 1982), 'social embeddedness theory' Granovetter (1985), 'structural holes theory' (Burt, 1993) and 'social capital theory' (Coleman, 1988).

Trustworthiness

Friendship and trust are main characteristics of the social exchange. In contrast to economic exchange, social exchange is signified by unspecified obligation as it involves the principle that one person does another a favour, and while there is a general expectation of some future return, its exact nature is not stipulated in advance (Blau, 1964). Diffused future obligations are created and are not precisely specified as in economic exchange. Social exchange requires trusting others to discharge such unspecified obligations. Trust is even considered as a major factor of the social integration of societies (Fukuyama, 1995; Hardin 2002). It is also referred to as social capital (Coleman, 1988; Putnam, 1995). Trust is therefore a key factor of marketing relationships (Morgan and Hunt, 1994), and is mostly related to the social network. From the institutional point of view, it is defined as trustworthiness in this book (Jansson, 1994a, 2007a, b; Jansson et al., 1995).

As illustrated in Figure 7.2, there are different types of trustworthiness. Organizational trustworthiness concerns the organization, for example a buyer trusting the selling organization to keep promises given on quality and delivery time. This is a relation between an individual and an organization, that is, combining the social and organizational aspects of the network. However, it does not mean that it is less emotional than other person-to-person relationships, since an individual may be highly involved in an organization, identifying with it through its brand in a very personal way. Reputation is an expression of this trust.

Individual trustworthiness regards persons and the friendship among them, that is, the social network. One type of individual trust concerns the individual as a representative of his or her company. This type of trust is defined as professional trustworthiness, since it has to do with how tasks are completed together with other individuals and is more instrumental than emotional. An employee can, for example, be expected to complete his or her tasks in a certain way, not being biased from undue influences. This relationship is personal and formal. The connection between the social and organizational networks differs from that for organizational trustworthiness. Professional trust originates from the organizational network, is established through the social network, and strengthens the organizational network. Another kind of trust is related to other individuals as persons. It has different friendship base from business, for example personal traits, membership of a social or cultural group, or the like. This is called social trustworthiness, since persons associate because they like each other, or because they belong to the same social or cultural group. This takes place in the social network and influences the organizational network in different ways.

Directions

Implied in the network metaphor is that relationships take place in various directions. A distinction is made between three types of such relationships. The traditional buyer–seller relationships

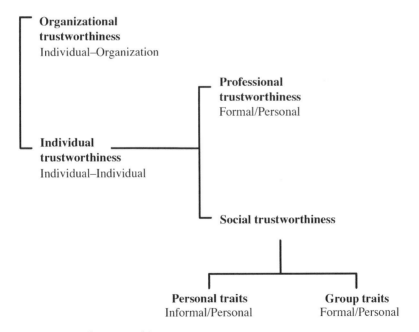

Figure 7.2 Main types of trustworthiness

along the vertical value-added chain are defined as vertical relationships. Networks for product development in industrial markets are often vertical, since they mainly involve suppliers and customers. Such vertical networks have already been reported on above, especially the GIN and the GVC as well as the global factory and supply chain management. Relationships with competitors, on the other hand, are defined as horizontal relationships, for example when proprietary innovations are licensed to competitors. Organizations outside the market, for example universities and government units, are often key members of market networks. Relationships with such persons and organizations for business purposes are defined as the diagonal part of the network.

Networks as structures

The network structure expresses a certain combination of nodes and relationships. Connectivity or the degree to which the organizations or persons are linked to each other is a major aspect of the network structure. The other two are the number of direct links and the number of indirect links that organizations have (Ahuja, 2000).

Arm's length and hierarchical networks

A distinction is made between arm's length (external) and hierarchical (internal) networks. Arm's length relations are formed to facilitate concerted action on the part of autonomous firms in situations where there is no formal authority to impose coordination concerning international business strategy. An arm's length network consists of both market and non-market relations. A network having an authority directly present within the network to control it is defined as a hierarchical network, such as an MNC. It is important to study how specific external networks are connected to the internal MNC network.

This means that the definition of organizational networks is broad and includes external relations between firms that lack formal authority over one another as well as internal relations where there is such a formal authority. Firms are linked to each other in different ways. Some are loosely connected, rather market-like autonomous organizations where entry into and exit from the network is relatively easy. Networks characterized by opposite traits are more similar to hierarchies. The degree of collective orientation, for example the degree to which organizations are committed to joint decision-making; to a unified division of labour; to common goals, values and definitions of the situation and ranking of priorities and to a single leadership segment; and the height of entry and exit barriers, is a critical factor.

Prescribed and emergent networks

Network activities can be prescribed by being planned in advance. But this might not be possible in highly turbulent environments of often changing network structures in emerging markets. In such situations networks more emerge than being prescribed.

Open and closed networks

Along the connectivity dimension of the social network, a distinction is made between open and closed social networks. Based on the idea that organizations are embedded in social ties

(Granovetter, 1985), the characteristics of these networks are also assumed to be valid at the organizational level of the network. The open network mainly concerns resource exchange, while the closed network focuses on social exchange, trust and shared norms. An example of an open network is one in which firms have direct social contacts with all their partners, but these partners do not have any direct contacts with each other. Such a zero-relation is defined as a structural hole (Burt, 1993). A high number of such holes in a network implies that people on either side of the holes have access to different flows of information, that is, it consists of few redundant contacts and is information rich. Burt (1993) argues that to enhance network efficiency an actor should only maintain primary contacts and let such first-tier organizations handle all the firm's indirect contacts. The selection of primary network partners is then to be based on how many contacts they have. Thus, an open network structure is suitable when the gathering, processing and screening of information is the primary purpose as well as when identifying information sources is important since it maximizes the number of contacts. The indirect linkages are then stressed, for example those relationships extending beyond the direct relationships between a firm and its closest partners. The loosely coupled intelligence network of Chapter 9 consisting of weak relationships is another example of such a network of mostly indirect linkages. The opposite is the tightly coupled closed network characterizing the inter-organizational industrial network, where all partners have direct and strong ties with each other. This network is centred on social capital, which is built through trust and shared norms and behaviour (Coleman, 1988).

Thus, there is a trade-off between a large network that maximizes information benefits and a smaller network promoting trust building and more reliable information. This contraction is studied by Soda et al. (2004) regarding the organization of project teams. They found that the best performing teams (action networks) are those with strong ties among the project members based on past joint experience, but with a multitude of current weak ties to complementary (non-redundant) resources.

Networks as process

Action and organization networks

Depending on the durability of the network organization, a distinction is made between action and organization networks (Aldrich and Whetten, 1981; Jansson et al., 1995). The action network is a temporary set of units which has been established out of different units in the organization network for a specific purpose, for example to solve and transfer a customer solution or for creating a new product/service. The organization network is thus a larger, more permanent social structure or the 'ordinary' hierarchical network of the firm, from which members are drawn for participation in temporary action networks. When the task of this internal/hierarchical network is completed, the action network is dissolved, the units remaining in the organization network then awaiting the formation of future action networks. The organization network of the MNC is elaborated on below, while action networks are investigated in Chapter 9.

The other four dimensions regarding network processes concern how they change and have already been taken up in earlier chapters.

Stable and turbulent networks

It is not only a matter of how durable a network is but also if it is continuous, that is, if it is stable or turbulent during its existence. As discussed earlier, market networks in emerging markets are usually more turbulent than stable.

Incremental and revolutionary change

Incremental and gradual changes in evolutionary network processes in emerging markets are often interrupted by irregular and drastic revolutionary changes.

These change aspects will be developed in further detail in Chapter 16 and the Appendix as institutional change.

THE BASIC NETWORKS MODEL

Based on the general network view, the MNC, markets and society are strategically related to each other in the basic networks model shown in Figure 7.3. The figure illustrates the external network environment of the MNC, that is, its relationships to major external parties in product/service markets and the government field. Financial market networks and labour market networks are also indicated in the model. As will be described in Chapter 11, network relationships are influenced by institutions. This is illustrated in Figure 7.3 as networks being embedded in the society at large, which is broken down into various institutional structures. They are defined as societal sectors, for example the educational system, the legal system, professional and interest organizations, and culture.

The importance of culture as an institutional factor is shown in the model by dividing culture into four factors: country culture, family/clan, religion and business mores (morale). Thus, the international network strategy of the MNC influences and is influenced by both institutions in the societal sector and different commercial actors in the product/service market and other markets, as well as major interest groups in the broader societal environment, in this case exemplified by major actors in the government sector.

As explained in Chapters 5 and 6, the main motive for the MNC to establish and run the international network strategy in markets is to maximize profits, while the main motive for such a strategy towards non-profit units in the government organizational field is to respond to policy. The MNC and its network actors in markets and government are influenced by institutional structures ('macro rules') surrounding these networks, for example systems of property rights ('relationships rights') and other legal rules such as judicial and penal systems. The impact of these institutional structures determines what goes on inside the networks. Other examples of institutional complexes of importance are family, clan, ethnicity, religion, culture, the political system in general, trade unions, business associations, and business mores and conventions. The state holds a special position in this model, since it participates as a collective network actor, having mutual contacts with MNCs. It is also seen as an institutional structure outside the network, having a one-directional influence on MNCs, for example represented by the national and local laws of the legal system. In a similar vein, religious norms might encourage or inhibit incentives for innovation and entrepreneurial activities. Hence the norms, values, cognitive factors and regulations inherent in such institutional complexes external to networks

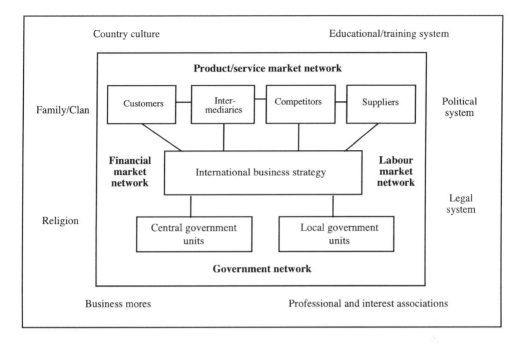

Figure 7.3 The basic networks model

have an impact on the MNC. This is also true of more proximate institutional structures in which market actors and government actors are embedded, that is market institutions. For example, the institutional context of a specific market might facilitate or hinder a certain strategy being implemented. Government policy could have a detrimental effect on resource mobility to and within a country.

THE OUTSIDE-IN PERSPECTIVE ON INTERNATIONAL NETWORK STRATEGY

The basic networks model relates the MNC to its external network context, which is now developed as the outside-in perspective on INS. The inside-out perspective or the internal organization network is taken up later in the chapter. Certain major aspects of the general network view in Figure 7.1 are combined to form the business-to-business (B2B) network marketing framework. The purpose is to lay the foundation for the international network strategy specified in Chapters 5–6 and developed in Chapters 8–10, as well as the internationalization in networks theory introduced in Chapter 4 and developed in Chapter 10.

According to Håkansson and Snehota (1995), a firm's role, development and performance in industrial product/service markets is explained by its ability to develop relationships. Volumes, market share, profits and growth depend upon how the company handles its relationships. Also, most costs and revenues stem from its business relationships. The inter-organizational approach to marketing in industrial markets builds on a broad view of relationships (Ford, 1997, 2002; Ford et al., 2006).

If compared to other approaches in marketing (Iyer, 1997), it is fundamentally different from most approaches to marketing in general (Sheth et al., 1988), relationship marketing (Sheth and Parvatiyar, 2000), including relationship marketing of services (e.g. Grönroos, 1995, 2000), and business-to-business marketing, in which traditional marketing concepts and tools are applied.

Industrial and consumer market networks

The global industrial networks at the inter-country and inter-company levels, the sustainability industrial networks and the local inter-organizational marketing networks are all industrial market networks. The differences between such industrial product markets and consumer product markets are normally so large and decisive that they motivate different theoretical approaches to marketing. The theoretical perspective taken in studying marketing on industrial markets is defined as the inter-organizational approach, while the perspective taken on marketing of consumer products and services is defined as the relationships marketing approach. The emergence of the inter-organizational approach towards business marketing is well described in Johanson and Mattsson (2006). It was originally developed in Sweden in the 1970s through close contact between industrial marketing/purchasing research and business practice. The discovery that this traditional marketing theory did not fit with practice led to a broad search for other theories, including outside the marketing field. A major reason for this was that the Swedish research in marketing in the early 1970s was based on 'earlier research about inter-organizational structures and change in distribution systems and industries and emerging observations of the nature of supplier–customer relations on international markets' (ibid., 2006, p. 265).

The major differences between industrial product markets and consumer product markets, normally referred to as the motivation for the inter-organizational approach, are outlined here (Jansson, 1994a). A first major difference concerns market structure. A second major difference in the marketing of the two types of products is that the interrelationships within the system are closer in the case of industrial products, especially in the vertical dimension. Dependencies are represented in industrial marketing theory in various ways, being expressed, for example, in terms of networks which involve both vertical and horizontal dimensions. The buyer–seller relationships are closer and the distribution channels more direct in industrial marketing than in consumer marketing. A third major difference between the two types of markets is that for industrial markets interrelationships between parties are more stable and long term. Various studies have shown that the industrial structure in many European countries is rather rigid, with a marked preponderance of large companies. For industrial markets, geographical concentration tends to be greater, the numbers of customers to be less, and the individual customer to be greater in size than for consumer markets, the competition often being oligopolistic. A fourth dissimilarity between the two markets has to do with the type of demand. Industrial needs are generally more complex and sophisticated, in particular from an engineering point of view, than are consumer needs. The awareness of these needs and means of fulfilling them tend to be organized in a more professional way in industrial markets. The buyers there are firms, not individuals. For this and the other reasons just mentioned, sellers are confronted with a different demand situation there than in consumer markets, as seen, for example, in the buying process, which is generally more complex in the case of the professional buyer.

Even though the inter-organizational approach has mainly been used to study relationships between firms in industrial markets, it has been shown to be valid for firm relationships with parties outside markets (Blankenburg and Johanson, 1992), for instance government and other stakeholders in the social environment (Jansson et al., 1995; Jansson, 2002, 2006a, b, 2007a).

Emerging market networks

The inter-organizational approach is suitable for international network strategy in emerging markets. The major reason is that emerging markets are not market societies in the European or North American sense. In embedded societies, where 'everything influences everything', it is hard to separate the marketing system from the rest of society. More stakeholders are involved in the system, and relationships are more personal and embedded rather than impersonal and confined to business alone. The inter-organizational approach (Jansson, 1994a) to relationship marketing stresses the general business relationship aspect rather than any particular type of relationship, for example customer or supplier relationships. The main reason for this is that it builds more on both organization theory and marketing theory compared to most relationship marketing theories. Parvatiyar and Sheth (2000) see relationship marketing as a new school in marketing and Vargo and Lusch (2004) develops a new dominant logic for marketing. These developments can be seen as an addition to the 12 schools earlier identified by Sheth et al. (1988). Judging from Gummesson (1995), Sheth and Parvatiyar (1995) and Vargo and Lusch (2004), this new relationship market school mainly builds on more traditional marketing thinking as represented by the managerial (marketing management) school and the (consumer) behaviour school. The broad approach of this book, however, is more related to the systems school and the organizational dynamics school, the latter of which deals with relationships between organizations in marketing channels. It is founded more on inter-organizational theory focusing on the marketing between organizations and not on organizations and individuals as in the mainstream marketing theories dealing with marketing of consumer products and services.

Industrial market network structure

Most marketing research based on the inter-organizational approach focuses on dyadic relationships, but it also focuses on sets of links within networks. In the latter case, the relationship focus is mostly kept by looking at the network as a number of direct (the dyadic aspect) and indirect relationships (e.g. Anderson et al., 1994). Dyads are connected to three major types of networks (activity patterns, resource constellations, actor bonds) according to the actors–resources–activities (ARA) model (Håkansson and Snehota, 1995). The inter-organizational approach is strongly sociological in its orientation (see, for example, Håkansson and Östberg, 1975; Håkansson, 1982; Johanson and Mattsson 1987, 1988). Originally it was applied to dyads between European firms (Hallén and Johanson, 1989), but was later extended to firms from Asia, North America and Australia (Håkansson and Snehota, 2000).

At the end of the 1970s, the need for a wider perspective on relationships was felt, since it was demonstrated time and time again that the direct buyer–seller relationships were influenced by indirect relationships, for example the buyer's customer relationships or the supplier's supplier relationships. The network aspect of industrial markets started to be developed, where relationships are seen to evolve through interactions within industrial networks. Instead of the research being mainly focused on dyadic relationships, it was extended to sets of links within networks. This development can be explained by the specific market structures prevailing in Western Europe in those days. One major characteristic was that they were more imperfect or closed than in the US market. Industrial economics theory, which became popular in the 1970s, was used to explain this difference. However, it was found to be insufficient, mainly because it was based on the analysis of one industry, while relationships took place between firms from different industries. Inspired by transaction cost theory, especially Williamson (1975, 1979) and to some extent systems theory, the 'Markets-as-Networks Approach' (Mattsson, 1997) was developed as an intermediate market form between the neoclassical pure market and the hierarchy. In Swedish research, the first major publications with this new network approach to industrial marketing came in 1982 (Johanson and Mattsson, 2006).

Industrial networks as process

Network relationships also concern flows or processes, for example the sequence over time of particular activities or that the nodes are connected to each other over time in a specific way. Relationship processes are usually divided into sub-processes, where each process consists of a number of stages or phases. Such a process model for how relationships evolve was developed by Ford (1980). Buyer–seller relationships over time are separated into five stages, where the first stage consists of marketing activities before the relationship begins. The next three stages show how direct buyer–seller relationships are established: their beginning and deepening. This development can be described according to a number of relationship factors, for example how the experience, commitment and adaptations of the parties increase and how the distance and uncertainty between them are reduced. The variable 'experience' indicates the amount of experience the respective parties have of each other. Both parties will judge their partner's commitment to the relationship. Commitment is to a large extent shown by the willingness to make adaptations. The variable 'distance' is multifaceted and can be split into the following types of distance: social, cultural, technological, time and geographical distance. Uncertainty deals with the fact that at the initial stages, it is difficult to assess the potential rewards and costs of the relationship.

For network processes past conditions are essential for understanding present and future network relationships, where a network structure at one point in time is a residue of diverse past processes. This is most obvious in emerging markets, where change is more pronounced than stability. For example, it becomes important to study various types of change in networks and at what levels they take place as well as different search and discovery processes for customers and suppliers (Johanson, 2004).

The inter-organizational approach specified

The main concepts of the inter-organizational approach to B2B marketing are summarized and illustrated in Figure 7.4, which builds mainly on Johanson and Mattsson (1987, p. 38), but also on Snehota (1990) and Håkansson and Snehota (1995). The various exchange processes through which relationships develop are analysed, as are the adaptation processes that take place between parties in the continuous evolvement of relationships, for example through product modifications, changes in production, delivery routines and other behavioural rules. The central idea is that of the establishment of network relationships creates bonds and dependencies between the parties involved, which make relationships continuous and stable. The more intensive processes of exchange become, the stronger the reasons are for adapting to each other and not replacing the other party. A mutual orientation is created which results in a preparedness to interact in a dyad. Change takes place within the relationship rather than in relationships with other parties. A mutual knowledge of and respect for each other's interests is established, which leads to cooperation and resolution of conflicts. Mutuality is thus clearly a characteristic of business relationships. This reciprocity is largely shaped by social exchange processes, but also by business and information exchange. One reason behind the complexity of relationships is these different types of exchange. Another is the many organizational units and large number of persons normally involved. Different forms of investment in relationships shape the future behaviour of the parties involved, since they affect the parties' access to resources. It is less expensive to trade with companies with which one has relationships than those with which one does not. Aiming at establishing linkages involves realization of the fact that resources are heterogeneous. The same line of reasoning can be applied both to dyadic relationships and to networks of relationships. In the latter case, in particular, it can have a strong systemic impact on the marketing and purchasing possibilities of the

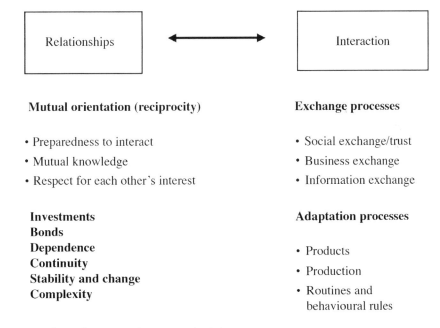

Mutual orientation (reciprocity)

- Preparedness to interact
- Mutual knowledge
- Respect for each other's interest

Investments
Bonds
Dependence
Continuity
Stability and change
Complexity

Exchange processes

- Social exchange/trust
- Business exchange
- Information exchange

Adaptation processes

- Products
- Production
- Routines and behavioural rules

Source: Based on Johanson and Mattsson (1987).

Figure 7.4 Relationships and interaction in industrial dyads and networks

firm involved. The firm's interactions are strongly affected by the access it has to resources from different types of networks. For example, how a seller interacts with its buyers depends partly on how the two-party relationships involved are connected to other, indirect linkages within the network or networks to which the seller has access, for instance influencing how the seller relates to its suppliers. Competitive strength is likewise affected by relationships. Within a given network different macro positions (relating to the whole network) and different micro positions (relating to given dyads) can be distinguished (Johanson and Mattsson, 1987). A fundamental ingredient of the inter-organizational approach is social exchange theory (Blau, 1964).

However, this theory often tends to be employed in the same way in analysing interpersonal social exchange as in analysing inter-organizational exchange. As Blau (1987) observed, there is the danger here of transferring basic concepts from the micro-level to higher levels of analysis. The objectives of individual organizations are reached by participating in various networks. This leads to dependency on other networks and subjects an organization to the manipulations and influence of other organizations outside its sphere of control. This dependency creates uncertainty, inter alia concerning the organization's capacity to acquire reliable and adequate resources to attain its goals, for example to maintain its competitive position. Managing this uncertainty without losing organizational autonomy is a chief concern for individual units within a network.

Resources are a key factor behind these concepts of the inter-organizational approach, where they, inter alia, are used to explain power-dependence relations based on social exchange theory (Emerson, 1962; Cook and Emerson, 1984; Pfeffer and Salancik, 1978). This approach to resources still dominates the inter-organizational approach, which, inter alia, is seen in how strategic issues are taken up. The inter-organizational approach deals with strategy (see for instance Axelsson, 1992; Ford, 2002; Håkansson and Snehota, 1995; Snehota, 1990), and resources are the basic factors of the ARA model. This fits with Gulati et al. (2000), who stress that the relationships in which firms are embedded profoundly influence their conduct and performance. Firms are therefore more properly viewed as connected to each other in multiple strategic networks of resources and other flows. Still, the dominant strategy theory developed during the last 30 years on resources and capabilities has not been incorporated, that is, the resource-based view (RBV). The main reason for this seems to be that this view is based on economics, which conflicts with the sociology base of the approach, for example expressed through its foundation in exchange theory and power dependency (Axelsson and Easton, 1992; Håkansson and Johanson, 1992; Håkansson and Snehota, 1995; Ford, 2002; Ford et al., 2003).

THE INSIDE-OUT PERSPECTIVE ON INTERNATIONAL NETWORK STRATEGY

As found in Chapter 6 on the hierarchy of resources and capabilities, resources are bundled together to create organizational capabilities. The latter are defined as the capacity of a collective entity to perform strategy. Capabilities can then be organized as cross-functional capabilities, or an entire organizational unit can be seen as an organizational capability. The internal network organization of such capacities is now developed as an inside-out perspective on international network strategy. Based on Jansson (2007b), and the internationalization of the organization of the MNC in Chapter 4, the MNC is defined as a hierarchical network, building on the formalization factor of network structure in Figure 7.1.

The hierarchical network organization of the MNC

The organizational subforms of the intra-organizational hierarchical network consist of three nets, which are illustrated in Figure 7.5. The directions aspect from Figure 7.1 is used to describe the relationships pattern of the hierarchical network, that is, the vertical, horizontal and diagonal dimensions. The planning aspect of the network structure is also applied. The authority net then consists of prescribed vertical relationships, where clusters of organization sets are linked to each other. This formal structure can be segmented in different ways, for example according to function, product, geography or matrix. It is designed so that decision-making is either centralized or decentralized, or some mixture between them, for example the global product organization. The lateral net is formal and consists of cross-departmental, divisional, or company relations, for example direct managerial contacts, temporary or permanent teams and project groups, task forces, committees, integrators and integrative departments. The social net is informal, based on social trust such as friendship, and consist of emergent linkages. Groups consisting of such non-task-oriented social relationships are defined as cliques. Coalitions, on the other hand, are temporary groups based on professional trust, consisting of task-oriented unexpected lateral and emergent linkages.

Three main interests compete through these nets over influence. The group interest represents the global overall interest of the MNC, while the global product or functional interest concerns the interests of the divisions. The local interest then represents the interest of the local company, often a subsidiary.

Action networks
Action networks are defined as temporary lateral nets organized for a specific task, for example the project groups, teams or task forces mentioned above. Group members are recruited from their permanent positions in the authority net, to which they return when the temporary work is over. The project organization of such action networks is taken up in Chapter 9.

Network controls
There are three major groups of controls of strategic activities and performance: process, output and input control. The first two are mainly formal, while the last is mainly informal. Process control involves direct controls of strategic behaviour effectuated through orders, advice and dialogue. Indirect control is done through formalized and standardized information stored in texts, for example written policies, job descriptions and standard procedures like manuals, charts and so on. Output control concerns internal performance, which is based on financial and technical reports and sales and marketing data, and is mainly organized through the planning and budget system. It also concerns external performance in the market, that is, market control through market prices and transfer prices. This output control system is a key information source for evaluating strategic performance. Input control regards socialization of the employees, building on the organizational

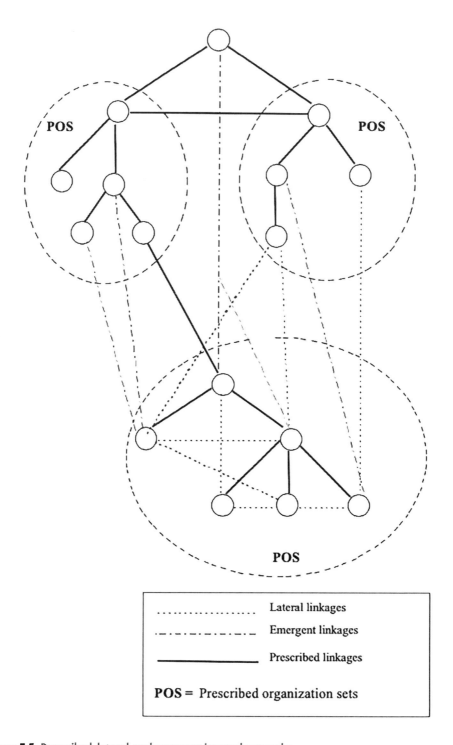

Figure 7.5 Prescribed, lateral, and emergent internal networks

culture of known and shared strategic objectives and values through training, transfer of managers, career-path management, measurement and reward systems, and informal communication.

CONCLUSIONS

International network strategy in this book is mainly studied at the organizational level and not at the level of the person or the individual, organizational networks thus being conceived of as a structure for coordinating organizational activity. Organizations are populated by people who represent formal organizational processes between firms. These inter-organizational networks are viewed as clusters of people joined by a variety of links through which they exchange goods and services, communicate by exchanging information and socialize by exchanging sentiments. Organizations within the network have their own interests, and at the same time are part of a larger collective with a right to carry out work on behalf of the whole network.

The network view is systematized into four models. The general network view is specified as three major aspects: networks as relationships, as structures, and as processes. The three other network models are developed based on this general model. The basic networks model illustrates the strategic network and institutional external context, while the inter-organizational approach to international network strategy itemizes how MNCs strategically act in such an environment. Both represent an outside-in perspective on INS, therefore constituting the foundation of the international network strategy in Chapters 8–10 as well as the further development of the internationalization in networks theory in Chapter 10 in order to study the internationalization process of multinational exporters. The fourth model on the internal network organization of the MNC as a hierarchical network organization represents an inside-out perspective on international network strategy.

8
International network strategy in industrial markets

As seen in Chapter 6, a vital strategic aspect of firms in industrial market networks is the ability to develop relationships in order to exploit the resources of the multinational corporation (MNC) as well as other resources of the local market network. The major type of industrial market network taken up in this book is the product/service market, which is chiefly defined as an efficiency-oriented organizational field in Chapter 5. Strategic marketing in such a market context mainly concerns business-to-business (B2B) activities between organizations. The international network strategy (INS) is then about bridging gaps through having relationships with various commercial stakeholders. Resources and capabilities play a key role both in conditioning this networking process and in creating competitive advantages. The international network strategy taken up in this chapter is therefore directed at economic agents, mainly customers and distributors, but also suppliers and other relevant parties in the product/service market.

Three major aspects of the INS are considered: the network map, the linkage mix and the competitive mix. Grounded in the basic networks model (Figure 7.3), a network mapping methodology is developed to analyse marketing situations in emerging industrial markets. The linkage mix concerns the composition of relationships used in marketing a product/service to the customers. To get a competitive advantage, it is vital to achieve first-mover advantages over time through having a certain competitive mix. The resource-based perspective is used to analyse the internal setting of the MNC from a network perspective. A typology is established of four major network capability profiles behind developing and maintaining network relationships.

THE INTERNATIONAL NETWORK STRATEGY MODEL

A major conclusion from Chapters 5–7 is that a network view on international business strategy (IBS) in emerging markets needs to build on a broad view of relationships, where the inter-organizational approach is found to be the most suitable. This is a business-to-business approach that has mainly been developed for industrial marketing and purchasing, building on major differences between the marketing of industrial products and consumer products. The main focus is on buyer–seller relationships, which often are well established and of long-term duration. They are complex, with contacts between the companies taking place on several different levels, particularly when complex products are involved. Business marketing is viewed as an inter-organizational matter, and it is regarded as fruitful to treat both the marketing and the buying behaviour of firms as organizational issues. This makes it possible to apply the same theory, of inter-organizational character, to both marketing and purchasing, the two being seen as two sides of the same coin, together representing the buyer–seller relationship.

This is fundamentally different from most approaches to marketing in general (El-Ansary, 1983; Sheth et al., 1988), relationship marketing (Sheth and Parvatiyar, 2000), including relationship marketing of services (e.g. Grönroos, 1995, 2000), and business-to-business marketing (e.g. Jackson, 1985; Bingham and Raffield, 1990), in which traditional marketing concepts and tools are applied.

The inter-organizational approach is limited to market relationships and rarely includes the non-market relationship aspect, for example government and other stakeholders in the social environment. Since the rationale behind doing business in the product/service market is based on efficiency, the whole idea is to sell and buy products at a profit. The justification in the government field, on the other hand, is to get approval for doing business in the market, for example to get a permit. This means that the whole idea is to be legitimate. The different rationales lead to differences in the type of relationship established with stakeholders in the market and those outside the market, for example government.

As was laid out in Chapter 7, the market structure of an industrial market such as the product/service market is usually concentrated and rigid, while demand is complex and sophisticated. The result is often tight interrelationships and strong dependencies between professional buyer and seller organizations. This market situation is looked upon as a network relating these parties to each other. This inter-relatedness is even more typical of emerging markets due to the embeddedness of the industrial markets in society, that is, where 'everything influences everything'. The basics of the inter-organizational approach developed for this market situation were specified in Chapter 7, this approach being the foundation of the international network strategy in this and the next chapter.

The INS model consists of a mix of three major strategic means: the network map, the linkage mix and the competitive mix, which are modelled in Figure 8.1. The network map concerns how the MNC relates itself to the whole market network, including buyers, distributors, competitors, suppliers and financiers. It builds on the discussion in Chapter 7 about network relationships taking place in various directions. The linkage mix regards how the seller creates and maintains different kinds of relationships with individual parties within the network. Typical of such a vertical market network is that the seller both cooperates and competes with the buyer for the resources involved in the exchange. The competitive mix, on the other hand, focuses on the competitors' network or the horizontal network. Unlike the linkage mix, its focus is on the position the seller takes or possesses in the competitors' network through the means of competition utilized. This mix then relates to horizontal competition, while the linkage mix involves vertical competition. A crucial aspect of the competitive mix is to get a first-mover advantage. One way to achieve this is to transform the composition of the market from a large number to a small number of parties by gradually reducing the number of competitors, for example by out-competing competitors or acquiring them. Another way to get a first-mover advantage is to be an early mover on the market in order to pre-empt it, the goal being to reduce the number of competitors by locking out potential entrants from the market. This is not only a question of entering early into the market but also of 'grabbing' the customers before the international competitors. From a network strategic point of view, the means behind this fundamental transformation process to change basic market conditions can be described as the spinning of a network so that the buyer is enclosed in the network and competitors are locked out.

Perceived customer value

The main goal of the international network strategy is to provide superior customer value, which is done jointly between the supplier and the customer. The supplying MNC needs to be familiar with the value-generating processes of the customers, that is, what solutions or packages customers want to purchase, and use that to create value for them. Different groups within the buying organization may have different perceptions of the supplier's value offering, that is, values created are subjectively perceived by the customer. This perceived value is defined according to Monroe (1991) as the ratio of perceived benefits relative to perceived sacrifices. The customer then makes a trade-off between benefits and sacrifices in the supplier's offering. Examples of perceived benefits are physical attributes related to the product, for instance productivity and durability of the product or ability to change features and applications of the products according to the customer's requirements. Other benefits concern service attributes such as technical support, availability of

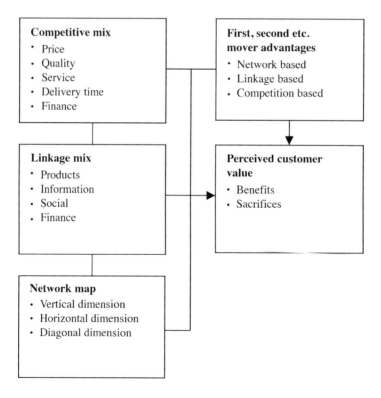

Figure 8.1 International network strategy in the product/service market

spare parts and ease of use for operators. Examples of perceived sacrifices are purchasing price, expected costs for maintenance and repairs, and risk of failure or poor performance.

Network mapping

Two main types of network marketing situations are analysed. One involves individual organizations as part of two-party relationships (dyads) or three-party relationships (triads), where industrial products and services of various types are exchanged, for example components, consumables, equipment and after-sales service. This situation will also be described and analysed in Chapter 10, mainly as an entry strategy. The other type is more complex and involves clusters of organizations. This network marketing situation is introduced in this chapter, but is mainly dealt with in the next chapter about networking processes and project marketing.

Before the MNC starts to build relationships in both these marketing situations, preparations are necessary, mainly to know what the market looks like by mapping it. A major result is a network map with possible 'routes' described and analysed. Network mapping is a way to handle the complexity of the INS in order to be able to know where to focus marketing efforts. After having identified relevant networks, they need to be described and analysed. In this analysis of the external environment, the following questions may be raised:

1   What does the network look like? Which are the relevant nodes and linkages? Should only direct linkages to the customers be included or should indirect relationships also be considered, for example to customers' customers?

2   How much of the network of a specific organizational field needs to be 'laid out'? Where is the network horizon? This outer-border question is difficult to answer, since there are no objective ways to delimit a network. As a consequence, the map of the network will vary with the marketing problem at hand.

3   What type of network is it? Is it a hierarchical or an arm's length network or is it a prescribed or an emergent network?

4   What does the network consist of? Which are the major bridges between the different parts of the network?

5   How should the network be structured? Does it consist of clusters? And how dense are these clusters? Is the network loosely or tightly coupled?

6   To what degree does the MNC reach out to different parts of the network, that is, what is its degree of connectivity?

Three main network dimensions are distinguished in Figure 8.2: the vertical dimension, the horizontal dimension and the diagonal dimension. The vertical dimension takes up the parties included along the value-added product chain: first-tier customers and second-tier customers such as customers' customers and so on; first-tier suppliers and second-tier suppliers such as suppliers' suppliers; various kinds of intermediaries. The horizontal dimension includes competitors, while the diagonal dimension concerns connections to other organizational fields such as the financial market network and the government network.

The organizations along the three dimensions are grouped at different levels or tiers. The primary part of the network or the first tier of relationships consists of direct relationships, which are manifested in linkages with external parties such as customers, suppliers, competitors, financiers and government authorities. The secondary part of the network consists of the second tier of indirect relationships of the MNC, for example suppliers' suppliers. They are only considered when they are of critical importance for business marketing in the primary network. Sometimes a third tier of relationships are included along the value chain, as when the seller (e.g. of a machine) wants to know the customer's (e.g. the manufacturer using the machine) customer (e.g. the buyer of the products produced by the machine) of its dealer (e.g. the distributor of the machine). In structuring the complex network, it is often necessary to assemble companies in different groups. A distinction is then made between macro and micro clusters. A macro cluster consists of individual first-tier companies or a mix of companies from different tiers, for example end users, main contractors, and consultants. A micro cluster consists of organizational units within a company, for example different departments involved in marketing a certain product or project.

The complexity of network mapping is illustrated for an MNC involved in a very complex type of network marketing, namely the marketing of projects. The reason is that the more complex the

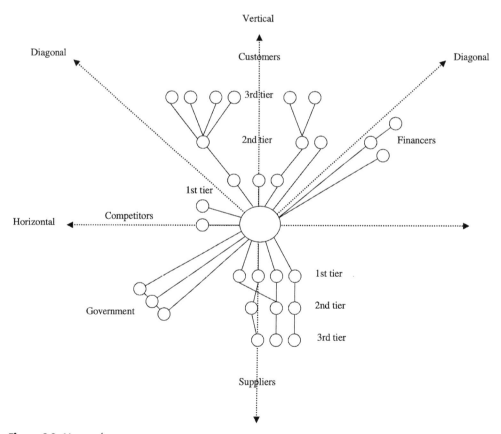

Figure 8.2 Network map

product/service sold, the more complex the process of linking up buyers and sellers. Usually, it also takes longer to handle change in networks involving complex products than those exchanging single products such as components and machines. However, the complexity of the market situation is reduced by limiting the example to a marketing situation, in which the MNC manages the business of the project itself. Consortia and similar cooperative arrangements between independent firms are therefore not taken up here. The MNC or micro cluster exemplified – Indpow – is a dominating MNC in most of its business fields throughout the globe. With its long and extensive experience of operating in transition countries, it is especially suited to illustrate marketing of industrial goods in emerging markets, in this case in India. Indpow and its marketing activities and organization in India are presented in the next chapter, since the case will primarily be used there to illustrate marketing. The project network identified in this chapter therefore also works as an input to the next chapter.

The first tier of relationships consists of direct business marketing relationships with external parties such as customers, consultants, suppliers, financiers and government authorities. Although no relationships are established with competitors, they are included in the primary network, the reason being that there is dependence through market competition. The second tier of indirect relationships of Indpow consists of customers' customers. Several parties such as end users, consultants and contractors are involved on the buyer side. Such parties represent a buyer cluster, which is a macro cluster. Complex projects consist of a large number of different products and services, supplied by several units that may either be separate companies or belong to the same MNC. These sellers form different seller clusters that compete with one another (competing clusters). Various governmental bodies are often involved as a government cluster, either as part of the buyer cluster or as a group of outside parties. Individual clusters are connected within themselves and with one another through a mix of four main types of linkages: product linkages, information linkages, social linkages and financial linkages. The focus here will be on Indpow as a particular seller micro cluster and its relationships with other clusters. The network marketing situation involved is analysed at the organizational level, individuals being seen as representatives of their organizations.

The vertical dimension: customer clusters

Direct relationships with customers are considered to be the most important of all relationships with external parties. For the project business exemplified here, they are characterized as long term, broad and flexible.

Although the customer structure varies, it is rather concentrated to big companies. These customers organize the purchasing situation in two major ways. Either the equipment for the project is bought in bits and pieces and put together by the buyer, or it is purchased in one package as a turn-key project. In the latter case, it is constructed by the seller or by a third party: a main contractor. This means that sometimes linkages are established with one buyer (the end user) and sometimes with two buyers (the end user and the main contractor). To adapt to these marketing situations, Indpow has created a strategic flexibility by developing a capability to act both as a main contractor and as a subcontractor. When Indpow is a subcontractor, the major strategic issue is to develop a linkage mix between the end user and the main contractor. Sometimes the end user only wants to deal with one party, whereas Indpow teams up with the main contractor in front of the customer. Other times, marketing is concentrated to the end-user linkage, in which case this customer makes a separate deal with Indpow and then tells the main contractor to buy from Indpow.

Whether micro clusters consist of public or private customers is an important strategic issue. Indpow often has a problem in getting public sector customers to understand the value of the turn-key arrangement, which is not the case in private industry. Public customers traditionally believe that it is less expensive to act as main contractor by breaking projects down into pieces, buy parts separately and assemble the plants themselves. However, this is usually more expensive, since public customers overestimate the technical competence of their engineers. Such assembled systems often do not turn out to work so well in the long run. This situation of customers having the main contractor facility in house is slowly changing with the liberalization of the industry.

Another difference is that public customers operate their plants differently, mainly looking at costs. Private customers are more quality conscious and better appreciate the value of technical solutions, and do not only focus on price. Relationships with private customers are also characterized by a more relaxed atmosphere involving more or less continuous discussions between the parties during the project process. Linkages with public customers, on the other hand, are more formal or strictly rule-bound, for instance involving sealed tenders, and where purchasing is organized in committees, which follow formal procedures by the book. This means that offers are picked at the lowest price conditional upon passing the requirements of the tender. Despite this formality, the contract often only becomes one stop on the road to the final order, with many changes and renegotiations taking place after the contract has been signed. This blend of formal and informal relationships is essential within this micro cluster. Even if purchasing committees are strictly rule-bound, members have some discretion, and friendship can smooth things out. They might become less rigid and to the letter, more understanding, give time for meetings and presentations, and become more open to giving and taking information and to influence. The micro clusters of Indian private industry, on the other hand, are dominated by the power and authority of the owner, who, when required, takes quick decisions.

Another important division of customers from a network perspective is between established and new customers. At Indpow, it is considered to be much easier to deal with old customers, although they might not be as profitable as new customers. The main reason for this is the good relationship already established. Competitors will usually bid very low, but if the relationship between Indpow and its existing customer works well, it will constitute a barrier for the customer when it comes to accepting the bid. With new customers, the cost of capture is much higher.

For another project-selling MNC studied in another Indian industry, technological issues are not an important part of the project marketing any longer, being looked upon more as a basic standard for competing. The reason is that all major competitors have similar competence, which makes technical solutions equal. Software, for example service offerings, delivery security and the ability to comprehend the purchasing decision processes of the micro clusters, therefore becomes more decisive for getting a competitive advantage. The informal parts of the relationships with the micro clusters have become more important, for example social calls, dinners and associating with customer personnel outside work. Overall, linkages are more privately oriented than in Scandinavia. Price is also more important. The customer often wants additional service but is unwilling to pay for it.

The behaviour of the customer changes with the stage of the purchasing process, and this is discussed in the next chapter.

The vertical dimension: consultants

Consultants are often a crucial third party in project networks. They are critical members of the macro clusters, where they play different roles. Long-term relationships with consultants are therefore of special importance when selling to projects, especially to large projects.

In most local Indian industries, where *Indpow* is involved, there are ongoing contacts with a rather limited number of consultants, usually about two to four firms. Most of them are technical or engineering consultants. But there are also some agent-type consultants, who provide commercial assistance on the basis of broad contact nets. Often their role in large projects is limited to being consultants: taking care of or coping with technical diversity and double-checking the conclusions reached by the customer staff. In one industry segment, for example, a project normally starts with the customer identifying a suitable consultant, who is then hired to investigate locations, work out technical specifications and handle various political processes. Therefore, consultants become important information sources regarding new projects. One important task is to make feasibility studies, especially for government projects financed by the World Bank or aid organizations. Consultants are also often involved in the writing of specifications and in the evaluation of bids. Sometimes they also more directly influence purchasing by giving recommendations about how to divide the project among suppliers. It could also happen that they are involved in the engineering design that takes place after the contract has been signed, as well as in the execution phase by being used for inspection, controls and supervision. Thus, sometimes consultants only participate during the initial phase of a project, and sometimes they participate throughout the whole project.

The vertical dimension: suppliers

The MNC also has long-term relationships with key suppliers in India, which are usually developed by means of education and training. Indpow considers these suppliers of strategic equipment as long-term strategic alliances, which take years to develop. Relations are normally kept up, even though projects are sometimes rejected and business lost. Many of them also supply competitors, but that is not a problem. Such world-class suppliers will not play tricks. As will be discussed further in Chapter 9, these key suppliers, unlike ordinary suppliers, also participate in the marketing of projects.

The horizontal dimension: competitors

Indpow has three main groups of competitors. First there are MNCs, with which competition takes place on equal terms. The second group consists of wholly or partially state-owned enterprises, which through their strong government connections get various favours. The third group consists of small companies, which compete on price. Indpow India keeps itself informed about the activities of the competitors through published information, rumours, social relations like surveying people within the Indpow group or former company employees, and customers. Social and informal relations are therefore important media in competitor analysis. The competitive situation often is concentrated to a few buyers and sellers.

The diagonal dimension: financiers

Since there is a trend towards finance as a major competitive tool, Indpow has established a finance function in India. The company provides its own financing to customers but also acts as an intermediary by having contacts with banks to provide project financing, especially to private customers. Some financial solutions are local, but most financial packages include a considerable element of foreign financing. Here relations are international and are taken care of by the group. With government projects, the financial aspect is not important, since public customers raise money internally or externally from the World Bank or aid organizations.

Because of the large sums and risks involved in very big projects, two or three banks cooperate in a syndicate, with one bank acting as lead bank. As part of investigating the future cash-flow of the project, banks demand the right to approve key contracts. In that way finance organizations are involved in evaluating very large projects, but not usually 'normal' projects. Indpow also has a project and trade finance company of its own, which can arrange finance for large projects and leasing arrangements for smaller projects. Through another group unit dealing with ventures, Indpow may also provide equity finance to a project. Banks are important information nodes, inter alia to get information about the financial strength of potential customers at an early stage of a project.

The diagonal dimension: governments

The importance of relationships with government officials decreased gradually during the 1990s due to liberalization, for instance licence issues became more and more unimportant (cf. Jansson et al., 1995). The discretion of officials at all government levels was reduced and more clear-cut rules led to greater transparency. However, there are still ongoing contacts with municipal- and/ or state-level authorities regarding practical issues related to manufacturing. This is discussed at length in Chapter 15, which is about IBS towards government.

The Group

The relationships the subsidiary has with different group units vary. Since the project business is mostly handled by the Indian companies of Indpow, there is less contact with internal units outside India. Because of the high independence and long history of being established in the country, these subsidiaries are Indian in character. Since the subsidiary receives little internal technical and marketing support, there are few contacts with various units within the group. With the build-up of local competence, independence from the group has become large.

Linkage mix

Using the network map, it is now possible to go into the network and find out how to act in parts of it, for example towards the customers or suppliers, to establish a linkage mix. This part of the INS pertains to vertical competition and concerns how to establish and run relationships along the vertical value chain. As discussed above, the linkage mix varies with complexity of the network map, for example whether single products are marketed to single buyers or a package of products to a cluster of buyers. The linkage mix, then, considers the complexity of both the spatial dimension of building and maintaining different types of relationships within a network structure and the time dimension of how long it takes to do this and at what point various linkages are used to establish, develop and decide on the value offering together with the customer. Chapter 9 is devoted to this time or process aspect.

As shown in Figures 8.1 and 8.2 above, a combination of four major types of linkages (product, information, social and financial) is involved, forming a specific mix of relationships. The general objective is to create customer value by building long-term and mutually beneficial relationships with customers, dealers and distributors in order to add value to the end product along the vertical product chain. A bond is established between the parties through a suitable mix of linkages. For example, when developing a new product, buyers and sellers might work together closely for an extended period of time. Through this process, they become enveloped in their relationship, making the substitution of either of them by another party difficult. The seller, for instance, becomes involved in various concrete problems of the customer, resulting in a very specific linkage. The distance to be covered between the start of the commitment and obtaining the results in the form of an exchange of products is often very long. Commitment grows gradually as the parties become more and more absorbed by the relationship. Strong mutual interdependence involves considerable dangers for both parties. The strong tie-up and the long-term character of business deals results in considerable trouble if anything goes wrong. If each solution to a customer problem is specific, most of the expenses are wasted if the business is taken by a competitor. In such cases, the degree of linkage specificity is high and switching costs are high, since it is hard for the parties to replace each other. It is then important that the parties protect themselves from the dangers inherent in this type of business dealing. This is usually done within the relationship through building up a mutual balance of gradual commitment of resources. The decisive judgements for both parties concern the degree of commitment to be made in each phase of the business process.

Thus, linkages in industrial product/service markets are often characterized by a low degree of substitution, investment in linkage-specific resources and capabilities, and a long-term character. In many dyadic relationships, for example, the parties have become so united that competitiveness is maintained, and the costs kept low through standardization of procedures, which serves as a barrier to competitors. It is then essential to not lose this competitiveness and first-mover advantage by letting the relationship become set in a fixed mode. Flexibility is kept up by making adaptations to a changing context. The linkage mix for projects concentrates on social linkages being established and maintained with key persons. Investing in such networking activities often represents the largest and most important part of the marketing investment in project selling.

There is a trade-off between the main types of linkages. The information linkage is often most important in the initial stages, where the parties build up knowledge about each other. This mutual knowledge together with the linking process itself make it increasingly possible to organize the relationship better by simplifying it. The social linkage seems to be important throughout the whole process. Creating trustworthiness through social contacts is in many emerging economies important in the initial stages and even a precondition for starting the commercial exchange. Later on, when parties have come further in their relationship, they learn to know each other, which further strengthens the relationship.

As more and more transactions are carried out, parties are able to reorganize to create further improvements. With the stabilization of relationships, knowledge of prices and other conditions tends to reach a steady state. Parties have learned much about each other and about competitors, and this in turn makes it expensive to change the price norm. Interest in prices has gradually decreased and price competition has been replaced by non-price competition.

When establishing relationships in new markets, there is always the danger of repeating behaviour from other markets, which might not suit the new market. Such habits of following invisible, taken-for-granted norms from the 'old' markets of Western Europe was noted in South East Asian markets (Jansson, 1994a), especially in the first years of operation. Local needs, for example, were taken more or less for granted, Swedish MNCs assuming them to be essentially the same as in Europe. Such 'easy ways out', however, could reflect poor local responsiveness, and an unsustainable long-term competitive position. This could amount to the marketing situation not having been properly analysed. Through necessary adaptations thus having been delayed, later costs may be considerably greater (e.g. due to lost sales) than such costs would have needed to be with better and more timely adaptation to local conditions.

Trustworthiness

As taken up in Chapter 7, establishing trustful relationships is a critical part of the networking process and then of the linkage mix. Such trustworthiness is mainly related to the social organization of the relationship, where a distinction is made between organizational trustworthiness and individual trustworthiness, the latter type being further divided into professional and social trustworthiness. As found by Jansson (1994a, 2007b) and Jansson et. al. (1995), the relation between social trustworthiness and emotions is complex. When trust is based on personal traits, friendship is mostly based on emotions and the relation is therefore personal and informal. This is the true personalized relationship. Still, when social trustworthiness comes from a common social or cultural background, a low degree of emotional affiliation may be involved. An arranged marriage could be a good example of this, especially if the partnership is founded more on instrumental factors like social position than on emotional factors like love. Relations based on social trustworthiness originating from group traits are personal but vary in their degree of formality.

Competitive mix

Since the competitive mix concerns various means of competition, it is related to horizontal competition. The seller offers a technical solution to a buyer's problem, which creates a favourable position in the competitors' network. The offering consists of various parts, for instance of hardware in the form of products of a certain quality and of software such as service, transfer of know-how and financing. The package is delivered within a specified time at a specified price. It is modelled in such a way that it distinguishes itself favourably from the competitors' offers.

An important part of competitor analysis or benchmarking is to analyse the competitors' international network marketing strategies, for example what products and projects they are involved in, how these sellers are evaluated by the customers, how they influence decisions, how they follow up on contracts, how they are paid, and how they deliver and install projects.

Price vs quality

Since it is usually hard to sell on quality in emerging country markets, price is the dominant element of the competitive mix in these markets (Jansson, 1994a). An important function of the market is to establish norms for the functioning of price, norms being critical constraints for the MNCs' competitive mix. How prices are fixed in various market networks is important for decisions on the competitive mix. In traditional market forms, prices are determined by the market and the market actors are therefore being mainly price takers. In other forms, on the other hand, the parties are the chief price makers. In most industrial product market networks, prices and products are not seen as given, as they are in the more classical markets such as many commodity markets. Rather, it is the other way around, prices and products being viewed as being first negotiated and then determined (product and factor prices). Market actors are considered as price makers and not as price takers. Pricing is usually a very difficult and risky task, the outcome of which determines the distribution of economic benefits between the parties. Prices are considered not only to be discovered but also to be influenced by the parties, as well as to be dependent upon the resource situation of the buyer and seller and of their competitors.

This situation is faced in the imperfect emerging markets, where it is expensive to find out about the price of a product, both for the buyer and for the seller. The seller, for instance, collects information about the segment of the market of relevance (customers and competitors) as well as information concerning one's own activities, for example objectives, strategies and various costs relevant to the product. In traditional Western markets, price provides a good approximation of efficient resource allocation, which is often less true in emerging markets. However, it is still in the interest of sellers to offer cost-effective products and for buyers to purchase such products in order to be efficient and competitive in the markets in which they sell their end products. Consequently, the resources spent are recovered through price, at least in the long run. Price is still the main approximation of an efficient allocation of resources between the parties to a linkage and between competing parties in the environment. Price reflects, therefore, not simply production costs but also other costs relevant for a certain type of business exchange. The lower these costs are, the less resources are used up in fulfilling needs. The lower the prices can be set, the more competitive the company is. This is the bottom line in pricing.

Thus, price is the most important component of competition, since it determines the economic outcome of the business for the parties involved. It can be seen as the very basis of competitiveness. However, as already indicated, it is particularly difficult in emerging markets to establish the relation between price, costs, efficiency and competitiveness. Pricing is more complex in these markets. First, it is difficult to calculate prices and to know whether they reflect an efficient resource allocation between parties. Second, non-price competition is also important. This type of competition largely dominates the marketing of advanced industrial products by MNCs, relegating price to the background in the competitive mix. Even if price agreements finally determine the resource allocation between the parties, quality, service and other competitive factors may be stressed by buyers and sellers. Complexity of needs makes it difficult to price an offer. The price must be related, for example, to a certain quality and service level as well as to delivery time. These parameters are determined collectively within the framework of the network. Price is one of various factors determined through such a process.

The high uncertainty involved in marketing in the complex emerging markets and the ensuing problems of fixing prices, making them less transparent, can be taken advantage of by an opportunistic seller. The buyer can be influenced into buying a product that is less than suitable for actual or future needs. Similar problematical results could come about through neither party having sufficient knowledge about the needs in question and the potential alternatives in the market. The non-transparent role of price as a competitive factor under such conditions may thus result in biased business.

Price tends to be evaluated in terms of expectations and promises or norms regarding such matters as quality, service and delivery time. Exchange only takes place if price is acceptable to both parties.

First-mover advantages

As shown in Chapter 5, which talks about the antecedents to IBS, most theory on competition is structural and therefore does not consider the timing of efforts to achieve competitive advantage. This is a crucial part of the INS, that is, to achieve a first-mover advantage. One way is to be the first in the field. An MNC that enters a new market before its competitors increases its chances of winning the game by being the first to offer its solutions to the customers. This means that the supplier that manages to establish the first linkage with a customer more easily gets a competitive advantage. Another way is to become the first supplier of a customer. This happens when the seller gets some kind of advantage over the competitors by becoming the primary supplier in the industry or on the market. When the business is renewed with the satisfied customer, parity between sellers no longer exists, since it is cost saving for the customer to do business with a company it already knows and trusts. Getting a first-mover advantage is then a question of both when the business marketing move is made (picking the right time) and how it is made (making the right move), for example by finding the best mix and sequence of network linkages over time.

First-mover advantages may be achieved through the information linkage, with the customer being influenced by and dependent upon information from the seller. It could also be achieved through the social linkage, by the customer becoming socially committed to the seller. In addition, such advantages may be achieved through product or financial linkages, the customer becoming dependent upon the seller's products and financing. Specific linkage mixtures may be found to be particularly advantageous at various stages in the building up of the relationship. In the marketing of projects, for example, social and information linkages are very critical at the initial establishment phases.

A first-mover advantage can also be achieved through a competitive offer. The strategy here involves a combination of a linkage mix and a competitive mix. The linkage mix creates a framework for the transfer of the competitive mix. But a first-mover advantage is also influenced by what the MNC as a seller can offer. An advanced technical solution far above the customer's present capabilities, for instance, requires a more long-term build-up of information and of social contact networks for transferring know-how. Likewise, if financing is an important marketing element of the offer, a financial linkage will become established.

If one MNC has already achieved a first-mover advantage, the strategic alternatives are more limited for the other firms, any of which can at most achieve a second-mover advantage. This is achieved by entering the market before the other remaining competitors, or by being a second supplier of a customer. Third- or fourth-mover advantages may not even exist on small emerging markets. The MNC that manages to acquire an earlier state-owned monopoly company in an industry also acquires its entire local customer network. By being able as a first mover to control the whole local industry, a large, sustainable, and durable competitive advantage is created in the form of large entry barriers for competing firms. Thus, due to the normally limited size of emerging markets during the initial development stages, the chances of establishing a sustainable number of customer relationships are reduced the later the company moves into the market. In cases where there is only room for two suppliers in a market, newcomers need to out-compete the incumbents by taking over their customer relationships. This is more difficult than being a primary supplier on the market. However, such third- or fourth-mover advantages may arise at later stages of market development with the fast growth of these economies. There is also a downside to being a first mover. The first to enter a market, for example, often has to make a higher market investment. Making way for others is costly. Furthermore, later arrivals may benefit from lower learning costs by being able to learn from the first entrant about what works well and what does not.

CAPABILITY PROFILES

Behind an international business marketing strategy that creates competitive advantages lays the MNC's internal resource/capability constellation to develop relationships. A local network strategy formed for the specific market in an emerging market can therefore only be executed if there are suitable capabilities present in the country or it is possible to draw on capabilities found within the group outside this country. The capability profile describes the mix of capabilities found at a local company for a certain INS, for instance knowledge and skills. A network strategy in a certain market environment, for example, may require either a specific knowledge about a few customers or a general knowledge about many customers.

The capability profiles show a company's ability to handle various types of networks and linkages. The grouping of the profiles is illustrated in Figure 8.3. First, a distinction is made between two main types of solutions that create value for the customer: those that satisfy specific customer needs and those that satisfy general customer needs. In the former case, solutions are made and adapted to individual needs, while they are not adapted in the latter case. Behind each type of a solution is found problem-solving capabilities. There are capabilities such as certain employee skills and technical systems as well as management systems in the form of certain problem-solving processes. Where the company has capabilities that make it possible to solve the individual problems of customers, the company is said to have a customer specialist profile. But where capabilities instead are arranged to solve the common problems of many customers, the company is said to have a product specialist profile. The reason for the latter name is that when linkages are managed towards solving common customer needs, they tend to converge on the product rather than the customer. Hence, in this case the product as representing a general customer solution is the key focus and not the specific individual customer solution.

Second, a distinction is made between how needs and solutions are bridged, that is, whether it takes place through direct linkages between buyer and seller or indirectly through a third party. The profiles of product and customer specialists are both oriented towards problem-solving through direct contacts in dyads. Where intermediaries are involved, the linkages of the supplying company with customers are indirect. Intermediaries are involved in solving customer problems for two strategic profiles. The distributor network specialist profile is based on a triad structure, where an independent intermediary is the main customer interface and plays a major role in solving customer problems, for example a dealer. To handle this kind of strategic situation, the MNC needs to have a capability profile that makes it possible to primarily manage linkages through the intermediary network rather than with final customers directly. A profile, on the other hand, where the MNC specializes in being the intermediary itself by having the distribution network 'in house' is called a distribution specialist. This is a dyad, where the MNC as a distributor does business directly with its customers.

A distinction is further made between marketing and manufacturing capabilities. Often manufacturing is important from a marketing point of view, since an efficient production of a solution/product is a condition for a good marketing result. For instance, some MNCs call attention to local production as an important factor of the competitive mix. When the profile is oriented towards production, there is a manufacturing specialist. Sales companies are also purchasing specialists, while manufacturing companies are manufacturing specialists or a mix of both. If a company is classified as a manufacturing specialist only, it has no capacity for marketing, for example a sub-contractor of machine capacity. Trading companies which specialize in sourcing products for the group are pure purchasing specialists. When the capabilities of a firm are classified according to this scheme, one profile or a mix of profiles is obtained.

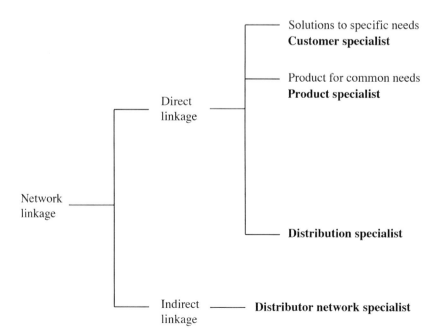

Figure 8.3 Capability profiles

Customer specialist

The ways customer problems are solved implies that each of the business marketing capability profiles introduced above represents a specific problem-solving capability. The capability typical of the customer specialist profile has the following characteristics: each customer is treated individually, business marketing activities are specialized to the individual customer, and information is collected about specific customer needs. Most tailor-made products as well as package deals such as various types of equipment for projects therefore belong to this category. The main feature of this profile is that the problem-solving is directly oriented towards the specific needs of certain customers. The emphasis is on the software aspects, chiefly the design or adaptation of technically advanced products to satisfy individual customer needs. Engineering is the key word. The business marketing activities denoted by this profile are characterized by long lead times and high sales costs in long-term relationships and broad contact nets. Production capabilities are subordinated to marketing capabilities and need to be flexible to make possible the production of individual solutions. The scope of the problem-solving capacity varies with how many different kinds of particular needs are catered for. Customer specialist capabilities tend to emerge through the continuous contacts with the customers, by learning and adapting to the customers' changing requirements. A deliberate planning of activities built on such capacities is difficult; hence continuous contacts are very important.

The degree of specialization of the problem-solving capability is high, making the specialization of resources and capabilities high because of the tailor-made products sold. This implies that the costs of switching between customers are substantial for customer specialists. Competition is need-positioned and oriented directly towards customers, to whom solutions are provided. Competition takes place between networks of specialized linkages.

Product specialist

Companies selling technically advanced industrial products with low or no adaptation to individual customer needs have another problem-solving capability and are therefore classified as product specialists. Networks and problem-solving capabilities are concentrated to the product rather than to the customer directly. These products are sold to customers who have a common need for a functionally high and consistent quality. For example, most components and steels sold directly to original equipment manufacturers (OEMs) are found in this category. A high engineering capability is essential if the competitive advantage of the first mover is to be maintained through the technical quality of the product. A product development capability is also critical. These engineering capabilities are high throughout the company, in marketing as well as in manufacturing and purchasing. The coordination of these capabilities is important to achieve a successful strategy. Economies of scale are important in all these activities. The need for flexibility in marketing as well as in production and of the problem-solving capabilities behind a certain flexibility is less than for a customer specialist. The specialization of resources and capabilities towards specific linkages is lower than for customer specialists. This means that the stability of networks is often more important than change. The networks of product specialists are characterized as being stable for long periods, but tend to change rapidly during rather short time periods. International network strategies are therefore more of the deliberate kind, since a certain strategy can be maintained for a longer period. A product specialist, contrary to a customer specialist, survives by exploiting an established network rather than by changing it. Competition is product positioned and oriented directly towards customers. Products are offered to customers and competition takes place between standardized networks.

Distribution specialist

Large ball-bearing manufacturers sell large volumes of products directly to OEMs like car companies as well as market small quantities through intermediaries to repair shops in the aftermarket. When the bearing producer is also a retailer taking care of its own sales in the aftermarket, it is a distribution specialist. If, on the other hand, it outsources the distribution to independent dealers, it is a distributor network specialist. Sometimes the high costs of establishing one's own distribution network are justified provided that pure distribution is important and that a sufficient number of customer linkages are involved. The number of customers and product varieties needs to be large enough to achieve economies of scope in marketing, inter alia an efficient use of the capabilities of one's own distribution network.

Establishing a company as a distribution specialist is the same as establishing both a distribution and a sales company, the company thereby becoming a distribution specialist as well as a product specialist. If the MNC is currently represented in the market by an external distributor, this could mean taking over this network. This is different to the case of establishing a sales company with a product or customer specialist profile by taking over an agent network. In both cases, however, the aim is to integrate forwards all the way to the customers in order to have direct linkages with them. The main difference lies in the types of marketing capabilities required. Product and customer specialists specialize their problem-solving capabilities directly to customer problems, while distribution specialists concentrate on their abilities to transfer these solutions to the customers, for instance skills in the assembly of an assortment of goods, and capabilities related to physical supply, transportation and storage.

Distributor network specialist

Many products are not economical to sell and/or distribute directly to customers. Being a distributor network specialist means that transfer capabilities related to distribution are outsourced to other parties. Distributors are set apart from agents. They are middlemen that besides buying and selling industrial goods also offer warehousing facilities, services and financing, for which they need relevant capabilities. Agents, on the other hand, only represent sellers, normally a limited number of sellers, and specialize their marketing capabilities to a certain geographical area and number of industries. Even if agents do have resources for carrying stocks, they mainly have capabilities concentrated to selling. The main marketing capacity of distributors, on the other hand, is distribution. Agents are therefore seen as an alternative to having one's own sales subsidiary.

It is usually more efficient to externalize resources and capabilities for distribution when economies of scope cannot be achieved in investing in one's own distribution network. This is often the case when there are long and extensive distribution networks, through which small quantities are sold of a broad variety of technically simple products to numerous customers spread out over a large area. In such cases, an intermediary makes a more efficient use of the resources than the producer. A distribution network can also be used as a channel for obtaining information about customers and competitors. Negotiating with intermediaries is also much less expensive than negotiating with customers directly. Moreover, the costs of controlling the prices of intermediaries is lower than enforcing them directly on customers, or through one's own distribution network. Informing oneself about the market and the intermediaries in order to control the prices of the distributors is one of the main costs for a distributor network specialist. These costs are lower for simple, standard products, since prices are mainly controlled by the market.

Availability of the products in the various parts of the industrial distribution network is a critical competitive factor for a distribution specialist or distributor network specialist. It is vital that the right product is delivered to the right customer at the right time. Then, resources and capabilities relating to delivery systems, inventory management, service levels and location of warehouses become critical. But in industrial distribution other functions such as sales, service and maintenance are important as well. An important issue is therefore how to divide up the capabilities behind these functions between the manufacturing MNC and the local distributors. A minimum requirement for the supplier is to have the capabilities that make it possible to control the marketing process of the distributor.

At a certain stage, it might even become more economical to integrate forward, that is, acquiring the distributor network or setting up one's own distribution network. Since this solution is very expensive, cost savings must be considerable. The establishment of such specialist structures involves high fixed costs. Another alternative is therefore to partially integrate forwards by setting up one's own sales company in order to participate in and control the distribution network on the spot. Then, with its stocks and marketing capabilities, the MNC moves closer to the customers. This makes the MNC a distributor network specialist, since products are supplied through distributors at the same time as most contacts take that route. A distinction is made between this type of distributor network specialist, where there is more of a joint action towards the customers, and another type consisting of mostly distribution activities as well as divided-up capabilities, where distributors operate more independently in a country. The MNC invests more in the distribution network in the former case than in the latter.

CONCLUSIONS

The international network strategy model was taken up in this chapter, being mainly relevant for the product/service market. Customers are the major type of actor in this market network. These customers are satisfied by creating superior customer value. To succeed in this, the supplier needs to be familiar with the value-generating processes of the customers, especially how customers subjectively make the trade-off between benefits and sacrifices. Having identified relevant market actors, the chapter then describes and analyses them using network mapping. This methodology is illustrated by an MNC selling projects. The reason is that the more complex the product/service sold, and the more complex and long-term the process of linking up buyers and sellers, the more difficult network mapping becomes. The organization of both the macro cluster and the micro cluster – and, consequently, the INS – is influenced by the type of customer, for example new versus established customer. Consultants are crucial members of the macro clusters, where they play different roles. The vertical dimension of the network map also includes the suppliers. The mapping of the competitors forming a horizontal network shows that there are three major types of competitors. Three actors found in the diagonal dimension of the map are important members of the network: financiers, governments and group units outside the emerging market.

The network map coming out of the mapping procedure lays the foundation for the INS. It is useful for making strategic decisions about which actors along the three dimensions to focus on, how to combine them, and how to sequence the relationships marketing over time to the various actors. Based on these decisions, the linkage mix is determined for each major party included in the network map. In emerging markets, it is of utmost importance to build trustworthiness, which is mainly done through the social linkage. Considering the network map at hand and keeping the network situation and linkage mix in mind, the ISN is completed by adding the competitive mix. As discussed above, the critical trade-off in emerging markets is between price and quality, while simultaneously considering other competitive parameters such as service level, delivery time and finance. In addition, how to compete over time through creating first-mover advantages play a critical role in achieving competitive advantages.

The outcome of the international network strategy also depends on a thorough mapping of the internal environment, which mainly consists of four types of composite organizational capabilities, specified as capability profiles: customer specialist, product specialist, distribution specialist and distributor network specialist.

The local INS will be elaborated on further in the next chapter by delving into the strategic international networking process and studying the network marketing of projects. In Chapter 10, the local INS in the foreign product/service market in marketing both industrial products and projects will be developed further by connecting it to the seller network through the internationalization process.

9
International networking processes

The previous chapter took up the international network strategy in the product/service market without going much into the change process itself. This chapter, which continues on from that chapter and builds on Chapter 7, is, rather, devoted to international networking processes. Such processes are best studied for very complex offerings such as in the marketing of projects illustrated in Chapter 8. This is especially true for the large projects, which are extremely complex and time consuming. Moreover, they create important business opportunities for many multinational corporations (MNCs) in emerging markets, since infrastructure development through constructing roads, airports, ports, houses, dams, power stations and industrial plants are a precondition for their high economic growth. There is a high demand for complex industrial products like capital goods for such projects, which are mostly sold in the form of a package deal consisting of hardware along with software such as services. Take a power plant for example. It can be designed in many ways, fulfilling a large variety of needs, thus creating a complex value-generating process. The equipment for the plant takes a long time to manufacture and put together by a large group of manufacturers and contractors. It is expensive to buy and therefore involves important financing matters not valid in marketing most other types of industrial goods. To succeed with such a project, numerous issues need to be solved together by buyers, sellers and other parties involved. Buying and selling activities as well as other activities involved become very complicated and take a long time to perform. Thus, the large investments made in building up infrastructure and industry in emerging markets create vast business opportunities for MNCs skilful in marketing complex business projects.

INTERNATIONAL NETWORK MARKETING OF PROJECTS

According to Jalkala et al. (2010), a number of changes took place in the project business arena during the beginning of this century which have important implications for project marketing theory and practice. First, the consultants as a third party of the customer network began to play a larger role in the definition of projects. Second, the customer base became more dynamic by being reorganized due to mergers and acquisitions (M&As). Third, the buying process changed due to an increased professionalization of the buyers, which increased customer power, inter alia making the business riskier for the seller. These changes in the customer cluster resulted in the sellers becoming more customer-oriented, for example they started to use key account management in project marketing. Suppliers also moved upstream by getting more involved in the early stages of the marketing process through participating in defining customer requirements. They also moved more downstream by offering maintenance services and training. Brand management became more important, as did references from satisfied customers. Many project sellers broadened their business beyond large complex projects to also become service providers and single product sellers. These major changes represent important strategic issues that need to be considered for the international network strategy. Most of them are covered below, since they have been important strategic issues for project marketing in emerging markets for a long time.

As found in Chapter 8, there are important differences between international network strategy for products or services, and projects consisting of a package of products and services. The complexity is larger in many ways for project marketing. First, business network marketing is of a more imaginary kind in selling projects due to the special mix of physical and service attributes of the package deal, and how they are manifested over time. The physical facility, for example, cannot be inspected until the project has essentially been completed. This means that project marketing mostly consists of a presentation of ideas and images, made concrete, for example, through sketches, drawings, models and simulations. Such an imaginary type of marketing increases uncertainty for both parties, implying that successful marketing, unlike in most other business marketing situations, depends more on the reduction of uncertainty through the establishment of trustful relationships.

Second, project business is of a more temporary character relative to the more continuous product/service business. It is often found that marketing activities related to the specific project take place within a limited, often well-specified time-span. However, this is questioned based on the findings by Jalkala et al. (2010) as well as the experience of other project marketers in emerging markets. They have a more long-term approach to project business, building relationships with the same customer, covering more than one project cycle. This chapter contributes to solving this contradiction.

Third, it takes much longer to form and develop customer relationships for projects than for products. Between its initiation and completion, a project passes through a sequence of events. In fact, this extensive evolutionary relationships process is the major difference between marketing of 'ordinary' industrial products/services and marketing of projects, and this is therefore the focus of this chapter. More precisely, the chapter is about the strategic aspects of this network relationship process. The focus is on how links or activity chains are initiated, developed and organized, meaning that actor bonds and resource ties are relegated to the background (Håkansson and Snehota, 1995).

Three major issues concerning international network strategy in the marketing of projects are taken up:

1.   The business marketing process is studied. Due to the long time-spans involved in project marketing, relationships take on a particular character, being both complex and of long duration. They follow an evolutionary path, which is divided into three different sub-processes. This develops considerably the normal way of dividing the project sales process into various stages, where the number of stages and the names given to them vary between authors.

There is therefore a need to define them better from a marketing point of view and ground them in a specific theoretical framework.

2. Some specific strategy issues in the business marketing of projects will be focused on. It has been established that mutual adaptations in long-term relations create strong interdependences and high switching costs. But how do these take place during the various cycles of the marketing process? For this and other reasons, project business is risky, with the high stakes involved. How are these uncertainties dealt with throughout the project cycle, particularly those created by tie-ups among the parties throughout the process? Furthermore, the winning sellers often emerge in the early stages of the process, even before tenders are published. It seems to be that the winners are those MNCs that manage to influence the tender specifications in their favour. Moving downstream by the project seller is thus a necessary strategic move in emerging markets. This key strategic issue is therefore penetrated further in this chapter.

3. The organization of project marketing is taken up, since a neglected issue here regards how marketing is organized or implemented along the evolutionary path, especially how project management is organized to integrate the marketing, construction and operation of projects.

The chapter focuses on the international network strategy in this project process, where it is mainly a question of establishing and maintaining a network of relationships with customers and other parties to get the order. An important knowledge source about such relationship processes is research on the life cycle of relationships for industrial products (Ford, 2002; Ford et al., 2006; Wilkinson and Young, 1994), which mainly builds on an industrial network approach. Research on the dynamic aspects of relationships marketing also provides relevant background (Dwyer et al., 1987; Gordon, 1998; Peck et al., 1999) as does research on the evolvement of inter-organizational relationships (Ring and Van de Ven, 1994). The international network process framework within which this project marketing process takes place builds on previous research on project marketing in emerging markets (cf. Jansson, 1989b, 1994a; Ghauri, 1983; Owusu, 2002; Owusu and Welch, 2007) and other relevant research in the project marketing field (Mattsson, 1973; Bansard et al., 1993; Cova and Hoskins, 1997).

INTERNATIONAL NETWORK STRATEGIC PROCESSES

The international network strategic processes for marketing of projects are grouped into three separate processes: the product/service process, the relationship process and the network marketing process. The product/service process concerns the fact that network marketing is different for different solutions offered by the seller. The process is divided into a number of periods. The more complex the product, service or package offered, the more periods involved. For the large projects studied in this chapter, there are four periods from the initiation of the project to its finalization: the formation period, the bidding period, the execution period and the termination period. The relationships process consists of four stages: the pre-relationship stage, the early stage, the development stage and the long-term stage. The main focus of this chapter is on the network marketing process, which is divided into a number of marketing cycles and phases relevant for the life cycle of a project made up of these relationship stages, and periods of the product/service process. Figure 9.1 shows how these three sub-processes are related to each other.

Product/service process

The product/service process normally consists of four periods. The project emerges and is specified during the *formation period*. Due to its complexity, it takes time to specify the need and how best to satisfy it. Since the customer is often not fully capable of determining this, help from experts such as technical consultants is required. Other issues than those relating to marketing and manufacturing also emerge, for example finance. Even if it can be established exactly what is needed, the buyer might not be able to finance the purchase. When a general need has been established, it is time to study the need in more detail as well as to compare it to what is available on the market. For the buyer, this means translating the need into more specific requirements for equipment and service, which takes place through writing the tender specification. This is an elaborate process involving many people. For the seller, it is a question of influencing the buyer to select the offer provided. The publication of the tender finalizes the formation period and starts *the bidding period*. Based on the specification, sellers are normally asked to submit tenders, either sealed or open bids. These tenders are evaluated by the buyer and the order given to the seller supplying the winning bid. This period ends with the signing of the contract. Then the *execution period* starts, when the project that has been ordered is implemented. The equipment is manufactured, delivered, installed and tried out. Thereafter, the equipment is ready to be run for many years to come. The project is finally transferred from the seller to the buyer, which means the end of their relationship for this project. This is the *termination period*.

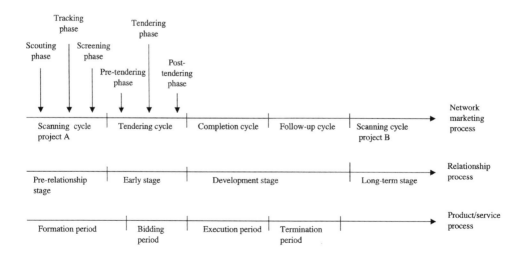

Figure 9.1 International network strategic process

Network marketing process

The network marketing sub-process of the international network strategy is the key process in selling projects (Jansson, 1989b, 1994a). It is divided into a number of major marketing activities. Each major activity tends to follow a cyclic pattern with gradually increasing and decreasing activities before the cycle is phased out and the next cycle starts along a similar pattern. These network marketing cycles are illustrated in Figure 9.2.

The network marketing process is divided into four cycles. The activities during each of these cycles are further divided into some major types of activities. In the formation period, the seller identifies the project and evaluates its profitability. Since most of these activities concern scanning, this cycle is called the scanning cycle. This marketing cycle is mainly about establishing and utilizing intelligence networks. It takes place during the pre-relationship stage, since it is too early to influence the buyer cluster. However, sometimes the seller starts to influence the buyer already during the end of this cycle, where it overlaps with the tendering cycle and shifts the relationship process into the early stage.

Most influencing activities take place during the tendering cycle, when the seller also creates and submits the tender. If the company gets the order and a contract is signed, the network marketing process continues with the completion cycle, when the equipment is manufactured, delivered and installed. This cycle also marks the beginning of the development stage of the relationship process. Finally, during the termination period, the project is finalized by making trial runs. Two major types of marketing activities take place in connection with this period: the follow-up cycle and a new scanning cycle, which marks the beginning of the network marketing process of a new project. If there is a follow-up cycle, the seller does not finish the marketing activities for the ongoing project upon

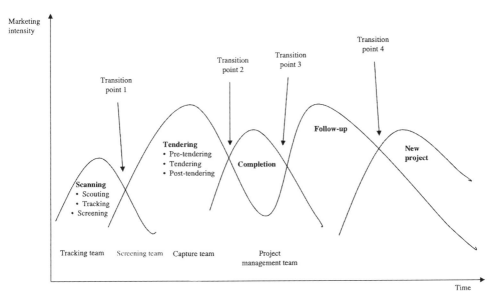

Figure 9.2 Project marketing cycles

entering the termination period. The project is followed up by, for example, servicing it and selling complementary products. So even if the project process has come to an end, it does not have to mean that the relationship with the buyer is terminated, since more projects may come up in the future. Rather, the relationship process enters the long-term stage with the start of a new project process, during which the relationship is kept alive by making courtesy calls, for example.

For a first-time project, most of the marketing activities during the scanning cycle take place in the pre-relationship stage, namely all activities up to transition point 1, when the outward marketing activities start to influence the buyer cluster. Throughout this lengthy network marketing process, described through four major cycles, a relationship with the customer has been institutionalized, or an already established relationship strengthened further and reproduced. The early stage of the relationship process has then been reached. The relationship might have reached some kind of habitual stage, where network relationships have become routine, and appropriate habits developed.

Integration of network marketing activities

The marketing activities during the four cycles vary as regards such project characteristics as project size, purchase form and how well known the seller is. A successful result requires that various network marketing activities along the project process are integrated. The organization of the project marketing process is seen as an action network consisting of teams formed for different tasks and that need to be integrated. For example, the tracking team does the screening, while the main task of the capture team is to win the bidding competition. There are already crucial marketing problems in the formation period, even before it is possible to identify what projects will be available. The seller tries to obtain first-mover advantages as early as possible. It is thus important to make a strong marketing effort early on, so as to get a lead over competitors. In that way, more is also learned about the business situation and about how to act in the various cycles. The own commitment increases, and with it the size of the network-specific investment, as more and more periods and relationship stages are passed. There are two crucial transition points or milestones. The first one occurs between the scanning cycle and the tendering cycle at transition point 1, when it is decided whether the MNC should close down the project or go on. The second critical decision takes place at the end of the tendering cycle (transition point 2), when the winning bid is selected.

NETWORK MARKETING PROCESS ILLUSTRATED

To illustrate the network marketing taking place during the various cycles and phases of the linking process, the same case is used as in the previous chapter, namely the project marketing activities of Indpow in India.

The case illustration – Indpow

Since the case is used more in this chapter, it is now presented in more detail. In 2000 Indpow had 10 500 employees in India. Since most of the resources and capabilities required for the local business had been established in India, little support was received from Europe. The majority of the shares of the local Indian group was owned by the European mother company, while the minority share was split between the government and the public. The factories were established a long time ago. The number of staff had grown slightly over the last few years of the 1990s, but the operations had grown very much more.

Organization network

Indpow India had a matrix organization, where one line of command was based on the product dimension and the other on the geographical dimension. The product part was divided into three major business segments based on type of customer demand (power, transmission and industry). The business segments in India were divided into business areas (BAs), which in their turn were divided into business units (BUs). The operational sales organization was divided into four regions. The regional office for the Northern region was located in Delhi, the office for the Southern region was found in Chennai (Madras) and the office for the Western region was located in Mumbai (Bombay), while Kalgata (Calcutta) was the base for the regional office covering Eastern India. The operations were handled by branch offices, with front sales people in various locations and a number of factories spread out over India. This matrix was managed from the country headquarters in Delhi, where the president and his staff were located together with two of the vice presidents for two of the business segments. The third segment – the industry business segment – was headquartered in Bangalore. The matrix in India was connected to the worldwide matrix of Indpow at the group level.

Each regional office covered the whole product range found at this Indian part of the MNC. The people at a regional office assigned to the various business areas reported to the business area HQ in India. The area marketing manager was responsible for the whole product range in his area. Inter alia, this system of marketing managers worked as a kind of information network covering all India, where, for instance, the local sales representatives got information, or 'early warnings', by talking to potential or existing customers. This is very important in India, where social nets are close with many meetings occurring face to face. In eight of ten cases, earlier information was received from these sources than from other sources like media channels and consultancy reports.

The power segment consisted of business areas, which were profit centres. These business areas had different capabilities for projects, for example. Some of them were almost fully self-sufficient, which applied to cases where the local market was considered big enough to carry many projects. In some cases, business took place on a global scale, with production of various parts all over the globe.

The industry segment was organized according to customer industry, which gave a good understanding of the needs and wants of the client. The seller learned about the customers' processes, which made it possible to make the customers' equipment more functional and more valuable, leading to leaner processes. This organization gave the customer a total solution across various business areas within this segment, one advantage being that the customer did not need to deal with a number of different persons from the MNC.

To facilitate contacts between Indpow units involved in project business, there was a global information system for projects, called PROMIS.

The transmission segment was a typical product business and was therefore quite independent from other group units abroad. The reason was that 95 per cent of the goods sold were manufactured in India, which meant that there was more local responsibility compared to the other segments in India.

At the regional offices, there were different groups assigned to different segments. Transmission business, being a typical product business, was the most decentralized activity. Regional units were self-sufficient for standard products, but not regarding customized products, for which support was given by headquarters. In the other segments, where there was more project business, foreign units were more involved. The responsibility for an action network like a core team was regional and the different groups within the team worked out different packages to offer. This was a way of ensuring a joint approach to the customer. Very large projects were usually handled from New Delhi, and they were also involved in forming a project team and assigning a project leader when the contract had been signed.

The regional office, in its turn, supported the branch offices in various locations, which also received some support from BUs and BAs at the segment headquarters. The larger, the more important and the riskier the project, the higher up it went, meaning that the size and number of teams grew. For complex products, there was support from the BU or BA, which prepared the actual offer. In these cases there was a transfer of responsibility to the BU or BA, but the field person stayed involved as an interface to the customer. The decision-making was informal and there was usually a consensus between branch, region and BA. Sometimes assistance from abroad was also involved, but not much. There was some import of items to the industry segment, but whether this import was direct or not was up to the customer. Often they felt more comfortable when the regional office handled the imports, since it was located closer to them.

Network strategy

The reader is urged to revisit Chapter 8 to look at the network map. The network mapping of the strategic network situation is followed up by illustrating some major strategic issues resulting from the analysis of the map. The network delimited in the mapping process is thus activated in the network strategy. As found in Chapter 8, marketing of projects is very much a question of coordinating the large variety of relationships of the market network.

A strategic decision made by Indpow is that different units should work together as much as possible in order to pull resources and to present a united front towards the customer cluster. The marketing is to be organized in project groups, where members change with the evolution of the marketing process. If Indpow's customer is an Indian company, then the local subsidiary has the customer interface network. Sometimes, the picture is more complicated. If the customer is a joint venture, there is a customer micro cluster with a foreign partner and an interface abroad as well. This is a sensitive situation that needs to be evaluated carefully. It is necessary to know about the relationship between the partners: how they get along, if they have different or even conflicting drivers, and so on. The experience of this MNC is that one party dominates the joint relationship, and it is necessary to find out who that is in order to have the right network strategy.

How consultants are included in the network strategy depends upon the role they play in the marketing process. Sometimes, linkages to them are only used as part of an intelligence network to get information. When consultants are utilized to investigate new projects, relationships are formed with them to learn about new projects. Consultants will also float inquiries to various companies. A most important capability then is a good relationship with both the customer and consultants, which needs to be constantly maintained, for example by keeping good relationships with these parties even between projects. When consultants are directly involved in influencing purchase decisions, the solution is sold both to the customer and to the consultants. Often consultants are used to go through the specifications, and therefore it is important to have good connections with them in order to influence this process to the advantage of the company. Since the consultants' recommendations are not binding on the customer, it is also essential to influence the customer directly to change the specifications if these recommendations are unfavourable to the seller.

When Indpow needs to organize finance, banks and other finance organizations are also linked up. Banks are used to arrange loans, since procurement of finance gives a competitive advantage. They are also used to get important information about new projects, particularly from the World Bank and aid organizations. But usually there is no lobbying with banks, since they are not involved in technical evaluations. An important competitive weapon then is to help the customer to find good financial solutions. Indpow uses its capability of having well-established contacts with banks to achieve this. Sometimes, the MNC's internal finance unit based in Europe also provides project finance. When equity financing is required, many times up to one-third of the investment, Indpow sometimes agrees to own a minority equity share of the customer for a period of about five years.

A few key suppliers of important components get involved as early as the pre-tendering phase and stay active throughout the project. Some go along with the company representatives on customer calls. Information is also shared with these long-term partners very early in a project. The subcontractor will assign representatives to participate in the project, who are usually well known to the customer. There is a pre-tender understanding between the main contractor and the subcontractor. When there is a list of acceptable suppliers, agreed upon with the customer, subcontractors are not normally brought along for joint customer visits.

Indpow has a lot of contacts with federal government authorities to facilitate imports of key components to projects. Meetings are held for discussing specific issues. Sometimes, assistance is also received from the customer on such matters.

Scanning cycle

During the scanning cycle, three major activities or phases occur: the scouting phase, the tracking phase and the screening phase. In the scouting phase, the MNC collects information to identify upcoming projects by surveying different organizations of the broader network that initiate projects. Then, a preliminary evaluation of their business potential is done in the tracking phase, followed by a more detailed assessment of a more limited number of projects in the screening phase. During the scanning cycle, the buyer is also engaged in investigating and evaluating the needs of the project customer and whether the suppliers are able to fulfil them. The buyer also searches for information from potential suppliers. A feasibility study is often done by the buyer or by a consultant. Some sellers also offer such studies to the buyer for free.

An important pre-relationship activity during the scanning cycle is to identify the project net-work. Purchasing of projects is normally a very complex type of business, implying that the network identification often produces a complex grouping of clusters. This was discussed and illustrated in the previous chapter, where a network consisting of four main types of clusters were singled out: buyer clusters, seller clusters, competing clusters and government clusters. As found there, several parties are usually involved in the various clusters, since complex projects consist of a large number of different products and services, which are supplied by several units that could either be separate companies or belong to the same MNC. Parts of the government cluster are often involved, either in the buyer cluster, for example as a public end user, or as outside authorities governing the network. Individual clusters are connected within themselves, for example a micro customer cluster, and with one another through a mix of the four types of linkages specified in Figure 8.1.

Intelligence network

To map the project network or other activities during the scanning cycle, it is a question of us-ing intelligence networks rather than influencing parties through the customers' network and the competitors' network. Moreover, in line with trying to achieve first-mover advantages, it is impor-tant to obtain information about a business opportunity, for example a project, as early as possi-ble so as to be able to start influencing the buyer cluster. An intelligence network could then be formed encompassing a variety of major organizations involved in a project in one way or another, allowing first-hand information about emerging projects to be obtained.

An intelligence network is exemplified in Figure 9.3. It has been established at the group level to get information about emerging new projects that could mean business for the group. The main idea is to cover those organizations that finance large projects and which evaluate project propos-als at very early stages. The network involves relevant UN organizations, World Bank organizations and aid organizations as well as foreign embassies. Information brokers specializing in contacts with these organizations are also hired and information about suitable contacts for interesting projects bought from them. The Swedish Trade Office in New York is also used for such purposes. This network is also linked to local information clusters at the regional offices and sales companies in various foreign markets, which scan local organizations for possible future projects and feed such information into the network. Effective surveillance within the network demands regular visits to the various organizations of the network, as well as an organization for receiving persons from the network, for example foreign missions and other important visitors being received at the central head office or at subsidiaries. Such activities are either carried out internally by the parent company and different subsidiaries or managed externally by consultants and trade offices.

One way for a company to take the initiative at as early a stage as possible is to create a project for a customer and then try to influence the latter to accept it. The company must have consid-erable knowledge of the country so as to know which projects could be in demand and what the project networks look like.

Scouting phase

Watch is kept at branch offices, regions, business areas and business units. There is a circulation of newspaper clips scanned into the computers and e-mails among units. For the spotting of new

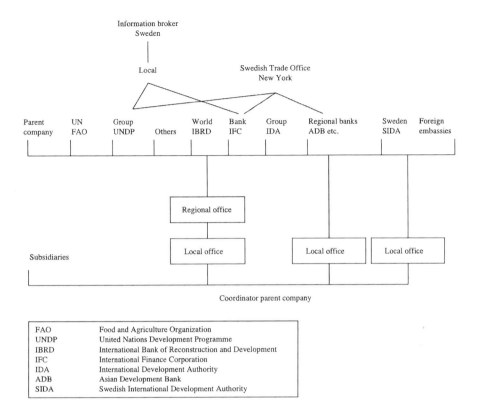

Figure 9.3 Intelligence network

projects, there is a marketing organization spread out across India, extracting information from customers. Indpow has organized the scouting for new business opportunities to be done by business development groups.

Some of the most important sources of information during the scouting phase are daily newspapers, government bulletins, market surveys done by the MNC, government general policies and big business houses. Other sources of information are customer talk, consulting firms and units within the MNC abroad with contacts with the World Bank or with foreign suppliers/subcontractors. There are also industry associations, and information is subscribed from special consultants who gather and sell information. Information might also be available from other parts of the world having contacts with the World Bank.

A first hint of a new project is often obtained from papers and magazines. Early warning signals also often come from face-to-face meetings with customers. Another source is consultants who are known well through having long-term relationships. A project in one business area usually starts with the customer identifying a suitable consultant, who will then investigate locations, work out technical specifications and handle various political processes. Big groups might not need consultants. They usually have enough in-house expertise. The consultants will also float inquiries to various companies.

Tracking phase

There is an 'opportunity tracking system' within the company, which produces an 'opportunity list' of new projects identified. Thereafter, a series of evaluation processes take place. At first, as much information as possible is searched for. This is important because of the large uncertainty with a project at this early stage. The information found is fed into databases, both local and global, which, inter alia, help global headquarters to see trends in different markets, also being of use for manufacturing units and technology centres all over the world. The tracking team is to come up with a 'yes or no' decision for investing in further screening, which is very important in emerging markets like India. There is a huge gap between supply and demand in the industry, which has the consequence that many inexperienced companies want to diversify into the power business by setting up power stations. This results in many unrealistic projects and a high drop-out rate.

So before the customer goes public with the plans, the seller follows up the results of the tracking phase by phoning different financial organizations or some four or five consultants doing feasibility studies in the field of business. If the customer is entering a new field, a feasibility study and the expertise of consultants are often required to get a loan. A project with a major public customer usually starts with a feasibility study by the government to find out about the possibility of a plant. This is mandatory when financing is sought from the World Bank and other aid organizations that need to approve the project. In the feasibility study, it is also stated whether a turn-key or split contract is to be used, something that can be influenced through good connections and relationships both with the customer and with the financiers.

Screening phase

A screening process follows next, where the appropriateness of the project and the risks involved are assessed. Before it is decided to go for a project, the financial circumstances of the project and the past record of the customer are investigated more closely. One important aspect analysed is whether the project will find financing. With government projects, this is usually not a problem. Public customers raise money internally, or they could borrow from the World Bank and similar financiers. With private industry, on the other hand, the financial issue is crucial. Even if Indpow can lend to the customer, other financiers are also needed.

Screening is organized differently depending on how demanding the task is, varying from being handled by teams of different sizes to being dealt with by one individual. For example, if an official announcement of a large and potentially profitable project is likely, a screening team is assembled. This follows from a decision by the tracking team to go on with the project. Since business units abroad are usually involved in a large project, it also has to be approved by the lead centre to which the business area reports.

Transition point 1

The first network marketing cycle has come to an end and may continue into a new cycle if the project is not aborted. This instance is defined as transition point 1, since one marketing cycle transitions into another. Based on the evaluations of the profit potential of the project, it is decided at the end of the screening phase whether the MNC should go on and submit a bid or close the project. This is a crucial decision point, since the preparation process during the next marketing cycle for a large project might take two to three years, involving considerable costs. Based on this decision, a capture team is set up to take over the marketing from the screening team. After having decided on a capture strategy and the partnering/financing concepts, the tendering cycle starts.

Tendering cycle

The influencing of the customer mainly takes place during the tendering cycle. This cycle is broken down into three major activities or phases: the pre-tendering phase, the tendering phase and the post-tendering phase. The pre-tendering phase is centred on the writing of the tender specification This is the phase where the seller tries to influence the specification so that it is adapted to suit its own products. In the tendering phase, the seller prepares the bid, which is then submitted to the buyer on a specific predetermined date. During the post-tendering phase, the various bids are opened (if the bids are sealed) and evaluated by the buyer.

There are important differences between a single and a two-step tendering process. The latter consists of a technical part and a commercial part, where the technical specifications are fixed after the tendering process and can only be influenced in exceptional cases. The outcome of the tendering cycle then depends on the price of those bids fulfilling the specifications.

A single tendering process is mostly used for technically simple items that are often purchased repeatedly. This situation is easier to influence. The customer will arrange the qualifying bids according to price, and the general rule is to accept the lowest priced bid. There is usually a buying committee of two to three more influential members, who all have their preferences. The final decision rests with the board, which does not always go for the lowest price. Some private customers do no float tenders. They know which suppliers have the best and newest solutions and contact these companies directly.

Public customers are obliged to float tenders. Here, the tender committee often consists of technicians, finance people and some senior managers. The composition of the committee depends on the purchasing process. With private customers, one to two persons often take the final decision. At public customers, different departments work out the specifications for their respective parts of the project. They often use vendor specifications of available equipment, since they cannot prepare better specifications themselves. Consultants often participate in evaluating the specifications. If the connections with the consultants are good, the process can be influenced to the advantage of the seller. Since their recommendations are not binding on the customer, it is also possible to influence the customer directly to change the specifications.

Pre-tendering phase

During the pre-tendering phase, the seller approaches the buyer with the start of outwardly directed and canvassing communication activities. The seller now knows about different potential projects and project purchasers and begins trying to influence them. The different parties do not yet know much about each other and still experience high uncertainty. For the buyer, this uncertainty may concern the seller's production capacities and solvency, as well as its propensity to keep agreements. The marketing activities begin in a general way before later on becoming more specific.

Indpow starts to influence specific parties of the clusters as early as the pre-tendering phase, which is mainly done through the network strategy. Two important parties to influence are the end user and the consultant. A common tactic in this phase with the end user is to try to affect the tender specifications through a suitable linkage mix. To facilitate this, the company endeavours to be on the spot long before a tender comes out, even before the work on it starts. The aim is to recognize what products the firm could supply in terms of the specifications. To achieve this, visits are made to key persons in the purchasing cluster, mainly the end user's technicians. The purpose is to create a contact net with them through promoting the information and social linkages. Sometimes, certain persons are employed by the seller cluster to create contacts, which mostly are maintained for many years. It is important to find out who writes the tender specification to be able to provide information to the right persons. Since very complex projects are hard to specify, outside information is required, which makes those writing the specification receptive to visits from suppliers. Consultants are often important, since they take part in writing the tender specification. Moreover, they carry out the feasibility studies on which the specification is based. It is therefore essential to include the consultants in the network strategy and build up good relations with them. To get a first-mover advantage at a very early stage, the seller may decide to prepare a feasibility study itself, thus bypassing the consultant. Such studies, on the other hand, are very expensive to carry out and there is no guarantee of getting the order.

Since the project does not materialize during the pre-tendering phase, marketing is very much a matter of selling project concepts. First-mover advantages are often created in this phase, since when the tender is published, many competitors enter the business process with their bids. Thus, the aim is to pre-empt the business by coming in earlier than competitors in an effort to get the specification adjusted to fit the company's products. Since competitors act in the same way, this is a difficult and delicate task. Customers vary in their inclination to be influenced at this early stage of their decision-making. Arranging seminars is a common marketing activity in this phase.

When a project is coming up, a sketch of a solution is presented to the customer regarding manufacturing, project management, after-sales services and financing. Customer representatives are visited in teams consisting of both technical and commercial people, and where support is received from the group when needed. The technology of the seller is presented along with what it can achieve. The goal is to influence the contents of the tender.

If the value of the project is large, a national capture team is set up. The team consists of at least three persons but often more. A project manager, who will take charge after the contract has been signed, might also be involved at this stage. The team members start interacting with the customer to make the tender specification more favourable with respect to the solution presented. The initial customer visits are with technicians, followed by purchasers. The customers' organization of the buyer cluster is important to analyse, for example which persons favour the seller and which favour different competitors.

It is much easier to set a deal with old customers, inter alia to justify a higher margin. The most important influencing factor with an old customer is a good and trustful relationship. Competitors will usually bid very low, but if the relationship is good, the customer will usually not accept the bid. With new customers, the cost of capture is much higher. Stiff competition might lead to several rounds of bidding before the price has been adjusted to specifications. Since it is difficult to justify a higher price based on value and performance, a reasonable price is most important as a factor with new customers. There is a trend towards financing as a major competitive tool, and a finance function has been established by Indpow in India. For large projects sellers often go in with equity, but this MNC usually arranges consortia of banks, which can provide loans on favourable terms.

Regarding contacts with other group units, there is a global system called PROMIS, to which all group units have access. Any job getting a 'yes' in the screening cycle and worth more than US$3 million is fed into PROMIS, where the status of the project is reviewed every fortnight.

Tender specification

After the strategy and action plan have been developed, the influencing of tender specifications starts, where technicians deliver technical arguments, finance people financial arguments and so on. The sales manager is the key person of the network, being the generalist who brings others along. It is important to know the decision-making process of the customer. If the customer is local, the Indian unit has the customer interface network. If the customer is a joint venture with a foreign partner, there is an interface abroad as well. The pre-tender discussions mostly concern technical matters. A key success factor in influencing is a good relationship with different members of the buying committee, to have a number of promoters. Another success factor is the previous experience of these members with the selling MNC. Still another important factor concerns the offering of various personal gifts to the decision-makers, which is done in about 30 per cent of the cases. It is important to act in a coordinated way so that contradictory and unrealistic promises to the customer are not made regarding prices and delivery times.

Tendering phase

The tendering phase starts with the buyer publishing the tender and the seller supplying a bid. A critical decision is how much to invest in a bid, that is, to what extent the seller should become further involved in the relationship. The stakes are high, since it is expensive to produce bids, particularly for large projects. As seen above, the chances of getting an order very much depend on how much the seller has managed to tie up the buyer in previous phases.

The contact frequency with customers and suppliers increases during pre-tendering and then stays rather even throughout the project. However, the nature of the contacts changes, since the marketing people of the early cycles are replaced by implementation people. The marketing department does then not function as the customer's main channel to the seller after the contract is signed. The subcontractors get involved as early as in the pre-tendering phase, and stay active throughout the project.

To make the actual bid or offer is a rather standardized process. A project team is assigned to work out the offer. Members from the capture team often participate to keep themselves informed about the process. The information-gathering activities go on continuously throughout the entire sales process. It is necessary to keep track of developments all the time. How much clearance is required from other group units depends on whether technology from other units is used or if they participate in negotiations. The division of work between units is set when the deal is signed and not when it is settled.

A key project-marketing issue of this phase concerns the relation between price and the technical quality of the tender specification. If the quality of the lowest bid is lower than the quality of the specification, the customer needs to consider whether the lowest bid is still good enough or whether to strictly follow the specifications. If the bid is higher and the quality better, the established relationship could be used to convince the customer of the usefulness of one's own higher-priced offer, arguing that the equipment is more expensive but lasts longer. The customer might then add an extra amount on top of the lower bids to bring the price up to the technological level of the bid supplied by the 'disadvantaged' seller, reversing the order of the bids. However, this might not be possible due to funding problems. This process is called 'loading' of the bid, where the purpose is to bring the prices of the other bidders up. Being in the opposite situation of having the lowest priced bid, it is very important to avoid being 'loaded up'. In this situation, it is of great importance to not add extras above the specification for which the customer is unwilling to pay. It is vital to bid exactly according to specifications, which reduces the chance of being 'loaded up'. Sometimes, a bid is submitted according to the specifications, although it is known that the specifications cannot be fulfilled. But once the order is placed, the relationship and the convincing ability of the seller are used to persuade the customer that a 100 per cent fulfilment of the specifications is not necessary. Another reason for the customer not to pick the lowest bid is delivery time requirements. Perhaps the lowest bidder cannot deliver in time.

Post-tendering phase

After the tender has been submitted to the customer, it is followed up. This is a critical phase and real 'action time'. A close watch is held on what is happening with the bid, trying to find out how the evaluation is done, for example if consultants are used. The MNC is working through its friends at the buyer. This is the time when the real selling is going on. The bid is presented in a favourable way, highlighting the good parts and keeping a low profile on the less good parts. A bid not actively marketed at this stage will be forgotten, even if it is the best offer. One major reason is that the competitors are always active, highlighting the less good parts of the offer. Sometimes it is possible to make post-tender changes to the bid, that is, to adjust the tender to the circumstances after it has already been submitted to the customer. The marketing process described applies to very large projects.

Sometimes the first part of the tendering phase, the evaluation of the bids, is open rather than closed, making it possible to influence the buyer. In such circumstances there is no clear demarcation line between the tendering phase and the post-tendering phase, which tends to be rather fluid. The bids are usually shortlisted and a few sellers selected, these being invited to discuss various types of clarifications. Such meetings tend to be extremely important. Since not everything can be formulated on paper, oral specifications may be decisive for the outcome of negotiations. Technical matters often dominate. Final negotiations of the contract for large and complex projects often take place even after an order has been accepted. Often it is possible to influence the buyer during the post-tendering phase, meaning that the submitted tender is not final. Negotiations are then critical, especially if the bidding process is open, and if two or three sellers are selected for further bargaining. Bargaining takes place in order to reach an agreement. Bids are evaluated in both technical and economic terms. Bidding usually starts with a preliminary bid followed by informal meetings to specify the final offer. After that, negotiations become more formal, before the buyer finally decides on the suppliers. The agreement reached is influenced by the state of the broader organizational framework. If the legal system cannot be used, stipulations not normally present in business contracts may be included, or a less formal agreement may be made based on trust.

Transition point 2

Usually it takes a long time before attempts to sell projects result in orders, with the tendering cycle itself sometimes lasting for up to two or three years. The overriding objective during this cycle is to get the order. If this happens, the relationship changes again, this time from the tendering cycle to the completion cycle. This point in time, where the relationship passes from the second to the third cycle, is defined as transition point 2.

Completion cycle

If the MNC wins the race and gets the order, the project process continues with the execution period, when the deal is implemented. The completion cycle of the marketing process has now been reached, and the hardware and software contracted for are manufactured, delivered and installed. After the contract is signed and the project has passed transition point 2, the marketing people hand over the execution of the project to the various business areas of the company to effectuate these tasks. However, marketing keeps in touch with the customer, still being the customer's channel for dealing with problems and questions and customer service in general.

Transition point 3

After the equipment has been tried out and proven to work, the completion cycle is over and the operation of the project begins. This is the final point or transition point 3, when the completion cycle shifts into a new network marketing cycle, the follow-up cycle. Since the seller is usually not involved in this stage, the project at hand is over as well.

Follow-up cycle

The follow-up cycle is an important network marketing cycle, since spin-offs from the project can be taken advantage of. So even though the individual project process is over, the contacts built during the early stage and so far in the development stage can be used for getting future business. A first-mover advantage might have been achieved which can be used to sell additional equipment and service through the follow-up cycle. Even if a company has lost a contract, there are sometimes possibilities for sales later during this cycle. A common heuristic is to try to bind the customer to the purchase of spare parts and service through a combination offer. The guarantee for the machines may be formulated so that it is no longer valid if spare parts from other suppliers are employed. Orders for supplementary equipment might also be received. These follow-up sales demonstrate how an initial order for main equipment can be worth more later on. This is often taken account of in international network strategy through the selling of basic equipment at a low price in order to gain access to a profitable after-sales market. In addition, the seller cluster may want to utilize the recently completed project as a reference object for future business. It is also important to maintain contacts with the buyer so as to obtain information about new projects. The relation is maintained by making courtesy calls and getting involved in other similar social activities.

Transition point 4

Even though the project process has come to an end, the network marketing process goes on, including the relationship process. This new scanning cycle bridges and connects the individual project processes, meaning that the relationship process enters the long-term stage. This point in time, when the old project process turns into a new project process, is defined as transition point 4.

After-sales service is mostly settled in the contract signed. However, long-term service contracts or after-sales services are often hard to sell in India, since there is no demand. The relationship with the customer is kept alive through courtesy calls, since the seller wants to develop the relationship further by entering the long-term stage or staying in it if there is already an established relationship. These calls are taken advantage of when a new project is coming up, in which case transition point 4 has been passed. Between projects, the contact frequency is low compared to the more frequent contacts with customers when tenders are being influenced. In the new project, the frequency of contact increases a great deal again, reaching a peak during negotiations, after which the regional marketing unit in Mumbai, for example, has much less customer contact.

Rehabilitation projects

In other marketing situations, the follow-up cycle plays a more important role, for instance regarding sales of plants delivered by the MNC and the competitors. These sales are important to follow up, since they might generate future business. Sales in between projects are important means of keeping customer relationships alive. In Indpow's case, rehabilitation sales constitute a specific type of follow-up sales, which work as a bridge between projects. After being run for many years, plants might be in need of rehabilitation. If so, this business is often large enough to motivate a separate project. To find new rehabilitation projects a list of suitable plants is kept, for example with their age, health condition and so on. When the appropriate time for rehabilitation has come, either contacts are made with the owner of the plant or the owner makes contacts with the seller. If a suitable project is then spotted, the close contacts with the customer are used to discuss what needs to be done.

ACTION NETWORKS

Action networks are defined in Chapter 7. Following the network view of this research, the organization of the project marketing process is viewed as an action network. As found above, the marketing activities throughout the different stages of the project process are handled by different marketing teams. This team organization of project networks is a typical example of an action network. Flexibility is a major characteristic of the organization of these temporary lateral nets. They are accommodated to a number of factors, for instance the size of the project, the number of parties involved in the clusters and the number of stages of the three sub-processes of the linking process: the product/service process, the relationship process and the marketing process. Another critical issue concerns the relation between this temporary action network and the more permanent organization network. People are taken from their permanent positions in the authority net to work for a shorter period in a lateral net, afterwards returning to their station in the organization network.

Action networks are formed around project teams, which are organized differently depending on the type of project. For small projects, there is often the same action network (project organization) throughout the linking process, for example a small team of up to three persons with a project leader responsible for forming the project and for tendering and completing it. For large projects, the organization of the team varies with the evolvement of the network marketing process, for example with separate screening, tracking, capturing and project management teams. The organization of marketing for medium-sized projects is a mix of these two extremes, where the screening activities, for example, might be organized separately, and where a few people belonging to a project management team will take care of all other activities.

Small and medium-sized projects

Marketing of electrical equipment and systems to industry, for example steel mills, consists of both turn-key projects including complete installations and sales of pieces of equipment. When Indpow gets involved in such a project, a project manager is assigned, who then picks a project team consisting of both technical and commercial people. The project manager is the single window to the customer. In the project team there is normally an 'execution project manager' (with the team from the start), to whom the overreaching responsibilities are transferred upon execution of the project. If the product/service is supplied from abroad, a second (foreign) 'shadow' project manager is often assigned for that overseas part, but the Indian project manager is still the leading one. The Indian unit takes the initiatives in these matters as well as regarding the assistance needed from other group units. In general, India gets all the assistance required from the group. Information might also be received from principals in other parts of the world, for example from those who have contacts with the World Bank.

Large projects

Tracking team
The tracking during the scanning cycle is usually done locally in India by a tracking team consisting of a regional sales manager and representatives of the business area HQ, where the regional sales manager has the main responsibility. In some cases, when the customer is a partially foreign joint venture, persons from the group units outside India are used in evaluating the foreign partner. The information found is fed into both local and global databases, which, inter alia, help global

units to see trends in different markets. These databases are also used by manufacturing units and technology centres found all over the world.

Screening team

If an official announcement of a project is likely, a screening team is assembled. This follows from a decision by the tracking team to go on with the project, a decision mostly taken in a consensus manner. Since business units abroad are usually involved in large projects, the decision to proceed has to be approved by the lead centre to which the business area reports. There it is considered what resources might be needed, whether Indpow has the right technology to pursue the project, and the priority of the project. Overall, there is close interaction between the business area and lead centre, since these units are seen as partners in this kind of business. The core technology resides at the lead centre. The global screening is conducted by a screening team composed of people from the lead centre, people from the business area in India and people from other local business units abroad. If the project can be expected to include financing or investment by Indpow, people from these overseas functions also participate. If the local unit is well developed, there might be local leadership of the screening team, the advantage being that such a leader will be close to the customer. However, usually someone from the lead centre assumes leadership, which means frequent visits to India to get to know the customer. The leader is usually not formally assigned, but emerges more or less spontaneously during the process, as the competent person taking charge. Whoever is the leader, local units have a considerable influence on things, since they know the customer and the local conditions.

Capture team

If the company decides to go on with the project, a capture team is set up to replace the screening team. This is a major decision that takes places at transition point 1. In the capture team persons are included who may contribute to a winning strategy. Some core members are always members of such an action network: a sales manager from the business area in India plus a technician. If Indpow in Europe is involved, they will contribute with a sales manager and a technician. Who takes the actual lead depends on the involvement of the parties in the project. If the core technology and the core equipment are from Sweden, then Sweden will lead. Usually there is a consensus regarding the lead roles, but one of the sales managers is always the leader of the process.

This core capture team has an initial brainstorming session where it is decided who else should be involved in the team or participate in team meetings. This depends to a large extent on which 'winning strategy' is preferred in the specific case, which in turn depends on the key drivers of the customer. The team starts interacting with the customer. For large projects within one business segment, these early visits are made by the leader of the BU, the group leader of the region, experts from BU and the project manager. The activities of a capture team begin with a full-team meeting, where the drivers of the customer are discussed and the competition analysed, after which a 'game plan' is laid. Along with the strategy, an action plan is jointly developed by the team.

A major problem is that attention from top-level people, who often are very busy, is required more and more as the process progresses. This leads to a sort of internal competition for top-level attention between capture teams, where the more aggressive team wins. Teams therefore sometimes feel powerless and constrained. One solution to this problem is to pick a number of particularly important customers and assign some senior resources as 'key account managers' to them. Another problem with capture teams is their diverse composition. They usually consist of people from different cultures with different languages, backgrounds, professions and so on, often leading to misunderstandings and lack of communication. People from different cultures operate differently, where some are soft and some are aggressive, reacting differently. Hence, it is very important to have managers with an international outlook, and who are experienced, cooperative, have a cultural understanding and know how the organization works. Actually, a 'superman' is required, who is a leader and not a manager. To find such a person, there are training programmes for capture team members, especially for potential future 'key managers'. In order to determine where to put the resources in the most sensible way, there is a business development function at Indpow making country plans and projections for different customers.

Project management team

The project management team is formed later on in the marketing process to complete the project. Usually members from this team are not very active during the tendering cycle, except when it comes to creating resource allocation plans and completion schedules later on in the sales process. The reason is that there are penalties if delivery times are not kept. If project management has previously worked with the customer, this team might have an important role as an interface early on. The same is true if another business area has conducted business with the customer before and the Indian subsidiary has not. If members of these units know the customer well, they might be called into the capture team meetings.

Control system

To assist the action networks in the network marketing process there is a control system in the form of a combined information, report and support system based on a specific software. This is global Indpow software which has been adjusted to Indian conditions. It consists of formalized procedures for every step of the process on the way to a finished project. Data are fed into a set of form sheets corresponding to the following steps:

1. Sales Pursuit
2. Bid and Proposal
3. Plant Design
4. Project Management
5. Supply Chains
6. Install/Commissioning
7. Service/Support

Among the sales pursuit sheets there is a forecast form containing the status and probabilities of a project. From this form there are direct software links to other pages associated with the successive screening steps, which makes it possible to follow the development of the project by comparing these pages. The software contains various parameters and questions, which result in opportunity analyses with scores helping to classify business, for example expected costs, customer opportunity profiles, the extent of customer contacts and the quality of these contacts (supporter, ally etc.). There is also a feedback from the software, with messages like 'customer contact is needed'. Another form gives information about the client's business. The data fed into these forms are seldom of an exact nature, so decision-makers have to rely on judgements and guesses.

For group contacts there is the PROMIS software, which contains information about very large ongoing projects from all over the globe worth more than a certain limited amount. In this database is found potentials and trends, but also ongoing reference projects. These reports, being of a rather short format, are probably studied by higher group management. The priority and status of various local projects are determined in India and fed into the system.

CONCLUSIONS

The influencing of the customer cluster takes place through a tri-part process consisting of the network marketing process, the relationship process and the product/service process, together forming the strategic international networking process. This chapter is mainly about the first and third process, while the relationship process will be taken up in Chapter 10 as part of the local international network strategy. The network marketing process usually begins before a specific project has been identified, that is, before the project process is initiated during the formation period. The most critical marketing activities for getting first-mover advantages take place during this period and the bidding period, while the execution period is not so important from a marketing point view, except towards the end, when the follow-up cycle starts close to the beginning of the termination period. The early start of the network marketing activities for projects means that the pre-relationship stage is important. Careful preparations during the scanning cycle are critical for bringing the relationship process through the early stage via efficient handling of the tendering cycle to win the project. The relationship is further developed through the completion cycle in the development stage. Hopefully, satisfied members of the micro cluster will then set the relationship off to a prosperous future through the relationship finally having reached the long-term stage.

During the scouting phase of the scanning cycle, the major organizational routine of the seller cluster concerns surveying different organizations of the broader network to identify upcoming projects through using various information sources and intelligence networks. After having identified projects, their business potential is evaluated, first preliminarily in the tracking phase, and then through a more detailed assessment in the screening phase. Based on the information and evaluations of the profit potential, it is decided at transition point 1 whether the MNC should commit itself to the project. A feasibility study is often done by the buyer, a consultant, or even sometimes by the seller.

The MNC starts to influence specific parties of the macro and micro clusters as early as the pre-tendering phase, this being mainly done through a suitable linkage mix. At this phase, the different parties know too little about each other and therefore still experience high uncertainty. Two important parties of the macro cluster are often influenced, namely the end user and the consultant. A common marketing routine in this phase is to try to influence the writing of the tender specification to get it adjusted to a project that can be offered by the seller cluster. The purpose is to pre-empt the business to achieve a first-mover advantage ahead of the competitors.

In the tendering phase, which begins the bidding period, the seller prepares the bid, which is then submitted to the buyer on a specific predetermined date. A critical decision concerns how much to invest in a bid, that is, whether the seller should become further involved in the relationship with a particular micro or macro cluster. The chances of getting an order very much depends on to what degree the seller has managed to tie up the buyer in previous phases, that is, how committed the buyer is. In the post-tendering phase, sealed bids are opened and evaluated by the buyer. This phase ends with the signing of the contract. Negotiations are a critical part of this phase, especially if the bidding process is open, and if two or three sellers are selected for further bargaining.

If the MNC wins the race and gets the order, the project process continues with implementing the deal. At this transition point (transition point 2) the network marketing process passes to the completion cycle, where the hardware and software contracted for are manufactured, delivered and installed. After the equipment has been tried out and proven to work, the completion cycle is over and the running of the project begins. Since the seller is usually not involved at this stage, the project is over as well. This is transition point 3, where the completion cycle shifts into the follow-up cycle.

Even though the project is over, the relationship developed can be used for follow-up sales and for getting future business, for example by using the project built as a reference object. Through this lengthy marketing process that has brought the relationship process to the doorstep of the long-term stage, the relationship with the customer has become on the verge of being institutionalized. The development of the project has evolved to transition point 4, which connects the individual project processes and makes the buyer–seller relationship long term.

Project marketing action networks are formed around project teams, through which the resources and capabilities are mobilized. The teams are organized differently depending on the type of project.

10
Entry strategy of multinational exporters

To develop further the process aspect of the local international network strategy advanced in the previous two chapters, it is now related to the internationalization process. This chapter deals with one of the major aspects of international business strategy introduced in previous chapters, namely 'geographic spread'. The different theories on the internationalization process taken up in Chapter 4 are developed more in this chapter to study entry strategy into emerging markets as part of the international network strategy. The 'with whom' issue, which has been mainly covered through the internationalization in networks theory, is elaborated on by integrating this theory with other socially oriented theories on internationalization processes. The exporting theory is combined with a relationship process theory into a five plus five stages of internationalization model. The internationalization through these stages is determined by organizational learning and institutional distance, which mainly originate from the Uppsala internationalization process theory. This extended internationalization in networks theory is primarily developed to study the international network strategic process of multinational exporters (MNEXs), their internationalization process and especially how they enter and establish network relations in emerging markets. Entry strategy takes place through the entry network, where network type, network position and entry node are key aspects. In the process of entering the emerging market, the MNEX establishes its foreign local business by successively operating in three networks. Initially the firm exposes itself to the foreign market through the exposure network, then it builds local relationships through the formation network and finally maintains the relationships and establishes new ones in the sustenance network. Thereafter, the chapter's focus is shifted to the beginning of the internationalization process, from MNEXs entering emerging markets to such local exporters exiting them. This exiting of the home market is defined as the take-off strategy. Before going into these entry and exit aspects of the international network strategy, the entry mode and the motives for investing in local emerging markets are compared for MNEXs and multinational corporations (MNCs).

ENTRY MODES

As introduced in Chapter 4, traditional research on the internationalization process is mainly about MNCs, for which the dominant entry mode is foreign direct investment (FDI) organized as a subsidiary or similar organizational arrangement (e.g. a joint venture) to sell, distribute and manufacture products for the local market or specializing in one or two of these activities. The FDI could also be in a joint subsidiary with other local business activities, or in an affiliated project selling office. The package deal of large projects could also contain both licensing arrangements and management contracts, which turns the local project arrangement into a combination of entry modes. One-time single large projects like those considered in Chapter 9, on the other hand, can be seen as a distinct mode and not as exports if a temporary organization is set up in the country to construct and operate the project. These entry modes are all classified as the FDI mode. But entry could also take place through being limited to exporting products via intermediaries in the foreign market such as agents, who only sell, and distributors, who also distribute. This entry mode is called the export mode. The first type of entry is typical for MNCs and the latter for MNEXs. Marketing investments in third parties like intermediaries are normally associated with low risk, while investments in a company of one's own are more of a high-risk undertaking. Sharing the investment with a party in a joint venture is then associated with medium risk.

Thus, entry mode has to do with economic aspects of international business such as degree of risk, control and commitment of resources, and return on investment. For example, Lu and Beamish (2001) found that the choice of entry mode by small and medium-sized enterprises (SMEs) highly affects their performance, for example profitability. It is affected by the firm's resources, where larger firms tend to have larger economic and managerial resources for the investments demanded for own representation in the market of entry than smaller firms. Nakos and Brouthers (2002) use Dunning's OLI framework to determine the participation strategy or entry mode for SMEs.

A major factor behind the choice of entry mode is the economic motive for doing the foreign investment. Resource-rich MNCs that invest in foreign production are usually divided into four types according to the primary motives behind their investment: natural resource seekers, market seekers, efficiency seekers and strategic asset or capability seekers (Dunning, 1981; Dunning and Lundan, 2008). The first type goes abroad for natural resources, for example oil, the second type in search of markets, the third type to increase the efficiency of production, and the fourth type to acquire assets, for example new technology. Dunning and Lundan also identify four main reasons for firms engaging in market-seeking investments in manufacturing. One reason is that firms follow their customers abroad; another that they invest to adapt their products to local market conditions. They have also found that the host government has a major influence on such market-seeking investments, for example by offering incentives and only allowing investments in certain industries. A third reason is that production and transaction costs are lower when serving the local market from an adjacent facility than from a distance. A fourth reason is that the MNC needs to have a local presence because its main competitors have one. However, all these motives only concern production and do not include investments in marketing. This therefore excludes the MNEXs that chiefly make such investments. Moreover, there might be more than one motive behind an investment and motives may change over time with additional investments in the country. Since internationalization processes are being studied, it is vital to include ensuing investments in the foreign market, for example investments in new types of operations 5–15 years after firms' initial entry.

Market-seeking entry modes

The FDI entry mode, then, mainly concerns how firms from mature markets became MNCs. In referring to the typology of international firms in Chapter 4, one notes that all types of MNCs included there have completed the establishment chain mainly by having internationalized through making FDIs. MNEXs, on the other hand, have not done that but instead stopped somewhere along this process by sticking with exporting. This difference between entry modes is studied by Jansson and Söderman (2019) in relation to Swedish firms investing in China over time.

According to the establishment chain of the Uppsala internationalization process theory, foreign investments first take place in marketing and then in manufacturing. The initial investments are in distribution during the indirect exports stage, and in sales or purchasing during the direct exports and foreign-sourcing stage, followed by investments in one's own marketing and distribution company, and finally in production (Johanson and Wiedersheim-Paul, 1975). Dunning and Lundan (2008) add two more phases: deepening and widening of the value-added network and the integrated network multinational. These phases concern how to organize the establishment chain once it is in place as well as how to organize further activities in the country. The former phase deals with how to integrate the various parts of the value chain already established, perhaps also adding new local activities. The latter with how to coordinate this local organization with the international organization of the MNC.

The study by Jansson and Söderman (2019) shows that market-seeking investments in China are either customer-market driven or supplier-market driven. In the former case investments are made in marketing knowledge to sell products/services through relationships with local customers, whereas in the latter case investments are made in relationships to buy products from local suppliers. Additional market-seeking investments could be made along the establishment chain in marketing, mainly distribution; in manufacturing; and finally in other types of activities, for example directly in competition by acquiring competitors. The sequence of investments along the establishment chain is illustrated in Figure 10.1.

Customer-market driven investments in sales and distribution

One type of customer-market driven investment is in marketing assets such as sales and distribution and another is in customer marketing and manufacturing assets. Two groups of investors in marketing assets alone were found in this study. One mainly invests in sales, while the other primarily invests in distribution but also in sales. Both these groups were dominated by MNEXs.

The market investment in mainly sales is based on products such as components with highly recognized quality standards, sold globally in a business-to-business (B2B) context through local distributors which they do not own. The Swedish SME Bona Chemical represents a company that carries out this type of investment. It established a regional sales office in Beijing in 1991 to sell its line of floor treatment products, especially varnish, through local distributors. Bona Chemical, then, delivers a superior product and service offering based on a self-constructed sales network. It is an interesting case, since the company hired a manager to establish a sales network in China – signing a management contract in 2001. It used an external resource, an experienced executive, as a consultant for three years in order to build up a network of sales points and to teach the newly employed, as well as the home office in Sweden, the Asian ways of doing business. This is an interesting experience that might be useful for other MNEXs establishing themselves in China. The main task of the manager was to teach Asian consumers to increase their appreciation of the products and services. As with any small exporter, the firm focused on adaptation and reconfiguration as its key need. This flexibility was increased through having a management contract.

This investor is representative of most Swedish MNEXs that have established a foothold in China through their own sales office. The main challenge is to find local customers and to construct a sales and service network of distributors. These are low-commitment investments that seldom reach further than the indirect customer stage of using agents or distributors. They want to maintain their flexibility, for example when accepting an alternative, Chinese-culture-inspired business model or platform. A prerequisite for these small exporter types is that the top management in Sweden, or preferably the founder or main owner, takes a personal and active part in crafting the business in China. Typical of these marketing investments is the intense local competition, since most products are available in China from local suppliers. To differentiate a product it is important to construct a specific individual distribution platform in order to be aligned with 'local needs'.

B2B marketing and manufacturing

Swedish companies have not only made marketing investments but have also invested in local production, either in factories or in service facilities, or both. Depending upon the type of marketing investment, five types of such combined FDI in marketing and manufacturing investments were found. Most of them are made by MNCs.

As seen in Figure 10.1, one type is the B2B marketing and manufacturing investment. This type is often a joint venture with a local partner. These joint ventures are created by established MNCs, mainly engineering firms, who have strong business concepts based on superior technology which

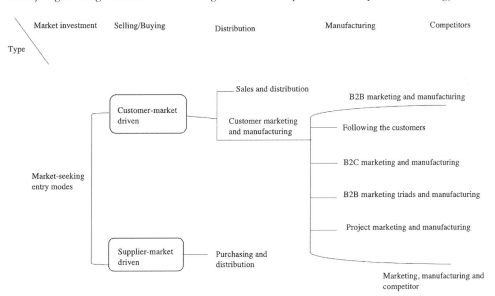

Figure 10.1 Entry modes

the Chinese government is interested in. Besides B2B marketing investments in sales and distribution, these firms have invested in their own manufacturing facilities in the local market, and thereby have invested in a larger part of the value-added chain and are more deeply involved in the local market. Many well-known Swedish MNCs in the engineering industry have committed themselves to the Chinese market by investing in factories to manufacture the components locally, for example SKF (ball bearings), Atlas Copco (compressors), Alfa Laval (separators) and Sandvik (tools). Sandvik opened its first office in China in 1985, just after China opened up to foreign investment. The first factory was opened in 1994 and produced tools for the Chinese market. Today's organization takes the form of a holding company, Sandvik China Holding, which was established in 1996 and is responsible for Greater China. Today, Sandvik has more than 65 offices, employees in over 100 cities in China, and has production units for all business areas at about 10 sites. In addition to sales, SKF has invested heavily in distribution. But most of its investment has been in manufacturing. SKF has, after opening their first factory, established more than a dozen factories all over China, which makes the investment very deep and the commitment very high. The SKF ball bearing is a key to the company's success, being sold to the expanding car industry but also to the railways. Alfa Laval is another example of a successful engineered brand, with its dominating technology in separation (centrifuges), fluid handling (pumps and valves) and heat transfer (heat exchangers). This investment involves a business model based on the manufacturing and sale of equipment with a highly recognized quality standard built on a strong global brand. Several of the joint ventures formed in the early days of the opening up of the Chinese market have been dissolved. The reason for this failure was the obligatory joint venture partnering, which was based on the government's ambition to get access to advanced technology and innovations through legal measures, but did not always work due to differences in strategic management styles and mind-sets.

Following the customers abroad

A specific group of investors in B2B marketing and manufacturing have followed their customers abroad. It mainly consists of MNCs, but there are also some MNEXs. One type of investor passively piggybacks its main customer abroad by being more or less 'recruited' to the foreign market. An example is IT service firms. Another type establishes itself more actively when most customers in its industry have moved to the foreign market. This type caters to the local needs of its Swedish client companies. The investments in their own service facilities of the four big Swedish retail banks – Handelsbanken (SHB), SEB, Nordea and Swedbank – represent this latter type of follower. The firms are service providers in the 'local needs' category, localized where Swedish firms are present. This type of customer market driven investment is based on trustful relationships with and an ability to adapt to the local foreign business of the customer followed.

B2C marketing and manufacturing

This market investment is in business-to-consumer (B2C) marketing of a global brand of an MNC, and in a distribution network of its own plus in manufacturing. The manufacturing of the high-volume products is local mainly due to government requirements. The motive is to expand its business and be more successful in the rapidly increasing local market, which is highly supported by government. Volvo Car Corporation is a Swedish passenger car manufacturer, which has been owned by the Chinese Zhejiang Geely Holding Group since 2010. Geely also wanted to bolster their position in Europe, and purchasing Volvo was a step in that direction. This FDI departs from the traditional internationalization process in that it is formally done by a local firm, which has acquired this Swedish MNC or global brand from a US MNC. All other types of FDI taken up here concern Swedish MNCs that have expanded their international business to the Chinese market by investing there. While China is currently the largest automotive market, Geely was unable to break into the top 10 in sales there. The technology and brand awareness associated with Volvo has helped them to move forward in China and overseas. The Chinese company allows Volvo to operate largely independently. Volvo has kept its manufacturing plants in Sweden and Belgium while opening up production facilities as well as expanding distribution networks in China. China has become Volvo's second home market.

B2B marketing triads and manufacturing

This type of investment is made by MNCs that market machines used in local production and need to know the business of their customers' customers. Firms belonging to this category provide sophisticated Swedish-developed technology, consultancy, components and systems to local customers, sometimes in joint ventures with local partners. Due to their close proximity to the customers, they also locate production close to the customers. Tetra Pak is a global food packaging giant that provides both packaging machines and packing materials, mainly to the same customers. Tetra Pak is developing new innovations in the packaging industry and therefore wants a total coverage of all potential customers. After-sales and operations are important features of Tetra Pak's 'one concept only company'. The Tetra Pak model includes business experts or specialists who are each responsible for a set of countries, and who are necessary to keep the service level high. To be fully utilized, the specialists need several countries to work. Yet, the cluster leader has the task of coordinating the overall corporate strategy in the entire cluster region, including the prioritization of customer development work. Many of Tetra Pak's customers within the food and beverages industry are expanding across borders at a fast pace. Therefore, suppliers such as Tetra Pak must follow these expansion routes. The challenge is to try local adaptation and work on reconfiguration. The Tetra Pak concept has several revenue streams, including fees from its consultancy service. Other sources of income include the charge for hiring the filling/packing (and so on) machines and the revenue from special multi-layer paper, which has to be bought from Tetra Pak. This has led to Tetra Pak's strong market position, with competitors attempting to blame or to sue the firm for its dominant position.

Such a firm as Tetra Pak is driven by a deep knowledge of the business logic of their customers' customers. Customer identification and customer development constitute systems for achieving dominance, together with experts with different skills and different country responsibilities. This coevolving system developer is a network creator. Since it provides important equipment to aid the development of the country, it is also an infrastructure builder. The business model focuses on competence in business development through superior knowledge and excellent hardware.

Project marketing and manufacturing

Firms investing in project marketing and manufacturing operations are involved in large projects, which are marketed to both private and public customers in China, mainly to state-owned enterprises (SOEs). This type of investor is well known from Chapter 9, where the project market-ing in India of one such Swedish MNC was analysed. The equipment sold by this type of investing MNC, or at least part of it, is manufactured locally in China. The business of this type of investor is based on a highly recognized quality and global brand. The firm might also be a standard setter or even a market creator, particularly if it is a world-leading brand. As seen in Chapter 9, marketing of projects is very much a question of networking, which requires a high level of inter-firm coopera-tion that in China needs to fit within the guanxi type of context. Ericsson is a telecommunications equipment provider of Swedish origin that established itself in China as early as 1895. The future is very challenging for Ericsson because increasing numbers of its new customers will be from China and other Asian countries. In 2007 deliveries to China were already worth as much as the compa-ny's aggregate global sales outside of Sweden during 2003. There is clear government support for locating Ericsson's activities in China, and Ericsson has employed a growing number of capable local engineers in what is a rapidly growing market. Another major challenge for Ericsson in China concerns its major competitor Huawei. This Chinese MNC is an 'insider' that is very familiar with the Asian environment. Ericsson has contributed to developing Huawei's competitiveness. This MNC has learned a lot from Ericsson in China and in Sweden through its subsidiary in Stockholm, being located close to Ericsson. Therefore, Ericsson's relationship to the Chinese government is ambivalent as the government is both a customer and supporter of Huawei. Being a first mover that believes in innovation has been important in the rapidly growing Chinese economy, especially in strategic industries such as the telecom sector. Technologies are changing but the government requires superior knowledge to raise and establish local standards. Domestic market demand has been extremely high due to the very high growth.

Marketing, manufacturing and competitor driven investments

This group of MNCs has initially invested in distribution networks and manufacturing facilities but have moved further into the Chinese market by acquiring a local competitor. Since this is a local brand, this additional investment is classified as asset-seeking.

With an expanding domestic demand, how should Volvo Construction Equipment (VCE), which produces wheel loaders and excavators, develop their marketing and branding concepts in China? An initial problem was that people were familiar with the Volvo brand because of their passenger cars, but not with the Volvo corporate brand that today includes construction equip-ment and other heavy vehicles such as trucks and buses. SDLG (Shandong Lingong Construction Machinery Co) is a joint venture in China, which since 1997 has been 70 per cent owned by VCE. They develop, produce and market a broad range of products, including wheel loaders, that are cheaper but not as sophisticated as VCE's own products. SDLG's products have been introduced to markets outside China as a complementary brand to that of Volvo, mainly in order to compete in lower-quality segments. As explained by Jansson and Söderman (2019, p. 258):

> it seems that these major firms respond to the Chinese threat to their global market positions by entering the low-price segment to compete head-on with Chinese firms. European MNCs have implemented this strategy in China by acquiring local competitors in this segment.

By taking on the new competitors in their home market, these newcomers will have fewer resources available to go for the high-price segment in foreign markets. This also opens up the possibility of internationalizing an acquired firm by establishing it in an emerging market, such as Brazil, to compete with other Chinese and local CE [construction equipment] firms in the low-price segment.

How Chinese companies compete in Brazil is further developed in Jansson and Söderman (2013).

Supplier-market driven investments

These MNCs make offshore cost-driven market investments by shifting supplier sources to the Chinese supplier market. Examples of such MNCs include international retailers. Marketing investments are made in the purchasing of locally produced goods and in the supply network, mainly in supplier development and control, where corporate social responsibility is important. This is a B2B operation in a B2C marketing industry. Supplied products are sold to customers worldwide through department stores.

Long ago there was a Swedish brand called Algots whose flannel shirts were famous for their classical style and endurance. Such shirts do not exist any longer in a highly competitive world with changing tastes, suppressed prices and a range of manufacturing options to produce 'in-house' or through 'outsourcing' to external manufacturers. This is the logic that international retailers such as H&M (having purchased from Asia since the 1960s) and IKEA (today buying a lot from China) also seem to base their business model on. However, since they do not produce themselves, they go for cheaper supplier sources. H&M designed, specified and assembled clothing in an extremely rapid manner and became known as a low-cost driver, served by well-reputed suppliers all over the world, most of them in Asia. With this business model, H&M has acquired a large, worldwide consumer base.

INTERNATIONALIZATION PROCESS OF THE MULTINATIONAL EXPORTER

As indicated above and introduced in Chapter 4, the multinational exporter (MNEX) is a smaller MNC that differs from the large ethnocentric MNCs by chiefly doing international business through the market. MNEXs might own a few subsidiaries in key markets, but the major part of the international business is done by external parties such as agents and distributors. The small traditional MNCs studied in Jansson and Sandberg (2008) are typical examples of MNEXs. Even though they are small (around 200–300 employees), they have access to certain resources, since they belong to a larger group, normally a larger MNC. These are highly specialized niche SMEs that are members of a larger group of companies, which will make final decisions on big strategic issues. The strategic base of these MNEXs is in a country region of their home market, where the major strategic units, sales, production and main sub-suppliers are located. Even though they have limited human resources, the growth is more constrained by their specialization to a certain niche market. This is tiny in most foreign markets, and does not allow for any economies of scale or scope. The

MNEX is therefore normally active on a small scale in many foreign markets at the same time as it is flexible enough to be able to increase or reduce market presence in accordance with the business cycle of the various markets. The foreign operations are mainly sales organizations, which mostly consist of agents and distributors but also a few own sales centres (e.g. local engineering offices) and sales subsidiaries. A few of the MNEXs locate a small part of their production abroad. These MNEXs became more global by growing in their existing markets and expanding to the emerging markets during the Third wave. Their strategic production base has remained more or less intact in the home region and did not undergo any major shift to Eastern Europe or China.

The internationalization process of MNEXs and the major factors influencing it are illustrated in Figure 10.2. The establishment and maintenance of network relationships in a foreign market tend to follow the pattern of five stages of relationships evolvement developed by Ford (1980) and earlier introduced as the process aspect of industrial networks in Chapter 7. These stages are covered in detail below. This local networking process is part of a larger internationalization process governing how MNEXs spread their activities throughout the globe between various foreign countries and regions. This transnational internationalization process follows the pattern of the exporting theory presented in Chapter 4 of five stages of gradual internationalization of exporting SMEs. These two processes are combined into a five plus five stages model, mainly relevant for the

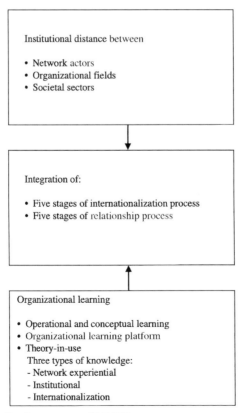

Figure 10.2 Internationalization process of MNEXs

MNEX. It is influenced by three major aspects of institutional distance and the three dimensions of the major internal driving force, namely organizational learning. This internationalization process is now described in more detail, starting with the relationship process.

The relationship process

Based on Ford (1980), the relationship process is described according to a number of relationship factors and learning, for example how the experience, commitment and adaptations of the parties increase and how the distance and uncertainty between them are reduced. The variable 'experience' indicates the amount of experience the respective parties have of each other. Both parties will judge their partner's commitment to the relationship, which is reflected in their willingness to make adaptations. The variable 'distance' is multifaceted and can be split into social, cultural, technological, time and geographical distance. Uncertainty deals with the fact that at the initial stages, it is difficult to assess the potential rewards and costs of the relationship.

The pre-relationship stage

The first stage takes up marketing activities before the relationship begins, for example network mapping in planning to take over a customer from a competitor (see Chapter 8). To start with, the seller might be looking for factors in the networks that can spark a switch of suppliers by the customer. This is where preparatory work takes place in order to evaluate new potential customers before networking starts. The experience of the customers in this stage is none, or low, uncertainty is high, distances are large and commitment and adaptations are zero.

The early stage

The next three stages show how direct buyer–seller relationships within networks are established. With networks mapped and relationships identified, the exploration of these start. Commitments are made to focus on specific customers, at most resulting in a sample delivery. Although still low, experience of customers is starting to build up. This is a mutual learning process, where the parties learn to know more and more about each other. Trust and commitment are being established and decisions are being made that also reflect personalities as opposed to the straight analytical decisions of the pre-relationship stage. The first adaptations are made but are still few. Suppliers experience high uncertainty and high distances to the customers. Together, these factors give a low degree of institutionalization of relationships.

The development stage

Business between the customers and the supplier starts to grow and resources are increasingly shared. Contracts are signed and there is a delivery build-up. Intensive mutual learning results in increased experience on both sides, as well as in reduced uncertainty and distances. Trust and commitments increase, which are signified by both formal and informal adaptations as well as cost savings. Relationships change character and become entirely focused on the dyad, in that way becoming deeper and broader. This means that the relationship is becoming institutionalized with common routines and habits starting to take form, backed by shared norms and values.

The long-term stage

After several major purchases or deliveries, the relationship becomes fully developed and now settles into a stable stage with continuous business going on between the parties. They have learned to know and trust each other, which means there is a high level of experience and uncertainty is perceived to be low. Distances are small and commitment high. Adaptations are extensive and cost-savings considerable. Relationships are now established and become more and more routine with mutually acknowledged norms of conduct and standard operating procedures. The main aim when building relationships is to reach the long-term stage, to gain an ongoing long-term relationship with the buyer. If this is not accomplished, the relationship may retract to an earlier stage, even to the pre-relationship stage. In the latter case the relationship-building process may start all over again, perhaps this time with a new partner.

The final stage

The relationship is very stable with high commitments. There is even a risk that the relationship gets stuck and becomes hard to adapt to ongoing environmental changes. The high trust, low distances and low uncertainty might lead the parties to become complacent. This makes the relationship sensitive to being broken, due to environmental changes and attacks by competitors.

Organizational learning

As discussed in Chapter 4, experiential knowledge is the key aspect of the internationalization process, being the major factor behind its stage character. This implies that a focus on the resource base of the firm and how it changes is necessary; organizational learning then becoming a key aspect of these knowledge processes. Firms gradually build up their knowledge about foreign operations through operating in the markets. They learn from past experience by transforming this experience into useful knowledge. This experiential knowledge about foreign markets is developed in networks (Blomstermo et al., 2004; Johanson and Vahlne, 2003). Such network experiential knowledge is gained by operating in local market networks, where institutional knowledge is also built up on the local market scene. Together, these two types of knowledge add to the internationalization knowledge, putting the firm in a better position to internationalize further. These three types of experiential knowledge are path-dependent and unique for every firm, often being defined as a 'theory in use' (Eriksson et al., 1997). Internationalization knowledge concerns general knowledge about how to operate in foreign markets, while network experiential knowledge and institutional knowledge are defined as knowledge about how to operate in specific local market networks and environments.

The organizational learning of experiential knowledge is twofold: operational learning that occurs within an existing organizational process and conceptual learning that is more strategic or path-breaking, more similar to explorative learning (March, 1991; Forsgren, 2002). This division builds on Sharma and Blomstermo (2003a), who argue that the existing knowledge state is restructured discontinuously or intermittently. The idea is also based on results from research on the internationalization of Western firms in emerging markets.

Firms with long domestic experience of certain types of markets may have a cemented knowledge platform that takes time to change when the company moves from one type of market to another, for example from mature markets in the West to emerging markets in the East. Each stage of the internationalization process is represented by such a knowledge platform, which is created through an organizational learning process.

Firms tend to internationalize to culturally similar markets, thereby building exports as much as possible based on their experience gained from the domestic market. The exporting model is built on a similar idea, where internationalization is viewed as an innovation. The firm moves from a domestic market focus to active involvement in exporting through a learning process, thereby becoming more international. This learning takes place in the pre-export stage and the experimental involvement stage. Then, more learning in international markets brings the firm to the committed involvement stage. New organizational processes for the international operations are discovered, learned through conceptual learning, and result in a new knowledge platform. From this base, a new operational learning and business process is set off.

Institutional distance

New stages of internationalization are established with the firm extending its business from one major type of market to another major type or from one type of foreign environment to another. These foreign country market environments or contexts are defined as institutional settings. The internationalization process is therefore determined by the institutional distance between country markets. As introduced in Chapter 1 and developed further in Chapter 11, this concept involves major differences between how societies are organized. It is a broader concept than psychic distance (Johanson and Wiedersheim-Paul, 1975) or cultural distance (Majkgård, 1998). It improves cultural distance as a concept for international business research along the lines suggested by Shenkar (2001), being changed from a country-level characteristic to a country institutional profile based on institutional theory (Kostova, 1997). The institutional distance is assumed to be large when internationalization processes take place from old EU countries to new members as well as to Asian countries. It is based on the institutional view.

Networks are influenced by the institutional structures of the society, for example systems of property rights, and judicial and penal systems. This is also true of more proximate institutional structures in which market networks are embedded, for example market institutions. The institutional context of a specific emerging market might therefore facilitate or hinder moves to internationalize. Internationalization concerns activities in network relationship processes with the purpose of bridging gaps or distances at three levels: between actors in networks, between institutions in markets and between institutions outside markets.

The five plus five stages model

The global internationalization process is now integrated with the local relationship process forming a more developed model of the internationalization of the MNEX. While the former process concerns how the international experience of the firm increases, the latter process is a good approximation of how international experience is gained in a specific local market. The more developed the customer relationships, the more experience the firm has of the particular foreign country market. The five stages of the relationship process are illustrated in Figure 10.3 as circles connected to each other. By establishing more and more relationships abroad the firm moves further and further along the internationalization process, starting in the experimental export stage. The larger the number of relationships established, the larger the part of the firm's resources and capabilities that is dedicated to international business, which means that they are increasingly located abroad, among other things.

During the pre-relationship stage, the experience of the customers/suppliers is nil or very low, uncertainty is high, distances are large and commitment and adaptations are zero. According to the exporting theory, for a SME that has a domestic market focus and starts to internationalize to a foreign country, the pre-relationship stage corresponds to the pre-export stage for the first foreign market (Gankema et al., 2000). The development of the relationships in the foreign country market starts in the early stage, when commitments and experience increase somewhat. According to the exporting theory, this is similar to the experimental export stage of an internationally inexperienced firm. This establishment of relationships is a mutual learning process, where the parties learn to know more and more about each other. The first adaptations are made but are still few. High uncertainty is experienced and high distances prevail between the parties. The early stage is followed by the development stage, during which business between the customer and the supplier starts to grow and resources are increasingly shared. In this stage, there is a further development of the buyer–seller relationship, signified by a delivery build-up and the signing of contracts. Intensive mutual learning results in increased experience on both sides, as well as in reduced uncertainty and distances. Trust and commitments increase, which are signified by both formal and informal adaptations as well as cost savings. Relationships become focused on the dyad. Next, after several major purchases or deliveries, the relationship is developed and settles in the

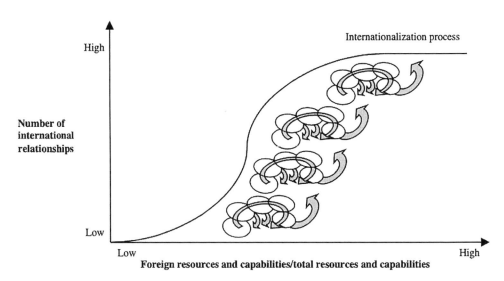

Source: Jansson and Sandberg (2008).

Figure 10.3 The five plus five stages model

long-term stage. The exporter and the importer have now learned to know and trust each other, distances being small and commitment high. The main aim when building relationships is to reach the long-term stage, to gain an ongoing long-term relationship. In the final stage, the relationship is extensively institutionalized with commitment being taken for granted, which might make it hard to develop and adapt the relationship to ongoing environmental changes.

Thus, relationships, being at the core of the internationalization process, follow a similar pattern as the internationalization process as a whole, by showing how the gradual build-up of international experience takes place. The more relationships in a foreign country that have reached later stages, the more internationally experienced and the higher the degree of internationalization of the firm. Further, the more countries where the company has established relationships, the more internationally experienced the firm.

ENTRY STRATEGY

Based on the five plus five stages model, the entry strategy aspect of the international network strategy is now advanced. The entry mode of MNEXs was denoted above as the export mode. However, building on the network view, the focus is now shifted to how firms plug into the country-specific business network. As noted by Agndal and Chetty (2007) and Forsgren et al. (2002), entry mode and other issues regarding entering foreign markets then become subsumed under this network aspect. As illustrated in Figure 10.4, the establishment of the international network strategy in the emerging market takes place through the entry network. The MNEX enters through three types of networks (dyads, triads and nets) to achieve a specific network position. The entry node is how the MNEX plugs into the local market through selecting such a network, for example by linking up to the customers directly through forming dyads or indirectly through establishing triads, using an intermediary such as a distributor or an agent. The entry process involves passing through three types of networks in establishing the international business in the emerging market: the exposure network, the formation network and the sustenance network.

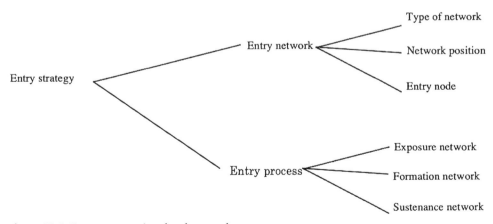

Figure 10.4 Entry strategy into local networks

Entry networks

The three dimensions of the entry networks are shown in Figure 10.4. Due to the fact that entry mode studies mainly deal with the economic consequences of entry, social aspects are under-represented. Another limitation is that these studies are based on FDI theories such as the OLI framework, internalization theory and other economic theories on the multinational firm and therefore have clear limitations regarding internationalization processes. They are mainly useful for explaining entry modes and other structural aspects on entering foreign markets, being insufficient for studying processes or social aspects.

The social side of entry and internationalization is therefore developed further, mainly through applying the network view to IBS described in Chapter 7. Entering foreign markets, then, concerns individual relationships which, in turn, are connected to other relationships in networks. The network established in a foreign market is defined as an organization set, the business network being centred on a particular node (Aldrich and Whetten, 1981): the entering firm.

Type of network

Depending upon the size of the organization network involved in entering, a distinction is made between three types of network structures: dyads, triads and nets. Dyads consist of two-party relationships, triads of three-party relationships and nets of many-party relationships. Smaller networks like dyads and triads differ in many ways from larger networks such as information networks. In accordance with Chapter 7, a multilevel perspective is taken regarding networks. Social and organizational networks are found at two separate levels of the local network organization, interacting so that activities at one level result in consequences for the other level. For example, the formal structure of linked organizations can be seen as an antecedent to the social network, influencing how individuals build relationships among themselves.

Criteria based on open networks (Burt, 1993) are used to analyse network structures, since they concern the gathering, processing and screening of information, as well as identifying information sources. This is a kind of information network stressing the indirect linkage (as shown in Chapter 9), which has mostly weak relationships and is loosely coupled, thus having a low degree of integration. The opposite is the tightly coupled closed network that is characterized by a high degree of integration, where all partners have direct and strong ties with each other. This network is focused on social capital, which is built through trust and shared norms (Coleman, 1988). How to become an insider then differs between these network structures. For example, there is a trade-off between a large open network that maximizes information benefits and a smaller, closed network promoting trust-building and more reliable information (Ahuja, 2000). Thus, open networks consist of many general and weak ties between many parties, while closed networks consist of a few strong social ties, which normally form the core of the local business network.

Network position

According to Chapter 4, internationalization through networks is the outcome of firms' actions to establish relationships by strengthening network positions. Firms establish new positions, develop old positions, or increase the coordination between positions in different country-based networks.

According to the internationalization process model above, an organization set is gradually established in the foreign market. Network-extending firms initially lack a local network position, meaning that they suffer from a liability of outsidership (Johanson and Vahlne, 2009). This liability is reduced by the firms strengthening their network position, which happens as firms learn, through their relationships, about their foreign counterparts, their preferences and various business opportunities. Firms develop trust in their counterparts, enabling them to further develop their network position. This relationships development process takes the entering firms from an outsider to an insider position. This enables a further commitment to the local business network and enables the firm to develop its network position towards an insider position.

This network position is defined as the degree of insidership by Hilmersson and Jansson (2012a). This is a critical aspect of networks for three reasons. First, it is closely related to the degree of coupling of the local network. The more integrated the firm becomes in the network, the more of an insider it is. Second, insidership is related to the control of the network. Third, the degree of insidership is closely related to competitive position. Thus, it indicates whether the entry has reached break-even, or if the exporter has achieved a first-mover advantage, since the firm has become a preferred supplier. Based on the discussion above, one can conclude that established dyads as closed networks have a high degree of insidership, while the degree of insidership varies for different triads. In nets the degree of insidership is usually low.

Entry node

Nodes used initially to connect to local firms and the relationships to customers initiated and developed through them are defined as entry nodes (Jansson and Sandberg, 2008). Through the entry node, the global seller network is connected to the local networks of the foreign market. As found in Chapters 8 and 9, the key local network for a seller is the buyer network. In principle, there are two major ways for a seller to connect to the buyer network in the foreign market or develop nodes through which to enter. Entries either take place directly with customers/suppliers or indirectly through intermediaries. Direct relationships are established between the buyer and seller in the respective countries. Such two-party relationships are either between a unit of the seller located in the buyer country or from the seller's location outside the buyer country. In the former case dyads are established through the entry mode FDI, that is, a subsidiary in the exporting/importing country. The latter case concerns MNEXs and is defined above as the export mode. Indirect relationships also concern this mode and involve some outside party or other type of entry node, usually an intermediary of some kind, for example an agent, dealer or distributor. Due to the involvement of such a third party, the entry network becomes a triad.

These two types of entry networks are now illustrated by a study made of the internationalization of firms from South Sweden to Poland during the 1990s and early 2000s, that is, when the latter country was in transition from a centrally planned economy to a market economy.

The *dyads* of international supplier relationships studied involved ordinary purchasing of components for the own production and outsourced products previously produced in Sweden, where the buyer took an active role in developing the quality of the output of the supplier. Communication between the parties was the major problem due to institutional distance, mainly language and cultural differences but also ways of organizing. The information linkage did not work so well and the social linkage was under-developed. For example, when a third person in the form of an interpreter is always present, it is hard to develop any deeper social relation built on trust. It was especially hard for the Swedish buyer to reach down to the operational levels through the tall hierarchy and to communicate with people at that level, for instance production planners, designers, foremen and workers. When representatives of the parties met, for example, only the upper echelons of the organizations were involved. This made it more difficult to check how the information given was perceived and acted upon. Institutional distance aggravated this situation further. For instance, Poles have a tendency not to admit to having made mistakes. However, due to the better knowledge of English at the Polish suppliers, the extent of these problems were less than for the exporter dyads at the same stage of relationship development. The main reason for this better knowledge seems to be that the importer as a buyer has more power and can demand that key persons at the supplier speak English, which was not possible for the exporters. Still, the buyer had to visit the supplier more often to discuss the problems face to face, since communication by telephone or e-mail was difficult.

A major challenge of the INS in *triads* is to make an effective trade-off between the strategy towards the third party and the strategy towards the final customer. This is a typical problem faced by an exporter doing international business through local intermediaries. The network strategy of the exporter towards the intermediary is dependent upon whether the intermediary has a strategy of its own towards the customers or a joint one with the exporter. This decides how to allocate the marketing resources between the intermediary and the customers. The Polish study also involved a classical sales agency case of the triad consisting of a strong relationship with the agent and a weak one with the buyers. It also included more balanced cases, where the seller made a more equal trade-off of the relationships between the agent and customers. In such balanced triads, there is more of a sharing of the customer relationships with the agent. In the former unbalanced triads, the seller is sometimes involved in the selling, but only on the initiative of the agent. The agent is taking care of the customer relationships and the seller is mainly involved in solving certain technical problems and in delivery matters, having more of a supportive role. Thus, the relationship with the agent provides the seller with a linkage to the market, but one which works differently depending upon the type of network strategy and the traits of the agent.

The management of the information or communication linkage is done differently. It varies with institutional distance in how to get information about the market and how to communicate with customers and other parties in the language belonging to another business culture. For example, the much more hierarchical organizational structures in Poland resulted in a top-down communication through official channels both with customers and with intermediaries. It was hard to develop a broad network of lateral relationships connecting buyer and seller staff at different organizational levels. Such contacts were often necessary to fully succeed with the INS, especially for technically complex products that require the exchange of technical information. It also became harder to implement deals at operational levels and to follow them up through after-market operations. Communication channels also became very long and slow, where the main information linkage between the seller and the agent took place at the highest levels. This meant that the control of the marketing process of the distributor/agent by the exporter was low.

This relationships set-up meant the triad developed very slowly or not at all. The institutional distance due to cultural barriers was still present, hindering communication and the information linkage as well as the social linkage from developing further, setting definite limits to growth. The MNEX was continuously cut off from the customers, particularly since it was in the interest of the agent to keep the seller in the darkness about market developments. Otherwise, the risk of the agent being replaced by another one increased, and likewise the risk of the seller taking over customer relationships through its own representation in the country. The remaining large social and cultural distances prevented the exporter from getting involved in the market, that is, from building up network experiential knowledge and institutional knowledge. Too little experiential learning by the seller took place, being mainly limited to the agent. This organizational learning by the exporter was especially low when the relationship with the agent was weak, for example when the agent represented a number of companies. Then, the seller had to compete with others for the agent's time and resources. A major conclusion from the study is that the agent often works badly as a mediator of information and knowledge. Another reason for the low learning of the seller is that experiential knowledge is mainly tacit, since it concerns experience, feelings and intuition. It is hard to transfer such know-how between parties and therefore it is necessary for the company to learn through operating in the market. Triads in emerging country markets are therefore paradoxical. Due to the high uncertainty experienced in these markets, low cost and flexible entry nodes such as triads are chosen. However, by not operating deeper in the emerging market, the seller is prevented from developing experiential knowledge about customers and the specific characteristics of the market. Uncertainty is not reduced or controlled for, which is necessary should the exporter want to expand business by investing more resources in the market.

This major problem of getting stuck in the triad is not so severe in the case of more balanced relationships, since the seller also has a direct relationship with the customer. There is even an example of the Swedish seller dominating Polish customer relationships. The exporter mainly handles the linkage strategy towards the customers, while the agent works more as a support organization in the local market, assisting the seller with sales and service, and working as a language and cultural interpreter. Here, experiential learning takes places through the more active and broader engagement of the exporter in the triad, creating better circumstances for market expansion. However, communication problems related to language and organization culture of the type discussed above are also found for this type of agency relationship. These problems are hard to solve in any major way as long as the representative in the market is an independent firm, being hard to control by the seller.

Entry process

The entry process illustrated in Figure 10.4 concerns how the network relationships entered are developed further to establish the INS and the firm in the foreign market and to sustain its business there. The entry networks described above – dyads and triads – are analysed further, now as a structural process. The focus is mainly on the individual relationships of these entry networks, using the five plus five stages model. These two-party and three-party networks will also be put into the larger context of the extended network, of which they are a part, that is, the net.

Many-party network
This process of the extended network is summarized as three major network structures found at

various stages of relationships development during the entry process of Swedish MNEXs (Hilmersson and Jansson, 2012a). They are the exposure network, the formation network and the sustenance network. They will be compared along the following characteristics: degree of insidership reached, types of ties developed, type of exchange taking place, and degree of coupling.

In connection with entering a foreign market, the firm exposes itself to the opportunities of the local business network. Initially, the idea is to keep this network as open as possible, which means that the *exposure network* mainly consists of weak ties. The focus of potential exporters is to find hubs through which to expose themselves to as many potential customers as possible. Thus, a potential exporter initially creates both information and social contacts to expose itself to various parties of relevance to the business in the new market. Next, it is mainly a question of starting to close the network by limiting the network being exposed to by linking up to certain entry nodes. Gradually trust and stronger ties develop, and these linkages are explored to locate parties of interest. The aim is to find a position in the business network through the exposure network, which mainly consists of customers and intermediaries. However, a more passive direct exporter may start with establishing one dyad and later enlarge the network by more dyads to find information hubs that expose the firm to more relationships.

In the *formation network*, the large open exposure network that maximizes information benefits is gradually transformed into a smaller, closed network by promoting trust-building and more reliable information. Exporters develop businesses by gradually transforming certain weak ties into stronger ones, either forming dyads or triads. In the latter case, the hubs of intermediaries and their social networks are instrumental for the establishment of a number of customer relationships in the country. Stronger relationships are developed through establishing social ties with persons at firms found throughout the exposure network. These relationships are then developed further with those selected as promising prospects. The organization set therefore gradually closes, which leads to the formation of the inter-organizational network, to which the social network is a precedent.

The goal in the formation network is to move forward with partners that were explored in the exposure network, and with whom sustainable business can be developed. But the MNEXs have now also gained enough network experiential knowledge such that new customers can be found. Therefore, in the formation network, they exploit hubs to expand the network based on the initial few nodes. Extending the size of the network is essential to create leverage effects. Thus, in the formation network, entering SMEs establish their positions in local market networks.

The limitations of the entry node triad discussed above can now be better understood by analysing the development of the Polish customer relationships of the Swedish exporters according to the relationship process model above. For the unbalanced triads, these relationships between manufacturer and customers had not moved beyond the early stage or the development stage. These stages were characterized by low commitment and few adaptations, since there were large social and cultural distances between the parties. The uncertainty perceived was high due to the parties having low experiential knowledge about each other. Since the agent was responsible for the customer relationships, the direct relationships would not develop further. Even in balanced triads, when the seller jointly participated in customer relationships along with the agent, the direct relationship was hard to develop further. The major reason for this was the language barrier and the cultural barrier between organizations. As found above, the language barrier makes it hard to communicate with the right people and learn to know them. The communication takes place with those that know English, but who often do not know enough about the actual problem. The tall hierarchy and high power distance of Polish firms make lateral contacts, which are necessary to succeed with the marketing of complex industrial products, almost impossible. Communication from the top level of the buyer to the seller is indirect, as it comes through the agent. The distances between the parties are not much reduced, which results in a low understanding of each other and few adaptations. Commitment grows slowly and the learning process is checked. Since trust is hard to increase, uncertainty remains high. This makes the seller less inclined to invest more in such relationships.

The question is whether the network strategy with the agent can compensate for the lack of development possibilities that arise from not having direct contacts with the customers. As noted before, this is only possible to a certain extent, mainly because the growth of experiential knowledge requires direct contact with the market and the customers. Moreover, compensation is made difficult if the control of the linkage strategy of the intermediary is insufficient.

In the *sustenance network*, exporters from mature markets establish themselves more firmly by replacing triads with dyads – by forming a joint venture or establishing a subsidiary. Over the long run, the business requires more structured relationships to secure production, marketing and sales, logistics and after-sales service. In the sustenance network, the aim is to move on with those partners with whom sustainable business can be developed or develop new partners. This is the final test of whether the exporter has managed to establish an insider position, that is, whether the organization set is closed enough to sustain the business.

A closer look is now taken at how the various relationships of the dyad can be sustained. The international supplier relationships of the Polish market discussed previously are all sustainable as they are found in the long-term stage. They are characterized by high commitment and extensive adaptations. The experiential knowledge of the parties is high. The technological, time and geographical distances are low, while the social and cultural distances consisting of language and organization cultural barriers seem to be moderate and therefore could possibly be reduced further. The uncertainty is low to moderate. Through the adaptations performed, the relationship has partly been standardized and made routine. The relationships studied developed mainly because the Polish suppliers willingly adapted the production system and the logistic system to the demands of the Swedish buyers. To make it possible for the supplier to improve the quality of the products, the buyers shared their knowledge with them. Due to the knowledge gap between the parties, the way of handling this transfer of knowledge involved the most crucial adaptations that lay behind the development of the relationship from the early stage to the long-term stage. This was especially true for relationships involving outsourced products, where the knowledge gap was large at the outset of the relationship. Communication through the information and know-how linkages played a critical role. Through these adaptations the technological, time and geographic distances had been more or less overcome. However, some institutional distance consisting of social and organizational barriers remained and were slowing down further developments of the relationship. Language problems and the very hierarchical organization of the seller rendered communication with the operational levels in both organizations difficult. Because of the large need to communicate, this was a big problem in subcontracting relationships, where products were designed in Sweden and produced in Poland. The social linkage was very important in these relationships, otherwise the communication would not work properly. The social linkage was closely related to the information and know-how linkages. When the parties trusted each other, the exchange of information and knowledge became more open and reliable.

However, as noted above, social relationships tend to be underdeveloped when barriers like these exist, which could represent a threat to the sustenance of the dyad. At the end of day, the number of supplier relationships in the Polish market was limited, since it took so much time and resources to develop and maintain them. Even though one very experienced buyer firm had managed to standardize the relationships through well-established organizational routines, the relationships did not last long, since they continuously needed to be changed in the dynamic emerging market.

TAKE-OFF STRATEGY

The focus is now shifted to the beginning of the internationalization process, from international firms entering emerging markets to local firms exiting them. But instead of taking up how MNEXs start to internationalize from mature markets as in the exporting theory, this section is about MNEXs exiting China. Internationalization of the individual Chinese firm starts either from the domestic market by building on the competitive advantages established there, or from foreign markets. The former situation is defined as horizontal take-off (HTO), while the latter is labelled vertical take-off (VTO). The distinction between these two ways of setting off is based on a metaphor from aviation. Horizontal take-off relates to how firms operating in the domestic market are transformed into international firms. It represents the internationalization process established for MNEXs described above in the five plus five stages model. The firm first establishes itself together with other firms in the local industry to build its competitive strength in the domestic market before it internationalizes. This is typical of HTO (before planes (firms) can take off, an airport (market) must be established). In vertical take-off, firms become international from inception without first developing an industry base in the domestic market. Competitiveness is, rather, developed abroad in the global marketplace. This way of starting to internationalize is defined as VTO (no airport is needed for helicopters to take off), being typical for the international new ventures (INVs) introduced in Chapter 4. Another take-off strategy is collective rather than individual, when a firm takes off as a member of a group of firms or of an action network (Sandberg and Jansson, 2014). However, this more uncommon take-off strategy of a collective internationalization process is not taken up here.

Take-off process

The take-off process is based on studies of the internationalization of SMEs from China, chiefly Jansson and Söderman (2012) and Child and Rodrigues (2005). Even if different, there are interesting similarities between the strategic thinking of these SMEs and that of the overseas Chinese SMEs (Haley, 1997; Haley et al., 1999).

The HTO process encompasses the initial three stages of the exporting model and an additional stage discovered in a study of the take-off strategy. It is called the indirect exporting stage and placed in between the pre-export stage and the experimental exporting stage. Here the producer uses a domestic representative, often a trading company, as a sales outlet for the foreign market. The sales usually take place in an international market outlet located in the home market, mainly trade fairs. The producer never leaves home and has no direct relation with the foreign country market. Further internationalization takes place through direct exporting, building on the experience gained through indirect exporting by starting to sell directly to parties on the foreign country market. This stage is more common in emerging than mature markets. An internationalizing firm that goes abroad after the pre-export stage has the choice between indirect and direct exporting to reach the experimental export stage.

The domestic market focus stage of emerging markets differs from mature markets. The situation on the domestic market is not normally included in internationalization process theory, since it is assumed that the exporter has developed a competitive advantage at home, which it takes advantage of in foreign markets. This assumption is not valid for emerging markets, where local markets in many industries are underdeveloped or even non-existent. The possibility of creating competitive advantages in domestic markets therefore varies with the development of the local industry market, that is, its marketization. As found in Chapter 3, local market development in China ran through three stages. Firms started to develop differentiation advantages during the third stage compared to having competed based on cost advantages in the previous stages. Competition on quality increased by virtue of the fact that companies relied more on the development of science and technology than on low price for their competitiveness. The motivation to go abroad became more real during this third phase.

VTO could take place at any of these stages, since it is not so dependent on local market development. On the contrary, the development of competitive advantages of the high-tech firm studied took place in foreign markets, which the firm later used to establish itself domestically, when the local market in China had developed.

CONCLUSIONS

This chapter deals with one of the major aspects of international business strategy introduced in previous chapters, namely 'geographic spread'. It is based on the models of internationalization processes discussed in Chapter 4, which are combined into an enlarged internationalization in networks model to study primarily the international network strategic process of multinational exporters (MNEXs). Their global internationalization process is combined with the local internationalization process to study how they enter and establish network relations in emerging markets. A chief aspect of the entry strategy – entry mode – is the inward FDI of Swedish MNCs in China, where the entry modes and investment motives of MNEXs are compared to those of MNCs. A stage model of the global internationalization process is combined with a stage model on local relationship development to form the five plus five stages model. Due to the large institutional distance between mature and emerging markets, MNEXs learn many new things when entering and expanding in and between emerging markets. Knowledge and learning are therefore key factors in internationalization to these markets. By defining learning as an organizational process and a way of making the resources and capabilities of the firm dynamic, the strategic aspect of INS is stressed. The MNEX enters through three types of network structures (dyads, triads and nets) to achieve a specific network position. The entry node is how the MNC plugs into the local market through selecting such a network, for example by linking up to the customers directly through forming dyads or indirectly through establishing triads. The entry process pertains to the passing through of three types of networks in entering the emerging market: the exposure network, the formation network and the substance network. While the chapter concentrates on the entry strategy, it also discusses the take-off strategy from one emerging home market, China, by looking at the internationalization of Chinese MNEXs.

PART VI

THE INSTITUTIONAL VIEW

Black-faced spider monkey – intelligent but endangered

Peruvian spider monkeys spend their whole life up in the trees, where they swing easily through the trees using their 'hooked' arms and tail, even being considered the trapeze artist of the jungle. As one of the most intelligent primates, these monkeys are not entirely programmed but can adapt to the local habitat. They have robust memories, using mental maps of the jungle to move through the forest canopy. Peruvian spider monkeys live in groups of 20–30 individuals. The size and dynamics of the groups vary with food availability and socio-behavioural activity. They hug each other when they meet to convey greetings and divert potential aggression. These monkeys have an essential role in the tropical rainforest ecosystem, especially in the dispersal of seeds as they travel over long distances. They have a life span of up to 20 years and eat mostly ripe fruit. They are currently listed on the IUCN Red List as Endangered. The sharp decline in their population is due to them being hunted for sale and consumption in the Amazonian bushmeat trade, their living area being developed for agriculture, and the habitat being polluted and destroyed by illegal mining activity. Reintroduction efforts have begun along the lower Madre de Dios River, where this photo is taken.

11
The institutional view of international business strategy

This chapter explores the institutional view of the network institutional approach (NIA) by explaining more how the complex and rapidly changing external environments of emerging markets work. A theoretical background to the institutional view is provided in the Appendix. Fundamental models for analysing the external strategic environment of these markets are developed, providing a basis for how to do international business there. According to the basic networks model introduced in Chapter 7, international business strategy (IBS) in the product/service market network is determined by the wider institutional framework divided into societal sectors. The background of this institutional part of the IBS is now developed by going into the institutional view, first to explain more what an institution is. Keeping the societal sectors intact, the basic networks model is next turned into the basic institutions model. This societal infrastructure consists of an embedded system of institutions, where a distinction is made between three analytical levels: besides societal sectors, also organizational fields and the organization. At the centre of the model is the multinational corporation (MNC) – the key institution or the micro institution of the book – which is surrounded by two layers of meso and macro institutions. Finally, the basic rules model is established by going deeper into the contents of the basic institutions model. This former model is based on the assumption that the organization of every society is founded on basic rules, thus being seen as the control infrastructure of the international business strategy. Four orders or ground rules are found behind this strategy, namely thought styles, values, norms and enforcement mechanisms.

NETWORKS AND INSTITUTIONS

The inter-organizational relations in networks takes place with outside organizations, where the direction, spread and substance of relations are determined by institutional factors (Mitchell, 1973). For example, the MNC could be accountable to a public audience for the societal effects of its customer relationships, such as not damaging the natural environment. This means that the firm should be legitimate. But, as noted earlier, the MNC primarily needs to be efficient or profitable. This difference between legitimacy and efficiency is expressed in the following way by Meyer and Scott (1983, p. 140):

> Networks operate in institutional sectors characterized by the elaboration of rules and requirements to which individual organizations must conform if they are to receive support

and legitimacy from the environment. Technical sectors are those within which a product or service is exchanged in a market such that organizations are rewarded for effective and efficient control of the work process.

The product/service market is such a technical sector, which, based on institutional theory, is here defined as an organizational field. MNCs are then viewed to operate in technical sectors demanding efficiently produced outcomes and in other institutional sectors demanding legitimacy-based outcomes such as government. According to Meyer and Rowan (1977) this means that 'organizations are special-purpose collectivities created to achieve goals, to perform work. Their meaning, their legitimacy, and their potency come from appearing to be rational systems' (Meyer and Scott, 1983, p. 160). Thus, the organization is also seen as an institution, which is also the approach of this book. These efficiency and legitimacy rationales often coincide, since efficiency is based on legitimacy-based rules. For example, governments in certain emerging markets are often sceptical towards the profit-'maximizing' rationale of MNCs due to the potential negative effects on the host economy such behaviour can have, for example the ecological and social impact. The MNCs then need to prove to the government that their efficient operations will not result in such adverse effects, that is, that they are legitimate.

This institutional view on the firm and its environment fits well with Whitley's (1992a, p. 6) definition of firms and markets as business systems. They are '… configurations of hierarchy market relations that become institutionalized in different market economies in different ways as the result of variations in dominant institutions'. This business systems theory is mainly used to compare markets within and between Western societies and East Asian societies, for example looking at the degree to which networks are institutionalized according to a number of aspects. This makes it possible to explore how institutions influence networks in markets, for example by expanding on the way the product/service market works according to the NIA. Some useful aspects found in Whitley (1992b) are as follows:

- Type of exchange. In Western markets, exchange takes place through ad hoc and short-term conflict-oriented relationships, where partners are changed continuously as prices change. In East Asia, on the other hand, there are more long-term cooperative relations between firms.
- The degree to which relationships are personal and trustful. Western market societies are characterized by impersonal relations and organizational trust (primarily being firm based), while trust and relations are personal in East Asian market societies.
- Types of actors, for example the significance of intermediaries in the coordination of relationships.
- Important characteristics of major actors, for example the stability, integration and scope of business groups. Where business groups dominate markets, as for example in South Korea and Japan, a large part of the domestic market network is internalized and monopolized by a few economic agents.

THE INSTITUTIONAL VIEW

The institutional view of the NIA is now developed further. As found earlier, an institution is looked upon as a societal system of rules due to the fact that human behaviour tends to follow certain patterns that repeat themselves over time. Institutions are defined as rule systems consisting of habits and organizational routines as well as beliefs and values typical of a legitimized social grouping of some kind. The major condition for the institutionalization of a certain behaviour is that this behaviour has been evaluated based on a value or norm and found to be acceptable internally or externally by outside groups, that is, it has been legitimized. Thus, members of a social unit behave according to the rules of the unit, meaning that individuals are provided with normative rules telling them which actions are legitimate and which are not. New members will imitate this behaviour, sometimes without being unaware of the rule behind it. This production and reproduction of material and symbolic life through established patterns of behaviour is valid for the individuals and the social unit to which they belong. Institutions subsist over time by being reproduced through institutional change processes.

A main characteristic of institutions is then their organizing nature, since rules determine how social behaviour is organized. Furthermore, rules facilitate and constrain the social behaviour among individuals and groups. The shared values, norms and meanings among them constrain their relations, thus resulting in patterned relationships. Lastly, regularities imply predictability. Due to the regular behaviour, institutions are characterized by predictability (Nabli and Nugent, 1989).

Traditions and habits

Since institutions concern groups, it is important to understand the difference between group behaviour and individual behaviour, for example between organizational and individual behaviour. This is exemplified by comparing traditions with habits. A tradition is an institution or socially acceptable behaviour that is repeated in the same manner over a long period, often for more than a generation. Traditions vary between different groups of people. Christmas, for example, is celebrated in one way in Sweden and another way in the US. Marriage ceremonies vary between groups. A 'love' marriage in Sweden is completely different to an arranged marriage in India. Traditions like Christmas and marriage are examples of institutions. Other examples of such institutional arrangements are the army, the Lutheran church, and so on. Thus society consists of a number of institutional arrangements like these. A sufficient number of group members will behave according to the tradition, otherwise it will not survive as an institution. However, a specific individual may choose not to follow a certain tradition, for example not to marry, or to quit the Lutheran church, instead preferring the tradition of another group, for example to marry in another way or become a member of the Roman Catholic church. The individual could also initiate a new tradition, for example by inventing a new way of accomplishing the same thing as marrying or by starting a new religious movement. Thus, individuals choose an institutional arrangement and mediate it through participation. The individual then becomes involved in social relationships and various forms of sharing. So from the perspective of the individual, traditions are carried over by being learned, which can be done either consciously or unconsciously. In the latter case, the individual just behaves like others without being aware of why, that is, the ideas, beliefs or other codes behind the behaviour are unknown. Even a consciously selected tradition may become habit by being repeated so many times that the act is taken for granted. This distinction between individual habit and tradition is important. Individual habits die with the individual, whereas traditions are group behaviour, which die harder by surviving the individual. Institutions live a life of their own different from the life of a particular individual. Therefore institutions, like traditions, are more than a number of individual social habits. They mainly involve collective patterned ways of thinking, and ways of enforcing the decisions behind the acts. This patterned behaviour needs to be 'underwritten' by specific norms and values for the institutionalization to go deep enough to survive. An example is an organizational process turned into an organizational routine.

An institution is then 'out there' and is above the individual; it may exist before any individual is born into it or chooses it; and it may survive all its present members. An institution as a system transcends the individual parts of it and is found among individuals rather than in them. Change in an institution is largely independent of what individuals know and how they act. As stressed by North (2005), institutions are societal, historical and cultural phenomena that normally connect generations of people. They become public through a social process that takes place between individuals, thereby transcending the private processes of the individuals. An institution is valid for a specific collective, for example Western society, a nation, or a company. The range of validity varies. A corporation, for example, through its traditions, lives a life of its own more or less irrespective of the specific individuals employed in it. Even if important individuals leave the company, its repeated acts, decisions and control mechanisms continue. However, the disappearance of certain key actors of critical importance to the reproduction of a tradition may make the institution disappear. These might be persons who are carriers of critical knowledge for the survival of an organizational routine.

The discussion of institutions so far is well summarized by Jepperson (1991, p. 145) as follows:

> Institution represents a social order or pattern that has attained a certain state or property; institutionalization denotes the process of such attainment. By order or pattern, I refer, as is conventional, to standardized interaction sequences. An institution is then a social pattern that reveals a particular reproduction process. When departures from the pattern are counteracted in a regulated fashion, by repetitively activated, socially constructed, controls – that is, by some set of rewards or sanctions – we refer to a pattern as institutionalized. Put another way: institutions are those social patterns that, when chronically reproduced, owe their survival to relatively self-activating social processes.

Institutions concern these behavioural regularities or self-activating social processes, and hence institutional change is about how they change. Institutional theory describes and groups organized regularities and explains their existence and change. Institutional theory implies a study of reality from an institutional perspective, mainly seeing the world as consisting of regularities or rules.

THE BASIC INSTITUTIONS MODEL

The rule-like behaviour patterns differ throughout society, being divided into different social groupings. Such a social unit is seen as an institution of its own, where behaviour follows the specific rules inherent in it. Besides having their own rules, these social units influence each other. What goes on within one institution is influenced both by the rules within this social unit itself, and by those of other social groupings outside it. Institutions then influence each other. The major institution of this book – the MNC – is defined as being organized according to institutional principles. Sets of rules and regulations govern strategies and operations that are executed collectively by the individual members of this social grouping. MNC strategy is therefore influenced by the rules within this social unit as well as by the rules of institutions outside it.

Hence, society is divided into different social groupings characterized by different regularities and rules. These groupings are embedded into each other, forming a multi-layered system of institutions. How one part of society is organized is influenced by how other parts of society are organized. This institutional world is, according to the basic institutions model in Figure 11.1, divided into three levels of description for the rules: micro institutions (e.g. the MNC), meso institutions (e.g. an organizational field), and macro institutions (e.g. a societal sector).

This world of institutions is looked at from the perspective of one institution – the MNC – which is found at the centre, and which is surrounded by institutions that impact it and which it impacts. These basic types of societal organizations linked to the MNC are segmented into two major groupings or arrangements of institutions: organizational fields and societal sectors. Organizational fields are described at two levels of abstraction. At the micro institutions level, specific institutions within organizational fields are taken up, for example the MNC and its stakeholders in one organizational field classified as the product/service market and another classified as the

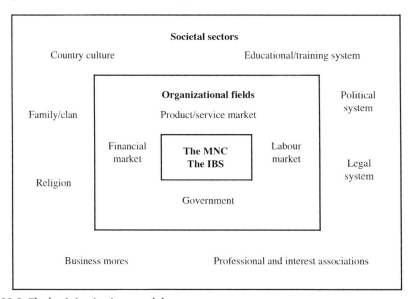

Figure 11.1 The basic institutions model

government. At the meso institutions level, social units are aggregated into whole organizational fields based on a common characteristic, for example the normative system. The product/service market is then an aggregate of various organizations such as customers, competitors and suppliers, which share common norms and values on how to operate in this market. The other organizational field – government – consists of ministries and authorities. These social units are aggregated based upon the fact that they share a common frame of reference and the typical rule-like behaviour following from this frame. At the most aggregated level, macro institutions are defined as societal sectors, for example the political system.

The influence of one institution on others is either bidirectional or unidirectional. The influence is reciprocal between organizations at the micro level of an organizational field, while it is mostly singular on the MNC from the organizational field as a whole, for example the market structure. There are therefore bidirectional influences between the market actors, while the influence on and by the market structure is mainly unidirectional. The influence of the societal sectors is direct and unidirectional on the organizational fields as meso institutions, and indirect on a micro institution such as the MNC. The grouping of institutions exemplified in Figure 11.1 varies with the strategic situation of the micro institution studied. In the figure, government is defined as an organizational field, and separated from the political system, which is defined as a societal sector. This means that there is an interplay between the MNC and government, while the influence of the political system on the MNC is unidirectional, either directly or indirectly through some organizational field. Other common broad ways of organizing society or macro institutions mostly influencing MNCs in emerging markets are the legal system, professional and interest associations, business mores or the business morale, family/clan, religion, and country culture. Thus, the meso and macro institutions link to each other in a certain way, creating a specific MNC emerging market environment, organized as an institutional framework of multi-layered organizations.

IBS depends on how the external environment as well as the internal environment of the MNC are organized, thus being influenced by institutional factors within the MNC (the internal institutional setting) and by the rules of outside institutions (the external institutional setting).

Organizational fields

In addition to the government, typical organizational fields in which MNCs operate are the products/service market, the financial market and the labour market.

Product/service market

As discussed in Chapter 5, if Porter's 'five forces model' is interpreted from the institutional view, there are a number of economic rules that determine how the product/service market works, for example rules regarding the way major actors relate to each other through competition. Another example of how to classify the product/service market from an institutional perspective is found in Williamson (1979). This economic institutional perspective on the governance of markets was introduced in Chapter 4 and is examined more in the Appendix. Still another example is provided by Whitley (1992a, b) and the business systems theory introduced above, which will be explored more below and in Chapter 12. The analysis of the product/service market can be developed further by dividing this large organizational field into smaller organizational fields such as sub-markets (e.g. an industry), or by subdivision according to stakeholder (e.g. one competitors' field, one intermediaries' field, one customers' field and one suppliers' field).

Financial market

A common way of characterizing financial markets from an institutional perspective is to distinguish between capital-market-based and credit-based financial systems (Whitley, 1992a, b). As is evident from the name of the former type of market, financial intermediation is controlled by the market. Specialized financial agents compete for capital and assets through market transactions, and the prices of financial assets are mainly set by market competition. Financial transactions are impersonal and rather short term. This is the equivalent of market governance in financial markets (see Appendix). Capital-market-based financial systems are mainly found in Anglo-Saxon countries, such as the UK and the US.

In the credit-based financial system, financial intermediation to a larger extent takes place through long-term network relationships between banks and specific large borrowers. Financial systems of this kind are found in, for example, Germany, South Korea and Japan.

Labour market

Whitley (1992a) makes a distinction between two types of labour market networks: market-based and organization-based reward systems. The purpose is to separate market-based and non-market-based systems. In the former type, individual professional and craft competencies are more important and persons more aware of their market value. According to Whitley: '... the extent to which labour markets are structured around publicly certified skills, and occupational identities are firmly attached to specialised certified skills, affect employee mobility and identification with distinct expertise' (Whitley, 1992a, p. 34).

In organization-based reward systems, labour market issues are not so much decided by the market but more by individual organizations, either by the employer alone, as in many Asian emerging country markets, or through negotiations between employers and labour unions, as in many European markets.

Thus, trade unions are an important institution (interest organization) in many markets. But since they are institutionalized differently between countries, it is often important to study them more closely, for example regarding their influence on reward systems, labour mobility and work organization.

STRUCTURES OF SOCIETY AND MIND

The basic institutions model concerns the social structure of a society. It is usually distinguished from the identity system, which is the realm of ideas of society or the ideational part. In certain cultural theory, this difference is expressed as the difference between social structure and culture (Keesing and Strathern, 1998). Two major social constructs express this distinction between social structure and identity system, namely role and social identity. Social identity (e.g. a lawyer or a management consultant) is based on shared meanings, expressing a mental capacity for certain social behaviour. A role is an enactment of the social identity, prescribing the behaviour appropriate to an actor in a particular capacity (e.g. how a lawyer should act in court based on his or her ability). The social structure concerns relationships and collectivities, which are described using terms such as roles, groups, values, status and trust. The identity system is described using words such as ideas, meanings, beliefs, codes, knowledge and learning.

The ingrained behaviour pattern typical of the identity system then comes from how humans think. According to the institutional view, human thinking tends to follow a certain routine that results in specific self-activated behaviour. Since thinking is habitual, behaviour is also habitual. Douglas (1986, p. 92) elegantly formulates how such cognitive rules organize human thinking into specific patterns, that is, what the structures of the mind look like based on institutional theory:

> Institutions systematically direct individual memory and channel our perceptions into forms compatible with the relations they authorize. They fix processes that are essentially dynamic, they hide their influence, and they rouse our emotions to a standardized pitch on standardized issues. Add to all this that they endow themselves with rightness and send their mutual corroboration cascading through all the levels of our information system. No wonder they easily recruit us into joining their narcissistic self-contemplation. Any problems we try to think about are automatically transformed into their own organizational problems. The solutions they proffer only come from the limited range of their experience. If the institution is one that depends on participation, it will reply to our frantic question: 'More participation!' If it is one that depends on authority, it will only reply: 'More authority!' Institutions have the pathetic megalomania of the computer whose whole vision of the world is its own program. For us, the hope of intellectual independence is to resist, and the necessary first step in resistance is to discover how the institutional grip is laid upon our mind.

Institutional theory integrates the structures of society and the structure of the mind by 'socializing' the mind.

THE BASIC RULES MODEL

Thus, there are two major types of societal rules: those of the identity system and those of the social structure. The relationship between them is seen as a complementary and mutually reinforcing. The first type of rules cannot then be fully understood without relating them to the other type of rules, institutional theory making it possible to integrate these sections of society into a coherent whole.

Based on this distinction and institutional theory, four ground rules are developed for how society is organized. The formal and informal rules valid for the MNC and the external and internal environment are condensed into four basic rules: thought styles, norms, values and enforcement mechanisms. Thought styles concern structures of the mind and originate in the identity system, while the other three rules concern the structures of the society and originate in the social structure. These are the basic external and internal rules that govern IBS, and are the major factors considered when matching the internal context with the external context. As a result, the informal rules dimension is developed more, since beliefs, norms and values largely concern this aspect. The basic rules model completes the institutional foundation of the NIA, thereby finalizing the institutional network template of the book.

Institutions determine strategic action, since they provide individuals with rules on how to act. In that way, behaviour is standardized by transferring rules, norms and ways of thinking between individuals. As found above, the institutions dealt with in this book are more like traditions than individual habits, and they give stability and meaning to social behaviour. To apply institutional theory to IBS, however, the regular self-activating social processes and their origins need to be defined in greater detail. The foundation of the basic rules model is the three institutional pillars found in the definition of institutions by Scott (1995, p. 33): 'Institutions consist of cognitive, normative, and regulative structures and activities that provide stability and meaning to social behaviour. Institutions are transported by various carriers – cultures, structures, and routines – and they operate at multiple levels of jurisdiction.'

This definition integrates different strands of institutional theory and contains three major factors: institutional content, carriers of institutions, and levels of analysis. Institutions are 'transported' or 'carried' through time by being reproduced many times as traditions over the centuries. Markets and hierarchies (such as MNCs) are examples of such carriers or 'reproduction units', which through their cultures, structures and routines transport institutions throughout the globe. The multiple levels of jurisdiction or the multi-layered system of embedded institutions have been a leading theme so far, for example expressed through the basic institutions model. So, if the MNC is defined as an institution in the form of a hierarchy (see Appendix), a specific MNC through its cultures, structures and routines is also seen as a transporter of this institution. But what does this institutional 'load' contain, or with what are the carriers 'loaded'? According to the specification above, there are three major types of content: cognitive, normative, and regulative structures and activities. These major institutional 'loads' of the MNC represent three main types of institutional aspects or 'pillars' as Scott (1995/2008) calls them. The cognitive dimension is then the institutional equivalent of the structures of the mind. The normative dimension, on the other hand, covers the social structures along with the regulative dimension. These aspects are specified as norms, values, thought styles and enforcement mechanisms. They are the major rules behind the regular behaviour patterns and provide behavioural stability through repetition. When these factors change, the patterns also change. Since the focus of the book is mainly on strategic thinking, the primary interest is in the thought styles and how they control strategic behaviour. But a thought world like this does not exist in a social vacuum; rather, it is influenced by social factors expressed as normative and regulative rules.

Thus, the three major contents of institutions ('pillars') are developed into four major types of basic rules as illustrated in Figure 11.2 They are valid for all institutions. For example, in the basic institutions model they are valid for MNCs as well as the organizational fields and societal sectors. The normative structure is divided up into norms and values. The cognitive structure is specified as thought styles, and the regulative structure as enforcement mechanisms. The four basic rules model is illustrated by a hypothetical example about an MNC that plans to enter an emerging market. The MNC is 'loaded' with a specific combination of basic rules that produces certain organizational routines. The question is whether these routines and the rules behind them are valid in the foreign market. A change of strategy and the development of a new organizational routine might then be necessary, which requires an adaptation to other values, norms, thought styles and enforcement mechanisms prevailing in this market. Therefore, to be an effective operator in a newly entered emerging market, the MNC might need to match the values, norms, thought styles and enforcement mechanisms prevailing there in order to adapt to the behaviour controlled by these rules. In order to know how to adapt to this situation, the MNC needs to make an analysis of the institutions in the external institutional setting, for example those exemplified in the basic institutions model (Figure 11.1). One societal sector – the legal system – is used as an example of an external institution that the MNC needs to analyse in order to adapt to it.

As seen in Figure 11.2, there are four basic types of rules controlling IBS contained in every institution: norms, values, enforcement mechanisms and thought styles. The MNC usually experiences the legal system as a regulative system, that is, as a number of enforcement mechanisms. The laws or formal written rules are learned from statue books, decrees and manuals. For the MNC, these external rules in the form of the enforcement mechanisms of a certain industrial policy become norms. Since norms specify how to act, these legal provisions become a norm for the MNC, influencing strategic behaviour. But usually it is not enough to study just these formal norms or rules, since they are limited to guiding MNCs in how they should behave. Companies could actually behave differently by following some rules but not others. This is a consequence of what was discussed above about seeing institutional arrangements as optional behavioural repertoires, containing various sets of rules. So, in addition to these formal rules, there might be other norms as well as other major sets of rules.

In this hypothetical case, this might be discovered when the laws are compared with actual practice or the organizational routines followed by local companies towards the legal system.

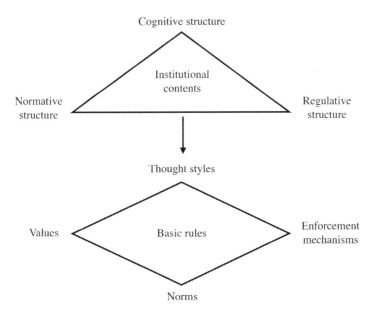

Figure 11.2 The basic rules model

Suppose there is a difference here, meaning that companies do not follow the law and are not punished for it. Then there is a mismatch between the organizational routines and the path or rule to follow expressed in written law. This difference is then analysed further by looking more closely at these enforcement mechanisms, for example at how the laws are executed. What are the direct and explicit controls over behaviour in the form of different rewards and punishments? Are the laws enforced in court? If not, there might be a lack of punishment because the risk of being sued is minimal when violating the rules. To analyse this gap further, a closer look could be taken at other basic rules of the courts: norms, values and thought styles. Regarding the values or the guiding principles of the legal behaviour, it could be found that values like honesty and impartiality are weak, implying that there could be a possibility for corrupt behaviour. Judges could be open to bribery. A study of the organizational routines of the courts might show that they tend to favour certain parties. Thus, in such a case, there is a mismatch between major rules, between certain enforcement mechanisms on the one hand, and other norms and values on the other. This leads to different strategies depending on which rules to follow. The institutional analysis of enforcement mechanisms, norms and values has now increased knowledge about why this institutional arrangement works the way it works, when it works.

This mismatch between institutional factors can be analysed further by looking more closely at the thought style behind the organizational routines of the courts and why this way of thinking takes place. For example, how are the formal rules expressed in the enforcement mechanisms thought about by the lawyers based on prevailing values? An analysis of how enforcement mechanisms, values and norms are transformed into action through the human mind may reveal more about mental processes. There might be certain prevailing ingrained ways of thinking that results in specific organizational routines in the courts, based on specific knowledge of the laws that gives a capacity to act as a lawyer. For example, a thought style of subjective decisions creating a low level of transparency could be found to be different from the one normally existing in a rationally functioning bureaucracy. If so, this adds knowledge about the difference between expected and actual behaviour originating from the formal law.

With this extended knowledge about a major constraining institution like the legal system in the emerging market, it is easier to create a fit between such external rules and the internal rules in the form of norms, values, thought styles and enforcement mechanisms, resulting in a suitable IBS. Different external rules then increase the flexibility of matching, since there is a broader repertoire of rules to select from. For example, if the main strategic behaviour of the MNC is to repeat established organizational routines between markets, it might be possible to find an external set of basic rules that matches the internal basic rules and ensuing organizational routines.

Cognitive structures

This institutional dimension develops the identity system or the structures of the mind. Every institution is a '… thought world, expressed in its own thought style, penetrating the minds of its members, defining their experience, and setting the poles of their moral understanding' (Douglas, 1986, p. 128).

The members of a collective share thoughts, make classifications and label reality in common. So cognitive structures and activities concern how strategists in MNCs think, why they think in common, the way they do it and what talk, decisions and actions result from this thinking. An MNC may even, because of its multicultural basis, be seen as an institution consisting of many thought worlds, where cognitive systems tend to vary between its various units. Cultural models that deal with cognitive aspects can be used to describe the different thought worlds, for example Hofstede's world view model (see below). To understand the various methods of strategic decision-making and organization prevalent in the MNC, it is necessary to know how employees categorize their behaviour, create order in their life and give life meaning. We need to know the programmes they use and their frames of reference, since they work as guidelines for sense-making and choosing meaningful actions. For the same reason it is also interesting to know how decisions are made: the rules of thumb or heuristics used, the logic behind them, for example as noticed in the categorizations and classifications that could be expressed as cognitive maps and themes. These concepts express established patterns of thinking and work as cognitive recipes for how people behave. Thus, from a cognitive point of view, institutions can be defined as established patterns of thinking or thought styles, which produce a self-activated regular organizational behaviour. Since these established patterns are reproduced over time, present-day thought styles can be seen as the crystallization of history into the minds of people.

Economic man

A critical thought style in MNCs concerns how decision-makers in various parts of the global organization think, for example how rational or logical they are. An extreme form of cognitive rationality is found in economics, mainly summarized in the ideal type 'economic man' (homo oeconomicus). This person is very able and perfect in many ways, especially at making calculations. He or she ('ze') is a perfectly rational and emotion-free individual who has complete information on all possible choices and who has the capacity to calculate and select the best alternative, that is, to maximize and even optimize. The values and norms behind this rationality were already developed in the 16th and 17th centuries by the mercantilists, and by the early economists in the 18th century, for example Adam Smith, and were finalized at the end of the 19th century in discussions on the emerging consumer society. This highly stylized thought world is more or less isolated from society. The roots of economic man are radical individualism or social atomism. Individuals are defined as independent, anonymous and individual market actors, acting only on price information. Society is based on values of selfishness or egoism, which is another value characteristic of economic man, for example expressed in economic theory in the utility-maximizing consumer. Behaviour is regulated by economic incentives and sanctions; that is, enforcement mechanisms are purely economical in kind. Another central guiding principle is that the individual is free to choose his or her own actions irrespective of background (e.g. group belongingness), thus being removed from his or her social background. Economic man has supremacy, since society is to be organized in such a way as to make this superrational economic behaviour possible. For example, another value premise is that the state should stay in the background and act as a 'night watch'.

This ideal representation of a completely rational decision-maker expressed as economic man is the foundation of the efficiency orientation of mainstream economics. However, it is too far from reality. This is a much undersocialized conception of man. Individuals do not have any social relations and are not part of any institutional context. Looking at decision-makers in a more realistic way, individuals have a more limited cognitive capacity and their rationality is bounded. Different ways for how people think when making economic decisions have been suggested, these ways mainly involving different forms of rules of thumb or heuristics. One decision routine emphasizes a satisfying behaviour rather than a maximizing behaviour, where a limited number of alternatives are searched for, evaluated and decided on in specific ways (Cyert and March, 1963).

Examples of a number of empirically based rules of thumb that are found include:
- People tend to look for information that supports a certain line of reasoning rather than for information that goes against it.
- People tend to simplify by overlooking what is remote in time and space.
- Acts of simplification are influenced by social norms and individual aspirations, perceptions and experiences (Sjöstrand, 1997, pp. 50–52).

Thus, these imperfect but more realistic 'logics-in-use' make the classical cognitive rationality represented by economic man rather unpractical. Still, these logics or heuristics are more realistic variants of this ideal rationality. They are defined as the logic of consequentiality in Chapter 5.

These negative and pessimistic assumptions about people are also valid in modern variants of economic theory. A later form of 'economic man' based on the same economic fundament is the 'contractual man', on whom transaction cost theory and agency theory are based. Here, man is not only egoistic but also deceitful and opportunistic. Therefore, control of individuals becomes the key issue in markets and firms, either by punishing them or by rewarding them. Transaction cost theory stresses the former aspect, that is, the importance of authority (fiat), the staff being tightly monitored and controlled (Williamson, 1975, 1985, 1991; see also Appendix). Agency theory stresses the latter part, that is, incentives, for example by making large stock options an important part of managers' compensation. Thus, as in most economic theory, enforcement mechanisms are pinpointed.

World views

How organizational decision-making is related to the social context can be better understood through using cultural theory. By studying theories that deal specifically with world views, the cognitive structure can be developed into a thought style. It is a question of finding the main informal rules expressed in the cultural theory. Hofstede (2001, pp. 9–10) defines culture as '… the collective programming of the mind that distinguishes the members of one group or category of people from another … mind stands for the head, heart, and hand – that is, for thinking, feeling, and acting, with consequences for beliefs, attitudes, and skills'. Thus, the people of a certain nation tend to behave in a common way due to the specific mental programme developed there. This is evidently a specification of culture as a cognitive system, or thought style. Values and norms are also included, since most mental programmes carry a value component. Values, or societal norms as they are also called, are seen as the major factor influencing mental programmes. Hofstede's work (1980, 2001) is a rich source of material for describing the major thought styles of several nations, including many emerging markets. The five dimensions of national culture are based on a number of aspects of a national cognitive system such as assumptions, views, preferences, themes, meanings, beliefs, attitudes, frames of reference, knowledge and skills:

- *Individualism* versus *collectivism* relates to people's self-concept, 'I' or 'we', and their preference for a loosely knit or tightly knit social framework.
- Large versus small *power distance* relates to how people view and accept unequally distributed power in society.
- Strong versus weak *uncertainty avoidance* stands for people's beliefs about uncertainty and ambiguity. Strong uncertainty avoidance leads to beliefs promising certainty and to organizations protecting conformity.
- *Long-term* versus *short-term orientation* relates to the choice of focus for people's efforts: the future or the present.
- *Masculinity* versus *feminity*, where, according to Hofstede (1994, p. 84):
  Masculinity stands for a preference in society for achievement, heroism, assertiveness, and material success. Its opposite, feminity, stands for a preference for relationships, modesty, caring for the weak, and the quality of life. This fundamental issue addressed by this dimension is the way in which a society allocates social (as opposed to biological) roles to the sexes.

Even though Hofstede's theory integrates mental programmes with values and norms, the theory is mainly cognitive. As a consequence, these five dimensions can be used to develop the thought styles of an institution.

Another useful cognitive cultural theory to specify the thought styles is found in Redding (1980). The six cognitive dimensions are as follows:

- *Self* concerns how people mentally relate to their social environment, for example if they look on themselves as belonging to groups or not. This dimension is close to Hofstede's individualism/collectivism dichotomy.
- *Morality* has to do with views on what is right or wrong, good or bad, and virtues, for example.
- *Work* concerns people's beliefs about their work, mainly expressed as a work ethic.
- *Causality* is a dimension that directly focuses on the mental process itself, for example whether the thought style is abstract or non-abstract, whether logical connections are made between categories, and whether linear, sequential explanations are made.
- *Probability* concerns how people mentally relate to the fact that the future is unknown, for example whether the future can be calculated or whether fatalism prevails. This cultural dimension is similar to Hofstede's uncertainty avoidance dimension.
- *Time* is about how people perceive time, whether it is monochromatic or linear, for example whether it is possible to divide up and measure time in a precise way. For example, the linear Western time perception is different from the Oriental circular time perception. Hofstede's fifth dimension – long-term versus short-term orientation – is related to this time theme.

A major conclusion from above is that human decision-makers are not removed from their economic and social background, but are part of it; that is, economic decisions are embedded in social relationships and institutional contexts. Strategic decision-making is then influenced not only by how people view the world and how they think, but also by the values they have and the roles they play.

Norms and values also influence how people think, and decisions, too, are influenced by these basic rules. For 'economic man' this influence is assumed away. Organizational behaviour is therefore also shaped by social factors such as the expectations created by norms and values. As noted above, the identity system cannot be understood without relating it to the social system, and vice versa.

Normative structures

Norms and values constitute rules '… that stipulate expectations for behaviour that are both internalized by actors and reinforced by the beliefs and actions of those with whom they interact' (Scott, 1994, p. 67). Structures and organizational routines are then infused and prescribed by normative structures such as values and norms.

Norms

Norms are specific normative rules or general expectations about a certain behaviour that are at least partially shared by a group of decision-makers (Heide and John, 1992). They work as guiding principles for how to act, a kind of decree about how one should act or how something should be constituted or organized. Norms can therefore be seen as the normal or acceptable behaviour in a social group, a convention or praxis. A system of norms is the normal pattern to which individual behaviour should conform. Thus, norms are a specific type of rule: a normative rule.

Values

Values are more generalized ideological justifications for norms and roles. Both norms and values then work as prescriptions or normative constraints for acting. Since such normative constraints are means of realizing states that are highly valued by the social group favouring them, norms are closely related to values and thus may be difficult to separate. Values also work as guiding principles and are therefore a normative rule as well. But values are more generalized ideological justifications for norms, that is, values are more abstract and have a wider applicability. They mean infusing the organization with value, for example by inculcating values in individuals. Such standards do not only involve broad goals like missions and other priorities, but also form the major part of the company culture in general, for example as core values. Values are at the root of cultures and behaviour. Important business values include hard work, honesty, self-discipline, financial success, and working towards common goals, personal achievement, creativity and respect for learning. Values are defined as '… conceptions of the preferred or the desirable together with the construction of standards to which existing structures or behaviour can be compared and assessed. This institutional factor sets the priorities. Norms specify how things should be done; they legitimate means to pursue valued ends' (Scott, 1995, p. 37).

Hofstede (2001) reserves values for mental programmes that are relatively unspecific, while the terms 'attitudes' and 'beliefs' are used for more specific 'mental software'. Values are defined as feelings with arrows to them, each having a plus and a minus pole, and exemplified in the following way:

- Evil versus good
- Dirty versus clean

- Dangerous versus safe
- Decent versus indecent
- Ugly versus beautiful
- Unnatural versus natural
- Abnormal versus normal
- Paradoxical versus logical
- Irrational versus rational
- Moral versus immoral.

A broad rule of one type is thus contrasted to its opposite. From this discussion it follows that values can be seen to take the form of dilemmas.

Regulative structures

Values and norms expressed as priorities specify the actions that a set of individuals regards as correct or incorrect, according to which they are expected to decide and act. But such normative rules do not specify what happens if expectations based on them do not materialize, that is, if behaviour that is supposed to follow on from the norms does not take place. So for behaviour to be effective in organizations, incentives and sanctions must also be present. The regulative aspect focuses directly on the sanctions and incentives in connection with the execution of rules: the enforcement mechanisms. So organizational behaviour is also controlled by various types of explicit regulations, and the way behaviour is monitored. Specific enforcement rules are set. Hence in addition to the explicit rewards and punishments, these formal enforcement mechanisms involve controls over behaviour such as measures for surveillance and assessment, and their application to reward conformity and punish deviance (Scott, 1994, p. 67). As mentioned above, this regulative dimension is stressed in organizational economics literature, which mostly has negative assumptions about man and therefore is biased towards issues of control.

Another important aspect of institutions, therefore, is that they produce economic and social control through direct regulation. A multitude of such explicit regulations exist in an MNC, for example specific incentives and sanctions used to achieve various performance goals.

Control infrastructure

As discussed above, the basic rules represented in Figure 11.2 constrain and give opportunities for individual strategic behaviour and organizational routines. This implies that the MNC is viewed as a control infrastructure, where thought styles, values, norms and enforcement mechanisms are defined as the four basic types of formal and informal rules. Organizational routines, cultures and structures are therefore governed by being framed, infused with value, prescribed and explicitly regulated by enforcement mechanisms. Enforcement mechanisms that operate as explicit controls have a direct effect on behaviour. Thought styles, values and norms, on the other hand, are mostly informal and work more as implicit controls, and therefore have a more indirect influence on strategic behaviour.

Together these four basic types of rules constitute a specific institutional framework within which individuals operate, and which opens up opportunities for action as well as restricting them. This institutional framework provides 'structures which individuals can reinforce, trespass upon or violate' (Sjöstrand, 1997, p. 77). The institutional setting does not entirely define actions by individuals; there is some freedom of action or agency. The main idea is that this infrastructure stabilizes strategic behaviour by reducing uncertainty. Common values are shared by a group of people, for example, which creates habitual group behaviour in accordance with these values. Thus collective strategic behaviour in MNCs and interacting organizations is characterized as a patterned behaviour, for example organizational routines. These routines are learned regular and predictable patterns of activity, made up of a sequence of coordinated actions by individuals (Grant, 1998/2002). The degree of institutionalization or routinization of this organizational behaviour varies with the different characters of the four basic rules.

As found in Chapter 6 and illustrated in Figure 6.2 and 6.3., the institutional controls can from a strategic perspective be seen as organizational capabilities.

CONCLUSIONS

The institutional view is laid out in this chapter as one fundament of the institutional network approach to international business strategy. The institutional view captures the major characteristics of the external context of emerging markets and the MNCs operating there: the embeddedness of groupings at different societal levels and how they are related. Institutions are carried over by being learned, consciously or unconsciously. An institutional arrangement is chosen and, as a consequence, mediated through participation. Institutions therefore constitute a behavioural repertoire. They standardize behaviour and transfer rules, norms and ways of thinking between individuals. These factors make institutions excellent instruments for describing, explaining and predicting actual organizational behaviour, thereby reducing uncertainty and risks in international business strategy.

This institutional perspective is made concrete through the basic institutions model. It consists of the MNC, four major meso institutions and a number of societal sectors. IBS is influenced by institutional factors within the MNC (the internal institutional setting) and by the rules of outside institutions (the external institutional setting). This institutional world is divided into three layers: micro institutions, meso institutions and macro institutions. It is looked at from the perspective of one institution – the MNC and its international business strategy – which is integrated into this institutional context, mainly being seen as a product of its internal and external environments. The influencing societal organizations are segmented into organizational fields and societal sectors.

The basic rules model is delineated to analyse the various types of institutions of the basic institutions model. It consists of thought styles, values, norms and enforcement mechanisms. An MNC is an organization consisting of many thought worlds, where cognitive structures vary between various units. Those employees sharing thoughts, making classifications and labelling reality in common have a unified thought style. These established patterns of thinking work as cognitive recipes for how people behave. Norms and values also influence how people think and act. Values are at the root of cultures and behaviour, working as standards for comparison. They set the priorities and function as guiding principles. Norms specify how things should be done. They work as guiding principles for how to act, a kind of decree about how one should act or how something should be constituted or organized. Organizational behaviour is also controlled by enforcement mechanisms. They concern how to construct the sanction and incentive system in order to reward or punish individuals and groups within the MNC, together with establishing surveillance and assessment systems to control its enforcement.

12
Analysing external institutional contexts

The paramount importance of the external environment to international business strategy (IBS) makes it necessary to establish a procedure to analyse and handle it, being especially relevant for the diverse and dynamic business environment of emerging markets. As introduced in Chapter 1, uncertainty can be coped with through either reducing or absorbing complexity (Child, 2001, p. 704). A classical way to reduce complexity is to improve decision-making by collecting information about the environment. This is an essential part of the rational decision-making praxis that was defined in Chapter 5 as the logic of consequentially and which is typical of the efficiency-based rationality. Since it is limited to economic data and information search in the market, it needs to be complemented by analytical procedures that also include the social environment.

The focus of the analytical procedure developed in this chapter is therefore on the logic of appropriateness, which is decision-making related to the social environment within which economic resource selection decisions are embedded. The major purpose is to identify and analyse strategic change situations. A broader and more holistic approach is then taken towards strategy and what influences it. It is a question of developing the ability to interpret environmental factors to understand the complexity and how to deal with it. For example, social networks are important for gaining access to information, enacting the environment through influencing it, and for getting early warning signals in order to be able to respond quickly to new developments.

Environmental analysis of emerging markets is seen as an organizational issue, being about organizing the analytical procedure so that complexity is reduced at the same as strategic flexibility is maintained to absorb complexity. The network institutional approach (NIA) is applied to the analysis of the external context. The institutional view provides an appropriate base for how to interpret external factors, while the network perspective is suitable when collecting information and for influencing it. In the latter case, it is necessary to have first-hand knowledge of environmental developments and suitable partners to network with, which is achieved through scanning and analysing the market environment. An example was given in Chapter 9 of an intelligence network used to scan the environment in the network marketing of projects, mainly done by the tracking team, and used by the screening and capture teams.

The environment is viewed to consist of a number of rule systems in accordance with the institutional models developed in Chapter 11. To be able to combine the strategies for handling environmental complexity in the right way to increase predictability and reduce strategic reaction time, the analysis of the external institutional setting is critical. An institutional view is assumed to make the environment more intelligible and predictable by looking at it in a uniform way, that is, focusing on the rules governing strategy. As shown in Chapter 11, this view provides the decision-maker with models to analyse, understand and predict the environment better from a strategic perspective. According to the basic institutions model (see Figure 11.1), for example, the environment is first divided into organizational fields and societal sectors, which largely corresponds to a division between task environment or operational environment and remote environment normally made in organization literature and followed in literature on environmental scanning (e.g. Stoffels, 1994). By breaking down these parts into smaller units, a basic model of the external environment is established. However, the specific breakdown illustrated in this figure is only one of several ways to specify the model. The division among organizational fields and societal sectors can be done in different ways, depending on the strategic situation of the multinational corporation (MNC) being analysed. It can be used, for example, to decide the size of the focal zone for each field and sector. The size of such a zone is determined by the quantity of resources the MNC commits to the scanning of each segment (ibid.).

INTERPRETING AND UNDERSTANDING EXTERNAL ENVIRONMENTS

A main purpose is to solve the strategic issue of the information paradox encountered in decisions on international business strategy matters in emerging markets, namely that there is an overload of information at the same time as information is lacking. This paradox is about the difference between information and knowledge. Numerous data are available on the web and through other channels. But they are often hard to interpret, since too little is known about the origin of the data and the context behind it, for example structural factors like country culture and political systems.

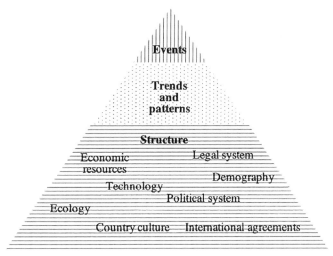

Source: Based on Van der Heijden (1996).

Figure 12.1 The 'iceberg'

This point is illustrated with the help of the 'iceberg' model illustrated in Figure 12.1 (Van der Heijden, 1996).

Knowledge about the environment is broken down into three categories: events, trends and patterns, and structure. The events are found at the tip of the iceberg, visible above the surface, and include information about companies and governments in different media. To place events into context in order to know more about them, underlying patterns and trends need to be investigated. Events do not happen at random but are related to each other through an underlying structure of connections between pieces of information, mainly of a cause and effect type. Behind the patterns are found certain structures, such as culture, policy, power distribution, regulation and technology. Generally, one can say that while newspapers and TV/radio mostly report on events, weekly news-magazines mainly report on trends and patterns and to some extent on structures. Sometimes there are special issues that go deeper into developments and problems by analysing trends and patterns in a certain field. However, since the structures behind the analysis are mostly not known from such data sources, one usually needs to read science-based articles that penetrate issues more deeply. Information produced is thus biased due to having been stripped of context consisting of structures such as culture and government policy. This makes data less intelligible for information consumers, especially for those from other cultures and societies. The problem is that this influence is not directly obvious from the information but is hidden behind the information. When collecting secondary information, for example, this bias is not seen directly from the information itself, because it has become detached from the underlying structures. The biased information is there, but not the producers influenced by certain structures. The interpretive process developed here is an attempt to re-establish this link between producer and information by analysing the structural background of the information, using a scientific approach.

THE INSTITUTIONAL VIEW OF ENVIRONMENTAL ANALYSIS

Applying the institutional view on environmental analysis makes it possible to uncover the societal origin of information. By learning about the institutional origin of information, the codes are unlocked to understand it. Tools are created from societal theory, mainly institutional theory. The idea behind this approach is that it is not possible to understand information about events in societies without a theory about how societies work, in this case based on institutional theory. The focus of this chapter then is on analysing and interpreting data rather than on collecting and compiling information. Models concentrating on environmental scanning are therefore only taken up briefly, since they are oriented too much towards data technical matters such as modes for collecting and sorting information as well as organizing databases, for example those methods and models dealing with management information systems, information technology, environmental scanning and business intelligence issues (e.g. Frankelius, 2001; Stoffels, 1994).

According to the scheme of environmental analysis developed by Fahey and Narayanan (1986), for example, the focus of this book is on the assessment stage rather than on the scanning, and monitoring stages. Knowledge is created through analysis. Institutional models are used to find patterns in the external environment of relevance to IBS and to analyse the structural factors behind these patterns. The institutional view makes it possible to develop a more coherent, penetrative and analytical method for IBS analysis than found in most textbooks on international business, marketing and management. Moreover, the institutional view goes both deeper and wider into the external environment than is the case in the literature on environmental scanning.

To reduce the high complexity of emerging markets or absorb it, a penetrative analysis needs to be made of not only the proximate market environment, but also of the wider environment outside the markets. The highly biased information on environmental factors in emerging markets can then only be understood through careful analysis. The tip of the iceberg is both less visible and harder to make sense of.

The analysis of the environment starts with the basic institutions model (Figure 11.1), which is examined further with the help of the basic rules model (Figure 11.2). Therefore, this chapter further develops the institutional view, inter alia by giving several examples of what is meant by institutions in an international business context. The institutions influencing the IBS are analysed at two main levels of description: organization fields in the inner rectangle and societal sectors in the outer rectangle. These levels correspond to the meso and macro environment used in environmental analysis in many strategy and marketing textbooks as well as being similar to proximate and background institutions (Whitley, 1992a, b). The purpose of the analysis of the external strategic environment of this chapter is then to identify, describe and analyse how and why the institutions in the two rectangles influence the IBS.

ANALYTICAL PROCEDURE

A distinction is made between two modes and three stages of analysing the external environment of the MNC in accordance with the institutional view.

Modes for approaching the external environment

Initially, it is necessary to choose a perspective from which to approach the external environment: the inside-out mode or the outside-in mode. The inside-out mode starts with the MNC and then moves in a stepwise manner further and further away from the company, that is, first doing the inner rectangle and then the outer rectangle. The outside-in mode also starts with the MNC, but then moves directly to the outer rectangle, from where the analysis of the environment moves closer and closer to the MNC. These two modes are normally combined, as the researcher iteratively moves back and forth between the three rectangles. The analysis can also start in the second rectangle or in the third rectangle.

The procedure followed depends upon the research object for which the environmental analysis is being done, that is, the unit placed in the centre rectangle, for example a specific MNC, a group of MNCs (e.g. the total foreign direct investment in a country), a specific industry or combination of industries, or a specific economic sector. Here, the individual MNC is located in the inner rectangle.

Stages of analysis

The analytical procedure is divided into three stages:

1. The identification stage
2. The explanation stage
3. The prediction stage.

In the identification stage, the environment is first scanned and monitored for institutions that might impact the IBS. The institutions found are then evaluated by making an institutional analysis, mainly by using the basic rules model (Figure 11.2) to describe them in more detail. The focus in this stage is then on the relation between individual institutions and the MNC. In the explanation stage, the focus is shifted to the system of institutions by analysing how the identified institutions influence one another and the MNC. In the prediction stage, the focus is on whether the system of institutions found for the MNC in the explanation stage is also relevant in the future. The reproduction of these institutions into the future is analysed.

Since the emphasis in these stages is on analysis, the main purpose is to find models that are useful for identification, explanation and prediction. Compared to most other types of environmental analysis, the procedure proposed involves a more thorough analysis of the environment. For example, an advantage of using an institutional approach lies in a deeper analysis of the identification stage by being able to focus directly on relevant environmental factors. Especially, this approach provides the researcher with a coherent theoretical base for carrying out environmental scanning, monitoring and analysis. Moreover, the institutional view does not preclude the use of analytical models that are not based on institutional theory, provided that they improve the environmental analysis.

A common characteristic of institutions is that they concern the fundaments of society. Since institutions are reproduced over time and usually persist over long periods, it is important to study the history of an institution in order to know how it works.

IDENTIFYING INSTITUTIONS

The scanning for potential institutions mainly follows the outside-in mode. The environment is first scanned for factors that might qualify as institutions for the particular strategic situation under investigation. Next, the institutions discovered are penetrated more fully to study their potential relevance. This is done by using institutional theory to dress them up as institutions.

Discovery

To make it easier to discover relevant institutions, a number of potentially useful models are suggested, namely the basic institutions model, the PEST and STEP models, and Terpstra's model.

The basic institutions model

From the point of view of environmental analysis, the basic institutions model (see Figure 11.1) provides a list of potentially relevant institutions, or suggestions for institutions that might be of relevance for a specific strategic situation of the particular MNC. But other factors in the environment related to the international business strategy could also be potential institutions. It might therefore be possible to find other models in the literature than the basic institutions model that propose environmental factors that qualify as relevant institutions. The PEST model is such a common model on the macro environment.

The PEST model

The Political, Economic, Social and Technological environment (PEST) model is widely used to describe the macro environment surrounding a firm (Fahey and Narayanan, 1986). It decomposes the relevant environment into four segments:

- The political segment deals with political progress in a society, and the regulatory framework that shapes codes of conduct.
- The economic segment concentrates on the general set of economic factors and conditions that confront all industries in a society.
- The social segment focuses on demographics, lifestyles and social values. The purpose of the analysis is to understand shifts in population characteristics, the emergence of new lifestyles, or changes in social values.
- The technological segment is concerned with the technological advancements taking place. New products, processes, materials, scientific activity and advances in fundamental science are the key concerns in this area.

The PEST model is seen as a guide to which segments to investigate and what the potential linkages are. It is mainly helpful in the identification stage, mainly for discovering potential institutions, but also as a background for translating environmental factors into institutions. It is also of some help in the explanation and prediction stages, as Fahey and Narayanan (1986) discuss the way the PEST segments are inter-related and propose a model for how to integrate them. However, this model is mainly descriptive by suggesting what the linkages between factors within segments and between segments may look like. Therefore, it only gives hints for the explanation and prediction stages. Due to its lack of theoretical foundation, this model cannot replace institutional analysis of the environment to find out how segments influence each other and the MNC.

Another similar model used for general environmental analysis is the STEP model. The same parts of society are taken up, only in another order: the social, technological, economic and political environments. This model is less useful than the PEST model, as it is more descriptive and offers less guidance on how to analyse linkages between factors and the ways they might change. Therefore, it is mostly helpful in discovering institutions.

Terpstra's model

Certain cultural models can also be used for the identification of potential institutional dimensions.

When culture, as in Terpstra and David's (1985) model, is viewed as encompassing every aspect of society, the similarities between seeing society from a cultural or an institutional perspective become more apparent. According to this model, culture is thought of as being able to transmit the entire social part of the repertoire of human action and its products as opposed to the genetically transmitted part. Society is divided into the following parts:

- Law (e.g. common law, code law, international law, antitrust policy, regulations).
- Politics (e.g. nationalism, sovereignty, power, national interests, ideologies, political risk).
- Technology and material culture (e.g. transportation, energy systems, tools and objects, communications, urbanization, science, invention).
- Social organization (e.g. kinship, social institutions, authority structures, interest groups, social mobility, social stratification, status systems).
- Education (e.g. formal education, vocational training, primary education, secondary education, higher education, literacy level, human resource planning).
- Values and attitudes (e.g. towards time, achievement, work, wealth, change, scientific methods, risk taking).
- Religion (e.g. sacred objects, philosophical systems, beliefs and norms, prayer, taboos, holidays, rituals).
- Language (e.g. written language, official language, linguistic pluralism, language hierarchy, international languages, mass media).

Because of the similarity between this model and the NIA, Terpstra's model may help to identify institutions in more detail, even giving clues for the explanation and prediction stages regarding how institutions found in the third rectangle influence one another and influence institutions closer to the MNC. However, because of its highly descriptive nature and strong similarity to the PEST and STEP models, it is mainly useful for discovering institutions, and for being able to provide a good base for describing them.

Description

The result of the first phase of the identification stage is the ascertaining of a number of relevant candidates for institutions with the potential to influence the IBS. They are already cast in a certain descriptive language, inter alia being labelled and described in a specific way, for example as country culture, family, and political system. Next, they need to be transformed into institutions by being translated into institutional conceptual language. As seen in previous chapters, institutions are commonly viewed as rule systems. North (1990), for example, defines institutions as the rules of the game in society or as constraints created by humans, which facilitate economic and political interaction. He makes a distinction between formal rules and informal rules, where the former include political and judicial rules, economic rules and contracts:

> Political rules broadly define the hierarchical structure of the polity, its basic decision structure, and the explicit characteristics of agenda control. Economic rules define property

rights, i.e. the bundle of rights over the use and the income to be derived from property and the ability to alienate an asset or a resource. Contracts contain the provisions specific to a particular agreement in exchange. (North, 1990, p. 47)

Informal rules are broadly viewed as including codes of conduct, norms of behaviour and conventions. These 'are part of the heritage that we call culture' (North, 1990, p. 37). Thus rules, inter alia consisting of norms and values, are a broad social concept expressing constraints on many aspects of human behaviour.

This rules aspect of institutions is developed further from this division into formal and informal rules. The main purpose is to describe the rules of the potential institutional candidates that relate to the IBS of the MNC under study, either by influencing the MNC or by being influenced by the MNC. The most relevant rules can be found in the following way.

Specifying relevant formal rules

A first step is to study whether the rules inherent in an institution become norms for the actors for which the rules are relevant. For example, for the legal system this could be achieved by studying the formal rules written in documents, such as how they are expressed in law books, statute books and decrees. If these formal rules are found to lead to expected behaviour, they are contextualized by describing the relevant context of the rules, for example the various courts of the legal system and how they are related. Since this has already been done to some extent in discovering institutions, this information can now be reworked and recast in a new form, specifying it as a rule to be followed. Usually supplementary information needs to be collected to get a more complete picture of the rule situation and how it evolved, for example how the rule has been enforced in one case compared to another.

Specifying relevant informal rules

If the written formal rules, viewed as laws in the current example, are not enforced, the analysis could be extended to understand why the intended conduct of the rule does not occur. The reason may be that there are other rules behind this conduct. For example, the conduct of the courts could be investigated, whether they are clogged up, or how lawsuits are filed and processed regarding a specific case such as the violation of property rights. The difference between the laws and this conduct is analysed to find out why the written formal rules are not followed. The focus is on the informal rules, for example the thought styles of the court members, or the norms and values behind the conduct.

This extended analysis involving the basic rules may also be done even if courts rule according to the law. There are many instances where one wants to have a deeper understanding of how an institution works. Some more examples are given in illustration A below.

Illustration A: the institutional dimensions of legal systems

Michael Backman, in his book *Asian Eclipse* from 1999 (pp. 11–14), gives an interesting description of major differences in the mix of formal and informal rules between Asian and Western legal systems, as shown by this extraction from the book:

The hierarchical order stressed by Confucianism tends to mean that many in Asia view power and authority as indivisible and immutable. The notion of 'natural' rights in the Western liberal tradition is foreign to the Confucian way. That the West could even suggest a viable alternative route is likely to be dismissed out of hand. The hierarchy reaches all the way up to one source of power; not several. There is an emperor. This indivisibility of power leaves little room for suggestions from the West. They might be listened to politely, after which the protagonists in Asia carry on regardless.

'Rule of law' is replaced by 'rule by law'. There are no constant truths. The law is used as a tool for whatever the ruler's objectives are; it isn't an end in itself. Tightly worded laws written at one time might not have validity in another time or context, so they are often deliberately vaguely worded to allow for discretion and reinterpretation. The separation of the judiciary from the government makes little sense in such an environment, so usually there isn't even the pretence of such a separation. Rather than be independent of government, the judiciary is an arm of it.

The ruler creates the rules but isn't bound by them. Those who can claim to be the agents of the ruler are also often not bound by the rules. This is one reason why corruption and patronage at senior levels is so pervasive in many Asian countries.

The reliance not so much on all-pervasive laws but on the arbitrary edicts of the ruler means that individuals tend to be utterly obedient when they are in the direct line of fire of the ruler and his agents, but very pragmatic when they are away from it.

If laws aren't fixed, then what role do contracts play? Obviously not a very precise one. Just like the emperor not wanting to share power with formal laws, many Asian business people don't want to share power with a contract. Contracts, after all, constrain flexibility. The more vague their terms, the greater the probability that they will be accepted. In most Asian countries, contracts are seen as more guiding than binding.

In the West, contracts, like laws, remain fixed with the passage of time. In Asia, they tend to relate to the prevailing conditions at the time.

The adversarial nature of Western-style legal systems is more of an affront to traditional 'Asian' ways rather than a complement to them. The very nature of contracts themselves is something of an affront – even in the relatively sophisticated economy of Japan. Complicated clauses that spell out punitive measures of various contingencies are laden with an underlying message of distrust. In the West, they are regarded more as a formality. In Asia, they represent a ceding of control.

Markets are usually looked at in a more technical sense or as a formal rule system; however, they can also be described as an informal rule system by viewing them as belief systems, stressing the cognitive dimension. An industry can be looked upon as a cognitive field consisting of a distinctive corporate language, constructs and frameworks that guide member organizations. The specific activities and forms of the industry are then assumed to be ruled by this mental structure of the industry expressed as shared beliefs about the competitive rules of the game and the structural freedom of action within the industry.

Translating cultural dimensions into institutional dimensions

According to the institutional view, culture is thus seen as an assembly of informal rules. This informal rule character of culture is demonstrated by the following quotation on a common way to describe organizational culture:

> As individuals come into contact with organisations, they come in contact with dress norms, stories people tell about what goes on, the organisation's formal rules and procedures, its informal codes of behaviour, rituals, tasks, pay systems, jargon and jokes only understood by insiders, and so on. These elements are some of the manifestations of organisational culture. When cultural members interpret the meanings of these manifestations, their perceptions, memories, beliefs, experiences, and values will vary, so interpretations will differ – even of the same phenomenon. The patterns of configurations of these interpretations, and the ways they are enacted, constitute culture. (Martin, 1992, p. 3)

This quotation gives a more detailed description of organizations, taking up several relevant features that can be viewed as informal rules valid for the organization. The description comes very close to an institutional description of organizational phenomena, and is therefore easy to translate into an institutional conceptual language and fit into institutional models. Thus the strong similarity between cultural theory and institutional theory makes cultural models useful when describing and analysing organizational fields and societal sectors in more detail. As is evident from the last part of the quotation, the description mainly takes up aspects belonging to the cognitive dimension, that is, the organization as a belief and meaning system. Culture is often a principal factor in institutional theory, for example being seen as a main carrier of institutions by Scott (1995). Note that the analysis still takes place outside the MNC and the centre rectangle, where companies are found in groups in organizational fields.

There are a number of models that may be of help in this process of describing institutions as informal rule systems, making it possible to penetrate institutions further by supplying thick descriptions of institutional dimensions. These models may give insights into how to classify an institution after preliminary discovery, and how to further describe it as an institution. Cultural models are particularly useful when developing the normative and cognitive aspects of an organizational field or societal sector. This is evident when culture forms a societal sector of its own, for example country culture.

The distinction between organizational fields and societal sectors is important to keep in mind when deciding on the type of cultural model to use. A prerequisite is that cultural dimensions and institutional dimensions are comparable in that they describe society in a similar way, mainly for groups at the same societal level. Hofstede (2001) distinguishes between three levels: national culture at the macro level, organizational culture at the micro level and occupational culture at the meso level. Thus, one has to be careful when using cultural theory, since it could be unclear for which societal level a theory is valid. Generally, it can be noted that for the organizational fields, organization culture models are useful, while country culture models are relevant for the societal sectors.

A main conclusion from the previous discussion of institutions is that there are many similarities between cultural and institutional theories, and therefore cultural models can be used in institutional analysis, for example to develop the informal rules. Judging from the literature, institutions and culture relate to each other in different ways. This discussion is strikingly similar to the discussion in Chapter 11 (structures of society and mind) between anthropologists and sociologists about the distinction between culture and social structure and how they are related. First, there are cases where the definitions of culture and institutions (or social structure in this other discussion) more or less coincide. This was exemplified above in discussing Terpstra's model, where culture is defined in such a broad way that it becomes similar to the definition of institutions. Second, culture is a factor of institutional theory, thereby being defined as a major institution. This definition of culture is found in Scott (1995) and means that culture can be included as a factor in institutional theory, being seen as a carrier of institutions. Third, culture and institutions (or social structure) are different social phenomena. These relations between culture and institutions are important to consider when cultural models are used as part of institutional analysis. When the first relation is present, the cultural model needs to be redefined as an institutional model. This is easily done, since there is a strong similarity between the definitions. According to the second relation, they are already integrated, since culture is an institution. Hence, there is no need to translate cultural dimensions into institutional dimensions. In the third case, where culture and institutions are defined as being different, culture needs to be redefined in order to become an institution, which is exemplified next.

Hofstede (1983, p. 76) views institutions as a consequence of culture:

> Within a nation or a part of it, culture changes only slowly. This is the more so because what is in the minds of the people has also become crystallized in the institutions mentioned earlier: government, legal system, educational systems, industrial relations systems, family structures, religious organizations, sports clubs, settlement patterns, literature, architecture, and even scientific theories. All these reflect traditions and common ways of thinking on which they are based.

Even though Hofstede (2001) distinguishes between culture and institutions, he considers 'the institutions-versus-culture dilemma' to be a non-issue. Societal norms or values shape institutions, which in their turn reinforce the societal norms. 'They are the chicken and the egg. Institutions reflect minds and vice versa' (ibid., p. 20). Culture is mainly defined at the national level as a general factor that lies behind institutions, and it is reflected in them, for example as the organizational culture of a company.

In this book, where culture is viewed as a rule system, it is a question of finding the main informal rules expressed in cultural theory. As shown in Chapter 11, some basic informal rule systems have been distinguished, namely values, norms, thought styles and enforcement mechanisms. Even though Hofstede's theory, as was found in this chapter, integrates mental programmes with values and norms, the theory is mainly cognitive. As a consequence, these five dimensions can be used to develop the thought styles of an institution. Another cognitive theory presented in that chapter – Redding's – can also be used for such a purpose. Which one to choose depends on the problem in hand.

Illustration B: the informal rules of the Chinese business network

This selection problem is now illustrated using research done on Chinese small firms (Jansson, 1987; Jansson et al., 2007; Jansson and Söderman, 2015). To explain the networking conduct of these firms the basic rules model (Figure 11.2) is used. The cognitive informal rules are specified based on Chapter 11, that is, Redding's six cultural dimensions (1980), and the normative informal rules based on Hampden-Turner and Trompenaars (2000). The enforcement mechanisms are also included. They are specified according to Whitley's theory (1992a), which is taken up below under the explanation stage.

These informal basic rules and their subrules behind how the Chinese business network works are illustrated in Figure 12.2 based on the research of these networks in China (Jansson and Sandberg, 2014). This research is based on studies of the cultural roots of the Chinese society, mainly Confucianism, for example Hofstede and Bond (1988) and Redding (1990), summarized in Drew and Jansson (2014). A classical study is found in Pye (1985) of Asian politics based on treating Confucianism and other Asian philosophies as political ideology.

Thought styles. The logic of Chinese network marketing is defined as the logic of symmetry. The major reason is that Taoism constitutes the foundation of the strategic thinking of Chinese firms. The core aspects of strategic marketing orientation, decision-making and strategic action are traced back to Taoism. Since this Chinese praxis of decision-making is dualistic or binary, thereby allowing major alternatives to coexist, it is different from both the logic of consequence and logic of appropriateness.

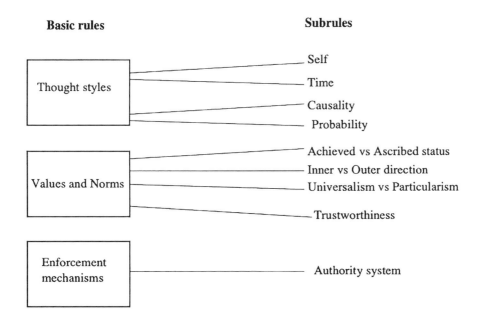

Figure 12.2 Informal rules of the Chinese business system

Based on this logic of symmetry, the major difference between Chinese and Western network marketing lies in how marketing managers think. Such thought styles influence how marketing managers decide, act, lead and control. Below, it is therefore discussed how such thought styles are influenced in their turn by norms, values and enforcement mechanisms. The firm's identity or 'Self' in the European business network is based on its own operations in an inter-organizational network. However, within the collectivistic Chinese business network, the firm is viewed as a cog in a social network that prevails over the firm, the identity thus being based on the networks the firm belongs to. The risks are then shared with other parties in the network rather than primarily being taken up by the individual firm itself. Thus, the world is perceived to consist of networks, which plays a key role in influencing how marketing managers think and do business. The 'Time' perspective is shorter, where the goal is to earn profits in the short run.

The thinking within the Chinese business network is binary: a kind of both-and thinking. It is based on the logic of symmetry, being holistic or contextual, intuitive, pragmatic and emotional. The strategic orientation is harmony, and opportunity seeking, opportunities being detected by acting in the market in a reactive way. Therefore, learning occurs through gaining more experience. According to most research on Chinese small and medium-sized enterprises (SMEs) in particular, the Chinese do not plan much. This influences 'Probability' so that firms relate to the future by being engaged in visionary thinking. No specific path is laid out. Instead, the path itself is important, where a vision is stated to where the path should lead, which can be seen as the 'Tao' of the firm. This is shown by the fact that neither deadlines nor forecasting are important. This lack of planning is also understood from the fatalistic time perception of the Chinese (Redding, 1980), that is, that future events are decided by fate.

Norms and values. The key role of relationships in Chinese society has been researched extensively. Most of this research is about 'guanxi' (Li, 2007; Luo, 1997; Park and Luo, 2001; Wong and Tam, 2000; Wong and Leung, 2001). Basically, relationships are 'Ascribed'. Different guanxi hierarchies are found in the literature based on the five classical relationships of Chinese society. They deal with how to build relationships dependent upon the hierarchical position of the group. 'Guanxi family' stands for the ego network, and 'guanxi net' for the entire network, meaning that organizational status is based on family connections. Relationships are personal, transferable, reciprocal and intangible, and are essentially utilitarian rather than emotional ('genxing'). 'Renqing', or unpaid obligations to the other party, is established through the exchange of favours. The network is 'Outer-directed', mainly through the importance of face ('mianzi'). It is a key component in 'guanxi dynamics', being an intangible form of social currency and personal status, originating from the Chinese shaming culture (Ho, 1976). 'Guanxi' is also 'Particularistic' by being based on cliques and nepotism, making relations informal, and non-bureaucratic. Business is closed and opaque to outside firms and blurred boundaries exist inside the firm. 'Trustworthiness' is a kind of implicit contract based on the business network, coming from relying on individuals rather than organizations. The internal and external organization therefore consists of personal external linkages to customers and suppliers. Relationships within the firm are trust based by being based on a benevolent boss and loyal employees.

Enforcement mechanisms. The organizational set-up of firms within the Chinese business network is characterized by being based on vertical social relationships, with a centrality of power and a high degree of strategic adaptability. The Chinese firm can therefore be seen as an organism, where the informality of the internal organization structure is high with nepotism, patronage and cliques, which creates a blurred boundary between formal and informal organization. '*Authority*' is based on vertical social relationships. The firm is also a typical hierarchy characterized by 'law and order', where everybody knows his or her place in a top-down authority structure. Actors are therefore monitored and controlled.

EXPLAINING INSTITUTIONS

Relevant institutions were discovered above and described adequately as institutions. The analysis is now developed further in order to find out which are the most relevant institutions in the societal sectors and organizational fields for the MNC being studied. This will make it possible, inter alia, to reach a better understanding of how the marketplace functions, by, for example, seeing how the cultural and social environment affects labour and government behaviour. The purpose is to look for rules in the form of explanatory factors or determinants in the third rectangle that explain institutional patterns (rules) and developments in the inner rectangle. This makes it possible to know how the institutions identified and described in the outer rectangle directly influence organizational fields and indirectly the MNC. In this explanatory stage, institutional theory is also used, primarily those theories that deal explicitly with how firms and markets found in the inner rectangle are influenced by institutional factors in the outer rectangle. Here, Whitley's business system theory stands out as being particularly helpful.

Business systems theory

This part on the business systems theory builds on Whitley (1992a, b). The major relationship of the theory is how the business system as an institution at the meso level is influenced by other institutions at the macro level. A business system is defined in terms of hierarchies and markets as '… configurations of hierarchy-market relations that become institutionalized in different market economies in different ways as the result of variations in dominant institutions' (Whitley, 1992a, p. 6).

The business system
The business system is seen as an organizational field found in the inner rectangle, which is described by three major factors: the nature of the firm, market organization, and authoritative coordination and control systems. These factors are described below based on Whitley (1992a, p. 9):

The nature of the firm
- The degree to which private managerial hierarchies coordinate economic activities.
- The degree of managerial discretion from owners.
- Specialization of managerial capabilities and activities within authority hierarchies.
- The degree to which growth is discontinuous and involves radical changes in skills and activities.

- The extent to which risks are managed through mutual dependence with business partners and employees.

Market organization
- The extent of long-term cooperative relations between firms within and between sectors.
- The significance of intermediaries in the coordination of market transactions.
- Stability, integration and scope of business groups.
- Dependence of cooperative relations on personal ties and trust.

Authoritative coordination and control systems
- Integration and interdependence of economic activities.
- Impersonality of authority and subordination relations.
- Task, skill and role specialization and individualization.
- Differentiation of authority roles and expertise.
- Decentralization of operational control and level of work group autonomy.
- Distance and superiority of managers.
- Extent of employer–employee commitment and organization-based employment system.

Background institutions

The institutions at the macro level are defined as background institutions, which largely match the societal sectors. Such background institutions are defined as social institutions that:

> … underpin the organisation of all economic systems and form the background to industrialisation and the development of modern market economies. Typically they are reproduced through the family, religious organisations and the education system, and often manifest considerable continuity from pre-industrial societies, especially where industrialisation has been relatively recent and fast. (Ibid., p. 19)

They belong to the outer rectangle, where the institutional characteristics of large societal groupings are found. In the explanatory stage, interest is primarily focused on the background institutions that influence business systems and what this influence looks like. In other words, there is a search for determinants that might explain the appearance or development of specific organizational fields. Whitley (1992a, p. 20) specifies six general characteristics of background institutions or societal sectors that influence the institutions of markets and firms, that is, the organizational fields in general.

Degree and basis of trust between non-kin. A market economy does not work if a minimum degree of trust is lacking between the economic actors involved, who usually do not know each other. This varies between societies and is more prevalent in Western mature markets than in Eastern emerging markets. The high importance of personal networks both inside and between business firms in the product/service markets of South East Asia, for example, is often explained by a lack of such society-wide trust. System-based trust mechanisms are reproduced through the societal sectors of the country culture or family system and the organizational field of business mores and product/

service markets. Thus Whitley (1992b) points to relations between societal sectors and organizational fields that might be of help in explaining the direct influence on organizational fields or the indirect influence on MNC strategy and organization.

Commitment and loyalty to collectivistic entities beyond the family. In societies where commitment and loyalty are bound to the family or some other smaller unit, cooperation with strangers is difficult. This makes it harder to form large company hierarchies or to employ and make people work efficiently in the local units of MNCs. This factor tells us about the importance of the family system and how it might influence certain organizational fields.

Importance of individual identities, rights and commitments. If a market economy based on the self-interest of the individual is going to work, individual rights and obligations are a prerequisite (see the discussion on 'economic man' in Chapter 11). These rules for human behaviour are normally specified formally in the legal system and in contracts based on it. This factor is often missing in emerging markets in which societies are collectively based with less space for the individual, especially in authoritarian societies such as China and Russia. In Western firms, roles and tasks are formally specified based on the individual. This characteristic is important when analysing the country culture, the legal system, and relations between these, as well as relations with the organizational fields.

Depersonalization and formalization of authority relations. Authority in firms is influenced by how authority is specified in the society concerned, for example whether authority rests on formal rules and procedures or whether it is of a more personal kind and based on the moral worth of the individual. Also, for this institutional feature there is a divide between the depersonalized and formalized authority characteristic of Western MNCs and the personalized authority found in many firms in emerging country market economies, for example in Chinese companies in South East Asia or in Korean chaebols.

Differentiation of authority roles. The same divide between mature market economies and emerging country market economies is often found regarding the way authority roles are differentiated, which is mirrored in companies.

Reciprocity, distance and scope of authority relations. In emerging country market societies, the distance and remoteness of authority roles in relation to the people is usually larger than in Western societies, resulting in less reciprocity between superiors and subordinates. In contrast to Western societies, power is less instrumental and authority less linked to expertise and less expressed through formally prescribed positions.

These six characteristics of the background institutions help to bring out key characteristics of the societal sectors, mainly the social system in Figure 12.4 and country culture in the basic institutions model. They could also be helpful in improving understanding of the political system and other societal sectors by explaining how these characteristics of the country culture are crystallized into these sectors. In such circumstances, political authority, for example, tends to be wider and not limited to the political sphere, inter alia giving wider responsibility to political leaders. This is one key factor behind the patron–client relationships in many South East Asian countries. The third characteristic mainly refers to the legal system. The six factors influence the organizational fields, such as the product/service markets or financial markets, either directly via the social system or indirectly through the other systems. The way to analyse this systemic impact is looked at next.

Influence of the third rectangle on the second rectangle

After having described and analysed institutions in both the third and second rectangles in greater detail and hinted at how they can be related to each other, it is time to focus more closely on the impact on the second rectangle of institutions in the third rectangle. A suitable method is illustrated in Table 12.1, namely an institutional matrix, where characteristics of background institutions (societal sectors) in the outer rectangle are specified in the rows, and characteristics of the business system (organizational field) are specified in the columns. The characteristics of background institutions discussed above are listed in Table 12.1. To facilitate the analysis only a few of the business system traits above are listed in the table. Two factors have been taken to represent the nature of the firm, namely the second one about the degree of managerial discretion from the owners, and the last one about the extent to which risks are shared with business partners and employees. Regarding the market organization, the first three factors are collapsed into one major characteristic about whether market relations are long or short term. The fourth trait is also included in the table, namely dependence of cooperative relations on personal ties and trust. The characteristics taken up from the third group on authoritative coordination and control system are decentralization of operational control; impersonality or formal relationships; differentiation of authority roles and expertise; and extent of employee commitment.

As observed in Table 12.1, the influence is summarized as being either direct (positive) by changing in the same direction, or diverse (negative) by changing in opposite directions. When the purpose is to find out about the impact of one particular background institution on the business system, the rows are related to the columns. A high level of individualism, for example, influences five business systems characteristics. There is a diverse or opposite effect on long-term risk sharing, market organization and employee commitment. This means that when the level of individualism is high, these three characteristics are low, for example there is a low sharing of long-term risk. There is a positive effect on reliance on formal procedures and rules as well as on role specialization. So when the level of individualism is high, there is also a reliance on formal procedures and rules, that is, the impersonality of authority and subordination relations being high.

When the purpose, on the other hand, is to analyse how a particular business system characteristic is influenced by the background institutions, the columns are related to the rows. For example, market organization is directly correlated with one background institution, and diversely correlated with two others. This means that when the markets are organized as long-term cooperative relations, the levels of institutionalized trust are low, the levels of inter-family cooperation and collective loyalty high, while the level of individualism is low.

PREDICTING INSTITUTIONAL DEVELOPMENTS

So far, institutional theory has mainly been used to analyse structures and patterns in the external environment. But it is also possible to use it as a basis for studying the dynamic aspect of the external environment. Predictability was defined in Chapter 11 as a major characteristic of institutions. Uncertainty is reduced by an anticipation that the behavioural regularities typical of institutions

Table 12.1 Relations between business system and background institutions

Background institutions	Business system characteristics								
	Managerial discretion	Long-term risk sharing	Market organization	Personal inter-firm links	Centralization of authority	Reliance on formal procedures and rules	Role specialization	Employee commitment	Distant, omni-competent managerial role
Low levels of institutionalized trust			+						
Low levels of inter-family cooperation and collective loyalty			-						
High level of individualism		-	-			+	+	+	
Low formalization and depersonalization of authority									
Low differentiation of power									
Aloof, non-reciprocal and omniscient conceptions of authority									

Source: Based on Whitley (1992b).

will repeat themselves in the future. An important part of environmental analysis is therefore to study whether the institutions previously discovered, described and explained reproduce themselves into the future or change. Predictions can be made at various points in the environmental analysis procedure developed in this chapter, for example during the explanation stage above, whether the product market network in the inner rectangle will be influenced by institutions in the outer rectangle in the same way in the future.

Since future institutional developments are uncertain, an important task of a prediction is to evaluate the probability of a specific rule system being prolonged into the future. A distinction is made between two types of risks:

- *MNC risk*. This type of uncertainty concerns how the strategic situation of the MNC is influenced by specific future institutional developments.
- *Institutional risk*. This is an evaluation of whether a certain institutional development will take place in the future, mainly independently of how the MNC concerned acts. This risk is dependent on the characteristics of the institution in question, for example how complex and dynamic it is.

There are a number of methods used to predict the future, such as trend extrapolation, time series analysis, cross-section analysis, econometric models, brainstorming, role playing and scenario development (Stoffels, 1994). The further into the future one looks, the more predictability goes down and uncertainty rises. According to Van der Heijden (1996), in the shorter term, when predictability is high and uncertainty low, forecasting is the planning mode of choice. When determining the medium-term future, scenario planning is the most effective tool. In the very long term, everything is both uncertain and unpredictable and attempts to plan can only use hope. The distance into the future varies between different environments, mainly dependent on how stable the environment is. The slower the incremental change of the environment is, the more suitable is forecasting. It projects the future on the basis of what was seen in the past, on historical precedent in the form of similar events. When environments are dynamic and changing quickly, future events will be more dissimilar to past events. This is typical of business environments in emerging markets, where forecasting is not a suitable method, particularly not in the medium term. Instead, due to high turbulence, scenario planning is more suitable for prediction here. Scenario planning is also more in line with the strategy focus of the book, namely that scenarios are policy development tools, while forecasts are decision-making tools. Scenarios are in effect perception tools that allow decision-makers to have a sort of peripheral vision.

Thus, because of the high complexity of external frameworks, it is not possible to make exact quantitative predictions, such as by using statistical forecasting techniques. Forecasts are quantitative predictions of events through establishing trends and patterns behind developments, that is, those parts constituting the tip of the iceberg and areas just below the surface (see Figure 12.1). Scenarios, on the other hand, are qualitative predictions focusing on structures, that is, the deeper lying parts of the iceberg. Therefore, scenario planning is suitable for predicting institutional developments. Or, conversely, basing scenario planning on institutional theory will improve this method and result in better scenarios. Another advantage of the institutional view of environmental analysis is that it provides the scenario planner with a perspective on the environment. It addresses one of the main problems of the scenarist: where to start looking.

MNC-focused path scenarios

A common way to make qualitative judgements about the future is then to use scenario planning. A scenario is the presentation of a possible future, usually made as part of strategy analysis. Because of their purpose of reflecting uncertainty through plausible future conditions, a number of scenarios are created, covering likely alternative futures and risks. They are based on the planner's judgements originating from a study of historical and present institutional developments, or based on others' judgements, for example experts in various fields. The type of scenario planning taken up in this chapter is the more advanced path or sequence-of-events scenarios. They differ from the simpler cross-sectional scenarios, which are limited to telling stories about future conditions and circumstances.

An important strategic issue in scenario planning is setting the ranges for the scenarios: the plausibility range, the time range and the geographic range (Stoffels, 1994). The plausibility range concerns what events to include in the analysis, considering how conceivable their future occurrence is. A distinction is made between events emerging from a probable future environment, a possible future environment or an improbable future environment. Uncertainty and time are related so that the further into the future one looks, the more uncertainty increases and the more predictability decreases, inter alia determining which prediction methods should be used. A critical question is then the time range selected, usually a five-year period. Regarding the geographic range, scenario development discussed here concerns an individual country market of an emerging market. The range settings determine the factors on which to base scenarios. The better this is done, the more exact the scenarios produced. However, there is always a risk of restricting the scenarios too much, thereby missing alternative factors and futures. This is discussed in greater detail below.

Usually scenarios are developed independently of the company for which they are supposed to be relevant, and are compared with the business idea and strategy of the company after they are finished. This approach is based on the assumption that environmental developments take place irrespective of what the company does. This is a doubtful assumption on many occasions, especially when making scenarios for a large MNC that might have a certain impact on the environment. A potential drawback then of this general approach is that investments are made in time and effort to develop scenarios that are of little relevance to the MNC. The approach to the environment risks being too broad, implying that too much information is collected and analysed for futures that are too general to be useful. To reduce this drawback and have a narrower perspective, an MNC-related scenario method is developed. However, this could have the opposite drawback, in terms of being too myopic, dealing with very limited futures for the MNC, and missing out on other vital factors. This bias could be reduced by complementing the MNC-focused inside-out mode with the outside-in mode. Still, the perspective on the environment would be narrower than the single outside-in approach of more traditional scenario planning.

Identifying key factors for future success

The procedure for scenario planning according to the institutional view is now developed. It takes up scenario planning primarily as the final phase of the three-stage model of environmental analysis. The process for creating scenarios starts with approaching the environment from the perspective of the MNC, that is, following the inside-out mode. The purpose is to determine the most critical structural factors of the environment influencing the future IBS of the MNC. They are defined as the key factors for future success of the IBS. The time range chosen is a five-year period. The key factors are extracted based on the previous stages of institutional analysis of the external environment. The aim is to divide the key factors into two groups: key factors that are possible to influence by the MNC, and key factors that are impossible to influence. This gives a preliminary division of key structural factors in the organizational fields (mainly possible to influence) and societal sectors (mainly impossible to influence). An overview of the current external environment has thus been achieved through identifying relevant factors and then explaining how they are related to one another. These key factors are next analysed to find out which are crucial for the future success of the MNC. Examples of factors that are possible to influence could be keeping delivery agreements, competitive product, financing to customers, increased spending on R&D, and performance-based salary system, while examples of key factors that are impossible to influence could be the financial system, globalization of markets, political reform and exchange rate.

Next, the key factors are studied further for the MNC and the environment respectively, beginning with the MNC as part of clarifying the relationship between the MNC and its environment. One way to do this is to carry out interviews with various people in various positions, asking them about what these factors will look like in the future. Relevant issues to study might be: Are the key factors extracted from secondary sources also future key factors? Are there other key factors? The strategic significance of a factor is further analysed by determining how it influences the strengths and weaknesses of the MNC.

Subsequently, the previous analysis of the external environment of the MNC is deepened by describing further the future state of the institutions identified through the key factors. These are relevant aspects of the organizational fields related to the factors possible to influence and relevant aspects of the societal sectors related to the factors impossible to influence. An important part of this analysis is to broaden the analysis of the environment and look for other institutional factors that might be important for the future development of the MNC. This could also include speculative and imaginative thinking regarding future developments.

The impact of societal sectors on organizational fields is analysed again as well as the influence of the environment on the MNC. This will provide further knowledge and understanding of how the organizational fields will function in the future, for example how the country culture affects the behaviour of the government, and how the government, in its turn, affects the MNC. The relationship between the values of the country culture within the social system and major values of the labour market may also be worked out, eventually connecting these values to the organization culture of an MNC.

Extracting Drivers and Stabilizers. The final aim of the process is to extract the institutional factors that drive change and those factors that create inertia by supporting stability. These drivers and stabilizers carry the institutional analysis into the future by pointing out the determinants of each relevant institution that could bring about change and which factors determine stability. The drivers and stabilizers can be related to the institutions as exemplified in Table 12.2.

Creating scenarios

It is now time to create the scenarios. Since only a limited number are to be created, the drivers and stabilizers need to be connected to each other to give a limited number of major combinations that can form the bases for the scenarios. It is a question of finding the most critical factors that have overriding importance for the future of the MNC. Based on these factors, scenarios can be structured following the deductive method, which:

> … aims to first discover a structure in the data to be used as a framework for deciding the set of scenarios to be developed, rather than let the scenarios emerge from it as in the inductive methods. The resulting framework identifies the scenarios in the set by means of a few crucial descriptions, mainly end-states, which are state-of-affairs in the horizon year, described in terms of the key dimensions. (Van der Heijden, 1996, p. 202)

Each scenario is described by relating the societal sectors and organizational fields to each other. This produces a specific configuration of societal sectors and organizational fields for each scenario. After having determined the basic structure of each scenario, they are filled in with available data or even with new data if necessary. Each scenario is labelled with a few words expressing the basic nature of its story line.

An example is given in Figure 12.3. Here, protectionism and the exchange rate were found to be the most critical factors. These critical factors originate in the product/service market (protectionism vs open market economy) and the financial market (high- or low-valued local currency), and are highly influenced by government and its policy to open up a closed economy and solve a financial crisis. Scenario 1 is assessed to be the most positive scenario for the MNC, and is labelled 'The sun is shining'. Scenario 4 is called 'Heavy nationalism' and is the least positive scenario. The other two scenarios are found in between these two. Scenario 3 is then evaluated to be more positive to the MNC than scenario 2.

Table 12.2 Exemplifying drivers for change and determinants for stability

Institutions within the organizational field	Drivers of change	Stability determinants
Financial markets	Performance-based salary systems	Protectionism
Labour markets	Performance-based salary systems	Country culture Social values and norms
Product/service market	Globalization	Low level of innovation

Source: Holst and Winzell (1999).

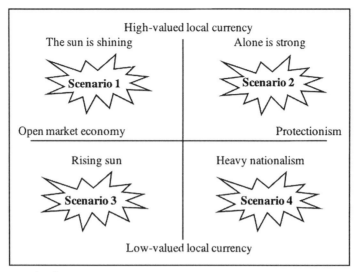

Figure 12.3 Example of a scenario matrix

Assessing impact on international business strategy

When the scenarios have been established, it is time to perform strategic analysis on them, which is illustrated in Figure 12.4. A SWOT analysis is done of each scenario to find out how the specific external environment described in the scenario influences the competitive advantage of the MNC, and then how the MNC should respond to the strategic situation of the scenario. First, each scenario is scrutinized for the threats and opportunities it will impose on the IBS, and by relating it to the strengths and weaknesses of the company, mainly its resources and capabilities. Based on this analysis, conclusions are drawn regarding the international business strategy to be undertaken by the MNC should the specific scenario occur, for example how to match the specific environment represented by the scenario, and what IBS to apply.

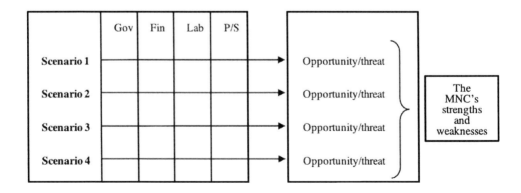

Figure 12.4 SWOT analysis of the scenarios

CONCLUSIONS

An analytical procedure for performing an institutional analysis of the external environment was developed in this chapter. The major idea is to develop the ability to reduce uncertainty through researching the complex environment as well as how to handle it by absorbing complexity. Such an ability is grounded in the NIA. The network view lays out how to collect information from the complex environment and how to handle the environment, while the institutional view provides an appropriate basis for interpreting external factors. Knowledge about the institutional origin of information is given, the idea being that it is not possible to understand information about events and how they relate to trends, patterns and structures without having a theory about society.

The institutional view develops a more coherent, penetrative and analytical method compared to most ordinary ways of carrying out environmental analysis, as it goes both deeper and wider into the external environment. Knowledge is created by finding patterns that are relevant to the strategic situation of the MNC, and analysing the structural factors behind these patterns, mainly with the help of institutional models.

The environmental analysis involves three stages of information search and model use. In the identification stage, models are identified and described that are useful for explanation and prediction. Potential candidates for institutions are evaluated through analysing them as institutions. A more penetrative analysis is introduced, where first formal rule systems are identified and described, and then the analysis extended to informal rules. After having discovered relevant institutions and described them adequately as institutions, the analysis continues to the explanation stage in order to find out more about how institutions are related to one another as a system. In this stage, it is also possible to benefit from institutional theories, especially the business systems theory.

Since predictability is a major characteristic of institutions, uncertainty is reduced by being able to anticipate that the behavioural regularities of institutions will repeat themselves in the future. An important part of environmental analysis is therefore to study whether the institutions identified and explained reproduce themselves into the future or change. MNC-focused path scenarios are developed, based on the assumption that the MNC can influence its environment. This type of scenario differs from the more common general scenarios. The practice of institutions-based scenario planning starts by identifying key factors for future success. Then drivers and stabilizers are extracted, which form the background for the creation of scenarios. Finally the impact of the scenarios established on the international business strategy of the MNC is assessed by carrying out a SWOT analysis.

How to evaluate the performance of the international business strategy executed based on this strategic analysis of the external institutional context is examined in Chapter 16.

13
International matching strategy

As stressed throughout this book, it is not possible to separate the world of business from the worlds of politics, ethics or ecology. Multinational corporations (MNCs) need to adapt to the combined challenges of climate change, biodiversity, social equity and human rights in a world of greater transparency, more explicit values and more fragile corporate assets. These issues are therefore of high strategic relevance in international business. Ethics becomes a critical consideration in this context, often being defined as basic values or moral principles in society. However, a more appropriate definition is provided by Treviño and Nelson (1999, p. 12): 'Ethics is the principles, norms, and standards of conduct governing an individual or group.' According to this definition, ethics does not involve only moral principles or values but also norms and standards of conduct. This definition fits nicely with the definition of institutions in this book, which includes norms and values as dimensions controlling conduct. Another conclusion from previous chapters is that ethics is relative, and varies between societies. The basic institutions model (Figure 11.1), for example, has such a foundation. If ethics is viewed in this way, a social foundation is provided for international business strategy. MNCs then conduct business in certain ways depending on specific societal values, norms, thought styles and enforcement mechanisms prevailing in society.

The societal performance of international business strategy (IBS) is developed further in this chapter and the next chapter, resulting in a broad perspective on competitive advantage, including sustainable business. As found in Chapters 5 and 6, it is vital for an MNC to have an ability to sustain its business from a societal point of view and not only possess resources and capabilities for achieving competitive advantage in the economic environment. The foundation for such sustainAbilities is that the MNC possesses organizational capabilities of the type illustrated in Figure 6.2. These capabilities are then utilized to achieve societal advantages and sustainable business. This is especially important for companies operating in emerging markets, where social and natural environmental issues are more pressing and the relations between business, the state and private non-profit organizations are different from Western mature markets. It is important to not solely create job opportunities, for example, but also to contribute to environmental protection, health, infrastructure development, education and so on. Taking social responsibility therefore becomes a means for the MNC to raise its level of legitimacy among many groups in society. Corporate social responsibility (CSR) issues become a critical strategic issue for the MNC, and an essential part of the IBS. These issues are therefore integrated into the international matching strategy (IMS).

The basic strategic situation facing the MNC regarding social issues is expressed in the same way as for economic issues in the market, as a question of finding the right trade-off between local responsiveness and global integration. To what degree is the MNC locally responsive to its social context through matching local natural environmental and social standards, and how does it integrate these with the group's standards?

This strategic dilemma is solved by having an effective matching strategy. As established earlier, matching involves linking the internal environment, consisting of resources and capabilities, with the external environment, consisting of various stakeholders, by making them compatible with each other. International matching strategy therefore focuses on the social environment. MNCs relate their own values, norms and beliefs to the values, norms and beliefs prevailing in the foreign market. The more immediate commercial environment of the MNC is composed of micro and meso institutions with which the MNC exchanges resources to effectively survive, for example customers, suppliers and financiers. The basic orientation of the IBS in product/service markets is efficiency. But achieving legitimacy through the matching strategy is also important, since the MNC must adhere to a number of rules such as regulations, values and norms related to the natural and social environments. In the government and political context, for example, legitimacy is the leading matching principle. This is taken up in this and the next chapter.

The international matching strategy is defined first, before developing the legitimacy issue as a strategic concept. The major strategic situations faced in matching is covered next, followed by major optional international matching strategies. Since the main claim made to obtain legitimacy with stakeholders is about being responsible, the CSR issue is introduced next and related to the legitimacy orientation of the IMS. Based on the definition of sustainability in Chapter 5, the sustainability business triangle is developed as a foundation for CSR. The focus is on two of the three values behind sustainable business, where the ecological value is separated from the social value as the specific value. Finally, the development goals of the Sustainable Development Agenda 2030 are integrated into to the international matching strategy as critical strategic environmental issues.

INTERNATIONAL MATCHING STRATEGY DEFINED

There are three main meanings attached to the word 'matching'. First, matching involves linking one thing with another, which from a strategic point of view is interpreted as the MNC linking its internal institutional framework to its diverse external institutional framework to gain sustainable competitive advantages. Second, matching also has the connotation of making something similar to or corresponding to something else, which here means making the internal framework compatible with the external framework, or vice versa. This meaning of the word fits with the praxis of decision-making taking place according to the logic of appropriateness, for example how to accommodate strategy to the norms of the external environment. If the customers belong to different cultures, for example, sales strategy is differentiated according to these cultures. Third, like a match or game, matching strategy also implies competition, and competitive strength in this book is based on the efficient use of resources and capabilities in a legitimate way.

Based on the three meanings of matching, international matching strategy is seen as the main mechanism for linking, in competition with other firms, the internal environment (consisting of resources and capabilities) with the external environment by making them compatible with each other. It is defined as the matching principle relevant for a number of organizational routines followed to accomplish this. For example, organizational routines aimed at manipulating the social environment are grouped together according to the matching principle they follow, and given a strategy name, in this case 'manipulation'.

How matching is done builds on the basic rules model (Figure 11.2). In matching, MNCs relate their own values, norms, thought styles and enforcement mechanisms to the corresponding basic rules prevailing in the emerging market. This implies that internal and external institutional environments are 'strategic twins' presupposing each other. However, matching does not mean that strategy is always in harmony with internal and external institutions, only that strategy builds on the capabilities suitable for a specific external institutional framework. Conflicts between the internal framework and external conditions are also conceivable, such as when the MNC breaks existing standards and creates new ones based on its internal resources and capabilities.

Thus, consistency between strategy and the external sources of competitive advantage, on the one hand, and consistency between the strategy pursued in the specific market environment and the resources and capabilities available for that environment, on the other, are achieved through matching.

LEGITIMACY-BASED STRATEGY

As noted in Chapters 5 and 6, international matching strategy is legitimacy based, where the MNC adheres to a number of basic rules in order to gain or maintain environmental support. Legitimacy is founded on the premise that MNCs operate in a country in sectors where there is a high level of technical development, demanding efficiently produced outcomes (e.g. firms), while simultaneously operating in sectors that are institutionalized in other ways (e.g. government). Legitimacy can then be achieved indirectly through the economic system as a whole by being efficient, thereby living up to the general values and norms as well as the cognitive and regulative structures relevant for the institutional rule complex found in a specific organizational field or societal sector. This can be done, for example, by demonstrating that the activities of the MNC in the country are justified; that is, they are taking place according to government norms and generally accepted societal values. Legitimacy can also be gained directly from stakeholders in such an organizational field. While efficiency is performance based, legitimacy is judged on valuations.

The issue of legitimacy of MNCs is coupled with the fact that organizations require resources from the environment to remain alive and to function, such as money, information and access to markets. Furthermore, their activities must be approved of by society, as generating income and employment or making a contribution in the long run to the development of the country, for example, not polluting the environment. An organization must prove to the environment it has a right to exist and therefore must prove itself to be beneficial to society; that is, it must gain legitimacy. Legitimacy in this sense is externally supplied and externally controlled. Such a claim for legitimacy is not given, and it is not achieved automatically; rather, it is worked for and can be influenced. A company must prove its right to be allowed to operate in a certain country or with certain stakeholders.

Legitimacy as a strategic principle is based on the definition of legitimation by Cipriani (1987, p. 1):

> Among the various possible meanings of what has been defined as legitimation, two should be borne in mind as more pertinent to sociological analysis: the attribution of validity to a given situation, action, function or authority (from below) … and (from above) the more or less motivated justification of what by itself would not be lawful or valid … In fact, claim, demand, recognition, ratification, acceptance – all are social and individual actions which presuppose endowing what is going to be done with meaning. … By way of further distinction, legitimation in reality is said to be based on two 'couples' of behaviour; from above, as a claim of validity only for what one is convinced of, or, instead, as a cynical claim of validity for what one knows is not justifiable; and from below, as a well-founded recognition of the legitimacy of something or, contrarily, as a de facto acceptance, though without foundation, of the legitimacy of something. The attribution of a 'foundation' simply means that this does not exist and so must be 'constructed', and on this depends the whole scaffolding of a complex of guiding ideas which orient attitudes and behaviour. And since, in general, a foundation is something in common, to be shared, its own particular character represents its potential for diffusion and ability to provide the sense of belonging to a group as to a party, a community or a whole nation.

Legitimation is further refined in this definition by Karlsson (1991, p. 3:4) as:

> … an act of communication through which desired or implemented actions are made meaningful. This act of creating meaning is strongly related to the valuations, norms, and rules of the group, to which the organization/individual that attributes validity to the actions belongs. To legitimate is thus to justify or rationalize.

To gain legitimacy or legitimation is thus a two-way process of creating a joint foundation and a sense of belonging to a group of like-minded people by sharing certain thought styles, values and norms. From above, it is a claim of validity for what one knows is justifiable. From below, this claim is justified according to the valuations, norms and other rules of a certain group. This means that the stakeholders and the MNC are involved in communication activities with each other, claiming and giving legitimacy.

Hence, matching strategy is guided by a quest for legitimacy, which is given to an organization by other organizations based on the actions of that organization. Such an acceptance is based on a test of these actions, where the criteria are based on styles, norms and values. The reasons behind the actions are tested to see if they can be justified. To gain legitimacy, organizations are involved in communication activities with each other, claiming and giving legitimacy. The way this is done in various countries, for instance, depends on how the organizational fields are organized.

The MNC strives to achieve legitimacy from stakeholders in various organizational fields and societal sectors. Legitimacy is related to the basic rules internal and external to the MNC, which have been institutionalized either into specific stakeholder groups or into society in general. In the first case, a stakeholder carries the values, norms and thought styles on which the MNC justifies itself. Legitimacy is based on the calculative self-interest of the stakeholder; that is, the MNC is supported by the members of an interest group if they receive some kind of benefits from the existence of the MNC. These benefits can be of an economic, social or ecological type. Another sort of legitimacy concerns the impact on society and its welfare in general, where the MNC and its activities are perceived as valid according to some socially constructed general value and belief system. According to Suchman (1995), the former type of legitimacy is pragmatic in kind, since it is based on calculated judgements regarding the immediate benefits for the legitimizing interest groups. This is not the case for the latter type of legitimacy, which is more of a moral type. However, this does not mean that self-interest can be disregarded as a basis for moral legitimacy. Rather, the perception of a group of what is righteous for society at large often has a tendency to intermingle with what is beneficial for the self-interest of that group.

Legitimacy can thus be obtained directly from interest groups or indirectly from society at large. In the basic institutions model, interest groups are mostly represented in organizational fields, while general values and beliefs are represented in societal sectors. The MNC might then need legitimacy directly from specific interest groups in the market, for example a labour union. Indirectly, legitimacy might also be claimed through the economic system by being efficient, thereby living up to the values and norms as well as the enforcement mechanisms relevant to the institutional rule complex found in a specific market system. However, in many countries this latter type of legitimacy cannot be taken for granted and is not automatically given, since 'efficiency', due to other values and norms, is interpreted in another way.

STRATEGIC MATCHING SITUATIONS

According to the logic of appropriateness defined in Chapter 5, organizational members create order by matching rules and situations and in using criteria of similarity or difference. How the MNC relates itself to a specific stakeholder to achieve legitimacy then depends on the major strategic situation in which the MNC finds itself. Four such situations are presented below based on the differences and similarities of this situation with the situation of the MNC. This makes classifications of the situation for the strategic decision important. The MNC therefore finds itself in different strategic situations when matching, for example the MNC is either following the rules of the environment or trying to make the environment follow the rules of the MNC. This adaptation issue relates directly to the major strategic dilemma in international business raised in previous chapters about local responsiveness versus global integration. Here, the MNC can be involved in four types of local responses: the MNC adapts its internal environment to the local external environment; parties in the external environment adapt to the MNC; both the MNC and outside parties adapt to one another; and no adaptations take place. Suitability then becomes a major selection criterion in adapting IBS to the rules of the internal institutional setting and to the external one.

MNC change

The MNC changes the international matching strategy mainly by matching the institutional controls of the internal institutional environment by adapting them to the external institutional framework. This is the classical local adaptation problem of the MNC when entering an emerging market.

External context change

This is the opposite situation to the former one, since the IMS is not changed but rather the external context. It could be an MNC push in the form of a product new to the foreign market brought in from abroad by the MNC. The product carries a new institutional arrangement that creates conflicts in the local environment and makes it adapt to the new situation.

Twin change

The international matching strategy is changed by adapting the internal institutional framework of the MNC to the external institutional framework, or vice versa. When the change originates in the external environment of the MNC as an environmental push, evolutionary or incremental change is most common. An example is a change of government policy, which the MNC matches by changing its internal institutional context. But change could also be revolutionary, where a strong build-up of conflicts and tensions leads to a radical shift of the multilevel system of institutions, making 'everybody' adapt swiftly. Examples of such major environmental transformations are the Iranian revolution and the fall of the Berlin Wall. But when resistance is very strong in one organizational field (e.g. politics), change could take time in another (e.g. the economic system). In Indonesia for example, the restructuring of some major conglomerates only started to take place in 2002, about five years after the Asian financial crisis hit the country. An example of a twin change originating in the MNC as an MNC push is when the MNC invents new rules for the market by introducing a new and more efficient product standard. Other stakeholders such as customers and competitors may also adopt this standard, making government change its policy to the new standard.

No change

IMS does not change and neither does the external institutional context of the MNC. There are no adaptations in the internal or the external institutional frameworks. Due to a suitable match between the internal institutional environment of the MNC and the external environment, global strategic arrangements are extended to the new external environment by being reproduced there. As established in Chapter 3, this is a rare situation in emerging markets, which are mainly signified by being transitional or changing. So the book is mainly about the other three situations.

IMS, then, concerns how the MNC responds in a particular strategic situation, for example if the analysis shows that there is a change or no change in the rules of the external framework. The strategic responses are of three major kinds. Either the MNC is proactive by impacting the rules of the external framework or it is reactive or passive in relation to the external environment. Matching strategy concentrates on how to best organize these actions by considering how the environment is organized. It may be organized as individual stakeholders at the micro level, organizational fields at the meso level, or societal sectors at the macro level. Due to shifting rules, matching strategies usually differ between stakeholders and organizational fields.

As stated in Chapter 6, suitability is a major criterion in evaluating the competitiveness of the international business strategy. This means that the internal framework should be suitable for the specific external framework to create competitive and societal advantages. Moreover, institutional change is characterized by inertia, which makes matching hard to accomplish in change situations. Rigidity is then a leading characteristic of the internal routines organizing the hierarchy of resources and capabilities.

MAJOR INTERNATIONAL MATCHING STRATEGIES

Based on the definition of the IMS above, there is a behavioural repertoire consisting of a number of potential organizational routines to be followed by the MNC in matching the internal and external institutional frameworks in foreign markets to each other. They are listed in Table 13.1. The proactive strategies and their organizational routines are presented at the top of the table, the strategic action then being reactive further down in the table. The reactive or passive matching strategies are mainly based on Oliver (1991) and her useful classification of strategic responses to external institutional pressures. They are presented after the proactive strategy and in the opposite order to her discussion. These different strategic responses put different demands on how these internal routines organize the hierarchy of resources and capabilities, mainly on the ability to adjust them to a specific response.

According to Table 13.1, MNCs could act to external influences such as demands from and changes in the external framework of the foreign market in various ways. At one extreme the MNC is proactive and is leading the environment, for example through setting quality standards. This is a kind of environmental leadership, where the MNC meets its self-imposed obligations to society and sustainable development. The strategic matching situation is here classified as a *twin change* situation. The MNC changes the IMS through developing a new set of rules, which are adapted to by the external environment. Innovation is a proactive strategy suitable for this strategic matching situation. By innovating, the MNC could, through following one organizational routine, generate change in the external institutional framework. One example of this routine is when a new industry standard is created through developing new products, this standard later being adopted by other companies. Another proactive organizational routine could be to move fast. The quickly changing world of today puts specific demands on the MNC's resources and capabilities, mainly with regard to flexibility and being able to concentrate activities quickly on certain innovation projects and areas within a short time.

In another proactive strategic posture, the MNC tries to manipulate stakeholders in the external framework by co-opting, influencing or controlling them, for example when the MNC wants to replicate its existing rules and routines in the new external environment. However, this could be difficult to achieve due to the high inadaptability of existing institutions. The manipulation strategy is typical

Table 13.1 International matching strategies

Matching strategies	Organizational routines	Examples
Innovate	Generate change	Developing a new product development routine
	Move fast	Creating flexible capabilities and organizational controls
Manipulate	Co-opt	Importing influential constituents
	Influence	Shaping values and criteria
	Control	Dominating institutional constituents and processes
Defy	Dismiss	Ignoring explicit norms and values
	Challenge	Contesting rules and requirements
	Attack	Assaulting the sources of institutional pressure
Avoid	Conceal	Disguising nonconformity
	Buffer	Loosening institutional attachments
	Escape	Changing goals, activities or domains
Compromise	Balance	Balancing the expectations of multiple constituents
	Pacify	Placating and accommodating institutional elements
	Bargain	Negotiating with institutional stakeholders
Acquiesce	Habit	Following invisible, taken-for-granted norms
	Imitate	Mimicking institutional models
	Comply	Obeying rules and accepting norms

of a strategic matching situation, where the external context changes but not the MNC. Here, the external institutional framework adapts to the internal institutional framework. Contrary to the innovation matching strategy valid for the 'twin change' situation, the MNC brings along rules that are new to the local environment but not to the MNC. According to the manipulation strategy, stakeholders can be persuaded to accept the new standard through influence or by controlling them through a dominating position, for example an MNC has a leading position in the product/service market. One way to neutralize an institutional demand is to co-opt the source of pressure, for example to buy or build close relationships with a supplier that is critical to the survival of the MNC. Co-option is then an organizational routine that makes room for a new standard by neutralizing an old standard.

The defy, avoid and compromise strategies imply a reactive posture, where the matching strategies have ingredients of both an active and passive choice behaviour. The defy and avoid strategies are mainly used when there are external pressures on the MNC to adapt to local conditions, but when change is resisted. In defying demands from the external institutional framework, the MNC may dismiss the demands, challenge them or attack them. Explicit new norms and values for MNC behaviour could be ignored if they are put forward by social groups lacking clout, in which case the MNC is not susceptible to external pressure. The company may also challenge new or changed rules and requirements, or even assault the sources of institutional pressure, such as when the MNC believes its privileges or autonomy are in danger. This could happen when a government tries to force an MNC to relocate its activities to an area that would make the company lose its competitiveness.

The organizational routines relevant for an 'avoid' strategy are exemplified by various ways in which the MNCs react to demands from governments in emerging markets. As emphasized by Oliver (1991, p. 154), 'concealment tactics involve disguising non-conformity behind a facade of acquiescence'. One example of this is saying one thing but doing another – an MNC informs government that it has decided to live up to a certain rule, but this promise is never fulfilled. In buffering, the MNC decouples part of its organization from the rest of the organization with the purpose of protecting it from certain environmental pressures, for example separating out the manufacturing unit in order to stabilize it and increase productivity. Another example would be when an MNC establishes different organizations in a country: a joint venture in cooperation with government for 'government-sensitive' business, and a wholly owned company for business that is not 'government sensitive'. In escaping, the MNC could change domain by leaving one country to go to another, for example because of pollution control rules that are too costly to match.

By applying defy and avoid strategies, the MNC does not respond to pressures to adapt to certain external rules. This means that an MNC change situation is turned into a no change situation, as the MNC refuses to change or avoids change. These strategies differ from the compromise and acquiesce strategies valid for the MNC change situation, where actual adaptations are made to external demands. Sometimes an MNC is confronted with openly conflicting institutional demands to which it needs to adapt, for example between customer demands for low-priced products and demands for more expensive but environmentally safe products. The MNC could compromise between these demands, for example by means of an organizational routine characterized by balancing the expectations of multiple constituents. Another tactic would be to pacify, that is, to partially conform to or accommodate one of these institutional elements. A third heuristic is to negotiate or bargain with these stakeholders.

According to the acquiesce strategy, the MNC adapts to the local external environment by following the various organizational routines relevant for these strategies. This is a strategic response of a passive MNC completely adapting to external demands by accepting the prevailing rules of the external institutional framework without protest. When following the habit organizational routine, the MNC is not aware that it is matching any pressures to change from outside, but blindly internalizes taken-for-granted rules and values. Imitation takes place consciously, as when following other MNCs' successful routines. When complying, the MNC incorporates external values, norms and institutional requirements into its own internal framework and adapts its strategy accordingly.

As suggested by Tsai and Child (1997), there is also a cooperative strategy option. This strategic response differs from the individual strategies in Table 13.1 in that the MNC cooperates instead of going it alone.

CORPORATE SOCIAL RESPONSIBILITY

Compared to markets in Western Europe and North America, MNCs in emerging markets focus more on social issues. This broadens their strategic repertoire and makes strategic components such as legitimacy and matching strategy important. The IBS is then founded on a different organization of society. When institutions found in Western societies are missing, the MNC needs to adapt to this other institutional environment. For example, if a social security system is missing, the company can respond to this situation through its IMS by creating its own system for the employees. In doing so, the objective is to win legitimacy by demonstrating to employees and government that the MNC is taking social responsibility for its business activities in the country. The employees then benefit at the same time as the MNC contributes to the welfare of society. Such social responsibility issues are therefore of high strategic importance for MNCs in emerging markets, and therefore are a natural part of the IMS.

Demonstrating social responsibility is then seen as a key way of achieving societal advantages and of making the MNC business sustainable from a societal point of view. According to Alkhafaji (1995, p. 294), there are five key elements in most definitions of corporate social responsibility (CSR):

1.   Corporations have responsibilities that go beyond the production of goods and services at a profit.
2.   The impact of corporations goes beyond simple marketplace transactions.
3.   Corporations serve a wider range of human values than can be captured by focusing solely on economics.
4.   These responsibilities involve helping to solve important social and ecological problems, especially those that business has partly caused.
5.   Corporations have a broader constituency than just their shareholders.

Thus CSR focuses on non-economic issues, social as well as ecological ones. This means that social and ecological values are created through socially responsible acts. According to the definition of ethics above, social responsibility is then achieved by the MNC relating itself to the norms, values, thought styles and enforcement mechanisms of the stakeholders. This implies that the way in which the laws and rules of the public sector organizations are followed is part of CSR. Even if the public rule system is mandatory, it is up to the MNC to decide whether to follow a rule or not by applying a suitable matching strategy. A vital part of the social responsibility of the MNC is then to be governed by the enforcement mechanisms of society, which are mainly formulated within the public sector and are valid for the social and ecological values. However, it is normally not enough just to stick to the public rule system in order to develop a sustainable business, since not all relevant norms, values and thought styles behind a sustainable society are expressed formally through public rules. There is also an informal rule system that needs to be considered. This is of particular importance in emerging market countries, where, due to their underdeveloped public sector, certain formal rules could be lacking or not enforced. The natural environment, for example, may be less protected by laws or government guidelines. Even if these are in place, public rules are not always enforced in these 'soft' societies.

CSR and legitimacy

Corporate social responsibility is thus closely related to legitimacy. A claim is made to the stakeholder that the activities directed towards it are socially responsible. If the actions or decisions taken by the MNC based on this claim are considered valid by the stakeholder in question and thus justified by it, the MNC has gained legitimacy from this interest group. Thus, by approving of the activities behind the claim for social responsibility, legitimacy is given to the MNC. Indirectly, legitimacy could also be gained with other constituents, for example government, as well as within society in general, by contributing to the welfare of society, for example in health, infrastructure or education provision.

Corporations can be socially responsible in various ways (Pava and Krausz, 1997), as shown by the following examples taken from The Prince of Wales Business Leaders Forum (*The Economist*, 1998, pp. 16–17):

- *In the labour market*. Training local managers and labour to be business partners. Developing local education capacity.
- *In the supplier market*. Developing local suppliers, products and services.
- *Infrastructure*. Assisting in the building of a social and educational infrastructure to contribute to economic development and widen the understanding of the role of business.
- *With government*. Input to public policy through economic environmental education and training policies.
- *Setting and raising standards*. Ethics and quality regarding environmental care, health and safety (e.g. improving the health and stability of the workforce and local community), and corporate governance.
- *Making social investments*. Social and economic partnerships projects regarding education, culture, community development and capacity building.

These are examples of actions for which the MNC could claim social responsibility and thus legitimacy. Hence the MNC might increase its legitimacy by gaining acceptance from governments, communities and interest groups as well as, potentially, critical observers, in that way improving its reputation. Legitimacy may be achieved by winning the support and commitment of employees, enabling them to contribute to wider civil society, as well as by improving the understanding of local issues, attitudes, culture and business partners.

THE SUSTAINABILITY BUSINESS TRIANGLE

A major conclusion from the definition of competitive advantage in Chapter 5 as profit driven is that IBS is efficiency based and takes place in the economic environment. As IBS is embedded into the social environment, profitable MNCs also need to be legitimate. The IBS must also be ecologically sound so that the possibilities for future generations to enjoy similar standards of living to the present generation are not compromised. Sustainable business then concerns the way economic value relates to social and ecological values. As defined in Chapter 5, the MNC achieves sustainable business by creating three major types of values according to the following formula:

Sustainable business = economic value + social value + ecological value

CSR focuses on the social and ecological values, where the latter value is separated from social value as the specific value inherent in protecting the natural environment and conserving resources so that nature is not destroyed. The benefits experienced by society from international business operations are social and ecological values created with stakeholders. Thus, the more the MNC has the capability to do that, the higher the values created with the stakeholders, and the higher the legitimacy achieved. So the more the MNC creates such values, the more sustainable the MNC's business is from a societal point of view. This also means that the societal advantage of the MNC increases. Societal advantages are then achieved by enhancing long-term stakeholder values through addressing the needs of relevant stakeholders.

Social value and ecological value may also add to economic value by creating more satisfied customers. In addition, how customer value creation affects the social and ecological values needs to be taken into consideration. These three values of sustainable business therefore constitute a 'triple bottom line' for the performance or effectiveness of the IBS. Such performance issues are taken up in Chapter 16. The links between these three types of values are now elaborated further based on Peralta-Álvarez et al. (2015). Figure 13.1 shows the interdependency between the values. It can be used as a tool in strategic analysis as a way of studying how to relate the values to each other when deciding on strategic goals. It can also be used as a basis for measuring performance along the three dimensions and to investigate how various combinations of the three values influence the sustainability of the international business strategy.

Figure 13.1 illustrates major trade-off options as various mixes of the three values created with stakeholders. Sustainable business is achieved by combining these values in effective ways. The more hypothetical alternative of not making any trade-offs at all is found at the corners. The left corner represents a strategy based on only economic considerations (the Economy–economy alternative), while the right corner represents an IBS based on only social values (the Social–social

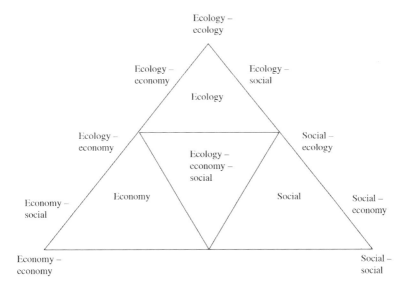

Figure 13.1 The sustainability business triangle

option). The former strategy is then entirely efficiency based, while the latter alternative is entirely legitimacy based. The upper corner represents the Ecology–ecology alternative, that is, to base the strategy on only creating ecological values. The trade-off options between the three values are found inside the triangle. The trade-offs dominated by mainly creating economic value, and less of the other two values, are shown by the lower Economy triangle on the left side, that is, showing the Economy–ecology and the Economy–social mixes. On the right side, within the Social triangle, creating social values dominates the mix as expressed by the major Social–ecology and Social–economy combinations. The upper middle triangle shows the ecology-dominated parts, namely the major Ecology–economy and Ecology–social mixes. Within the lower middle triangle, the mix is not dominated by any of the three values, instead representing more equal mixes between them, for example creating a balanced mix between the ecological, economical and social values.

The sustainable development goals of Agenda 2030

It is now shown how the sustainable development goals of Agenda 2030 can be used to decide on suitable goals for achieving sustainable business according to the sustainability business triangle. As stated in Chapter 5, clear-cut goals are a precondition for an effective IBS and for being able to control performance. This agenda contains a guide for business action on the development goals: The SDG Compass. Since the stakeholder approach of this guide fits well with the network institutional approach of the book, it will be used here and in the next chapter. It also works as a general guide for MNCs' international matching strategy, since it covers critical strategic environmental issues. The 17 sustainable development goals (SDGs) of Agenda 2030 are shown below:

1.   End poverty in all its forms everywhere.
2.   End hunger, achieve food security and improved nutrition and promote sustainable agriculture.
3.   Ensure healthy lives and promote well-being for all at all ages.
4.   Ensure inclusive and equitable quality education and promote lifelong learning opportunities for all.
5.   Achieve gender equality and empower all women and girls.
6.   Ensure availability and sustainable management of water and sanitation for all.
7.   Ensure access to affordable, reliable, sustainable and modern energy for all.
8.   Promote sustained, inclusive and sustainable economic growth, full and productive employment and decent work for all.
9.   Build resilient infrastructure, promote inclusive and sustainable industrialization and foster innovation.
10. Reduce inequality within and among countries.
11. Make cities and human settlements inclusive, safe, resilient and sustainable.
12. Ensure sustainable consumption and production patterns.
13. Take urgent action to combat climate change and its impacts.
14. Conserve and sustainably use the oceans, seas and marine resources for sustainable development.

15.   Protect, restore and promote sustainable use of terrestrial ecosystems, sustainably manage forests, combat desertification, and halt and reverse land degradation and halt biodiversity loss.

16.   Promote peaceful and inclusive societies for sustainable development, provide access to justice for all and build effective, accountable and inclusive institutions at all levels.

17.   Strengthen the means of implementation and revitalize the Global Partnership for Sustainable Development.

Most of these goals are too general to be directly useful in formulating goals for the IBS. They are more to be seen as a background against which the MNC can formulate its own more specific goals, for example working as a checklist for identifying the key strategic issues for the IMS on its CSR policy. Some of them are generally valid for societies at large, that is, sustainable energy (7), sustainable cities and communities (11) and peace, justice and strong institutions (16). But most of them are more specific, making it possible to refer them more directly to a certain type of sustainable business value. The goals of clean water and sanitation (6), climate action (13), conservation of life below water and life on land (14) and sustainable terrestrial ecosystems (15) are referred to as ecological values, since they relate to the natural environment. The SDGs on no poverty (1), zero hunger (2), good health and well-being (3), quality education (4), gender equality (5) and reduced inequalities (10) mainly concern the social environment and therefore social values. SDGs related to the economic environment and economic value are responsible consumption and production (12), decent work and economic growth (8) and building infrastructure, promoting sustainable industrialization and fostering innovation (9). They are specific enough to initiate an analysis of how to mix these values in order to have the best possible sustainable business, that is, an effective IBS. The SDGs can also be used as a background for discussing the strategic profile of the firm, for example whether it should have an Economy-social profile, an Economy-ecology profile, or a suitable combination of the three dimensions.

CONCLUSIONS

The international matching strategy is defined in this chapter and related to the legitimacy issue, which has been developed as the major strategic concept. Based on the definition of the IMS, a potential behavioural repertoire is presented as a number of matching strategies and their related organizational routines that the MNC could follow in matching internal and external institutional frameworks in emerging markets. MNCs could act to demands from and changes in the external framework of the foreign market in various ways. At one extreme the MNC is proactive and is influencing the external environment by meeting its self-imposed obligations to society and sustainable development. The MNC also tries to manipulate stakeholders in the external framework by co-opting, influencing or controlling them. Other matching strategies imply a reactive posture, where the matching strategies of defy, avoid and compromise have ingredients of both an active and passive choice behaviour. According to the acquiesce strategy, the MNC adapts completely to external demands, through the organizational routines of habit, imitate and comply. All matching strategies are adapted to four major strategic situations faced in matching. Since the main claim made to obtain legitimacy with stakeholders is about being responsible, the corporate social responsibility issue is related to the legitimacy orientation of the IMS. The sustainability business triangle is developed as a foundation for the IMS and how to relate it to the IBS. The focus is on the mixes based on the ecology and social triangles, which are related to the economic value. The ecological value is then separated from the social value as the specific value inherent in protecting the natural environment and conserving resources. The development goals of the Sustainable Development Agenda 2030 are integrated into the international matching strategy and CSR as critical strategic issues. In the next chapter, these general aspects are developed into a stakeholder management framework for international matching strategy towards stakeholders.

PART VII
INS + IMS = IBS

The flight of the California condor – again

This is '70-Fuego', born in 2008, cruising along Highway 1 together with other members of the Big Sur flock. To save the California condor, Ventana Wildlife Society began in 1997 to release birds raised in captivity into the wild. This famous wildlife conservation programme began in the 1980s, when the drastic step was taken to catch the last 27 wild condors and start a breeding programme at the Los Angeles and San Diego zoos. 'Fuego' was reared by his foster parents after arriving in Big Sur in his egg in 2008. He got his name from surviving, as a chick, two large wildfires close to the nest. Today about 300 condors are found in California, Utah, Arizona and Baja California. To keep track of the birds, they have been marked with tags. The programme is still ongoing, as the goal of having two sustainable wild populations and one in captivity has not yet been reached. So, if you happen to see '70-Fuego' and others in the flock, report them on www.condorspotter.com and say hallo from me.

14
International stakeholder strategic management

The central task of the stakeholder approach to strategic management is to manage and integrate the relationships and interests of the groups that have a stake in the business so that the long-term success of the multinational corporation (MNC) is ensured (Freeman and McVea, 2001). Since corporate social responsibility (CSR) issues are mostly integrated into stakeholder management, an MNC can be defined as an 'extended enterprise' (Post et al., 2002) or a 'civil corporation' (Zadek, 2001). Its long-term survival is then determined by its entire network of relations, business as well as non-business. To direct a course for such an MNC in a local emerging market, it is necessary to consider how this extended firm can affect the diverse natural and social environments and how these environments may affect the firm. The key strategic challenge is to develop a consistent policy that deals with the diverse stakeholders in the markets as well as outside the markets, a challenge that is even greater in the complex and dynamic environments of emerging markets. Since stakeholder management contains both a network and institutional part, its international strategy aspect can be developed by taking a network institutional approach (NIA) and using the international business strategy (IBS) model (Chapter 6). By mainly being about CSR and acting in social and natural environments, international stakeholder management also becomes a crucial part of the international matching strategy (IMS).

The IBS model is therefore applied to stakeholder management to integrate international matching strategy with international network strategy (INS). The main questions to be answered are: Which groups in society influence the MNC and are influenced by the MNC? How can the MNC match their norms and values? How can it establish and maintain relationships with these stakeholders?

Thus, as part of international stakeholder management, the international matching strategy model is established and applied to an MNC case concerning local stakeholders in one emerging market, Malaysia. To identify and analyse the relevant stakeholder network, the network mapping methodology developed in Chapter 8 is used, while an analysis is undertaken of the external and internal institutional settings to provide a background to the CSR issues. This latter analysis is founded on the basic institutions model and the basic rules model. Relevant basic rules are searched for by following the analytical procedure developed in Chapter 12 for analysing the external environment. This broader analysis is then narrowed down to identify the high impact areas and which stakeholders to engage. The CSR matrix is the major tool used, which is a kind of mapping instrument similar to those suggested in the SDG Compass. The key environmental issues found are also related to the sustainable development goals (SDGs) in Chapter 13. Based on this two-step analysis, the stakeholder-specific international matching strategy of the company is analysed. Finally, the strategies for the mix of stakeholders and issues are assessed separately for each key social responsibility issue and for the key stakeholders.

INTERNATIONAL MATCHING STRATEGY TOWARDS STAKEHOLDERS

As established in Chapters 5 and 6 and developed as a sustainability business triangle in Chapter 13, the MNC achieves sustainable business by creating three major types of values. The IMS concerns the non-economic aspects of the IBS, focusing on how the social and ecological values are generated with stakeholders. It is studied how they influence the MNC and are influenced by the MNC by establishing and maintaining relationships. The main considerations involved in effectuating the international matching strategy towards stakeholders in an emerging market are depicted in Figure 14.1. As shown there, the first step is to analyse the present strategic matching situation of the MNC, for example to establish the relevant network of stakeholders according to the mapping procedure introduced in Chapter 8. This stakeholders' network operates in an institutional environment of organizational fields and societal sectors, being influenced by various values, norms, thought styles and enforcement mechanisms. For example, labour is not only to be considered as an economic input but also as a stakeholder with social and ecological interests.

The MNC can gain, maintain or lose legitimacy through different actions, such as the provision of a stimulating working environment. Lost legitimacy can also be repaired. Legitimacy is influenced by the benefits and sacrifices experienced by the stakeholders based on their interests, which in their turn may create social and ecological values and result in societal advantages for the MNC. This claim for legitimacy is based on the fact that the MNC has a good idea of

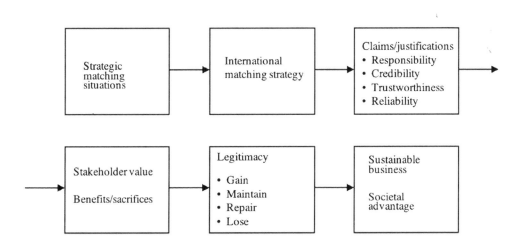

Figure 14.1 International matching strategy towards stakeholders

how its activities influence the sacrifices and benefits of the stakeholder, that is, how values are created taking into consideration the norms, values and thought styles of the stakeholder. Thus, legitimacy gained or repaired creates societal advantages, while legitimacy lost creates societal disadvantages. Legitimacy is achieved when the MNC's activities are recognized, accepted or ratified by the stakeholder. This happens if the expectations of the stakeholders are fulfilled. For example, if the MNC claims to be socially responsible for its actions, it works as a promise to the stakeholder. This, in its turn, leads to an expectation by the stakeholder that the MNC will act in the way promised (claimed). Such an expectation of a party acting in a responsible way is defined as a norm in Chapter 11. Other claims that create expectations among stakeholders and norms for the MNC to follow are credibility, trustworthiness, and reliability. These norms are not absolute but vary in strength and interpretation. So the more the MNC is perceived to be responsible, credible, trustworthy and reliable, the higher its legitimacy, and the higher the societal advantages.

The degree to which actions claimed are accepted depends on how closely the promises made and expectations of stakeholders match, which is decided by how the claimant acts, that is, if the MNC lives up to its promises. The more it does, the more benefits that are experienced in relation to the sacrifices made. But the benefits could also decrease if promises are not kept. The level of legitimacy is thus dependent on the level of benefits experienced and sacrifices made by the stakeholders, that is, the values created. Ultimately, this determines to what degree the MNC is perceived to be responsible, credible, trustworthy or reliable.

Hence, the IMS is a strategy aimed at creating societal values. The MNC influences the value level of the stakeholders through having various legitimacy creation resources. This ability to use the resources of the MNC to show responsibility, trustworthiness and so on is defined as an organizational capability in accordance with Chapter 6. Societal advantage and social and ecological values are therefore closely inter-related. The higher these values are, the higher is the societal advantage of the MNC. So, the better the MNC manages to fulfil its societal objectives at the stakeholder level, the higher its societal advantage.

INTERNATIONAL BUSINESS STRATEGY TOWARDS STAKEHOLDERS IN MALAYSIA

The IBS towards stakeholders is illustrated for a world leading MNC in the bearings industry, looking at its operations in one emerging market, namely Malaysia. The analysis is based on a study of the CSR of the MNC in this industry carried out by Johansson and Larsson (2001), mainly with regard to its factory in the country.

The internal institutional environment

Analysis of the internal institutional setting of the MNC is an important part of matching strategy. The internal environment of this MNC has already been analysed in Chapter 6, and therefore the reader is referred to this chapter, especially Figure 6.3.

The external institutional environment

Since the IMS concerns the natural and social environments, it is necessary to make a broad analysis of the society, to move far beyond the task environment of the firm. The institutional analysis of the external institutional setting of the bearings industry revealed a number of characteristics of the Malaysian organizational fields and societal sectors, which are summarized in Figure 14.2. Even though still largely relevant, this specific configuration of Malaysian society reflects the situation at the beginning of the 2000s.

Organizational fields

Five organizational fields were identified and the important characteristics of each field reduced down to between two and five factors per field. The organizational fields are the product market, the labour market, the financial market, official establishments and public interests.

The product market consists of the customers and distributors, the suppliers and the competitors. It is characterized by product differentiation, equal bargaining power between sellers and buyers, geographically oriented customer preferences, homogeneous rule systems in the market regarding customers and suppliers, and networking.

The labour market is characterized by brain drain, regional differences in the supply of skilled labour, high power distance between employers and employees, and a lack of trust in people who are not part of the family.

The financial market is characterized by foreign values and norms, powerful foreign analysts and increasing long-sightedness after an earlier stage of short-term orientation and speculation.

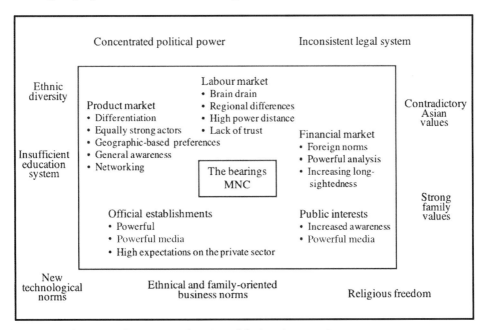

Figure 14.2 The external institutional setting of the bearings MNC

Official establishments incorporates organizations the MNC is directly involved with, such as government authorities and non-governmental interest organizations that are closely related to the government. These organizations are powerful, inter alia the government regulating the product, labour and financial markets. However, due to a lack of monitoring and control capacities, the enforcement of these regulations is uneven and selective, with foreign companies often being more regulated than domestic companies. There are also high expectations of the private sector, with the government often wanting it to take more responsibility than is mandated by law, for example expecting MNCs to apply the higher environmental standards of the home country rather than those of the host country. Due to the relative power of the interest organizations within the private sector, the interests of companies are often taken more into account than the interests of consumers.

Public interests represent an organizational field that includes the community, the general public and the media, as well as consumer interest groups. The activities of the public interest groups have led to increased pressures on MNCs to behave well. The media, through their increased power to change public opinion, have altered the rules of how companies should behave. By setting new rules, companies need to change their strategy from one based on a 'trust me' belief to one characterized by 'tell me' and 'show me'. They must now prove that they do actually act, not only promise that they will. This is a good example of how the granting of legitimacy changes from claims being based on 'talk' to being based on action. The globalization of media has also made information more accessible to the general public and led to a situation where a mistake in one part of the world might have implications for the image and reputation of the company elsewhere. Another factor contributing to the increased awareness of the general public is the appearance of various non-governmental organizations (NGOs).

Societal sectors

Nine major characteristics were found in relation to the societal sectors.

Ethnic diversity. Such diversity is typical of Malaysia, where the country's mix of Malays, Chinese and Indians is reflected in society in many ways. It has a direct or indirect impact on all the other societal sectors and results in a very particular and complex national rule system. Within each major ethnic group there are particular thought styles, norms and values, which often conflict with those of other groups. One essential thought style of Malaysian society, for example, is the view that there is harmony between the different groups, which is mainly asserted by the Malays, who form the majority group. This could, however, be considered a rose-tinted view of reality, and if you can scratch beneath the surface some resentment can be found among the minority groups (the Chinese and the Indians). There are also particular occupational norms related to ethnic origin. For example, the Chinese dominate the business occupations. Based on the basic rules characterizing the ethnic groups, a government policy has been instituted to improve the situation of the Malay population. This so-called Bumiputera policy, inter alia, partly regulates the employment and investment behaviour of the MNCs.

Contradictory Asian and Western values. Even if some Asian values hold true in Malaysian society, the expression 'Asian values' does not exist in a normative way in the daily life of Malaysians. Nevertheless, certain Asian values do appear. The dislike of Westerners is occasionally present, but this thought style could change quite swiftly with the next generation, which, as many of the members of this generation have studied abroad, is more open to Western influence and has different norms and values. The fact that community takes precedence over individuals and social and economic rights take precedence over civil and political rights is very visible in all the policies of the government or the prime minister, but especially in the comprehensive Bumiputera policy and the so-called 'Vision 2020'. Hence, all the values can be viewed as formal norms established by the Malaysian government. One can have different opinions of the extent to which democracy and human rights exist in Malaysia, but it has to be remembered that it is a former colonial country that has not enjoyed independence for long. Consequently, a certain degree of suspicion towards the attempts by the 'West' to impose its rule system as the universal standard is understandable, and therefore democracy and human rights might have other meanings in the Malaysian thought style.

Strong family values. The thought style is strongly based on family values. The family itself constitutes its own rule system, where everybody is obliged to put family before anything else, including work and individual freedom. Societies with strong family values and loyalty are often characterized by a lack of trust for people outside the family (Whitley, 1992b). This is true for Malaysia. In business life, for example, this means that business contacts normally function at the personal level.

Religious freedom. As a result of its rich mixture of different ethnic groups, Malaysia has many different religions each with different thought styles, values and norms. The government has not placed any restrictions on the practising of religion, although it does claim Islam as the official religion of the country. There is personal freedom of choice when it comes to religion, and people do sometimes convert to other religions. There seems to be a common thought style in the form of a mutual understanding between the different religious groups that is detached from ethnic considerations.

Ethnic and family-oriented local business norms. As observed above, business relations in Malaysia follow ethnic cultural borders, mainly due to the strong influence of ethnic and family values. An unofficial rule is that the use of English is routine when persons from different ethnic groups meet, despite the formal rule stating that Bahasa Malayu is the official language. Another informal norm is that business life and private life are not separated in the same way as they are in the Western world. Due to this integration of work and personal life, criticism at work could be perceived as personal criticism, and so it might be more appropriate to communicate through a third person instead of approaching the person concerned directly. Other thought styles include high power distance and hierarchical thinking, which makes criticism of superiors almost impossible. A particular thought style shared by all the ethnic groups, but is particularly strong for the Chinese, is the fear of 'losing face', which has important implications for the way business is done.

Concentrated political power. With political power strongly concentrated in the prime minister, there is a strong resemblance between the thought styles of the prime minister and the government, the system of government being most closely akin to an autocratic dictatorship where everything becomes politics. Another characteristic of the political thought style is that it is based on the strong presence of racial and religious values. Most of the political parties in Malaysia are ethnically based, focusing on racial and religious objectives and values. One expression of this is the Bumiputera policy referred to above, by means of which the government tries to create harmony in society through a racial political structure. Another complex and comprehensive thought style is found in the political programme 'Vision 2020' established by the government during one of Prime Minister Mahathir bin Mohamad's previous regimes. Important formal rules for the future are stated, for example that the government will continue to interfere in business whenever necessary. It seems the government wants to maintain its powerful position that enables it to control both foreign MNCs and domestic companies, while simultaneously expecting the private sector to engage in social issues. With an inadequate social security system and limited public social services, combined with increased general privatization, views on who will provide the missing elements are changing, from being the public sector to being the private sector and charitable organizations. The rule system for foreign MNCs is contradictory. Foreign direct investment (FDI) is both encouraged and discouraged. Major formal rules include requirements regarding local content, technology transfer and the number of expatriates working in the company. Another area where there is heavy governmental interference is decisions on where foreign companies should establish themselves.

Inconsistent legal system. Part of Malaysia's inheritance from the British era is its rule system for the financial sector. However, some of the standards and procedures in place are not very effective, especially the lack of enforcement mechanisms regarding companies that are not obeying the law. It is important to remember that this emerging market lacks the longer history of enforcement mechanisms that can be found in mature markets. However, the governmental authorities seem keener on monitoring and controlling foreign MNCs than on doing so for domestic companies.

Insufficient educational system. Despite the presence of both public and private universities, the educational system has not managed to support the demand for labour, particularly skilled labour. There is increasing participation of the private sector in the education system, which will change the

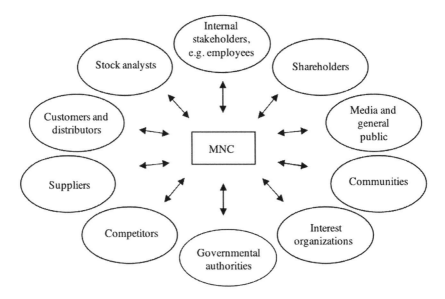

Figure 14.3 The stakeholder network

values and norms. The habit of the Malaysian middle class of sending their offspring to study abroad, the result of which is 'brain drain', is a clear sign of the insufficiency of the educational system.

The stakeholder network

Based on this analysis of organizational fields and societal sectors, the stakeholder network was established. It is represented in a network map and illustrated in Figure 14.3. Eleven key stakeholders (labelled A–K) are listed in Figure 14.4 on the CSR matrix. They correspond to those in Figure 14.3 except that internal stakeholders are not seen as one unit but split into 'Group and division' (A) and the 'Employees' (D).

The CSR matrix

Another major result of the environmental analysis is the identification of the key corporate social responsibility issues found to be of interest to the MNC. They are related to the key stakeholders above through the CSR matrix as illustrated in Figure 14.4. Such a CSR matrix is an important strategic tool that is used to relate the major findings of the external and internal institutional settings of the MNC to each other. The importance of each issue for each stakeholder is shown by the different shading in the cells. The line-filled boxes are the most important ones to focus on for the MNC.

The contents of the matrix are made more concrete by applying the matrix to the situation of the bearings MNC operating in Malaysia. The stakeholders and the key CSR issues are listed in Figure 14.4. Environmental care (1) stands out as the issue that most frequently arises in the empirical material, and includes ecological issues such as adjustments to ISO 14001, discharge systems for industrial waste, and education of employees and their families in ecological matters. It is possible to relate this and the other nine issues to the SDGs of Agenda 2030. The relevant SDGs are therefore given for each of the issues in Figure 14.4 and commented upon in connection with the stakeholder-specific matching strategy below.

The four stakeholders with most interest in the local subsidiary in Malaysia are the group (A), the employees (D), the governmental authorities (H) and the local community (J). Four other stakeholders have less strong interest in the factory: the customers and distributors (E), the suppliers (F), professional and interest organizations (I) and the media and general public (K). The three remaining stakeholders have even less interest in the social and ecological issues involved, that is, the shareholders (B), the stock analysts (C) and the competitors (G).

The IMS mix for CSR issues

The matrix gives a good picture of the strategic situation of the MNC regarding social responsibility issues and the stakeholders involved, but not of how the company is to demonstrate social responsibility in order to earn legitimacy with its stakeholders, that is, its matching strategy. The selection of IMS is also based on this analysis of the external institutional environment and the internal institutional setting as exemplified above. The matching strategies for the mix of stakeholders and issues are first analysed for each key social responsibility issue listed in Figure 14.4

and then for the key stakeholders. The first issue concerns how societal advantage is achieved by creating ecological value, while the other issues relate to social value.

(1) Environmental care

Environmental care is one of the most important issues within both the group and the local subsidiary. The MNC is quite proactive when it comes to this issue, having specific environmental policies and reports, and being certified according to the ISO 14001 standard in 2001. The majority of the respondents at the company therefore mentioned environmental care as an important issue. Regarding the SDGs, environmental care in this case mainly concerns water management (SDG 6), energy (SDG 7), climate change (SDG 13) and terrestrial ecosystems (SDG 15).

The three stakeholders with the strongest interest in the subsidiary's environmental care are the employees (D), the governmental authorities (H) and the local community (J). The MNC largely *complies* with the expectations of these stakeholders (the *acquiesce* strategy), since it is at

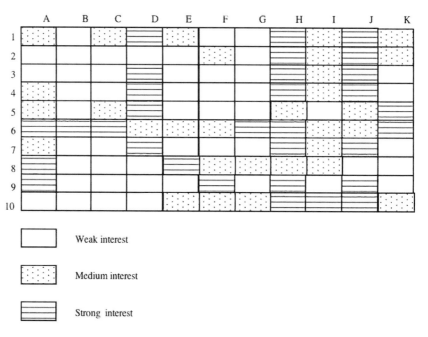

Notes: Key issues/key stakeholders: 1) Environmental care; 2) Creation of employment opportunities; 3) Employee's family benefits; 4) Education, training and personal development; 5) Working conditions; 6) Auditing and reporting; 7) Community development; 8) Customer development; 9) Supplier development; 10) Technology transfer and market development.
A) Group and division; B) Shareholders; C) Stock analysts; D) Employees; E) Customers and Distributors; F) Suppliers; G) Competitors; H) Governmental authorities; I) Professional and interest organizations; J) Community; K) Media and general public.

Figure 14.4 CSR matrix of the bearings MNC

the forefront of environmental issues, and applies standards that are above average. Simultaneously, since the company is active in the field, it has used the *manipulate* strategy, where there has been an influence on the immediate surroundings. The MNC has, for example, educated local companies close to the factory in environmental issues and the employees have also been educated in environmental care. Regarding the group and product division (A), the subsidiary *complies* with the norms of this stakeholder. There is relatively little room for own initiatives and the annual environmental report is made for the whole group, not specifically for the local subsidiary. The increased interest in environmental care among the stock analysts (C) and customers and distributors (E) is also *complied* with, which is shown by the implementation of the ISO 14001 standard, which was initiated as a result of demand from the major customers and the requirements of membership of the Dow Jones Sustainability Index. The local subsidiary further *complies* with the norms of the professional interest groups (I) and the media and general public (K) through its environmentally friendly approach and environmental reports.

This shows that the MNC is aware of the importance of having a sustainable business in Malaysia, which is achieved by creating ecological value. By complying with the demands of a number of groups, these groups in turn benefit from the operations of the MNC. This makes them justify these operations, and hence legitimacy is gained through the ecological values created at the stakeholder level.

(2) Creation of employment opportunities

This and the next issue concern the promotion of full and productive employment and decent work for all (SDG 8). Together with issues 4 and 5 they also relate to the labour market as an organizational field. For issue 2, the MNC mainly follows organizational routines belonging to the *acquiesce* matching strategy. Being the first foreign MNC to locate a factory in the area, the subsidiary has created many employment opportunities. Almost 500 locals have been employed and the number of expatriates in the area has decreased steadily. Hence, the strong interests of the governmental authorities (H) and the local community (J) in increasing the employment rate in the area have been *complied* with. However, during the Asian financial crisis at the end of the 1990s, the subsidiary had to reduce its workforce and the company is not utilizing many local suppliers (F). Following such an organizational routine is clearly a result of the general norms within the group (A) regarding the creation of employment opportunities, and the subsidiary has therefore followed *habits*. The interest of the professional associations (I) and the media and general public (K) in the subsidiary's creation of employment is more of a general nature, where the expectations are that the company should contribute to the increased overall welfare of the country. Thus the subsidiary has *complied* with these expectations, and thereby gained legitimacy from the social values created.

(3) Employee's family benefits

This issue also concerns healthy lives (3). The employees (D) at the local factory have high expectations of the company when it comes to providing them and their families with benefits, such as appropriate salaries, medical care, pensions, loans for houses and social activities. Even though the company is above average regarding salaries (economic benefits), many requests are still made for improvements such as more social activities, better health care and increased transfers to the pension funds (social benefits). Thus, the subsidiary has utilized a *compromise* strategy, where the expectations of the different employees have been *balanced*. Regarding the governmental authorities (H), the subsidiary has pursued an *acquiesce* strategy, where the norm of greater benefits for the employees than regulated by law has been *complied* with. The pension system and health insurance are typical examples of what the governmental authorities expect from MNCs like the one studied. Also, professional associations (I) have the same kind of expectations and argue that CSR has to start internally with the employees and their families. Finally, the rather small local community (J), with its limited resources, largely depends on the company. Benefits experienced by the employees and their families will promote the community, since most of the employees come from the area. The health-care system, summer employment for the employees' children and the yearly family day are signs that the subsidiary has not only complied with the expectations but also *influenced* the community and caused a change, further adding to social value, and thereby gaining legitimacy from these stakeholders.

(4) Education, training and personal development

This issue primarily relates to quality education and lifelong learning (4), but also to gender equality (5) to some degree. Since the MNC values education, training and personal development highly, activities related to these issues are classified as following the *innovate* and *manipulate* strategies. Employees in the local factory (D) and the local community (J) also value education and personal development highly, as many of them are rather uneducated and dependent on the large local companies. Many of the employees also mention this issue as the main reason for choosing the MNC as an employer. However, these beliefs have not always been present locally, and the subsidiary can therefore be said to have *generated change* among the employees and in the community. It was necessary to provide education, since initially there were no people available with the right skills. However, the extensive education and training might also be a result of this being the norm within the group (A). Hence, there might have been the organizational routine classified as *habit* as well, along with a need to *comply* with the group. The governmental authorities (H) and professional interest associations (I) expect the MNC to develop the labour market through its education, training and personal development policies. Such expectations are also *complied* with in order to gain legitimacy.

(5) Working conditions

This issue also relates to SDG 8, which shows that employment and decent work are vital social issues for the company in Malaysia. Having a long tradition of operating production plants, providing good working conditions is natural for the MNC. The local factory is relatively newly established and equipped with good facilities and a good working environment. Hence, the subsidiary has *complied* with the social issue of providing good working conditions. This is in the interest of the group (A), which cares about the image of the company and the well-being of the employees; the stock analysts (C), who increasingly value companies according to, for instance, internal working conditions; and the governmental authorities (H) along with the media and general public (K), who have become increasingly aware of companies' internal working conditions. There have been even more active strategies towards the employees (D), the zero-accident programme, which can be seen as the *innovate* matching strategy, having had a large impact on working conditions. However, the employees have a couple of requests concerning a deficiency in working conditions that have not yet been fulfilled, thus requiring a *compromise* strategy to be pursued by the subsidiary. These requests pertain to a lower level of noise in the factory and having more and better facilities. There is also the suggestion that the facilities could be used by the local community (J), but the subsidiary has taken on an *avoid* strategy towards the community on this issue since this has not been done yet. No claim for CSR has thus been made here, which means that no social value has been created. This might result in the legitimacy gained with these stakeholders through other means being reduced or even lost, which could cancel out the part of the societal advantage coming from these stakeholders.

(6) Auditing and reporting

Transparency, that is, the extent to which the performance of the MNC in the social and natural environments is audited and reported to stakeholders and others in society, is a critical CSR issue. One way to improve transparency is through better auditing. In the bearings company case, all the key stakeholders find it important that the subsidiary measures and reports on its operations. The subsidiary therefore *complies* with the group's rule system of reporting (A). Regarding shareholders (B), stock analysts (C), customers and distributors (E), suppliers (F) and competitors (G), the subsidiary does not report to them separately, instead including them in general reports produced by the group. Regarding the employees (D), there seem to be different opinions about what should be measured and what should be reported. In general, there are requests for more information from many of the employees, which implies that there is an *avoid* strategy at the subsidiary. It is, however, unclear whether this strategy is deliberate through wanting to *conceal* performance.

The government authorities (H) and professional associations (I) are especially keen on foreign MNCs reporting on social and ecological issues. They expect a lot from them and require their commitment to Malaysian society. However, the subsidiary does not provide special reports to these stakeholders, indicating an *avoid* strategy. Nevertheless, there have not been any real problems in the subsidiary's relations with either the government or the interest organizations. When a problem occurs, such as an oil leakage, the subsidiary *complies* with the expectations of how they should be solved. The local community (J) and the media and the general public (K) increasingly demand appropriate reports on the company's performance, mainly because there has been a movement from a 'trust me' to 'show me' culture. The subsidiary, true to its thought style based on openness, wants to be transparent by showing what it is doing, but does not take much action, especially since there have not been any complaints.

Nevertheless, there does not seem to be any specific formal reporting within the company on CSR-related issues, which means that the MNC has *avoided* the requirements from all stakeholders to a certain extent. This is reflected by the different opinions among the respondents regarding the extent to which the specific matters related to CSR are reported within the group and the subsidiary. The mere existence of such differences in opinion implies that the reporting on CSR cannot be very good. Moreover, the MNC is a low-profile company, and its performance is not stressed externally. This issue is not so important for the MNC and not used much as a legitimacy-creating factor. Therefore, the potential for this issue to gain legitimacy seems to be under-estimated by the MNC.

(7) Community development

This issue is related to SDG 11 about making cities inclusive, safe, resilient and sustainable. Community development is most important for the employees (D), who mainly come from the local community; the governmental authorities (H), which want to develop the local area; and the local community (J) itself, which is rather dependent on the large companies. The MNC's mere presence in the area has had a great *influence* on the community through a *manipulation* strategy, even having some *control* over the local community, for example by providing employment; giving benefits to the employees' families; engaging in community projects together with other companies, such as those relating to fire protection and road tolls; giving smaller donations; and inviting the surrounding companies for education in environmental care. Furthermore, it is important for the group (A) to have smooth community interaction wherever in the world the MNC chooses to establish itself. Thus, the subsidiary has *complied* with the norms and values regarding community interaction within the group.

The pioneer status further signifies a smooth integration into the Malaysian society and the governmental authorities' (H) satisfaction with the MNC's local establishment and operations, thereby validating its legitimacy. Actually, as it was the first foreign company to establish itself there the company *complied* with the government's expectations of attracting companies to the area. Similarly, the rule systems of the professional organizations (I) have been complied with, since the company's local presence can develop not only the area but also industry and other manufacturers. Some respondents, however, believe that there should be more facilities at the factory which could be utilized by the people in the area and that the MNC could contribute more in the way of donations, social activities and so on. In any case, community development is mentioned by the respondents as one of the company's achievements in Malaysia, indicating that this is a key area of responsibility, which is of critical importance for getting societal advantages by gaining legitimacy through the social values created. Nevertheless, there seems to be even larger potential for creating societal advantages by gaining more legitimacy through increasing the benefits available to community groups.

(8) Customer development

Together with the next two issues, these classical CSR issues are mainly about promoting inclusive and sustainable industrialization as well as fostering innovation (SDG 9). The present issue is also about ensuring sustainable consumption and production patterns (SDG 12). The MNC's activities towards the customers and distributors (E), for example training in using the products, have influenced the market. The factory is a separate company within the group and is therefore not supposed to have any direct contacts with customers. In spite of this, visits to customers are sometimes paid when an error occurs, which implies a proactive approach. Hence, the norm within the group (A) of treating customers as important is *complied* with. Participating in raising quality through customer development also influences other market actors, namely suppliers (F) and competitors (G), as well as increases the MNC's legitimacy with government (H) and professional and interest organizations (I). The norms of other stakeholder groups with an interest in customer development, such as government, have therefore been matched with *manipulation*. So, by exceeding expectations in terms of customer development, legitimacy is improved with other stakeholders as well.

(9) Supplier development

Since many of the suppliers (F) are internal to the group, they are developed in an appropriate way, and the local factory follows the requirements set by the group (A) for suppliers. There is then an *acquiescence* strategy present towards the suppliers of the MNC. However, this strategy leads to a lack of utilization of local suppliers, because the group demands are too high for them regarding quality and delivery time, for example. Moreover, this combined *acquiescence* strategy towards the group and *avoidance* strategy towards suppliers and the governmental authorities (H) is possible, since there are no local content rules for the MNC to adapt to. Thus, as with customer development, a similar impact is created with other stakeholders, but this time it is negative, which may mean the MNC risks losing legitimacy. Indeed, the MNC could be more ambitious regarding this CSR issue and increase its impact on Malaysian society, thereby raising its legitimacy and creating a higher societal advantage. To find out more about how big an impact it is possible to achieve, the company could perform a value-chain analysis in accordance with the recommendation of the SDG Compass. The MNC should then analyse the inputs into the factory and the output, both in Malaysia and abroad, that is, the subsidiary as part of the 'global factory' or any of the global industrial networks.

(10) Technology transfer and market development

The governmental authorities (H), the professional organizations (I) and the local community (J) find technology transfer very important. As described earlier, the subsidiary has utilized a *manipulative* matching strategy and has *influenced* the Malaysian industry sector, as their technology and processes are rather uncommon in Malaysia. The MNC has also *influenced* the quality norms of the customers and distributors (E), the suppliers (F) and the competitors (G).

The IMS mix towards stakeholders

To study the importance of each stakeholder, they are ranked according to their degree of interest in the ten issues. As seen in the CSR matrix (Figure 14.4), two stakeholders stand out as having a strong interest in most issues, namely governmental authorities (no. 1) and the local community (no. 2). The interest of the other stakeholders in the CSR issues are more uneven. For example, the employees (no. 3) have a strong interest in five issues, a medium interest in one issue and a weak interest in four issues. The interest organizations (no. 5) have a strong interest only in technology transfer and market development but a medium interest in seven issues. Five stakeholders are only important for the MNC for certain issues, for example customers mainly for customer development and suppliers mainly for supplier development.

The mix of the IMS towards each of the three key stakeholders (nos. 1–3) is now summarized based on the section above about the IMS mix for the CSR issues. The mix of the IMS towards the government authorities is dominated by the *acquiesce* strategy, since the MNC is complying with the rules of the government for seven issues. It is also practising an *avoid* strategy by disguising nonconformity for two issues (auditing and reporting; supplier development) and *manipulating* government on supplier development. The IMS mix towards the community is more equally shared between three strategies. The MNC is complying with the rules (*acquiesce*) of the community for three issues, avoiding three issues by concealing its real behaviour. The IMS is active for two issues, where the local community is *manipulated* and proactive (*innovate*) regarding education, training and personal development. A similar IMS mix is found for the fewer issues of the employees.

CONCLUSIONS

The international strategic aspect of stakeholder management is developed by integrating the international matching strategy and international network strategy. The IMS is then elaborated further by analysing international matching strategy towards local stakeholders in emerging markets. The institutional view of the NIA is deepened by looking at socially oriented matching strategies towards stakeholders. The international matching strategy model is established and applied to the case of an MNC in Malaysia. A network map is generated of the relevant stakeholder network, and the external and internal institutional contexts are extracted through institutional analysis as a background to the CSR issues and the IMS.

Although all international matching strategies are used, *acquiesce* and *manipulate* are found to be the leading ones. As expected, the *manipulate* strategy of influencing standards is an important issue in emerging markets. Since the bearings MNC is at this time the only foreign producer in its industry in Malaysia, it set standards to manipulate norms and values. This shows the stakeholders that the company is powerful in the market, which enhances its legitimacy and creates social values and a good reputation. The employees at the factory had a large interest in the company's ability to set standards regarding salaries, benefits, working environment and so on. However, since part of the reason for the establishment of the factory in this local area was the low labour costs, European standards regarding salaries were only partly followed. Hence the MNC *compromised* between the group and the Malaysian stakeholders on this issue.

For the market actors, higher standards will lead to a developed market and new business opportunities. The Malaysian government, the professional interest groups, the local community, and the media and general public, had an interest in the subsidiary's ability to set new social standards, because this might help to develop the country. Creating transparency through establishing suitable auditing and reporting routines was shown to be a critical part of CSR when it comes to improving legitimacy with stakeholders.

All in all, IMS is stakeholder specific. For each specific issue, the strategy varies between the stakeholders, as well as there being some variation in strategy for a specific stakeholder. For example, through avoiding the requirements of formal reporting within the company on CSR-related issues as well as lacking in terms of supplier development, the MNC risked losing legitimacy. The lack of reporting is also a sign that CSR as a practice was inadequately institutionalized within the subsidiary, as well as within the group.

The CSR matrix is found to be a valuable tool for analysing the strategic situation in international stakeholder management. It gives an overview of the degree of importance of each CSR issue and each stakeholder. Moreover, it provides a profile of the importance of the issues for each stakeholder, as well as making it possible to analyse the common and conflicting issues for the stakeholders. Based on the matrix, the international matching strategies for the mix of stake-holders and issues were analysed separately for each key social responsibility issue and for the key stakeholders.

Government was found to be the most important key stakeholder. The MNC studied has solved the critical IBS dilemma of local responsiveness versus global integration by complying with the rules of this stakeholder at the same time as it has acquiesced with the rules of the group. Some compromise between local and global rules has been necessary, which has created a good fit. The IMS towards this primary stakeholder is developed further in the next chapter by going more into how to combine IMS and INS to achieve sustainable competitive advantage through the IBS.

15
International business strategy towards government

This chapter builds directly on the previous chapter in three ways. First, international stakeholder strategic management is deepened by concentrating on one major stakeholder, namely the government. In addition to usually being the most important stakeholder for the multinational corporation (MNC) outside the market, the government is both a social and economic actor. This makes legitimacy important, as well as how legitimacy influences the profitability of the MNC. Second, the international network strategy (INS) and international matching strategy (IMS) are more explicitly combined by analysing how they are integrated to achieve a sustainable competitive advantage for the international business strategy (IBS) as a whole, that is, INS + IMS = IBS. By going into the INS and relating it to the IMS, a more complete picture is given of the IBS. The chapter is chiefly about the strategy towards the executive parts of government, that is, the authorities and other administrative bodies engaged in implementing government policy. MNCs are mostly engaged with government at this more operational administrative level rather than at the political level. Third, the legitimacy-based strategic orientation is developed further by adding three major types of legitimacy of special relevance for this stakeholder.

The INS is taken up first, which is executed through the MNC–government network (MGN), where MNCs both cooperate on common causes and compete with one another. A model for

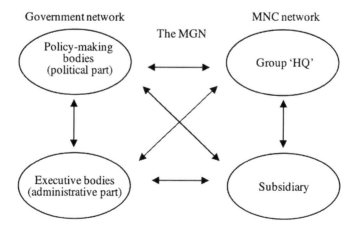

Figure 15.1 The multinational corporation–government network

international network strategy towards the administrative part of government follows next. It is grounded in the international network strategy model in Chapter 8, illustrated in Figure 8.1. Based on a network map, it takes up the main strategic objectives, the linkage mix, and the process of forming relationships with government actors. First-mover advantages are achieved through these relations and by taking into account another main stakeholder, namely the competitors in the product/service market.

The INS is combined with the IMS in an IBS model towards government. IMS is related to the INS through the network position, which is defined based on the extent of cooperation and conflict between the MNC and government. A major thought style is established for each position: domination, consensus, peripheral and harmony. How the MNC relates itself to a specific stakeholder to achieve legitimacy then depends on the strategic matching situation the MNC finds itself in, such a situation being defined as a network position.

THE MULTINATIONAL CORPORATION–GOVERNMENT NETWORK

The inter-organizational network established with various government units by the MNC is defined as the MNC–government network (MGN). This network forms part of the general network map previously illustrated in Figure 8.2. This specific part that connects two sub-networks is illustrated in Figure 15.1. One of these sub-networks is the hierarchical intra-organizational MNC network introduced in Chapter 7, which consists of the two main prescribed organization sets: the local subsidiary and group headquarters. The other is the government network consisting of two other sub-networks: the political part, that is, the policy-making bodies, and the administrative part, that is, the executive bodies. Companies could cooperate with the purpose of ensuring the policies favour their industry, such as by making critical resources available to it. Firms in a particular industry or in a number of industries engage in cooperative strategies and form cooperative organizations (industrial associations, for example) to plead for government favour. This may involve lobbying the government. The network organized for such joint action is defined as an action network. However, it is more common that firms within the same industry compete with one another through each firm maintaining its own contacts and developing its own inter-organization network in the bureaucracy.

MAIN OBJECTIVES OF THE INTERNATIONAL BUSINESS STRATEGY

There are two main reasons for MNCs to participate in the MGN, one related to legitimacy, the other to efficiency. They are viewed as the two major objectives of the MNC:

1. To gain a societal advantage by achieving legitimacy from government: this is the primary reason for contacts being established with government. By obtaining licences, for example, legitimacy is achieved.

2.   To gain a competitive advantage and become more profitable than the competitors in the market. This is mainly achieved indirectly via the government. One common way is to utilize the rules in competition with local firms or other MNCs, in order to favour one's own firm, for example to block competitors from introducing new products.

The relation between these two major objectives is often direct. The more an MNC can gain a societal advantage by improving its legitimacy position in the government network, the easier it often is to also reach efficiency goals such as competitive advantage in the market. For example, by winning the right to import high-quality materials for the local production site, the company's competitive advantage could be improved. In this respect, the relationship between legitimacy and efficiency or between societal advantage and competitive advantage is direct and mutually influential. The trade-off between these two major objectives could be complicated by the fact that they might be interpreted differently by various units within the MNC network. For instance, there could be conflict between the major interests. Compared to the group interest, where problems are viewed from a global perspective, the local subsidiary interest could favour legitimacy aspects more than efficiency aspects. Conflicting interests regarding technology transfer, imports and ownership may arise within the MNC as a consequence of such differing interests.

Thus, an MNC could be interested in influencing the implementation of a policy in order to obtain a licence before its competitors, or to hasten the processing of a permit. A company might win a competitive advantage by, for example, obtaining a licence ahead of its competitors to manufacture a new product, or import new products. A competitor could, on the other hand, stop or delay such actions and thereby keep its advantage through having a good position of influence with the authorities, with the result that such a position of legitimacy impacts on the competitive strength of the MNC. This major strategic dilemma between competitive advantage and societal advantage is analysed more below.

The MNC participates in the authorities' decision-making processes through the MGN. The granting of permits to do business in a country, for example, does not happen by itself, since the decision processes of the government network are very complex, with a high degree of discretion for individual decision-makers. Moreover, authorities are often dependent on information from MNCs to solve the complex issues involved. Also, the low capacity and rationality of the government can be improved with help from MNCs.

One characteristic of this rather informal process of the government network is that individuals are prone to extract monopoly rents. Government and company officials are not completely impartial and incorruptible, where only public or company interests are pursued. Government officials do not only grant permissions, but also have something to sell, just as MNC officials have something to offer. Individual parties could try to dispense favours to increase their influence. 'Buyers' at the MNC may offer favours to 'sellers' in government to obtain the right service. The temptation to bend the rules in favour of certain parties is strong, particularly since there is a shortage of such monopolized services. Favours can be created in ways other than through bribery to get government officials to take an interest in the welfare of the MNC, for example by providing valuable information for government decisionmaking, or jobs for relatives and friends.

Anyhow, decision-making within the government network can basically be classified as rational by following the administrative rationality logic. This makes linkages to government within the

MGN mainly a rational, clean process. Even if there are often reasons to question how professional government officials actually are, contacts within the MGN still take place between professionals.

INTERNATIONAL NETWORK STRATEGY

The MGN is now developed further through being focused on the linkage between the subsidiary and the executive bodies, namely the lower part of Figure 15.1. In most emerging markets, the IBS towards the government bureaucracy is the most critical part of the MGN, mainly to obtain operational permits such as licences. A model for the INS towards the executive part of government is therefore developed and illustrated in Figure 15.2. This model mainly builds on Figure 8.1, being about INS towards government rather than towards companies in the product/service market. It is complemented by the relationship process taken from Figure 9.1. There are important similarities between the MGN and industrial market networks. In both cases, network relationships are direct, long term, complex and stable; actors are professional; exchanges are complex; and decision processes complicated on both sides, involving many units and persons. Public actors are those organizations that administer and effect industrial policies, for example different processing units within the central bureaucracy and state bureaucracy that 'supply' licences. The other party of the MGN is the MNC subsidiary and parties affiliated to it, which claim that licences are granted.

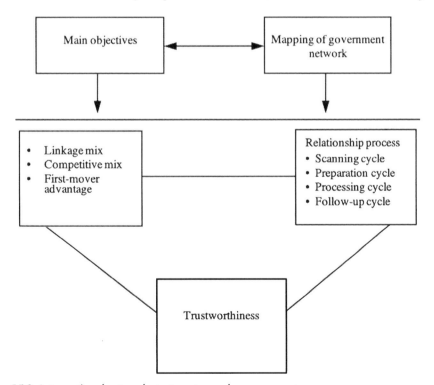

Figure 15.2 International network strategy towards government

As noted above, MNCs also cooperate to influence the government through joint action. A common way of organizing such cooperation is through forming an interest group, such as an industrial association. Companies therefore normally participate in two main types of networks to influence governments: action networks and organization networks. There are some major reasons for the MNC to participate in action networks in connection with acquiring permits. The government could be influenced to interpret a rule in a way that favours a group of companies, for instance local firms rather than competitors from abroad. Another reason for membership of an industrial organization could be to get first-hand information on the policy formation process, such as what is to be expected in the regulation of a certain industry. This can also be achieved through direct contacts with the government.

The main objectives of the IBS were stated above. They are also valid for the INS, since it is a sub-strategy of the IBS.

Mapping of government network

Most rules applied by governments towards MNCs mainly concern enforcement mechanisms. They are meant to attract or restrain firms, with some governments relying more on incentives and others more on restrictions. A chain of events or decisions normally takes place between different government authorities during the process of implementing an industrial policy, for example in issuing licences. An MNC mainly participates in such a horizontal process to obtain a permit, especially if it is not allowed to operate in the country without it. However, the implementation of the policy through the complex decision procedure, which often involves several authorities and ministries, is not 100 per cent strict. There is often some room for discretion, which makes it possible for the MNC to affect the decisions and sometimes even the policy itself.

After having mapped this government process network as an inter-organizational routine, one can go deeper into it by magnifying particular parts. Certain vital government units can be broken down into different organizational levels to look more closely at how these levels are connected to various organizational levels in the MNC network, and to study the relationships between them. The linkages consist of exchanges of material resources, information and communication, social exchange and influence.

Linkage mix

Deciding on the linkage mix is a critical part of the INS. Normally, it is a matter of combining the information and social linkages to create influences through the main phases of the relationship process, the purpose being to achieve an effective mix between the competitive and societal advantages. As was observed by Jansson et al. (1995), MNCs and the Indian government often worked together for long periods during the preparation and processing cycles (see below). The MGN was stable, intense and rather informal, where contacts were seen to be frequent and mostly personal, social, durable, professionally based and trustful. The strategic issues involved in these contacts were observed to be either information based or socially based. It was further established that when developing and implementing a project in the form of a new product to be manufactured and sold on the local market, inputs such as permits were needed. When acquiring these, the parties became enclosed in their relationship, making it difficult to substitute each other for a third party. The government, for instance, tied itself to a few MNCs' solutions for the needs of the country. The more resources the MNC invests in the country, on the other hand, the more its flexibility to divest is reduced. This tie-up grows gradually as the parties become absorbed into the relationship, and the flexibility of both parties is reduced. The stronger the interdependence becomes, the higher the switching costs of replacing each other.

Costs of acquiring permits could be considerable, with expenses often already high in the early phases of the MGN – the scanning and preparation cycles – because of the contacts that had to be cultivated with the government to create influence and trust. The cost of preparing documents for the applications could be large, too. The largest costs involved, however, were more indirect and concerned business aspects, for instance the preparation of investment proposals or lost profits in cases where applications were turned down. Since each solution was company-specific, most of the expenses were wasted if no licence was received. The degree of specialization of the linkages was normally high, which meant that it became costly to re-establish the linkages if they were terminated. It was therefore important for the parties to protect themselves from the dangers of such a relationship situation. This was usually done within the relationship by building up a mutual balance of gradual commitment of resources. The decisive judgements for both parties concerned the degree of commitment for each phase of the process leading to a licence being applied for, processed and maintained.

Relationship process

After a pre-relationship stage, the relationship process for bridging the gap between the organizations of the MGN consists of the establishment stage and the habitual stage. The habitual stage is the period when the relationship has been built up and is routinized, and habits have been developed.

First there is the scanning cycle, which mainly takes place during the pre-relationship stage. An investment proposal or similar investigation is made to study the feasibility of operating in the host country – to establish a factory, for example, or to import a new technology. Towards the end of this phase, the MNC also looks into how the government views such a project and what permits are needed. But actual contacts with the administrative units to find out about the licence opportunities start during the preparation cycle and runs until the licence application is filed. In the next cycle the licence is processed. During the follow-up cycle, which starts after the licence has been approved, officials are contacted to keep the relationship going while awaiting future applications. These cycles are common to all types of licence relations, although the characteristics of each cycle are different. Moreover, the importance of each cycle varies with the main type of licence. They are all important for complicated licences, as these take a long time to establish and keep going. For simpler licences, on the other hand, the marketing process mainly consists of the processing cycle.

The first two cycles mostly concern information collection. The parties collect information about each other on different aspects of the requirement and its solution. A lot of resources are spent on obtaining first-hand knowledge about the parties and about competing solutions as regards the needs of the country. This information-dominated phase is usually terminated when the licence application is filed. Negotiations may also be part of the preparation cycle, for example to reach a basic agreement, which is then followed by the licence application being filed. A basic agreement covers the reason for the application, for example that the MNC wants to build a new factory or to import a new machine, but negotiations can also take place during the processing cycle if there is no such basic agreement. The outcome of this cycle is the licence. In the follow-up cycle, it is important to develop the established relationship.

The length of the processing and follow-up cycles varies for different licences. In these phases the parties come together, thereby excluding other parties. The regular contacts through these licensing procedures establish a long-term relationship, potentially leading to a first-mover advantage through the barrier created against the competitors.

Trustworthiness

The study in India made by Jansson et al. (1995) also shows the critical importance of the social network and trust for the functioning of the MGN. The bonds between the MNC and the government were strengthened and sustained by the social linkage, of which trustworthiness was a critical part. Face-to-face interaction with bureaucracy was superior to impersonal contacts for more complex communication patterns and in creating trust. Such face-to-face contacts developed into durable, stable and reliable networks. Friendship was important and was shown to be closely related to trust. It was however also found to be rather calculative and instrumental, and can mainly be characterized as professional personal friendship; private personal friendship was uncommon. Social relations were also established for other reasons. Belonging to the same social groups, mainly kinship, as well as membership of professional groups were found to be behind important connections. Cultural groupings, primarily language groups but also to some extent regional groups, were also part of the connectivity of the organizations. Caste groups and religious groups, however, were unimportant.

Competitive mix

The competitive mix is another critical strategic decision of the INS and is more directly related to competition with other MNCs. To gain a competitive edge, various types of linkages are available to the MNC within the MGN, for example to create different favours, give information about the MNC itself and its products, and inform about how the company can benefit the country. These diagonal linkages to government were used to achieve sustainable competitive advantages while also considering the horizontal linkage to the competitors. Information and favours are packaged to differentiate the MNC from its competitors and are communicated through a suitable linkage mix, mainly personal transfers of information and social influence. The MNC may sometimes be assisted or supported by a third party, such as the home government, embassy or trade association.

First-mover advantages

A crucial part of the international network strategy is to find the best mix and sequence of linkages over time, with the ultimate aim of finding the right combination of the two main objectives: legitimacy and efficiency. One way is to transform the competitive situation from one with many parties to one with few parties, the number of actual competitors being gradually reduced. This is accomplished by building and maintaining network relationships in such a way that government bodies are enclosed at the same time as competitors are locked out. These activities are interpreted as aiming at creating and maintaining first-mover advantages over competitors. A firstmover advantage is achieved either through the resource linkage or through the social linkage, when the government unit is socially committed to the MNC. Other alternatives are product and financial tie-ups that make the government dependent on the MNC's products and technology.

A first-mover advantage is achieved by finding the right linkage mix for various stages of the build-up of the relationship, or through a competitive offer that differentiates the MNC from the competitors. The INS, then, consists of the right combination of linkage and competitive mixes. Which package the MNC can offer depends on the capability profile of the firm.

INTERNATIONAL MATCHING STRATEGY

As is known from previous chapters, the major rationale behind strategy in the government organizational field is legitimacy, which is given to an organization or person by other organizations/persons as a result of the actions of that first organization or person. Such an acceptance is based on a test or assessment of the actions. The outcome of the test is in turn dependent on the basic rules governing the ratifying organization. Gaining legitimacy is a twoway process, where the MNC and the political and administrative actors of the government are involved in a two-way communication process, claiming and giving legitimacy. What this procedure looks like in various countries depends on how the political system and executive bodies work.

As found above, the main objectives of the MNC in the MGN reflect the difference between efficiency-based and legitimacy-based strategy. To achieve a favourable strategic position in the market, it should be possible to characterize the MNC network as a rational structure of high technical development with a collective orientation towards efficiency. But since the MNC is also embedded in other institutionalized contexts, for example government and politics, this is also reflected in the network as having an orientation towards legitimacy. A local unit within the MNC network reflects these two major strategic orientations in its organization by having a structure legitimated through being efficient in markets and/or another structure that reflects the political interest.

The issue of legitimacy of MNCs with government is coupled to the fact that organizations require information from the environment to remain solvent and to function, such as money, information and access to markets. Furthermore, their activities must be approved of by society, for example generating income and employment, or making a contribution in the long run to the development of the country, and not, say, destroying the natural environment. An organization must prove to the government its right to exist and therefore it must prove itself beneficial to society; that is, it must gain legitimacy. Efficiency has two connotations. In a technical sense, MNCs must be efficient in order to be competitive and survive in the markets. In a non-market and more ideological way, efficiency is a societal value through which such behaviour is legitimized by society. From an ideological perspective, efficiency is regarded as a more fundamental legitimacy category, for instance justifying the technological and scientific or rational orientation of the modern welfare state. At this level legitimacy is seen as a concept expressing the MNC's adaptation to dominant values and attitudes within the society concerned. Society is large and complex, consisting of several groups and sub-groups with varying norms, values and beliefs of what constitutes legitimacy. Therefore, legitimacy was defined above from the perspective of different stakeholders (interest groups or coalition members) of the company.

Three major types of legitimacy

In a parliamentary system, governments are expected to reflect the dominant values and norms that prevail in society. Such a government, thus, can be considered to be reflecting and pursuing the dominant concept of legitimacy in society. Besides government, and as discussed in the previous chapter, legitimacy might also be extended to other stakeholders of relevance to the MNC, legitimacy being defined from the perspective of different stakeholders of the company. In this chapter, these various sources of legitimacy are looked at in terms of the major stakeholder in society: the government. Legitimacy achieved from government is divided into three main types: technical legitimacy, regulative legitimacy (including procedural legitimacy) and social legitimacy (see Figure 15.3).

Technical legitimacy

Host country governments often evaluate MNCs on three main grounds, the first being market based and focusing on the behaviour of companies in markets. This situation, where the company is evaluated on a commercial or technical basis, is defined as technical legitimacy, for example whether MNCs contribute to host country industrial and technological development by improving market

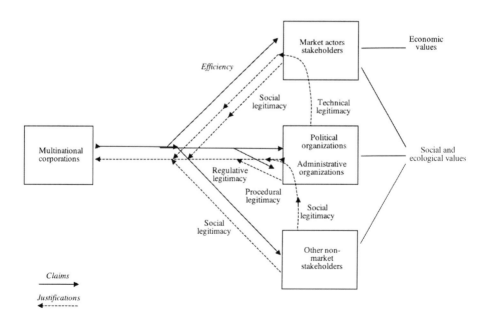

Figure 15.3 Types of legitimacy with government

efficiency. The efficiency concept is defined as market efficiency, that is, how efficiently companies are operating in the markets. This is a value-laden concept that is viewed differently by various interest groups in society. It is confined to the economic performance of the firm, which is related to its output and input. Technical legitimacy connects efficiency and legitimacy, since market efficiency is viewed from the viewpoint of a stakeholder.

One vital question is what this efficiency normative value looks like in a specific host country, for example expressed in terms of government policies and rules, and how it affects the MNCs. Are, for example, the typical values and norms of a Western market economy shared by this government? If not, how does a company justify its efficiency goal? Governments also attribute validity to MNCs on other than economic grounds, chiefly their general behaviour, such as whether the laws, regulations and customs of the host society are followed. For example, a way for an MNC to gain technical legitimacy is to transfer state-of-the-art technology and introduce higher-quality products than local manufacturers, thus contributing to raising the quality level and efficiency of the whole local industry. Technical legitimacy can also be achieved in the labour market by contributing to its efficiency, for example influencing labour groups through new values and standards brought in from abroad.

Regulative and procedural legitimacy

The second type of legitimacy concerns the wider effects of the market behaviour, such as adherence to and respect for host country government laws, rules and regulations, designed to guide, direct and regulate the MNC and its operations. This type of more pragmatic legitimacy is defined as regulative legitimacy. Since the regulative role is mainly the responsibility of government, it is vital to know how political and administrative organizations themselves gain legitimacy. This will improve the possibilities for MNCs to act politically, by learning the rules of the game and how to gain legitimacy. The various priorities of industrial policy documents, for example, are often public, and their content known. An informed and experienced MNC knows about these and adapts by including them in the proposals submitted to government. Such conformity to publicly declared policies increases the chances of gaining approval. MNCs also gain procedural legitimacy from administrative units by learning the rules and procedures of the bureaucracy and sticking to them. Hence, legitimacy is achieved by adapting to both political and administrative interests. While technical legitimacy concerns market efficiency, regulative and procedural legitimacy largely concerns administrative rationality.

Social legitimacy

Moreover, in an even wider and more ideological way, efficiency is a societal normative value, through which such behaviour is legitimized by society. This is the third ground for legitimacy, which is more moral in kind than the former ones based on a private company rationale and an administrative rationale. It incorporates such aspects as the technological and scientific or rational orientation of the modern welfare state, and concerns the question of the MNC's adaptation to fundamental values and attitudes in society. This third ground relates to the way the MNC contributes to the social and ecological needs of society. It is a type of moral legitimacy, which is defined as social legitimacy, and which is expressed through CSR. As shown before, labour, for example, is not only an economic input but also involves various social needs. Moral legitimacy in this field can be increased by improving CSR, for example how the company behaves with regard to labour, such

Table 15.1 Matching strategies

Degree of conflict	Degree of cooperation	
	Low	High
High	**Domination** –Manipulate –Defy –Avoid	**Consensus** –Defy –Avoid –Compromise
Low	**Peripheral** –Acquiesce	**Harmony** –Compromise –Acquiesce

as providing appropriate facilities for its employees and so on. An MNC could also demonstrate social responsibility and win moral legitimacy through promoting welfare projects. How to gain or lose social legitimacy with various stakeholders was analysed at length in the previous chapter.

INS + IMS = IBS

The IBS towards government mainly focuses on the IMS, which is related to the INS through the network position. As found earlier, such a position can be defined in different ways, for example in Chapter 7 as a macro or micro position, and in Chapter 10 as an insider or outsider position. However, in the MGN, the network position is defined based on the extent of cooperation and conflict between the MNC and government, being further characterized according to how the MNC views a certain position. Four network positions are developed and illustrated in Table 15.1, expressing different degrees of conflict and cooperation between these parties. A major thought style is then also established for each position: domination, consensus, peripheral and harmony. As established in Chapter 5, in deciding on the IMS, organizational members create order by matching rules and situations and in using criteria of similarity or difference. As further developed in Chapter 13, how the MNC relates itself to a specific stakeholder to achieve legitimacy then depends on the strategic matching situation in which the MNC finds itself. For example, the MNC is either following the rules of the environment or trying to make the environment follow the rules of the MNC. Such a strategic matching situation is here defined as a network position.

Domination

In the case of a high degree of conflict and a low degree of cooperation, the thought style based on the network relationships between the parties is viewed as domination. Three main types of matching strategies are conceivable in this situation. In the manipulate strategy each party tries to dominate the other by shaping its values and decision criteria. However, either one or both may conceive the demands made by the counterpart as illegitimate. Another organizational routine of this international matching strategy is to co-opt, where one party brings on board influential stakeholders, for example an MNC employing former government officials. One party may also try to control the other by dominating institutional stakeholders and processes. How well this will succeed depends on the bargaining power of the parties. The use of bargaining power may, however, cause the quality of the relationship to deteriorate, and may even put an end to it. As the bargaining power may then tilt more in favour of the counterpart, difficulties may arise. This could therefore be an unstable situation. Defy is another possible matching strategy in this conflict-prone situation. A strong MNC may dismiss government demands by ignoring explicit norms and values. It could also challenge the government by contesting rules and requirements, or even attack it by assaulting the sources of institutional pressure. If the MNC's bargaining position is low, the avoid strategy might also be conceivable, for example by disguising nonconformity (conceal) or escaping by changing goals, activities, domains or even country. One conclusion from Jansson et al. (1995) is that the manipulate and defy strategies based on conflict are not typical for India and not suitable to use with the Indian government. One might even say that these strategies have been practised more by MNCs from the US than by European or Japanese MNCs, and therefore these strategies may have a certain institutional bias. American companies are often strong advocates of the 'free-market' ideology as well as being considered to be more conflict-oriented than Asian or European MNCs.

Consensus

The network position of a high degree of cooperation as well as a high degree of conflict is complex and contradictory. The major thought style characterizing this situation is defined as consensus. Here, the avoid and compromise matching strategies seem to prevail. The compromise strategy was found by Jansson et al. (1995) to be typical of the way European MNCs acted in India as there was a high degree of dependence among the parties and the alternatives were few. This created a basic understanding of each party's position and the fact that they needed each other, at the same time as there was awareness of the basic conflict between MNCs and governments. In such situations creativeness and ingenuity are called for to find solutions that accommodate these conflicting positions. It is important to balance the relationship by avoiding securing gains at the cost of the counterpart, where the adjustments by the parties may be introduced either through the goals, or through the means to achieve the goals. Another alternative is to avoid each other by decoupling along the time dimension (buffering), which makes it possible for both parties to achieve their goals but not at the same time. It is plausible to believe that in such instances subsidiaries of MNCs enjoy a particular advantage, since they are part of a worldwide network. This may provide the subsidiary with a better possibility of developing a mix acceptable to the government in return for appropriate treatment. The possibilities of reaching a satisfactory deal with the Indian government were rather good, since it was a coalition of interests, where a number of ministries with conflicting views on what needs to be done participate in the decision-making process. MNCs could try to create balance between these conflicting interests by offering to satisfy a few ministries in exchange for their support against others.

Peripheral

When both the degrees of cooperation and conflict are low, the MNC–government relationship is defined as a peripheral situation on the part of the MNC. This is a typical situation when MNCs do not deal much with governments and therefore can concentrate on the business or efficiency aspects. In case the MNC needs to have anything to do with the government, it would be convenient to follow a matching strategy based on acquiesce, for example to comply by obeying rules and accepting norms or imitate by mimicking institutional models.

Harmony

The thought style characterized by harmony is signified by high cooperation among the parties, while the conflict level is low. In this situation, the government as well as MNCs are familiar with each other's needs and find that they are complementary. This situation is relevant for MNCs that are in a very strong position with the government in that they are in high demand because of their advanced technology or good export potential, that is, because they are considered to be highly efficient. This situation excludes the more conflict-oriented matching strategies, for example manipulate and defy, in favour of the less conflict-prone ones, for example acquiesce and compromise.

The situation of high cooperation and low conflict is typical of countries that have a friendly attitude towards MNCs, for example South East Asian countries such as Singapore and Thailand. These countries favour industrial policy founded on Western market ideology, where foreign companies are mainly evaluated on market performance, changing the mix between technical, regulative and social legitimacy. Since the parties here are more or less 'institutional twins', for example sharing norms and values, this matching strategy is characterized by a kind of mutual acquiescence, with both following invisible, taken-for-granted norms, mimicking each other's institutional models and obeying and accepting each other's rules and norms. There are shared interests between the parties, since the authorities are often dependent on MNCs for decision-making, such as when trying to get information. Therefore, the capacity and rationality of the government can be improved with help from the MNCs. However, as shown by the illustration of the CSR of the bearings company in the previous chapter, it is still very important to achieve social legitimacy, in particular with stakeholders other than the Malaysian government.

Illustration: international business strategy towards Indian governments

Another study of the IMS of a Swedish MNC in India, this time of Volvo Truck Corporation (VTC), revealed that there was a change from the consensus thought style to harmony, that is, a reduced level of conflict (Jansson, 2002). This also involves changing matching strategy: from more conflict-oriented strategies of defiance and avoidance to more cooperative ones, such as the compromise strategy. There is more room for negotiation. This is one effect of the liberalization of the Indian economy, where the attitudes of both the federal and the state governments towards MNCs have changed.

VTC was the first foreign MNC in the automotive sector that was allowed a 100 per cent foreign-owned subsidiary in India. This illustrates how attractive VTC's investment was to the Indian government, and also the change in government thought. VTC, as a global truck manufacturer, has a legitimate position in the eyes of the state and federal governments, and this factor was used in various ways during the establishment process in India. For example, VTC received many incentives from Karnataka State in the form of sales tax exemption and immunity from any new taxes imposed on it in the future. Moreover, Karnataka State built a new substation for power supply and laid a completely new fibre-optic cable to Bangalore (40 km from the plant). These are examples of how important Karnataka State believed the establishment of VTC's plant was for the region, the industry and the local community.

Thus, VTC cooperated by compromising. The MNC was very much adjusting and working according to the rules existing in India. VTC gained legitimacy with the state government in different ways. In its contacts with government officials, VTC was open-minded and showed respect for the local values and norms. VTC was also transparent in its operations, inter alia to reduce suspicion regarding its plans and intentions, and to create a trusting relationship. An example of the good relationship is the fact that VTC had immediate access to government officials and one official was appointed as a special 'personal' contact. If the MNC were having any problems with low-level bureaucrats who were demanding 'favours', for example, VTC could approach a higher-level official to get the matter resolved. The degree of cooperation was high as both parties stood to gain from the relationship. From a government point of view, VTC brought high technology, created new jobs and raised quality standards. Moreover, VTC shared its knowledge on environmental issues, creating a debate that the government advocated. From VTC's perspective, a good relationship with the government meant that it could more easily cope with the Indian bureaucracy and could focus on operating efficiently.

VTC also proved its commitment to the Indian market by introducing its latest models and technology. This manipulation of organizational fields by raising standards contributed to VTC attaining legitimacy from the government. Legitimacy was also improved by employing mostly locals, through which VTC gained legitimacy from the government via the labour market. Additionally, by contributing more money than was mandatory to the employees' pension funds, VTC assisted in improving its employees' social security. Last, but not least, the job opportunities created and the local economic improvements generated by VTC's establishment in Bangalore were other factors that increased VTC's legitimacy with government.

High legitimacy improved VTC's efficiency, since, for example, the state government viewed VTC as an asset and assisted in providing the right conditions for VTC to succeed. VTC, on the other hand, could concentrate on its core activities. Still, conflicts between efficiency and legitimacy did occur, as exemplified by the inspections made at the local factory. VTC's daily work in India was sometimes interrupted by state government officials' visits, the so-called 'Inspector Raj', to the plant in Hosakote. The officials came to check that VTC operations complied with existing rules and regulations, such as labour protection laws. At these visits, VTC presented relevant information to the officials and several VTC managers attended the meetings. These types of government activities resulted in VTC managers 'wasting' time on these issues instead of being able to concentrate on more crucial issues, such as operating the plant efficiently. Thus VTC's efficiency was somewhat distorted due to these government interventions. Initially, these visits were not always announced in advance and were quite frequent, but later most visits were scheduled and the number of visits decreased.

Liberalization has very much changed the way of achieving legitimacy compared to the pre-liberalization period. The INS strategy towards government as well as towards other stakeholders was also adapted to this continuously changing situation. The diagonal dimension of the network map was slowly shifting from being concentrated on relationships with federal government units to being focused on relationships with regional and local units, and from more to less complex networks. A strategy founded on the sustainability of the competitive advantage through high legitimacy due to government protection became even more unsettled, since liberalization promotes efficiency aspects. Technical legitimacy became more important than regulative legitimacy, which increased the importance of relationships in the product/service market at the expense of relationships in the government organizational field. Sustainable competitive advantages will then be based less on achieving societal advantages with government and more on achieving societal advantages with other stakeholders.

CONCLUSIONS

International network and matching strategies were combined in this chapter to analyse international business strategy towards government as the major stakeholder and as a follow-up to the international stakeholder strategic management in Chapter 14. The INS is executed through the MGN, where MNCs both cooperate on common causes and compete with one another. The former joint activity is defined as lobbying and takes place outside the MGN. First-mover advantages are achieved in the MGN through a different linkage mix and competitive mix. Face-to-face contacts are developed into durable, stable and reliable networks. Trustworthiness is closely related to friendship, which is found to be quite calculative and instrumental. Social relations are also established for other reasons, such as kinship, and membership of professional groups.

The IMS is then added to the INS. The MNC creates a mix between these two major types of strategies towards government in order to achieve three types of legitimacy: technical, regulative and procedural legitimacy. Technical legitimacy is gained by improving market efficiency, while regulative and procedural legitimacy is gained by following the rules and regulations of the government and following the procedures of the administrative bodies. Social legitimacy is more indirect, as it is closely related to CSR.

The INS and the IMS towards government are then combined more explicitly by analysing four strategic situations. They are defined as thought styles for typical network positions: how the MNC views the network position with government regarding cooperation or conflict. These thought styles were found to change with the liberalization of the Indian emerging market: from consensus to harmony. This made the domination thought style less relevant for India. Liberalization has very much changed the way of achieving legitimacy compared to the pre-liberalization period.

16
Evaluation and change of international business strategy

A broad view is taken when evaluating the international business strategy (IBS), where it is not only a question of evaluating strategic performance but also how the multinational corporation (MNC) could act based on the outcome of the analysis. The performance is related to strategic change by being included in a broader strategic management process, where strategy is continuously evaluated. Possibilities to change and how to change then depend upon the characteristics of this process.

The chapter then looks closer at the strategic management process to study how and when to make adaptations of the kind discussed in previous chapters. To evaluate the effectiveness of the IBS, strategic performance is analysed based on Chapter 14. First, an organizational life cycle sustainability assessment is made of various mixes of the ecological, economic and social values. As defined in Chapter 5, effectiveness concerns the degree to which objectives are fulfilled in relation to creating such values with the stakeholders. Thus, the higher the combined value of the mix, the greater the degree to which the objectives are achieved. Based on this first assessment of strategic performance, how sustainable competitive advantages are achieved by making a trade-off between legitimacy and efficiency is analysed. To succeed in making such trade-offs, one needs to explore how societal advantage and competitive advantage are related to each other.

Assessing strategic performance is then part of a continuous process of strategic evaluation regarding when and how to change strategy. Based on the network institutional approach (NIA), this change process is analysed as institutional change taking place within the hierarchical network organization of the MNC developed in Chapter 7. This change is constrained and induced by contradictory institutional arrangements at the meso and macro levels. The conflicts and tensions originating from such inconsistencies spread to the intra-organizational network, possibly causing internal conflicts between different interest groups. How they are solved influences the change outcome, as does the dynamic interaction between the resources and capabilities. When the basic rules are arranged so that conflicts are kept at bay, for example by norms such as trustworthiness, no change takes place. The basic rules then work as dispositions for change by being stabilizers or facilitators, while the capacity to change is determined by the resources and capabilities of the MNC. If and how change occurs is then decided by the capability to learn, that is, the organizational learning process.

EFFECTIVENESS OF THE IBS

To evaluate the effectiveness of the IBS three tasks are performed. Initially, an evaluation of strategic performance is done by making an organizational life cycle sustainability assessment of various mixes of the ecological, economic and social values. The organizational life cycle develops the process aspect of the sustainable global industrial network (SGIN) introduced in Chapter 4. Moreover, the assessment of this life cycle is founded on the sustainability business triangle introduced in Chapter 13. Next, how management, based on such an evaluation, makes an effective trade-off between legitimacy and efficiency to achieve sustainable competitive advantages is taken up. To succeed with this, management also needs to know how to transform societal advantage into competitive advantage, which finalizes the performance evaluation part.

Organizational life cycle assessment

Of the corporate social responsibility (CSR) issues for the bearings company in Malaysia illustrated in Chapter 14, ecological impact was one of the most important among those identified. It was also relevant for most stakeholders according to the CSR matrix. The MNC was quite proactive when it comes to environmental care, had specific environmental policies and reports, and was certified according to the ISO 14001 standard. These policies mainly concerned four sustainable development goals (SDGs), namely water management, energy, climate change and terrestrial ecosystems. However, as introduced in Chapter 1, environmental care is a much more important strategic CSR issue today than it was for this MNC in the early 2000s. This higher importance is also reflected in the current CSR standard, ISO 26000:2010 (ISO, 2017). Due to the critical importance of the ecological issue, the MNC could highlight this issue even more and relate it to social and economic issues. Such an analysis would show in a concrete form how ecological issues are institutionalized into the economic and social environments of a specific organization such as an MNC.

This sustainability business issue is now examined more by doing an organizational life cycle assessment according to the four-step methodology developed by Finkbeiner et al. (2010) and specified in ISO 14044:2006 (ISO, 2016). Such an assessment is primarily used in this chapter to evaluate performance and not for strategic planning. The first step is to determine the boundary conditions of the system. Next, data is collected on potential environmental impacts. These could be complementary data, if strategic analysis of the external and internal contexts has already been done, as exemplified in Chapter 14, and in accordance with the analytical procedure developed in Chapter 12. These results are then assessed and interpreted based on the goals defined and the scope of the study. The organizational life cycle assessment differs between the two global industrial networks (GINs) introduced in Chapter 2, namely the cradle-to-grave and the cradle-to-cradle industrial networks. The reason is that they represent different definitions of the boundary conditions. The latter circular network involves more activities than the former network regarding product use, disposal and recycling. The ambition is also higher, since the purpose is for nature to regenerate the products so that the materials are returned to the biosphere as organic material, that is, being neither synthetic nor toxic (Peralta-Álvarez et al., 2015).

An organizational life assessment of either of these two GINs expands the CSR analysis done in Chapter 14 by focusing on the time dimension, since the MNC takes on a life cycle approach to its activities. From a natural environmental point of view, it compiles, analyses and evaluates the inputs and outputs of the organization along the life cycle. Based on the formula for sustainable business, this life cycle sustainability assessment involves an integrated analysis of the three types of external environments with the purpose of creating ecological, economic and social values with the stakeholders. The organizational life cycle sustainability assessment (LCSA) then consists of three parts: a life cycle assessment (LCA) of the effects of the MNC's activities in the natural environment, life cycle costing (LCC) on the impact of these effects in the economic environment, and a social life cycle assessment (SLCA) on the impact of these effects in the social environment (Finkbeiner et al., 2010). A combination of these three types of assessment produces an overall assessment of the sustainability of a business; in other words, LCSA = LCA + LCC + SLCA.

Life cycle assessment

The organizational life cycle assessment is thus based on the LCA, where the ecological impact is studied throughout the life cycle of a product system, that is, the physical flow of resources and energy (Finnveden et al., 2009). An impact assessment can be done by grouping the total emissions from all life cycle stages into environmental themes according to the impact they have on broader issues of concern such as human health and ecosystem quality. Five impact indicators have been identified. Data had earlier been collected for inputs and outputs at each stage of the life cycle, for example for inputs such as energy, land and water use and for outputs such as products and waste leaving the system at each stage. Emissions are estimated for each of these, for example CO_2 emissions for the energy use in a factory process.

It is a well-known fact that the depletion of the ozone layer has human health impacts such as skin cancer, sunburn and skin ageing. Ozone-depleting substances are halogen gases containing chlorine and/or bromine, which have the potential to break down ozone in the stratosphere. They are measured in tonnes and weighted by their potential to destroy ozone. Increases in photochemical smog can also contribute negatively to human health. Photochemical smog is characterized by the formation of high concentrations of oxidants and aerosols in the atmosphere through chemical reactions. High concentrations of ozone (the most important photochemical oxidant) have adverse effects on human health, mainly causing severe sickness or premature death.

Together, three other environmental processes could have severe effects on ecosystem quality, namely acidification, eutrophication and ecotoxicity. Ecosystem quality often affects the preservation of species and populations, impacting on survival and reproduction rates. Acidification is measured as the decrease of the pH value of freshwater ecosystems. Eutrophication refers to a sharply increased growth of algae and other microscopic plants resulting from the supply of nitrogenous and phosphorous nutrients to natural water courses. A common measurement is micrograms per litre of water. Ecotoxicity pertains to how chemicals interact with organisms in marine, freshwater and terrestrial environments. Organisms at risk from chemical exposures include plants, fungi and algae as well as worms, bugs, fish, reptiles, birds and mammals.

Life cycle cost assessment

To study the eco-efficiency of the resource and energy use during the life cycle, the LCA is extended to include the economic impact of a product system throughout its full lifetime. The life cycle cost (LCC) then summarizes all costs caused by a product network during its entire life cycle (Finkbeiner et al., 2010). Examples are costs of inputs from land, water, energy and human resource as well as manufacturing costs of materials, components, equipment and inventory, transport and marketing costs, and costs of using and recycling the product. External costs are also included, that is, costs incurred by society above the more direct life cycle costs mentioned above. They occur outside the market, and include, for example, the costs incurred as a result of reduced ecosystem quality discussed above. Such effects quantified above are internalized into the market by being monetized and given an economic value, for example in a specific currency like dollars. This is often highly problematic, since it is hard to translate ecological effects into market values. For example, it is very difficult to value an effect on the ecosystem quality like a lower survival rate of a population of animals (such as tigers in Asia). For those effects impossible to value and perhaps also quantify, qualitative indicators can be found or developed. This is often also the case in assessing social sustainability, which is discussed next.

Social life cycle assessment

The social life cycle assessment (SLCA) adds the social conditions in the production, use, disposal and recycling of products in a global industrial network, that is, the social impacts of all of a product's life cycle activities from cradle to grave (Benoît et al., 2010) or from cradle to cradle (Peralta-Álvarez et al., 2015). The activities at various life cycle stages are associated with the locations where they are carried out (e.g. mines, factories, homes/offices, recycling firms, disposal sites and distribution outlets). Social impacts in relation to the stakeholders are then studied at these locations. According to the Guidelines for Social Life Cycle Assessment of Products (Benoît et al., 2010), the social sustainability of the firm is assessed by evaluating the existing stakeholder context through using various subcategories such as qualitative and quantitative social impact indicators related to specific key issues for each stakeholder. The guidelines include five major stakeholders: workers, consumers, other value-chain actors, local community, and society. These stakeholders are familiar from Chapter 14. For example, three major CSR issues concerning the workers were listed in that chapter, namely employment opportunities, family benefits and education. The guidelines list a comprehensive set of social impact indicators for the five stakeholders; for example, for consumers: health and safety, feedback mechanism, consumer privacy, transparency and end-of-life responsibility. Furthermore, qualitative indicators are suggested as are quantitative indicators for measuring the subcategories, for example typical unit process activity variables such as worker hours and value added. Either secondary data are collected on such established indicators or, if missing, primary data. Social effects are usually easier to monetize than pure ecological effects, for example the ecological impact on human health discussed above.

An impact assessment is done in accordance with the formula LCSA = LCA + LCC + SLCA, by which the impact on the natural, economic and social environments by the individual product networks are aggregated to make a complete organizational life cycle assessment for the firm as a whole. A major problem in adding up various impacts is the risk of double counting, especially of external effects. For example, if certain costs of reduced human health due to negative ecological impact are included in the LCA, they need to be omitted from the SLCA. Similarly, if the employee benefits have been internalized as a reduced social cost for society in the LCC, they should only be included in the SLCA if an additional social effect is contributed.

The sustainability business triangle

The sustainability business triangle illustrated in Figure 13.1 is now used to discuss how to evaluate different trade-off options between the three values (see Figure 16.1).

The results from the three assessments above are aggregated by adding up quantitative information and/or through summarizing qualitative information. The set of impact categories are aggregates of subcategories, which in turn are aggregates of indicators. It was exemplified above how the impact of the three subcategories acidification, eutrophication and ecotoxicity on ecosystem quality could be quantified. However, the different scales used need to be normalized by being adjusted to each other through a common scale. This is a tricky task, often resembling the classical problem of comparing apples and oranges. Moreover, the importance of each subcategory must also be decided.

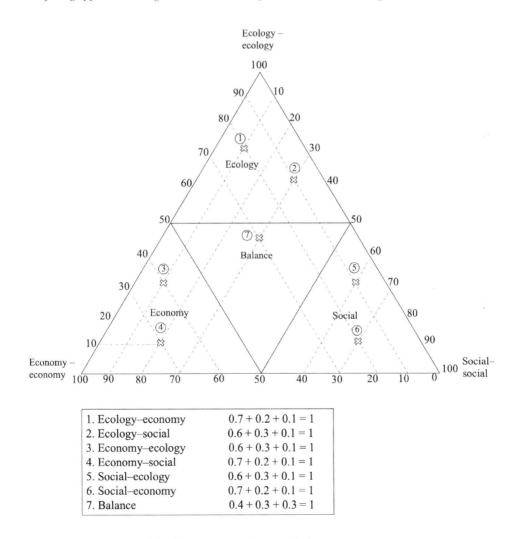

1. Ecology–economy	$0.7 + 0.2 + 0.1 = 1$	
2. Ecology–social	$0.6 + 0.3 + 0.1 = 1$	
3. Economy–ecology	$0.6 + 0.3 + 0.1 = 1$	
4. Economy–social	$0.7 + 0.2 + 0.1 = 1$	
5. Social–ecology	$0.6 + 0.3 + 0.1 = 1$	
6. Social–economy	$0.7 + 0.2 + 0.1 = 1$	
7. Balance	$0.4 + 0.3 + 0.3 = 1$	

Figure 16.1 The sustainability business triangle quantified

This is usually done by giving each subcategory a weight in order to be able to calculate a weighted average for the ecological impact, specified as a certain category, for example ecosystem quality. The choice of weighting method is a controversial issue because it requires the incorporation of social, political and ethical values (Finnveden et al. 2009). This is especially problematic at higher levels of aggregation, for example when making the trade-off between the ecological value 'ecosystem quality' and the social value 'human health' at the next step of aggregation. In one common type of method used, a panel is formed to ask a group of people about their values. Another common type of method is monetization, where values are expressed in monetary terms. This is easier for the social impact (social costs) than for the ecological impact. All panel methods and some monetization methods are based on stated preferences, where people are asked about their preferences. Monetization methods are usually based on preferences revealed in certain behavioural situations. After having determined the weighting factors, they are first used to calculate the sustainability utility value of each category by multiplying the subcategory values by a weighting factor and then adding them together. The same procedure is next used to calculate the sustainability value of the categories, that is, to find the best possible trade-off between the categories for each major value.

Finally, the ecological, economic and social values are balanced against each other. The trade-off options at this high level of aggregation are illustrated in the sustainability business triangle. Figure 16.1 shows the different weighting sets between the three values (Finkbeiner et al., 2010). At the corners, the weight is 100 per cent or 1 for each single dimension, for example the Ecology–ecology option at the upper corner. Mixes dominated by one value are illustrated as different points in the triangles. At point 1, found in the Ecology–economy part of the Ecology triangle, the mix is 0.7 + 0.2 + 0.1 = 1 between the ecological, economic and social values. At point 2, in the Ecology–social part, the mix is 0.6 + 0.3 + 0.1 = 1 between the ecological, social and economic dimensions. In the Economy triangle, at point 3 the mix is 0.6 + 0.3 + 0.1 between the economic, ecological and social values, and 0.7 (economy) + 0.2 (social) + 0.1 (ecology) at point 4. At point 5 and 6 are found mixes dominated by the social value. At point 7, a more balanced mix is illustrated, being 0.4 + 0.3 + 0.3 = 1 between the ecological, economic and social values.

A variety of such combinations are evaluated by determining the mix with the highest sustainability value. At best, an approximation of the total sustainability value is achieved. As discussed above, there are plenty of pitfalls during the complicated aggregation procedure of lumping levels together. It is hard to quantify all effects, let alone to value them in a unified way, especially since a combination of objective data and subjective judgement is used. As shown above, this is a complicated procedure, where numbers and qualitative criteria are related to each other. One way is to first calculate, based on quantitative data, the mix that represents the highest sustainability value. This value is then evaluated further by comparing it with qualitative estimates based on various indicators. This analysis is finally used to relate the ecological efficiency (the Ecology–economy trade-off) to ecological legitimacy (the Ecology–social trade-off) in order to analyse the effectiveness of the IBS.

Sustainable competitive advantage

To complete the evaluation of strategic performance, the competitiveness of the combinations with the highest sustainability values is examined. The trade-off between efficiency and legitimacy or competitive advantage and societal advantage of these combinations is analysed, along with how such an exchange affects sustainable competitive advantage. This analysis is done in two steps. First, the trade-off between competitive advantage in markets is related to the societal advantage in the government organizational field. This does not only concern various trade-offs focusing on the ecology value as assessed above. It is generally valid for all combinations of Figure 16.1, that is, also those involving focuses on the economic and social values such as various economy–ecology–social trade-offs. Second, the societal advantage achieved in the product/service market is added to the one achieved with government. The purpose is to finally evaluate the sustainable competitive advantage achieved, which is done by transforming societal advantage into competitive advantage.

Trade-off between legitimacy and efficiency

According to Figure 8.2, a critical aspect of the international network strategy (INS) concerns diagonal linkages, which are defined as the relationship the MNC has with parties outside the product/service market. Relationships with customers and suppliers in this market are defined as vertical linkages, whereas relationships with competitors are defined as horizontal linkages. Diagonal linkages, then, connect the government network with the product/service network, implying that the legitimacy-based international matching strategy (IMS) in the government field is related to the efficiency-dominating INS in the product/service market. A major reason behind a strong relationship between these organizational fields is that efficiency is defined differently in various countries or cultures. This produces a strategic dilemma in the IBS towards government of aligning two organizational fields based on different strategy rationalities.

The question is then how to make the trade-off between competitive advantages in the product/service market organizational field and societal advantages in the government field, with the aim of achieving sustainable competitive advantages. As stated in Chapter 15, the kind of legitimacy that expresses the direct link between these two organizational fields is defined as technical legitimacy. If this type of legitimacy is achieved, it means that the way of doing business in the product/service market to achieve competitive advantage is approved of by the government. This justification by the main representative of society gives the MNC a societal advantage.

As found in Chapter 6, a societal advantage leads to a sustainable competitive advantage if competitors cannot duplicate the resources and capabilities on which the societal advantage is based. Before this is discussed below, a closer look is taken at the way different combinations of efficiency and legitimacy create different conditions for such sustainability. Achieving societal advantage creates a positive basis for gaining sustainable competitive advantage. The origin of this strategic dilemma is that efficiency and legitimacy are related to each other and are present simultaneously for the MNC. There is conflict or a negative relation between the two because of competition over the common resource and capability base of the MNC. More of one may lead to less of the other. Limited resources must suffice for many demands, such as acceding to ecological and social norms regarding pollution, regional development, customer and supplier development, and so on. There is also a positive relation between legitimacy and efficiency, so MNCs can improve their competitive advantage through legitimacy and societal advantage. There is a potential synergy effect between the two major types of advantages that gives the MNC favourable conditions for a sustainable competitive advantage.

This major diagonal strategic dilemma of the IBS is illustrated in Table 16.1. It shows four typical situations of this balancing of efficiency (to gain competitive advantage) against legitimacy (to gain societal advantage). Cells 2 and 3 represent stable cases. An MNC found in cell 3 is in a bad competitive position, since it has a weak competitive advantage and a low societal advantage, meaning that the conditions for achieving a sustainable competitive advantage are bleak. An option is to withdraw from the host country voluntarily, or be forced out by competition or by the government. Another option is to improve the competitive position through the right combination of increased efficiency and legitimacy. The opposite position is found in cell 2, where the high legitimacy is mainly technical and has been achieved by being efficient. The potential for sustainable competitive advantage is good based on a high competitive advantage and societal advantage. In cells 1 and 4, the balance between efficiency and legitimacy is unstable. In cell 1, the position with the government is good at present, since the MNC is protected from competition by government through its high legitimacy. But since efficiency is low, this legitimacy position does not rest on a solid market competition ground. In the case where the MNC has a sustainable competitive advantage, it is mainly upheld through protection, which could be undermined in the future by a change of government. Such a precarious state of sustainability could jeopardize the MNC's competitive advantage if the protection is taken away. Cell 4 shows that it is not enough to have a sustainable competitive advantage based on a high competitive advantage, since there is low societal advantage. The low legitimacy here gives low potential for sustainability, at best making the competitive advantage temporary. This is a classical issue regarding the effects of MNCs on host emerging markets. An efficient MNC may drive less efficient local firms out of business and monopolize domestic markets. It may also hinder the emergence of domestic firms, in that way stifling local entrepreneurship. When host country governments fear such consequences, it is harder for the MNC to justify its operations in the country, and to be seen as a good citizen.

Overall, the MNCs studied in India until the beginning of the 1990s by Jansson et al. (1995) were found in cell 2, where a good trade-off between efficiency and legitimacy had been found through operating in India for many years and thereby gaining lots of experience of the country and learning how to achieve this sustainable business trade-off of resources and capabilities between efficiency and legitimacy achievements, making competitive advantage sustainable by means of having societal advantages. One main result of this research is knowledge on how the continuous trade-off between efficiency and legitimacy perspectives took place with changes in markets, both within MNCs and within governments. Social norms and values changed over time as did demand and competition in the market. As a consequence, both technical and regulative legitimacy were in a state of flux and tension, where the main strategic issue was to seek the right trade-off between the two in order to sustain competitive advantage.

When shifting the perspective to the government side, it can be noticed that one problem faced by governments when trying to change industrial policies and implement them, is how to 'soften' the strong legitimacy positions and high societal advantages enjoyed by firms through other means than efficiency. This justification of business operations in other ways (regulative and social legitimacy) than through being efficient (technical legitimacy) can be stressed as one main reason for the low efficiency found in the formerly highly protected markets of many emerging markets.

Table 16.1 Trade-offs between legitimacy and efficiency

Legitimacy (societal advantage)	Efficiency (competitive advantage)	
	Low	High
High	Cell 1 Unstable SCA	Cell 2 Stable SCA
Low	Cell 3 No CA	Cell 4 Temporary CA

Note: CA = Competitive advantage; SCA = Sustainable competitive advantage

Thus, even if the MNC enjoys sustainable competitive advantages through protection or other similar means, its business might not be sustainable from a societal point of view, since it is too inefficient.

Transforming societal advantage into competitive advantage

To be able to know how various trade-offs between efficiency and legitimacy influence sustainable competitive advantage as analysed above, societal advantage needs to be transformed into competitive advantage. The societal advantage achieved in the product/service market is added to the advantage achieved with government above. This additional societal advantage is generated through a CSR analysis like the one done in Chapter 14. Societal advantage has a positive influence on competitive advantage if it leads to higher profits earned in comparison with competitors. This effect is either direct or indirect. The direct effect occurs through creating stakeholder customer value rather than the classical customer value, that is, when social and ecological values are added to economic customer value. This may increase social complexity and causal ambiguity, which makes it harder for competitors to duplicate the resources and capabilities on which the societal advantage is based. As found in Chapter 6, sustained competitive advantage is achieved when competitors are unable to imitate the profitable international business strategy.

The indirect effect takes place via the asset base of the company (the hierarchy of resources and capabilities) to improve the current competitive advantages for the future, making them more sustainable. In the bearings company case in Chapter 14, it was found that the activities directed at specific stakeholders gain legitimacy with this stakeholder, which improves the societal advantage of the MNC. The stakeholders benefit from the situation, and social and ecological values are created. The business of the MNC becomes more sustainable through the higher ecological and social values created. More benefits for stakeholders improve the reputation of the MNC. Satisfied stakeholders may thus improve the public image of the MNC. Such a reputation is defined as an intangible resource, equivalent to brand equity. It works as a promise for the future and therefore becomes a resource of the MNC. Reputation concerns the identity system of the MNC and the images (thought styles) held by stakeholders about the MNC. It is also influenced by the brand image of the MNC, that is, brand equity as a commercial intangible resource. Reputation is therefore seen as a joint capability bundled together from social, ecological and economic resources. It then works as a link between resources that create combinations of social, ecological and economic values.

This characteristic of reputation makes it possible to link societal advantage with competitive advantage. The process of turning reputation into a competitive advantage is illustrated in Figure 16.2. Increased reputation from improved legitimacy can be transformed into competitive advantage through the sources of competitive advantage. A high reputation, for example, could in its turn become the source of a differentiation advantage by making pricing concessions possible (differentiating price), enhancing opportunities for product differentiation, or increasing strategic flexibility. It could also become the source of a cost advantage, for example if more legitimate actions result in more satisfied workers in the factory and making it possible to better take advantage of economies of scale in production. If the societal advantages originating from the higher ecological and social values of the stakeholders and government are to improve the competitive advantage of the MNC, they need to result in higher profits being earned in comparison with competitors. This competitive advantage is sustainable if competitors cannot duplicate the resources or capabilities on which it is based. Reputation is one such major intangible resource. It is closely related to the identity and images of the MNC, which also originates from other intangible resources, such as the brand. Societal advantage and competitive advantage are linked to each other via the link between reputation and brand equity. Increased reputation from improved legitimacy is converted into competitive advantage through the sources of competitive advantage.

If Figure 16.2 is combined with the international matching strategy model (Figure 14.1), one may conclude that there is also a major future connection between reputation and legitimacy, namely that a high reputation already established might facilitate achieving legitimacy. Since reputation can be generalized between different activities, a certain reputation earned from one activity could be transferred to another activity. For example, if the MNC has a global reputation for protecting the natural environment, this might facilitate legitimation locally.

THE INSTITUTIONAL NETWORK APPROACH TO STRATEGIC CHANGE

Assessing strategic performance is a continuous process of evaluating if, when and how to change strategy, and is thus a critical part of the strategic change process. This entire process is now analysed. The network institutional approach is applied to strategic change in international business by using institutional theory to explain further how change takes place in the internationalization

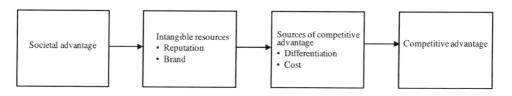

Figure 16.2 Transforming societal advantage into competitive advantage

processes and networking processes of previous chapters. But before explaining such strategic change from an institutional theoretical point of view, the key dynamic aspects of networking and internationalization are summarized. The key process constructs of these theories are italicized.

The internationalization and network processes revisited

As found in the previous chapters about networks, the internationalization process is evolutionary, where the establishment and maintenance of network relationships in a foreign market follow a pattern of *five stages of relationships evolvement*. This *local networking process* is part of a larger internationalization process concerning how firms spread their activities throughout the globe between various foreign countries and regions. This more *overall internationalization process* takes place through *five stages* in accordance with the exporting theory. Three major network structures are found at various stages of relationships development during the entry process. This *relationship process* is also relevant in the marketing of projects, in addition to the *product/service process* and the *network marketing process*. The product/service process is divided into a number of *periods*, and the network marketing process into *marketing cycles* and phases relevant for the *life cycle* of a project.

In the *international evolutionary process*, companies commit themselves to doing international business through a *gradual learning* process, which then is *incremental* and occurs when business is practised abroad, that is, *knowledge* is *experiential*. This gradual learning of experiential knowledge is then a key factor behind the stage character of the internationalization process. The new knowledge is interpreted and evaluated within the existing *theory-in-use* or cognitive structure associated with a particular *knowledge platform*. When this theory is no longer workable, it is restructured into a new theory-in-use and knowledge platform. For example, firms with long domestic experience have a rigid knowledge platform that takes time to change. This change process comes closer to *revolutionary change* than *evolutionary change*. *Organizational learning* is a key capability that will make the *stock of resources and capabilities dynamic*. *Commitment* is to a large extent shown by the willingness to make *adaptations*. The longer the firm has been involved in foreign operations, the more *knowledge* is *accumulated*, and the less uncertain the foreign market is perceived to be. *Uncertainty* varies with the stage of internationalization. For example, at the initial stages, it is difficult to assess the potential rewards and costs of establishing relationships with new customers. The uncertainty experienced is influenced by *psychic distance* or *cultural distance*. When foreign country market contexts are defined as institutional settings, the distance between them is defined as institutional distance rather than psychic distance or cultural distance. The uncertainty perceived when extending the business from one major type of market to another major type is therefore influenced by the institutional distance between country markets. This concept then involves major differences between how societies are organized. The institutional context of a specific emerging market might therefore facilitate or hinder the implementation of internationalization moves, which could create uncertainty.

The establishment of network relationships creates *bonds and dependencies* between the parties involved, which make relationships *continuous* and *stable*. A *mutual orientation* is created which results in a preparedness to interact in a dyad. A mutual knowledge of and respect for each other's *interests* is established, which leads to *cooperation* and the resolution of *conflicts*. This makes the *switching costs* high, meaning *change* normally takes place *within the relationship* rather than chang-ing to new partners. *Mutuality* or *reciprocity* is thus clearly characteristic of business relationships, being largely shaped by *social exchange* and *information exchange*.

Since this section of the chapter is about strategic change within the MNC, the process theories above concerning external networks are complemented by the theory on the hierarchical network organization of the MNC developed as an inside-out perspective on INS in Chapter 7.

Strategic change as an institutional process

To be able to change strategy based on the evaluation above, a new strategy analysis needs to be done of the external institutional context by following the procedure in Chapter 12, inter alia in-volving a prediction of institutional developments and a SWOT analysis. In analysing the opportu-nities and threats of the strategic change, it is especially important to study the external stabilizers and facilitators. This also goes for analysing the strengths and weaknesses of the internal environ-ment, especially the capacity to change specified as the hierarchy of resources and capabilities depicted in Figure 6.2.

The evaluation of effectiveness is thus related to strategic change. As noted in Chapter 12 and the Appendix, a major characteristic of institutions is their predictability due to being stable and rigid. Still, they do change, and this takes place through institutionalization or deinstitutionaliza-tion processes. When connected to international strategic management, this means that strategic change is a matter of reproduction or reconstruction of institutions consisting of formal and infor-mal rules that make behaviour habitual, such as an organizational routine. Strategic change is then about whether the mix of such routines are prolonged into the future or changed by being modi-fied or transformed into a new mix. For example, whether a certain mix of the strategic manage-ment processes represented by the organizational routines of the international matching strategies (summarized in Table 13.1) will be followed or changed into a new configuration.

According to the literature reviewed in the Appendix, the process of changing these rules is mostly characterized as path-dependent, where initial conditions and history have a lasting im-pact on a slow and incremental evolutionary process. The scale and pace of upheaval is different from a revolutionary process, where change is swift and influences most parts of the network simultaneously. Convergent and rapid change differ from these. The pace of change is generally higher for formal than informal rules. Different layers of institutions are distinguished based on the pace of change, for example 'meta institutional rules' are mainly informal and take centuries to change, while 'operational rules' are mainly formal and change as often as weekly. Institution-al theories differ in how formal and informal rules change, why they change, and how habitual behaviour is affected. Most theories are about how external institutions influence organizational structure, whereas only a few take up how organizations respond to outside pressure, by going into the agency aspect. This kind of strategic behaviour is of interest in building the international busi-ness strategy and therefore used in the book, including below. Even fewer articles deal with how the responsive behaviour influences the external context. This means that most of the literature on institutional change concerns the outside-in perspective and very little the inside-out perspec-tive on IBS. Of the articles summarized in the Appendix, mainly Seo and Creed (2002), but also

Greenwood and Hinings (1996), constitutes work describing and explaining institutional change at the organizational micro level.

Since institutions are embedded in each other, institutional change at the organizational level is constrained and induced by institutional arrangements at the meso and macro levels. In following these two articles, the internal change process is seen to be influenced by external constraints and inducements. The contradictions resulting from incompatible institutional arrangements lead to conflicts and tensions that drive the internal institutional change process. External conflicts spread to the intra-organizational network, causing the dynamic interaction between the resources and capabilities of the hierarchy depicted in Figure 6.2. The basic rules or institutional controls work as dispositions by being stabilizers or facilitators of change. The capacity to change is determined by the resources and capabilities at hand. Finally, if and how change occurs is decided by the capability to learn, that is, the organizational learning process. If the external drivers are of such a magnitude that no change occurs, existing institutions are reproduced further into the future. New institutions are developed either in an evolutionary process by modifying existing institutions or by creating new ones, sometimes leading to a transformation of the entire structure of institutions as in revolutionary change.

Thus, the conflicts and tensions due to the incompatible external institutional context spread to the internal institutional arrangement of the intra-organizational network, which then also is an arena for conflicts and tensions between incompatible institutions. The group interest competes with the global product interest and the local interest over influence, creating conflicts within the organization. The resolution of the conflicts depends upon the influence positions of these interest groups.

Internal stabilizers and facilitators

From the institutional change point of view, the network controls of the hierarchical network organization specified in Chapter 7 become institutional controls. They are viewed as internal stabilizers and facilitators, working as dispositions for change. The process and output controls of the MNC hierarchical network are mainly formal rules enforcing behaviour, thus being enforcement mechanisms. Input controls, on the other hand, are mainly informal rules related to thought styles, norms and values. The socialization of employees is seen as the institutionalization of thought styles, norms and values into the organization, forming the organizational culture. Values and thought styles were earlier exemplified as institutional controls for the bearings MNC in Figure 6.3. The basic rules then work as four types of learned dispositions of change signifying the interest groups of interactors of the internal network. The character of the institutional controls then determines how the conflicting interests and tensions about strategy are solved and whether this results in the IBS being kept or changed. In the former case of no change, the basic rules are arranged so that conflicts are kept at bay, for example by norms such as trustworthiness. Rather, the basic rules could change when they are disposed so that conflicts and tensions lead to an increase in the awareness of a necessity to change, that is, reshaping interactors' thought styles. If the organizational routines are impacted, there is change. For example, changing norms might influence changes of organizational routines, since they create expectations for a certain new behaviour. Thus, institutional change of organizations happens when organizational routines are brought into alignment with changes in basic rules through the praxis phase (Seo and Creed, 2002). This phase or strategic change process mainly involves an evaluation of strategic performance in accordance with the analytical procedure above and the strategic analytical procedure developed in Chapter 12. As discussed in the Appendix and based on Figure A.1, the change period for informal rules is normally longer than for formal rules, sometimes being extremely long.

Dynamic organizational capabilities

If and how change occurs is also determined by the availability and dynamism of the resources and capabilities, especially the capacity to learn taking place through the organizational learning process. As noted in Chapters 5 and 6, organizational capabilities are made dynamic through establishing routines for change based on learning. The importance of dynamic capabilities and organizational learning in change processes are then developed further by looking at such change from the institutional point of view. As found in Chapter 8, local INS is conditioned by the capability profile. The MNC needs to have certain resources and capabilities located in the country to have the capacity to effectuate the INS there. The capability profile then describes the mix of capacities found at a local company for a certain INS, for instance knowledge and skills. IMS adds the basic rules as institutional controls and organizational capabilities.

The analysis of external institutional contexts in Chapter 12 and the performance evaluation above can be seen as one big organizational learning process. As found earlier, organizational learning sets the hierarchy of resources and capabilities into motion. It is therefore a key factor of the organizational change process. As summarized above, organizational practices for the international operations are found to be discovered and learned in an organizational process based on a new knowledge platform. This step-like pattern fits well with institutional theory and its emphasis on inertia. The platform-like organizational learning of the internationalization and networking processes fits well with the evolutionary pattern of these processes. This stepwise arrangement of practices also shows that these organizational processes are path-dependent. Moreover, the firm's capacity to learn was found in Chapter 6 to consist of four types of organizational learning capabilities and three orders of learning, namely proto-learning (single- and double-loop learning), deutero-learning and trito-learning. The pattern of organizational learning of experiential knowledge characterizing the evolutionary change of the internationalization and network processes (Chapters 4 and 10) is mainly based on proto-learning.

The aspects of the dynamism of the organizational capabilities behind this internationalization process pattern are now expanded by adding deutero-learning as well as two new dimensions on organizational learning in order to find out how organizational learning is institutionalized in MNCs, that is, how the accumulation of experiential knowledge that gets stored in organizational processes becomes a routine. These new aspects are integrated with the organizational learning capabilities and organizational learning platforms into an organizational learning model, which is illustrated in Figure 16.3. The dynamic aspects of organizational learning are developed further by going more into the learning process. The knowledge is generated through an organizational learning cycle by being gradually institutionalized into organizational capabilities, making them change, and giving them a dynamic quality. Learning according to this cycle includes the individual and collective learning at the group and organizational levels. As seen above, this learning process is influenced by the thought style and other basic rules behind organizational processes, for example the world view of the strategist. Such assumptions behind a certain strategic decision routine is defined as a learning style. It is the thought style or major thinking behind how learning takes place. It is an antecedent to learning as well as being influenced by the learning, eventually. Due to variation in thought styles, people have different learning styles. Thus, learning is institutionalized through an organizational learning cycle and linked to the thought style as a disposition through the organizational learning style.

Organizational learning cycles. The learning on the platforms is developed further with the help of two feedback loops distinguished by Crossan and Berdrow (2003). The feedback learning cycle starts at the organization level and moves down into the organization. Learning at the organizational level influences the learning of groups and individuals further down in the organization. Established knowledge about how to do things is exploited throughout the organization. The opposite learning cycle is defined as feed-forward learning. It is a bottom-up process that starts with individual learning, leading over to collective learning at the group level, and is finally institutionalized at the organizational level. Through this cycle, knowledge is explored through four processes, namely intuiting, interpreting, integrating and institutionalizing. Intuiting is preconscious recognition of the pattern and/or possibilities inherent in a personal stream of experience, which can affect the intuitive individual's behaviour. When interpreting, the individual makes sense of an experience either on his or her own or in interaction with others. In the latter case, a collective meaning structure is being created through the shared understanding of the experience being developed. In integrating, mainly through deutero-learning, a shared understanding among organizational members is created and coordinated action taken by making mutual adjustments. This process will initially be ad hoc and informal, but if the coordinated action taken is recurring and significant it will be institutionalized. Tasks are defined, actions specified, performance evaluated, and tasks repeated or redefined, and so on.

Organizational mechanisms are put in place to ensure that certain actions occur and are evaluated. Then learning through strategic analysis that has been carried out by individuals and groups

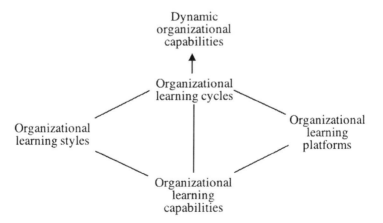

Figure 16.3 The organizational learning model

is embedded into non-human elements at the organizational level, such as structures, systems, procedures and strategy. For example, a new organizational routine is institutionalized, meaning that an organizational process will take place in another way than before.

Organizational learning styles. The learning process is also institutionalized as a learning style, which originates from a certain thought style. Due to variation in thought styles, people have different learning styles, complicating, for example, learning within a Western MNC with units in emerging country markets. For example, as illustrated in Chapter 12, there are major differences between the thought styles of Chinese and Swedish managers in the subsidiaries of Swedish MNCs in China. Since a learning style is a world view on learning, it could differ between such groups of managers. The learning process is broken when the learning style or the thought style behind it is changed, the current experiential state of knowledge being changed.

While proto-learning mainly goes on in evolutionary change processes, deutero-learning mainly characterizes revolutionary change when changing from one platform or template to another. A deutero-learning capability then involves a capacity to continuously redefine the assumptions on which the IBS is based, making it possible to repeatedly sustain competitive advantages. Thus, to be able to make the three major types of learning capabilities continuous by institutionalizing them into the organization they need to be supported by certain assumptions and attitudes. These learning styles, in their turn, need to be supported by specific norms (e.g. failures allowed), values (e.g. creativity and high-quality products) and enforcement mechanisms (e.g. performance measurement).

Trito-learning

According to Figure A.1 on layers of embedded rules, proto- and deutero-learning are mainly about institutional change at layers 1–2, that is, operational rules and collective choice rules or governance structures and institutions of governance. Deutero-learning is mainly about layer 2, since it is a matter of learning how to learn by questioning how an organizational process works and in considering the institutional controls behind it. In trito-learning one further step is taken by questioning these rules through reflecting upon how the basic rules of the MNC are influenced by external basic rules housed in an organizational field or in society at large, for example to learn about the firm's role in global society after having realized the urgent need to change the IBS due to drastically increasing pressures from the natural environment. Trito-learning is then about how institutional change of constitutional rules or high-level formal rules affect strategic change. One does not only question if the IBS is right in relation to the basic rules of the organization, but also whether it is right in relation to the basic rules of the country or even generic human values such as the SDGSs of Agenda 2030. Trito-learning also encompasses the change in the fundamental rules of society, that is, the meta constitutional rules or the institutions of embeddedness. This collective learning process then spans institutional layers of larger collectives at the meso or macro levels. An example is a coalition involving employees from various units of the global organization and external experts representing relevant external organizations. The work on Agenda 2030 is an example of trito-learning at the supranational level, where scientists from all over the world jointly learned about global ecological changes. A major problem in trito-learning is the large variation in learning styles of such a large collective. However, this problem is probably less in a group such as the Agenda 2030, since the members there have more of a joint learning style based on the values of the scientific community. This third-order learning capability then concerns the relation between the organizational context and external contexts at higher levels, for example in studying a learning situation for a firm that is replacing its organizational culture completely, including how it approaches strategic management. This is an advanced form of collective learning, where members of an organization agree on which common basic rules of the organization to follow after having agreed on which basic rules of society to follow. This requires that the basic rules of society and of the organization are known, along with how they are related.

The challenges in trito-learning are illustrated based on the work of Drew and Jansson (2014). They explore how changes in meta constitutional rules affect the leadership behaviour of Swedish MNCs in China. The question studied is how change of an organizational archetype such as leadership style in a Chinese context is affected over time by change in the fundaments of the country culture. It involves the basic organization of leadership in society, and how it relates to strategic management in firms. It was found that a major institutional stabilizer or meta constitutional rule behind the reproduction of the Chinese leadership style is the cultural theme of harmony. It forms the core of the major deep-seated Chinese traditions of Taoism, Confucianism and Legalism and has been carried by these meta cultures over millennia, being institutionalized into Chinese organizations. Even though China has experienced several discontinuous transformations, even highly systems-breaking revolutions that have transformed much of the institutional structure, this theme has survived. It has repeatedly been crystallized into new institutions and thereby organizations, being a major stabilizer behind the leadership style and authority pattern. Even today harmony infuses the core of private and political organization. Two other meta constitutional rules of the Chinese society also influence the lack of change in leadership style, namely face and patriarchical relations. These three meta rules are found to have been the major stabilizers of the Chinese leadership style and organizations over time through their disposition for reducing conflicts. This also explains the well-known trait of Chinese culture being highly conflict-avoiding, and the specific authoritarian way of solving conflicts, that is, by dictate. Thus, this stable leadership style and stable authority patterns are unlikely to change in the short to medium term. Thus, certain basic rules and organizational routines will be more resistant than others and take a long time to change, especially those that are informed by two or three meta constitutional rules. These deep-seated cultural traits will also constitute the cornerstones of the Chinese learning style, explaining how collective organizational learning takes place in the loyal, conflict-avoiding and harmonious Chinese collective. A major conclusion regarding trito-learning is then that there are limits to organizational change, even in the very long run, since certain new knowledge will never be learned and implemented. It therefore seems almost impossible that Chinese firms and perhaps also political organizations would change to a leadership style that is not based on harmony, face and patriarchical relationships. The tight and authoritarian direct controls by the government of the one-party state will most likely persist. For example, the three societal fundaments have been institutionalized in new control arrangements founded on artificial intelligence and consisting of public video surveillance and closed-circuit television (CCTV) systems, face-recognition techniques and the social credit system of assessing the economic and social reputation of individuals and firms.

Trito-learning is then inter-organizational learning taking place among people representing many organizations or countries, either at the meso level, the country level or the supranational level. The Chinese leadership illustration is about changes of a common leadership style of a collective of companies at the meso level, being impacted by the country culture at the macro level. Organizational learning in a UN organization takes place at the supranational level by people representing organizations at the macro or meso levels.

CONCLUSIONS

To evaluate the effectiveness of the IBS, an evaluation of strategic performance was done by making an organizational life cycle sustainability assessment of various mixes of the ecological, economic and social values created with the stakeholders. The organizational life assessment expanded the CSR analysis done in Chapter 14 by focusing on the time dimension, since the MNC takes on a life cycle approach to its activities. It involves an integrated analysis of the three types of external environments with the purpose of creating ecological, economic and social values with the stakeholders. The assessment consists of life cycle assessment, life cycle costing and social life cycle assessment, being formulated as LCSA = LCA + LCC + SLCA. Various combinations of ecological, economic and social values are evaluated through deciding on the mix with the highest sustainability value and in using the sustainability business triangle. This is a complicated procedure, where numbers and qualitative criteria are related to each other. An organizational life cycle sustainability assessment also improves the possibilities to specify the goals as exactly as possible by operationalizing and even quantifying them, which could be valuable for the next round of strategic planning. To complete the evaluation of strategic performance, the sustainable competitiveness of the combinations with the highest sustainability values is examined. The trade-off between efficiency and legitimacy is analysed, along with how such an exchange affects sustainable competitive advantage. A critical part of this trade-off assessment is to analyse how societal advantage and competitive advantage are related to each other.

Assessing strategic performance is part of a continuous process of strategic evaluation regarding when and how to change strategy, and is thus a critical part of the strategic change process. Based on the NIA, this institutional process takes place within the hierarchical network organization of the MNC made up of three nets. Since institutions are embedded in each other, institutional change at the organizational level is constrained and induced by institutional arrangements at the meso and macro levels. The contradictions resulting from incompatible institutional arrangements lead to conflicts and tensions that drive the internal institutional change process. These tensions spread to the intra-organizational network, creating internal conflicts between different interest groups. How they are resolved influences the change outcome, as does the dynamic interaction between the resources and capabilities. The basic rules work as dispositions by being stabilizers or facilitators of change, while the capacity to change is determined by the resources and capabilities. Then, if and how change occurs is decided by the capability to learn, that is, the organizational learning process. It is institutionalized through the organizational learning cycle and linked to the thought style through the organizational learning style. Change depends on the organizational learning capability at hand, and the type of change situation, if it is an evolutionary and gradual learning on an organizational learning platform or a more revolutionary change from one platform to another. When no change occurs, existing institutions are reproduced further into the future.

In trito-learning, one further step is taken compared to deutero-learning, by questioning whether the basic rules of the organization are right in relation to the basic rules of the country or even generic human values. It is a collective inter-organizational learning process, where the MNC is involved in a much larger collective at the meso, national or supranational levels. Trito-learning also involves other large inter-cultural groups working together to solve fundamental societal problems like transforming society into a sustainable society according to the goals of Agenda 2030.

Appendix – The institutional view: theoretical background

Institutions are defined in Chapter 1 as habits and routines shaped by the rules typical of a legitimized social grouping of some kind, either explicit formal rules such as laws or implicit informal rules such as beliefs, values and norms. Basically, institutional theory then deals with how society is organized. Within a grouping such as a firm is found rules (e.g. a formal hierarchy and a specific belief system) typical of this specific group, which result in a certain habitual and routinized behaviour. These institutions are related to each other in a multi-layer embedded hierarchy of rules, for example in the basic institutions model in Chapter 11. Institutions vary in scope and are found in various 'locations' at various levels of magnification. At the multinational corporation (MNC) level, for example, there is one particular configuration of rules at play resulting in specific organizational routines. This internal configuration of rules is influenced by the rules of other institutions outside the MNC, for example the legal system. Such an embedded approach makes it possible to break institutions down into different levels of magnification and show how these levels affect each other. In this book the MNC is then viewed as an institution that is related to various external institutions. The MNC is found in organizational fields together with other agents, for example other companies and government agencies, being influenced by these agents, by the common rules of such a field, and by societal sectors such as country culture and the political system. The MNC is conceptualized as an institution surrounded by other institutions. The international business world is organized and consists of institutions, where strategies and operations are reproduced in a rule-like fashion as organizational routines.

A MULTI-LAYER SYSTEM OF INSTITUTIONAL THEORIES

The institutional theories examined in this appendix are grouped as a multi-layer nested system. There are three levels of institutions, the micro institutions level (e.g. the MNC), the meso institutions level (e.g. industry markets, organizational fields) and the macro institutions level (e.g. culture, political system). The scholars behind the institutional theories explored for each of the three levels are listed in Table A.1. A distinction is also made between institutional theories based on economics and institutional theories with a socio-economic disciplinary background. Institutional theories based on economics are included since they provide a significant background to the efficiency rationale of the MNC developed in the book. North's (1990, 2005) institutional

Table A.1 Major scholars of institutional theories

Level of grouping	Disciplinary background	
	Economic	Socio-economic
Macro	North (1990, 2005)	Myrdal (1968) Ostrom (2005)
Meso	Coase (1937) Williamson (1975, 1979, 1985) Buckley and Casson (1976) Dunning (1988a, 1988b, 1993, 2005)	Hodgson (1988) Whitley (1992a, 1992b, 1994, 1999a, 1999b)
Micro	Miller (1992) Sjöstrand (1985) Jansson (1994a, 1994b)	Meyer and Rowan (1977) DiMaggio and Powell (1983) Powell and DiMaggio (1991) March and Olsen (1989) Scott (1987, 1995/2008) Sjöstrand (1997) Greenwood and Hinings (1996) Seo and Creed (2002) Westney (1993) Kostova (1999) Kostova and Zaheer (1999) Kostova and Roth (2002)

theory discussed below is classified as a macro-economic theory, the reason being that it deals with institutional development at the country level and is based on transaction-cost economics. The relevant theories for this book dealing with general economic aspects of firms and MNCs are classified as theories at the meso level, that is, the works by Coase, Williamson, Dunning, and Buckley and Casson.

Among the more general institutional theories with more of a socio-economic background, the theories developed by Myrdal (1968) and Ostrom (2005) are classified as macro theories. The institutional theory on business systems established by Whitley, on the other hand, is located at the meso level, since it deals with groups of firms. To open up the black box and develop the individual MNC as an institution, it is necessary to go to institutional organization theory. There is not much literature on the individual large corporation as an economic institution, or the MNC for that matter. A few attempts have been made to open the black box based on Williamson's internal organization forms (e.g. by scholars such as Miller, 1992; Sjöstrand, 1985, 1997), in particular to develop the M-form into an international M-form (Jansson, 1994b). Research into the organization from a socio-economic perspective or a pure social perspective, on the other hand, has grown into a large and very important field in organization studies. According to March and Olsen (1989, p. 22), for example, organizations are then generally seen as consisting of rules, which are defined as:

> … the routines, procedures, conventions, roles, strategies, organizational forms, and technologies around which political activity is constructed. We also mean the beliefs, paradigms, codes, cultures, and knowledge that surround, support, elaborate, and contradict those roles and routines. It is a commonplace observation in empirical social science that behaviour is constrained or dictated by such cultural dicta and social norms. Action is often based more on identifying the normatively appropriate behaviour than on calculating the return expected from alternative choices. Routines are independent of the individual actors who execute them and are capable of surviving considerable turnover in individuals.

Although aimed at non-profit organizations, this description of what a rule system within an organization consists of is also relevant for the MNC. The core of the network institutional approach (NIA) to international business strategy (IBS) has mainly been developed from such micro institutional theories, for example that of Scott (1995/2008). Most of these socio-economic institutional theories at the micro level are taken up and explored in various chapters, except those by Westney, Kostova, Kostova and Zaheer, and Kostova and Roth. Still, the theories by the latter scholars are included in the table, since they are seen to provide an important general theoretical background to the book.

THE ROOTS

The institutional view of this book can be traced back to the first American institutional economists, who were active at the beginning of the 20th century, mainly John Commons and Thorstein Veblen. They in turn were very much influenced by the German historical school from the end of the 19th century. Already then, and still today, institutional ideas in economics build on calling into question the validity of mainstream neoclassical economic theory. The basic idea is that this economic theory is too narrow, since it does not place the economy into its societal context. It is like studying the bloodstream without studying the body. The major ideas that united these early institutional economists are well summarized by Carlson (1995):

1. The static and mechanical general equilibrium theory should be replaced by a dynamic theory about evolutionary processes. Economics should be inspired by Darwin's world view based on biology rather than on Newton's world view based on physics.
2. The economy cannot be studied in isolation from the rest of society. This holistic idea implies that the economist should work in a cross-disciplinary way and benefit from knowledge in psychology, sociology, anthropology and law.

3. Neoclassical theory builds on unrealistic assumptions about the individual as a utility maximizer in a market characterized by perfect competition. This simple idea should be replaced by more realistic models on the market and a social-psychological perspective on the individual, who is both egoistic and altruistic.

4. The evolutionary process is not about invisible hands controlling individuals in harmonious ways, but about individual and organized interests that sometimes clash and sometimes cooperate.

5. To reduce individual choice and reduce the risk of conflict, habits and collective control mechanisms, namely institutions, evolve. Individual behaviour influences the institutions and the institutions influence individual behaviour.

6. There is interplay between institutions and technical development. Mostly, changes in production technologies result in changes in institutional arrangements. Since groups are influenced differently by technical changes, some groups will change their behaviour faster than others, which leads to conflict.

7. In modern industrial society, there is a basic conflict between production technology that makes large-scale production possible, and the business mentality which is to earn as much money as possible. Since production is subordinated to the business mentality, production capacity is not fully utilized. This is the well-known conflict between the long-term oriented industrialist and the short-term oriented financier.

8. The price mechanism does not work as a seamless coordination mechanism in an economy consisting of both competition and monopoly parts. It does not allocate resources between various activities in an efficient way, creates unfair income gaps and does not manage to keep economic activity at a high and permanent level.

The works of these institutional economists only became important from the 1960s onwards. One major reason was the growing importance of socio-economic issues, where the limits of neoclassical economic theory became too obvious to neglect. Examples of such issues concern labour, the environment, developing countries, globalization, big business and multinational corporations. Another major reason was the crisis in Keynesian economic theory (Carlson, 1995). The new institutional school is one major school that developed. Its basis is in transaction cost economics, an idea that originates from John Commons. The most well-known scientists promoting this institutional orientation are Ronald Coase, Oliver E. Williamson and Douglass North, where 'law and economics' is one major new research field. As will be discussed below, the study of the MNC as an economic institution builds heavily on this tradition.

However, the new institutional school is not very holistic in its outlook. It resides within the economics discipline. It is a broader economic theory, where some basic assumptions of neoclassical theory have been replaced by more realistic assumptions, such as those about perfect information, perfect markets and fully rational decision-makers. It mainly relates to one non-economic institution, namely the legal system, which is studied from an economic perspective. Thus, it is not much of a holistic and cross-disciplinary theory and has therefore not been found to be suitable for studying the very broad international business problems of emerging markets. Except for North and other economic historians, transaction cost theory is static, and does not deal with economic development processes.

INSTITUTIONAL THEORIES AT THE MACRO LEVEL

The most well-known economic theory dealing with institutions at the macro level is that of North (1990, 2005). He defines institutions as the rules of the game in society or as constraints created by humans, which control economic and political interaction. A distinction is made between formal rules and informal rules, where the former include political and judicial rules, economic rules and contracts. Informal rules are broadly viewed to include codes of conduct, norms of behaviour, and conventions. These rules relate to what is usually called culture.

Institutions are separated from policies or organizations. Institutions represent the rules of game, while organizations represent the players. Institutions are influenced by beliefs. They are therefore determined by consciousness and human intentionality. There is a deliberate effort by human beings to control their environment. According to North (2005, p. 49):

> There is an intimate relationship between belief systems and the institutional framework. Belief systems embody the internal representation of the human landscape. Institutions are the structure that humans impose on the landscape in order to produce the desired outcome. Belief systems therefore are the internal representation and institutions the external manifestation of that representation. Thus the structure of an economic market reflects the beliefs of those in a position to make the rules of the game, who enact rules that will produce the outcomes (that is, the sort of market) they desire, whether those desires are to create monopoly or to create a competitive market (always with the caveat that their beliefs may be incorrect and produce unanticipated consequences). When conflicting beliefs exist, the institutions will reflect the beliefs of those (past as well as present) in a position to effect their choices.

Change takes place continually through interplay between institutions, organizations and beliefs. The key to understanding the process of change is defined by North (2005, p. 3) as 'the intentionality of the players enacting institutional change and their comprehension of the issues'. Dominant beliefs result in the erection of an elaborate structure of institutions in response to policy-making. Institutional change is elaborated more below. This institutional matrix imposes constraints on the choices of entrepreneurs, who then react by trying to modify these constraints. The path dependence that results makes change incremental, a process that is occasionally interrupted by radical and abrupt institutional changes. Institutional change is developed in further detail below.

A more socio-economic oriented institutional theory was developed by Gunnar Myrdal. It is well described in his last major work *Asian Drama* (1968). According to him, all non-economic factors must be included in the analysis: political, social and economic structures, institutions, attitudes and human relations in general. The reason is that societal problems are broad and complex. There are no economic, psychological or sociological problems, just problems. It is necessary to take a holistic approach that stresses institutional factors and the cross-disciplinary nature of the social sciences. Myrdal especially stressed the importance of studying values and assumptions. He even extended this to the researcher as an individual. Since science is subjective and biased, the value premises on which research is based should be clarified. Following the heritage of the American institutionalists, Myrdal also developed an institutional change model at the macro-institutional level, according to which the change process is circular, cumulative and causal, following a pattern of virtuous and vicious circles.

INSTITUTIONAL THEORIES AT THE MESO LEVEL

The MNC as an economic institution

Internalization theory
The theory of the MNC is to a large degree based on transaction cost theory. As introduced in Chapter 4, two main theories help to explain the organization of the MNCs on a very general and abstract level: internalization theory, where transaction cost explanations play a prominent role; and the branch of transaction cost theory represented by governance forms (Williamson, 1979, 1981, 1985). Inspired by Coase (1937), internalization theory aims to explain why multinational corporations exist in the first place (see, for example, Buckley and Casson, 1976; but also Buckley, 1987; Casson, 1987; and Rugman, 1981). This also goes for other closely related research, such as by Hennart (1982). According to internalization theory, international trade theory, location theory and theories from industrial economics do not explain the existence of MNCs. These latter theories can be used to explain where MNCs choose to locate (location-specific advantages) and how firm-specific competitive advantages come about due to various market imperfections (firm-specific advantages), but they do not explain why international transactions are organized in firms rather than through markets. A number of contractual forms for international business have been developed, ranging from market contracts to internal contracts such as the MNC itself. This is explored more in Chapter 4.

The extended OLI paradigm
The most comprehensive new-institutional framework on the MNC is the OLI paradigm or the eclectic paradigm developed by Dunning (1981, 1988b, 1993). As developed more in Chapter 4, it integrates internalization theory and other major economic theories into one coherent theory on the multinational firm.

Dunning (2005) makes an interesting attempt to extend the OLI paradigm in the socio-economic direction. He argues that:

> 20/21 globalization and the emerging approach to understanding the goals and challenges of development is compelling business scholars to give institutions a centre stage treatment. This also requires that both micro and macro incentive systems be integrated more explicitly into the mainstream paradigms and theories of IB activity. (Dunning, 2005, p. 37)

Institutionally related variables are proposed that need to be incorporated into the eclectic paradigm. These variables mainly concern belief systems and values. A major reason is said to be that one of the unique features of contemporary capitalism is that it interconnects different behavioural morals and belief systems. In particular, Dunning stresses incentive structures and enforcement systems and their underlying belief systems. In that way the proposed theory comes close to how North (2005) has developed the new institutional economics theory by focusing more on belief systems. But Dunning ventures further away from the mainstream by also including values. Still, the extended OLI paradigm stays within the limits of the dominant new institutional economics approach. The result is an economic-social institutional theory rather than a socio-economic one. Therefore, it is placed in the same cell in Table A.1 as the original eclectic paradigm.

Dunning's (2005) extended OLI paradigm represents a major contribution in developing the MNC as an institution. It is also a very important attempt to develop international business theory with the help of institutional theory, much in line with what the present book tries to do.

Governance-forms theory

According to Williamson's new institutional governance-forms approach, the MNC is seen as a hierarchy that functions as a regulative structure or a governance structure. Williamson (1975, 1981, 1985, 2000) translates the common organization structures of corporations into three distinctive governance forms or types of hierarchies. The unitary form (U-form) has striking similarities with the classical functional organization, whose structure is often depicted as a pyramid. This type of hierarchy is signified by unitary control of the company by top management. The multi-divisional form (M-form) represents the divisionalized organization type. Here, control is differentiated by being executed through a separation of the company into smaller internal companies or divisions, implying that the efficiency of this form builds on the advantages of decentralized organization. Instead of a uniform hierarchy, there is a structure of multi-units. The H-form has many similarities to the M-form, but here the key controls are financial in kind, taking place through a holding company. In this form the conglomerate organization of the enterprise is recognized. These forms concern big companies in general and not multinational corporations in particular. Building on this inadequacy, Jansson (1994b) develops the M-form into a transnational M-form, which is one major base of this book.

The market as an economic institution

Markets and hierarchies are structured differently, since rules prevailing in markets are different from those found in hierarchies. They constitute two separate efficiency-oriented social orders, which are institutionalized differently depending on the institutional context in which they are found, for example with regard to the type of legal support. Markets in turn are separated into three major governance forms: market governance, bilateral governance and trilateral governance (Williamson, 1979). The market as an institution according to the governance forms model is developed for the product/service market in Jansson (1994a). The main characteristics of the non-hierarchical or external governance forms are presented in Table A.2.

Market governance

Market governance as defined by Williamson (1979) is a better theoretical representation of a price-dominated type of market institution. It comes close to the perfect market, but the congruence

Table A.2 Main characteristics of the external governance forms

	Market governance	Trilateral governance	Bilateral governance
Main type of information carrier	Price	Rules	Praxis
Extent of bargaining	Low	High	Moderate
Main type of enforcement (controls)	Formal	Formal/Informal	Informal/Formal
Main type of transaction	Discrete	Occasional	Repetitive
Main type of 'contract'	Rules	Agreement	Relation
Main type of trust	Organizational	Organizational/Professional	Individual/Organizational
Importance of trust	Unimportant	Important	Very important
No. of parties	Many	Very few	Few

Source: Jansson (1994a, p. 75).

is not complete, since there are costs for transacting. The assumption of atomistic competition contained in the perfect-market model is retained. The identity of individual actors in the market is thus irrelevant and discrete transactions are emphasized. The closeness to perfect competition is evident in the fact that the entry and exit to the market is unregulated. Knowledge of the market is high, the future being predictable and can be related to the present through information about prices, products and quantities. Such assumptions make it possible to specify contracts in detail. Market governance represents the main governance structure for non-specific transactions. It is based on classical conceptions of contracting, in terms of which 'third party participation is discouraged. The emphasis is thus on legal rules, formal documents, and self-liquidating transactions' (Williamson, 1985, p. 69). Note that the functioning of a specific legal system is assumed, in Williamson's case the US system. Market governance is signified by discrete transactions, price being determined by the market itself and cannot be influenced by any single buyer or seller. Markets for standard industrial products such as chemicals, carbon steel, computer terminals and shipping services resemble commodity markets in that price is the dominant information carrier. In addition, relationships are unimportant, transactions are repetitive and switching costs are low.

Bilateral governance

Bilateral governance provides a relevant background for how the markets are organized for other industrial products, for example components and minor equipment. In such markets the relationship is focused upon and not discrete transactions or the agreement. Established relationships are used for such transactions instead of going to the market. Business is not seen as a process of continuous adaptation to changing conditions, but rather as adaptations made within continuous relations. Business exists and takes place through a network of contacts that are bound by rules or routinized arrangements of a formal and informal nature. Price is chiefly supplemented by informal sanctions as a main control mechanism. Trust is established in order to get the behaviour routinized.

Trilateral governance

In trilateral governance transactions are safe-guarded in a different way. Assistance from a third party is sought to solve disputes between sellers and buyers and to evaluate the outcome of their joint business. The emphasis is then on the individual agreement between two parties arranged by a third party. This form of governance is typical for how markets are organized for very complex products like machines and projects. Transactions take place to develop the formal contract, interactions subsequent to the agreement being guided by it. Price is then supplemented by formal rules as another control mechanism.

The MNC as a socio-economic institution

Transaction cost theory is seen by Jansson (1994b) to express very well the main rationale behind MNCs originating from and mainly operating in Western market economies. Dominating orientation, basic beliefs, values and behaviour are elevated through this theory and the 'soul' of this type of MNC, as is illustrated by the following quotation:

> As the Western cultures derive their main orientations from the Judeo-Christian or Graeco-Hellinist traditions, order, symmetry, linearity, and individuality are the bases of an epistemological framework. Organizations are the systemic hierarchy of individual parts. As such, their efficiency and efficacy can be analysed down to the smallest unit, that is, individual. The unit's individual outcomes can be aggregated to obtain the results of the whole outcomes. As the organisation compares and contrasts the efficacy of different units, the systematic allocation of resources among them becomes of prime concern. In fact, the Western economic concept is mainly built on allocation of resources or allocative efficiency. On the other hand, if organisations are regarded as symbiotic relations of heterogeneous parts mutually benefiting all concerned, the precise demarcation of contributions is not possible and will not be attempted. Instead, measurement will be based on the totality of the system than on individual parts. The results of these divergent views can be observed in the ways the American and Japanese organisations measure their efficiency results. The American organisation, the prototype of the developed system in the West, emphasises the decentralisation and individual unit measurement.

The wave of decentralisation unit and accountability that had overtaken American businesses in the seventies is indicative of how the concept of allocative efficiency has carried itself to its logical extreme. On the other hand, Japanese companies are always looking for the contributions of synergetic relationships, because synergy is considered the basis of organisational relations. Thus, American firms will look for precise measurements of each sub-unit's performance in the shorter term, while Japanese firms are interested in fostering systems of relationships that will contribute to synergetic results. Thus, they will be more concerned with overall and long-term effects rather than with short-term and individual results. They are willing to tolerate the organisational units which may be inefficient by themselves but may produce positive effects in relation to others. In fact, the whole Japanese approach is aimed at the totality rather than the parts. The Japanese industrial system – Miti and the whole complex of individual companies – is aiming for total efficiency rather than their individual unit profits.

That is the difference which makes the Japanese organisation so formidable. Though this approach is clearly seen in the Japanese companies and culture, other Asian cultures share the totality concept in varying degrees. (Khin, 1988, pp. 217–18)

According to this quote, and in accordance with the institutional approach, all firms are underpinned by social institutions. This means, inter alia, that values and beliefs internal and external to the organization play a significant role in determining organizational structures and strategic behaviour.

Inspired by the governance forms theory, Powell (1990) sees networks as neither market nor hierarchy, that is, as an intermediate form between these types of governance. But the most developed theoretical framework from such a perspective is the business systems approach (Whitley, 1992a, b, 1999a, b, 2003). While the governance structure approach sees the MNC as an economic institution, the business systems approach views the MNC more broadly as a societal phenomenon including social aspects. The hierarchy now becomes an authority and control system. In both these approaches, the MNC is integrated into its environment, mainly being seen as a product of the environment. This means that the MNC as an internal institution is related to various external institutions. In the governance forms approach this is evident from the fact that it is also called the markets and hierarchies approach. The hierarchy as one major institution is closely linked to the other major institution: the market. As distinguished from the governance forms approach, the business systems approach also relates the company to its wider environment outside the markets. This wider environment is expressed as 'dominant institutions' in the definition of business systems as configurations of hierarchy–market relations. A distinction is made between markets and the state on the one hand, these being defined as proximate social institutions, and other factors of the environment on the other, these being defined as background social institutions. The former are found at the meso level and the latter at the macro level. Economic institutions like the MNC are not only confined by other, non-economic institutional frameworks such as culture and the state; rather, they are socio-economic entities themselves.

Thus, there are striking similarities between Western economic institutions because they share a wide variety of institutions, for example market-based wage systems, professionally oriented occupations and commitments to individualism, which together result in characteristics common to such economic institutions as the MNC.

Although Western MNCs share many common institutions, there is also a difference between them. Continental Western European firms, for example, are different from companies of Anglo-Saxon origin (Whitley, 1992a, p. 14). They share:

> … a common reliance on legal-rational norms and bases of legitimacy. Similarly, the prevalence of capital market-based financial systems, and the reliance on 'professional' modes of skill development and organization, in Anglo-Saxon societies means that dominant businesses in Britain and the USA seem to share a preference for financial means of control of operations and subsidiaries, and accord the finance function higher status than many continental European firms. This major institutional difference is disappearing. The complex system of cross-holdings and long-term relations between companies and banks typical of continental and North Europe have increasingly been replaced by arms-length market operations. The main reasons behind this change are falling profitability and the big growth of capital-market instruments. The European MNCs' change to American ways is demonstrated by the listing of the corporations in New York, more explicit setting of profit targets, increased use of financial manoeuvres and share options, deconglomeration of the companies, more efforts to control management through corporate governance and increased shareholder activism.

MNCs based in Western Europe and North America share particular traits that distinguish them from companies indigenous to Eastern Asia. This makes it possible to identify what tends to be characteristic of a specific Western European approach to business and to compare this with what can be termed the Japanese, the Korean or the Chinese business approach, these constituting the three most dominating business systems in Eastern Asia.

The market as a socio-economic institution

Market governance comes rather close to the markets found in the pure competition model, which makes the model unrealistic. The condition that the future be completely known is relaxed in order to make market governance more similar to Hodgson's (1988) less formal definition of the market below. Still, the most important characteristic of Williamson's definition of market governance has been retained, namely that most of the information is contained in the price. Price is a carrier of information about products and quantities, as well as about incentives, coordination and the allocation of resources. In commodity exchange, for example, trading is structured and information is published in order to help in the formation of price expectations and of norms. However, price is not completely determined by the market. When the degree of uncertainty is high, as in complex and volatile markets, guideline information is published so that agents can cope.

Hodgson (1988, p. 174) has shown that markets are defined in economics as a place where transactions take place and commodities are exchanged:

> We shall here define the market as a set of social institutions in which a large number of commodity exchanges of a specific type regularly take place and to some extent are facilitated and structured by those institutions. Exchange … involves contractual agreement and the

exchange of property rights, and the market consists in part of mechanisms to structure, organize, and legitimate these activities. Markets, in short, are organized and institutionalized exchange. Stress is placed on those market institutions which help to both regulate and establish a consensus over prices and, more generally, to communicate information regarding products, prices, quantities, potential buyers and potential sellers.

Some institutions within the market are associated with exchange and contracts in an elemental sense (such as the legal system and the customs which govern the contract). … These would be present even if a formal market did not exist. Other institutions are specifically to do with the development of a market and the coordination of a large number of exchanges in an organized manner.

Hodgson (1988) provides a definition of a commodity market here, but the description fits other markets as well.

Markets as well as hierarchies are in turn influenced by non-economic or social institutions, such as government, the political system, the legal system and culture. So market exchange does not take place in a vacuum but will look different depending on how other institutions in the environment work. The legal system plays a key role in controlling the market, as demonstrated by the following quotation:

Market exchange requires a combination of both state and customary institutions. For any developed system of commodity exchange there must be a legal system inscribing and protecting rights to individual or corporate property. There must be a body of contract law with criteria for distinguishing between voluntary and involuntary transfers of goods and services, and courts to adjudicate in such matters. In addition, however, the evolution of law is not simply a matter of legislative construction; a great deal of law grows out of custom and precedent. Property and contract law are not exceptions. Consequently, the existence of property and exchange is tied up with a number of legal and other institutions. (Hodgson, 1988, p. 150)

INSTITUTIONAL THEORIES AT THE MICRO LEVEL

Sociological institutional theory started to be developed for organizations in the middle of the last century by Selznick (1957) and others. Initially, research focused on the organization itself by taking up issues of influence, coalitions and competing values along with power and informal structures. Later, the focus shifted to the external institutional context by studying how it impacts organizations. The most extreme form of such external control of the organization is neo-institutional theory, where organizational structure is entirely determined by external institutions (DiMaggio and Powell, 1983; Powell and DiMaggio, 1991; Meyer and Rowan, 1977). The institutional context is an organizational field consisting of a network of vertically and horizontally interlocking organizations. They are all passively under pressure from the context to converge towards common organizational archetypes or templates of organizing. There are strong mimetic, normative and coercive processes at work. This stream of theory is then broader than early institutional theory. It not only emphasizes the normative, such as values and moral frames, but also the regulative (coercive) and the cognitive (mimetic). The stability of organizational arrangements and inertia rather than change are stressed.

A pioneering work in using this stream of institutional theory on the MNC is that of Westney (1993), who applies theories developed by DiMaggio and Powell (1983), Powell and DiMaggio (1991) and Friedland and Alford (1991) on the relationship between subsidiaries and headquarters. The works of Kostova (1999), Kostova and Zaheer (1999) and Kostova and Roth (2002) also provide a good background to the book regarding how to combine institutional theory and legitimacy theory to study the transfer of organizational practices between different units within an MNC.

But neo-institutional theory is not used directly in this book, only providing a background. The focus on conformity or isomorphism makes it too deterministic for a book on strategy. The behaviour of the MNC is entirely determined by its environment, the MNC only reacting to environmental pressures towards conformity.

This agency problem is dealt with much more in new-institutional organization theory (see, for example, Scott, 1987, 1995/2008). As mentioned above, most such theories at the micro level of relevance to this book are presented and discussed in various chapters and are not repeated in this Appendix.

INSTITUTIONAL CHANGE

Institutions change in various ways. According to Greenwood and Hinings (1996), the scale and the pace of upheaval and adjustment are less for evolutionary than revolutionary change. The former occurs slowly and gradually, while the latter occurs swiftly and influences almost all parts of the system simultaneously. Evolutionary and revolutionary change are different from convergent and radical organizational change. Convergent change is fine-tuning the existing orientation, while radical change is about transforming it.

Kingston and Caballero (2009) identify two broad streams of theories dealing with processes of institutional change at the societal level: collective choice and evolutionary processes. These processes are now accounted for based on this article.

Formal rules

In the former political process, the formal rules of institutions are deliberately designed and implemented in a coordinated and centralized way, either by an individual (e.g. a manager of a firm) or by a group. There are then both external and internal causes of the change of such formal rules. The process of change is mostly path-dependent, meaning that it is a dynamic stochastic process that does not converge to a stable equilibrium. In such a process, initial conditions and historical accidents have a lasting impact on the institutions. Due to vested interests in preserving the status quo, these political processes are usually incremental, since it is often easier to achieve consensus on small adjustments than to effect major changes to existing rules. Another impediment to efficient institutional change is the bounded rationality. Many theories give the state, individuals or interest groups consisting of judges and politicians an independent role in the making of formal rules. For example, according to Commons, the judiciary plays a key role in mediating the creation of new rules, especially the courts. Most collective-choice theories have a problem explaining why formal rules are ignored or do not result in the intended outcome. A major reason is that they say very little about informal rules, for example social norms like trust. Such institutions are often self-organized and evolve in a decentralized way, which does not fit into these theories.

Informal rules

Theories on evolutionary change are much better in dealing with informal rules. These rules evolve either spontaneously or by design, undergoing a decentralized selection process as they compete against alternative institutions. There is no central mechanism as institutional change occurs through the uncoordinated choices of many agents. When change comes from deliberate actions, learning, imitation and experimentation are often important factors. Evolutionary change is defined as consisting of processes that satisfy the core Darwinian principles of variation (mutations), selection (survival of successful traits) and inheritance (replication of such traits). Successful institutions then spread through the population, while others die out. Veblen's evolutionary economic theory on 'habits of thought' belongs to this stream of theories (ibid.). This is also true for the evolutionary theory focusing on routines developed by Nelson and Winter (1982). Here, evolutionary selection of successful routines occurs due to the pressure of market competition and spread to other firms by being replicated (copied). Similar mechanisms of change are also found in the transaction cost theory referred to above, mainly agency theory and governance-forms theory.

According to Kingston and Caballero (2009), Hayek sees expectations, rather than rules, as the fundamental source of order in society. Similarly to Veblen, he considers the co-evolution of institutions with the individual mind as the product of the social environment. The mind does not make rules but consists of rules that govern action. The evolution of the mind does not happen through the selection of individuals with innate characteristics, but through the selection of culturally transmitted institutions.

The societal orientation of the economic theories referred to above causes the evolution to differ from biological evolution in that the successful rules, habits or routines spread by imitation and learning, rather than being passed down directly through replication or sexual reproduction. All of the economic theories also regard external parameter changes as a basic source of the impetus for institutional change.

Formal and informal rules integrated

North (1990) integrates theories on the formation of formal rules with theories on the emergence of informal rules. Formal rules are deliberately changed through a political process, while informal rules change alongside, and as extensions of formal rules. The change is slow through an evolutionary process of cultural transmission, which cannot be changed deliberately. Informal constraints are therefore the major source of institutional inertia. The impetus to try to change formal rules can come from external or internal parameter changes, including learning. Institutional change is then incremental rather than sudden. There is an accumulation of many small changes rather than occasional large changes. The process is path-dependent because individuals learn, organizations develop and ideologies form in the context of a particular set of formal and informal rules.

Long-term institutional change is generally seen as a consequence of historical and slow processes, where formal and informal rules are eliminated and replaced over time (North et al., 2009).

The past can constrain the future in many ways. One way is represented by Myrdal's (1968) fully developed socio-economic theory on institutional change. The change process is circular, causal and cumulative. It contains virtuous and vicious circles, where reinforcing feedback loops cause the societal aspect studied (e.g. population or economy) to grow by increasingly higher amounts. The virtuous circle leads to integration and the vicious circle to disintegration.

Layers of embedded rules

According to Williamson (2000), formal rules are embedded in informal rules. Depending upon how rapidly they change, he distinguishes between one layer of informal rules and three layers of formal rules (see Figure A.1). The informal institutions are found at the top of the hierarchy, being called 'institutions of embeddedness' and including culture and norms. The reason is that they take

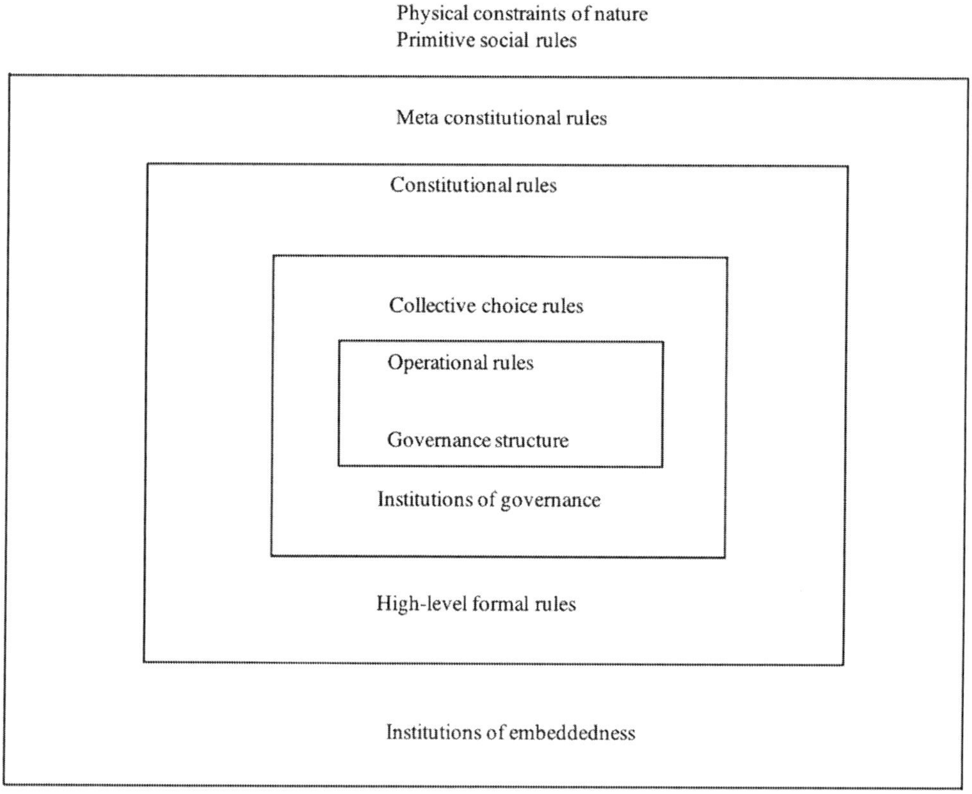

Physical constraints of nature
Primitive social rules

Meta constitutional rules

Constitutional rules

Collective choice rules

Operational rules

Governance structure

Institutions of governance

High-level formal rules

Institutions of embeddedness

Figure A.1 Layers of embedded rules

centuries or even millennia to change. They constrain the 'high-level formal rules' in the next layer, for example constitutions, laws and property rights. Here changes take decades or centuries. In the next layer, 'institutions of governance' set the rules for 'governance structures' in the lowest layer. These structures then control the contractual relations of the day-to-day interactions. Changes in the third layer take years, while adjustments of prices and quantities are continuous in the fourth layer. As noted above, new institutional economics operate with formal rules in layers two and three, and the informal rules are then treated as external parameters in the highest and most general layer, controlling the layers of formal rules below. Formal rules then change more often than informal rules.

Ostrom (2005) develops a similar multi-layer nested hierarchy of humanly devised rules. The layers are the same except for their names, reflecting that they originate from another institutional theory and consist of both formal and informal rules. For example, 'contractual relations' are found in the same layer as 'operational rules', since they restrain day-to-day interactions. 'Collective choice rules' control the selection of these 'operational rules'. 'Constitutional rules', in their turn, restrain the 'collective choice rules', while the 'meta constitutional rules' at the top of the hierarchy control the 'constitutional rules'. This highest layer consists of the most fundamental societal rules. Further on, at an even more basic societal level, Hobbe's state of nature may be found, representing a primitive society consisting of fundamental rules originating mainly from language, in addition to the dominating physical and biological constraints of nature.

Institutional change at the micro level

A more recent evolutionary change theory at the micro level is found in Hodgson (2013). It is about social evolution of complex populations of organizations, which evolve according to the Darwinian principles of variation, selection and retention. The replicator–interactor distinction is the main causal mechanism controlling this organizational change process. Replicators are informational mechanisms found in interactors, being classified as causal mechanisms, since they determine if change happens. Individual habits are the most elementary replicators of social evolution, while routines are replicators at the organizational level.

This theory and most of the institutional theories above do not go much into the change process itself. The agency aspect is then poorly developed. As noted above, there is no agent present in neo-institutional organization theory, since the behaviour of the organization is determined by its environment, only passively responding to environmental pressures towards conformity.

Greenwood and Hinings (1996) develop a less deterministic institutional change model, where organizations respond differently to the external institutional pressures plus competitive pressures from the market context. Responses of the individual organization to external pressures are rather reactive than passive. Change is radical and is a function of the dynamic interplay between four internal characteristics. The intensity of the internal pressures for change is a result of the way in which interest dissatisfaction and value commitments are linked with the external market and institutional contexts. Interest dissatisfaction originates within a coalition with different interests. How this dissatisfaction is directed depends upon how committed actors are to the current and alternative organizational arrangements, while being aware of their weaknesses and strengths.

The response to these pressures is determined by two enablers, namely positions of power within the intra-organizational network, and the groups' capacities to manage the transition process from one template to another. This ability concerns the availability of skills and resources within an organization and their mobilization by leaders. Experience increases the capacity for organizational change. How members of interest groups react then depends on their network positions, skills, commitments and histories.

However, the theory ends here and does not include the impact of the organizational change on the external contexts. Since change is limited to reactive organizational behaviour in general, the agency aspect is still insufficiently developed from a strategic change point of view. This also goes for the process of change. It is linear, being a product of sequential interactions between a given set of variables. The authors speculate about how such radical organizational change could proceed over time periods by being a product of processes that are oscillatory and iterative, consisting of different combinations of interactions between the four internal factors. For example, a cycle is a specific oscillatory and iterative process that fluctuates and repeats itself in a wave-like way.

Seo and Creed (2002) go more into how organizations can influence their environment (the agency aspect) as well as into the process of change by focusing directly on the organizational action process, which they define as the praxis phase. Compared to above, agents are now active through mediating between institutional contradictions and institutional change. Praxis is the construction of social patterns by partially autonomous social actors on the basis of reasoned analysis of both the limits and the potentials of present social forms. The theory mainly deals with evolutionary but also revolutionary change, which are both seen as bottom-up processes. As above, the adequate institutional pattern is determined through competition between different interest groups within the organization. Likewise, the internal change process is influenced by external constraints and inducements, consisting of contradictory multilevel and interrelated social arrangements. They are incompatible, resulting in conflicts that drive the institutional change process. These tensions reshape actors' consciousness through a reasoned analysis of both the limits and the potentials of current social forms. This reshaped consciousness starts the praxis phase, which involves the further critique of existing social patterns, the search for alternatives, mobilization and collective action. Through this process the existing social pattern is reconstructed.

Oliver (1991) elaborates the agency aspect even more by going deeper into various ways that agents actively respond to external pressures, and develops a typology of strategic responses. Non-profit organizations resist pressures in various ways, ranging from passive conformity to proactive manipulation. Due to this more advanced agency and types of change, it is used as a key source to develop the international matching strategy. It is therefore referred to more in Chapter 13, where it is also applied.

Still, most of these theories are of limited value in explaining strategic change, since they mainly consider responsive behaviour, leaving out proactive behaviour. They provide an input for developing the outside-in perspective on IBS in Chapters 5 and 6. But only Seo and Creed (2002) and Oliver (1991) contribute to the inside-out perspective by taking up how the organizational behaviour of internal mediators impacts the external context.

References

Agndal, H. and S. Chetty (2007) 'The impact of relationships on changes in internationalisation strategies of SMEs', *European Journal of Marketing*, **41** (11/12), 1449–74.

Ahuja, G. (2000) 'Collaboration networks, structural holes, and innovation: A longitudinal study', *Administrative Science Quarterly*, **45** (3), 425–55.

Aldrich, Howard and David A. Whetten (1981) 'Organization-sets, action-sets, and networks: Making the most of simplicity', in Paul Nyström and William H. Starbuck (eds), *Handbook of Organizational Design*, vol. 1, New York: Oxford University Press, pp. 385–408.

Alkhafaji, Abbass F. (1995) *Competitive Global Management: Principles and Strategies*, Delray Beach, FL: St Lucie Press.

Anderson, E. and H. Gatignon (1986) 'Modes of foreign entry: A transaction cost analysis and propositions', *Journal of International Business Studies*, **17** (3), 1–26.

Anderson, J.C., Håkansson, H. and J. Johanson (1994) 'Dyadic business relationships within a business network context', *Journal of Marketing*, **58** (4), 1–15.

Ansoff, I. (1957) 'Strategies for diversification', *Harvard Business Review*, **5** (35), 113–24.

Argyris, Chris and David Schon (1978) *Organizational Learning: A Theory of Action Perspective*, Reading, MA: Addison-Wesley.

Argyris, Chris and David Schon (1996) *Organizational Learning II: Theory, Method, and Practice*, Reading, MA: Addison-Wesley.

Axelsson, Björn (1992) 'Corporate strategy models and networks – Diverging perspectives', in Björn Axelsson and Geoff Easton (eds), *Industrial Networks: A New Reality*, London: Routledge, pp. 303–22.

Axelsson, Björn and Geoff Easton (1992) *Industrial Networks: A New View of Reality*, London: Routledge.

Axelsson, Björn and Jan Johanson (1992) 'Foreign market entry – The textbook vs. the network view', in Björn Axelsson and Geoff Easton (eds), *Industrial Networks: A New View of Reality*, London: Routledge, pp. 218–34.

Backman, Michael (1999) *Asian Eclipse, Exposing the Dark Side of Business in Asia*, Singapore and New York: John Wiley & Sons.

Bain, Joe S. (1956) *Barriers to New Competition*, Cambridge, MA: Harvard University Press.

Bansard, D., Bernard, C. and R. Salle (1993) 'Project marketing: Beyond competitive bidding strategies', *International Business Review*, **2** (2), 125–41.

Barney, J. (1991) 'Firm resources and sustained competitive advantage', *Journal of Management*, **17** (1), 99–120.

Barney, Jay B. (1994) 'Bringing managers back in', in Jay B. Barney, J-C. Spender and Torger Reve, *Does Management Matter? On Competencies and Competitive Advantage*, The 1994 Crafoord Lectures, Institute of Economic Research, Lund University, pp. 1–36.

Barney, Jay and William Ouchi (1986) *Organizational Economics: Towards a New Paradigm for Understanding and Studying Organizations*, San Francisco, CA: Jossey-Bass.

Bartlett, Christopher (1986) 'Building and managing the transnational: The new organizational challenge', in Michael Porter (ed.), *Competition in Global Industries*, Cambridge, MA: Harvard Business School Press, pp. 367–401.

Bartlett, Christopher and Sumantra Ghoshal (1989) *Managing across Borders: The Transnational Solution*, Boston, MA: Free Press.

Bartlett, Christopher and Sumantra Ghoshal (1992) *Transnational Management: Text, Cases, and Readings in Cross-Border Management*, Homewood, IL: Irwin.

Bartlett, C. and S. Ghoshal (1998) 'Beyond strategic planning to organizational learning: Lifeblood of the individualized corporation', *Strategy and Leadership*, **26** (1), 34–9.

Bell, J. (1995) 'The internationalization of small computer firms: A further challenge to "stage" theories', *European Journal of Marketing*, **29** (8), 60–75.

Bell, J., McNaughton, R., Young, S. and D. Crick (2003) 'Towards an integrative model of small firm internationalization', *Journal of International Entrepreneurship*, **1** (4), 339–62.

Bello, D.C. and T. Kostova (2014) 'From the editors: Conducting high impact international business research: The role of theory', *Journal of International Business Studies*, **43** (6), 537–43.

Bénétrix, A.S., O'Rourke, K.H. and J.G. Williamson (2012) 'The spread of manufacturing to the periphery 1870–2007: Eight stylized facts', Discussion Paper Series, Department of Economics, No. 617, Oxford University.

Benoît, C., Norris, G.A., Valdivia, S., Ciroth, A., Moberg, Å., Bos, U., Prakash, S., Ugaya, C. and T. Beck (2010) 'The guidelines for social life cycle assessment of products: Just in time!', *International Journal Life Cycle Assessment*, **15** (2), 156–63.

Berry, H., Guillén, M.F. and A.S. Heidi (2014) 'Is there convergence across countries? A spatial approach', *Journal of International Business Studies*, **45** (4), 387–404.

Bilkey, W.J. (1978) 'An attempted integration of the literature on the export behaviour of firms', *Journal of International Business Studies*, **9** (1), 33–46.

Bingham, Frank G. Jr and Barney T. Raffield III (1990) *Business to Business Marketing Management*, Boston, MA: Irwin.

Björkman, I. and M. Forsgren (2000) 'Nordic international business research – A review of its development', *International Studies of Management and Organization*, **30** (1), 6–25.

Blankenburg, D. and J. Johanson (1992) 'Managing network connections in international business', *Scandinavian International Business Review*, **1** (1), 5–19.

Blau, Peter (1964) *Exchange and Power in Social Life*, New York: Wiley.

Blau, Peter (1987) 'Microprocess and macrostructure', in Karen S. Cook (ed.), *Social Exchange Theory*, Beverly Hills, CA: Sage, pp. 83–100.

Blomstermo, A., Eriksson, K., Lindstrand, A. and D.D. Sharma (2004) 'The perceived usefulness of network experiential knowledge in the internationalizing firm', *Journal of International Management*, **10** (3), 355–73.

Brass, D., Galaskiewicz, J., Greve, H. and W. Tsai (2004) 'Taking stock of networks and organizations: A multilevel perspective', *Academy of Management Journal*, **47** (6), 795–817.

Brouthers, K.D. (2002) 'Institutional, cultural, and transaction cost influences on entry mode choice and performance', *Journal of International Business Studies*, **33** (2), 203–21.

Brouthers, K.D. and G. Nakos (2004) 'SME entry mode choice and performance: A transaction cost perspective', *Entrepreneurship Theory and Practice*, **28** (3), 229–47.

Buckley, P.J. (1987) *The Theory of Multinational Enterprise*, Acta Universitatis Upsaliensis, Studia Oeconomiae Negotiourum 26, Uppsala: Almqvist & Wiksell.

Buckley, P.J. (2009) 'The impact of the global factory on economic development', *Journal of World Business*, **44** (2), 131–43.

Buckley, Peter J. and Mark Casson (1976) *The Future of the Multinational Enterprise*, London: Macmillan.

Buckley, P.J. and P.N. Ghauri (2004) 'Globalization, economic geography and the strategy of multinational enterprises', *Journal of International Business Studies*, **35** (2), 81–98.

Burt, Roland S. (1993) 'The social structure of competition', in Richard Swedberg (ed.), *Explorations in Economic Sociology*, New York: Russell Sage Foundation, pp. 65–103.

Campos, N.F. and F. Coricelli (2002) 'Growth in transition: What we know, what we don't, and what we should', *Journal of Economic Literature*, **40** (3), 793–836.

Carlson, Benny (1995) *De Institutionalistiska Idéernas Spridning* [The Diffusion of the Institutionalist Ideas], Stockholm: SNS.

Casson, Mark (1987) *The Firm and the Market: Studies on Multinational Enterprise and the Scope of the Firm*, Oxford: Basil Blackwell.

Caves, R.E. (1979) 'Industrial organization, corporate strategy and structure', *Journal of Economic Literature*, **18** (March), pp. 64–92.

Caves, Richard E. (1982) *Multinational Enterprise and Economic Analysis*, Cambridge: Cambridge University Press.

Cavusgil, S.T. (1980) 'On the internationalization process of firms', *European Research*, **8** (6), 273–81.

Cavusgil, S.T. and G. Knight (2015) 'The born global firm: An entrepreneurial and capabilities perspective on early and rapid internationalization', *Journal of International Business Studies*, **46** (1), 3–16.

Cavusgil, S. Tamer, Ghauri, Pervez N. and Milind R. Agarwal (2002) *Entry Strategies for Emerging Markets: Entry and Negotiation Strategies*, London: SAGE Publications.

Chandler, Alfred D. (1962) *Strategy and Structure: Chapters in the History of the American Industrial Enterprise*, Cambridge, MA: MIT Press.

Chen, Min (1995) *Asian Management Systems: Chinese, Japanese and Korean Styles of Business*, London: Routledge.

Chetty, S. and D. Blankenburg Holm (2000) 'Internationalization of small to medium-sized firms: A network approach', *International Business Review*, **9** (1), 77–93.

Child, John (2001) 'China and international business', in Alan M. Rugman and Thomas L. Brewer (eds), *The Oxford Handbook of International Business*, Oxford: Oxford University Press, pp. 681–715.

Child, J. and S.B. Rodrigues (2005) 'The internationalization of Chinese firms: A case for theoretical extension?' *Management and Organization Review*, **1** (3), 381–410.

Cipriani, R. (1987) 'The sociology of legitimation: An introduction', *Current Sociology*, **35** (2), 1–20.

Coase, R.H. (1937) 'The nature of the firm', *Economica*, **4** (16), 386–405.

Coleman, J.S. (1988) 'Social capital in the creation of human capital', *American Journal of Sociology*, **94**, 95–120.

Collis, D. (1991) 'A resource-based analysis of global competition: The case of the bearings industry', *Strategic Management Journal*, **12** (1), 49–68.

Collis, D. and C.A. Montgomery (1995) 'Competing on resources: Strategy in the 1990s', *Harvard Business Review*, **73** (4), 119–28.

Cook, K.S. and R.M Emerson (1984) 'Exchange networks and the analysis of complex organizations', *Research in the Sociology of Organizations*, **3**, 1–30.

Cova, B. and S. Hoskins (1997) 'A twin-track networking approach to project marketing', *European Management Journal*, **15** (5), 546–56.

Coviello, N.E. (2015) 'Comment: Rethinking research on born globals', *Journal of International Business Studies*, **46** (1), 17–26.

Coviello, N.E. and A. McAuley (1999) 'Internationalisation and the smaller firm: A review of contemporary empirical research', *Management International Review*, **39** (3), 223–56.

Coviello, N.E. and H. Munro (1997) 'Network relationships and the internationalization process of small software firms', *International Business Review*, **6** (4), 361–86.

Crossan, M.M. and I. Berdrow (2003) 'Organizational learning and strategic renewal', *Strategic Management Journal*, **24** (11), 1087–105.

Cyert, Richard M. and James G. March (1963) *A Behavioral Theory of the Firm*, Englewood Cliffs, NJ: Prentice Hall.

Czinkota, Michael R. (1982) *Export Development Strategies*, New York: Praeger.

Day, G. (1994) 'The capabilities of market-driven organizations', *Journal of Marketing*, **58** (4), 37–52.

DiMaggio, P. and W.W. Powell (1983) 'The iron cage revisited: Institutional isomorphism and collective rationality in organizational fields', *American Sociological Review*, **48** (2), 147–80.

Douglas, Mary (1986) *How Institutions Think*, London: Routledge & Kegan Paul.

Doz, Yves (1985) *Strategic Management in Multinational Companies*, Oxford: Oxford University Press.

Doz, Y., Asakawa, K., Santos, J.F.P. and P. Williamson (1996) 'The metanational corporation', paper presented at the AIB Annual Meeting, Banff, Canada, September 26–29.

Drew, A. and H. Jansson (2014) 'Why has the Chinese leadership style prevailed over millenia? Towards an evolutionary theory of leadership', paper presented at the AIB annual meeting, Vancouver.

Dunning, John H. (1981) *International Production and the Multinational Enterprise*, London: Allen & Unwin.

Dunning, John H. (1988a) *Explaining International Production*, London: Unwin & Hyman.

Dunning, J.H. (1988b) 'The eclectic paradigm of international production: A restatement and some possible extensions', *Journal of International Business Studies*, **19** (1), 1–31.

Dunning, John H. (1993) *Multinational Enterprises and the Global Economy*, Wokingham: Addison-Wesley.

Dunning, J.H. (2005) 'Towards a new paradigm of development: Implications for the determinants of international business activity', unpublished paper.

Dunning, John H. and Sarianna M. Lundan (2008) *Multinational Enterprises and the Global Economy*, 2nd edn, Cheltenham, UK and Northampton, MA, USA: Edward Elgar Publishing.

Dwyer, F.R., Schurr, P.H. and S. Oh (1987) 'Developing buyer–seller relationships', *Journal of Marketing*, **51** (2), 11–27.

Easton, Geoff (1992) 'Industrial networks: A review', in Björn Axelsson and Geoff Easton (eds), *Industrial Networks: A New View of Reality*, London: Routledge, pp. 3–28.

ECB (2013) 'How have global value chains affected world trade patterns?' *Monthly Bulletin*, May, 10–14.

El-Ansary, Adel (1983) 'The general theory of marketing: Revisited', in Shelby D. Hunt (ed.), *Marketing Theory: The Philosophy of Marketing Science*, Homewood, IL: Irwin, pp. 271–6.

Emerson, R.M. (1962) 'Power-dependence relations', *American Sociological Review*, **27** (1), 31–41.

Eriksson, K., Johanson, J., Majkgård, A. and D.D. Sharma (1997) 'Experiential knowledge and cost in the internationalization process', *Journal of International Business Studies*, **28** (2), 337–60.

Fahey, Liam and V.K. Narayanan (1986) *Macroenvironmental Analysis for Strategic Management*, St Pauls, MN: West Publishing Company.

Farrell, D. (2004) 'Beyond offshoring: Assess your company's global potential', *Harvard Business Review*, **82** (12), 82–90.

Finkbeiner, M., Schau, E.M., Lehmann, A. and M. Traverson (2010) 'Towards life cycle sustainability assessment', *Sustainability*, no. 2, pp. 3309–22.

Finnveden, G., Hauschild, M.Z., Ekvall, T, Guinée, J., Jeijungs, R., Hellweg, S., Koehler, A., Pennington, D. and S. Suh (2009) 'Recent developments in life cycle assessment', *Journal of Environmental Management*, **91** (1), 1–21.

Ford, D. (1980) 'The development of buyer–seller relationships in industrial markets', *European Journal of Marketing*, **14** (5/6), 339–53.

Ford, David (ed.) (1997) *Understanding Business Markets: Interaction, Relationships and Networks*, London: Routledge.

Ford, David (ed.) (2002) *Understanding Business Marketing and Purchasing*, London: Thomson.

Ford, David, Gadde, Lars Erik, Håkansson, Håkan and Ivan Snehota (2003) *Managing Business Relationships*, Chichester: John Wiley & Sons.

Ford, David, Gadde, Lars Erik, Håkansson, Håkan and Ivan Snehota (2006) *The Business Marketing Course: Managing in Complex Networks*, 2nd edn, Chichester: John Wiley & Sons.

Forsgren, M. (2002) 'The concept of learning in the Uppsala internationalization process model: A critical review', *International Business Review*, **11** (3), 257–78.

Frankelius, Per (2001) *Omvärldsanalys* [Environmental Analysis], Malmö: Liber Ekonomi.

Freeman, R. Edward and John McVea (2001) 'A stakeholder approach to strategic management', in Michael A. Hitt, R. Edward Freeman and Jeffrey S. Harrison (eds), *Blackwell Handbook of Strategic Management*, Oxford: Blackwell Business, pp. 189–207.

Friedland, Roger and Robert R. Alford (1991) 'Bringing society back in: Symbols, practices, and institutional contradictions', in Paul J. DiMaggio and Walter W. Powell (eds), *The New Institutionalism in Organizational Analysis*, Chicago: University of Chicago Press, pp. 232–66.

Fukuyama, Francis (1995) *Trust: The Social Virtues and the Creation of Prosperity*, London: Hamish Hamilton.

Gankema, H.G., Snuif, H.R. and P.S. Zwart (2000) 'The internationalization process of small and medium-sized enterprises: An evaluation of stage theory', *Journal of Small Business Management*, **38** (4), 15–27.

Ghauri, Pervez (1983) *Negotiating International Package Deals: Swedish Firms and Developing Countries*, Acta Universitatis Upsaliensis, Uppsala (dissertation).

Ghoshal, S. (1987) 'Global strategy: An organizing framework', *Strategic Management Journal*, **8** (5), 425–40.

Ghoshal, S. and C. Bartlett (1990) 'The multinational corporation as an interorganizational network', *Academy of Management Review*, **15** (4), 603–25.

Ginsberg, A. (1994) 'Minding the competition: From minding to mastery', *Strategic Management Journal*, **15** (1), 153–74.

Gordon, Ian H. (1998) *Relationship Marketing*, Toronto: John Wiley & Sons.

Granovetter, M. (1973) 'The strength of weak ties', *American Journal of Sociology*, **78** (6), 1360–80.

Granovetter, Mark (1982) 'The strength of weak ties: A network theory revisited', in Peter V. Marsden and Nan Lin (eds), *Social Structure and Network Analysis*, Beverly Hills, CA: Sage, pp. 105–30.

Granovetter, M. (1985) 'Economic action and social structure: The problem of embeddedness', *American Journal of Sociology*, **91** (3), 481–510.

Grant, R. (1991) 'The resource-based theory of competitive advantage: Implications for strategy formulation', *California Management Review*, **33** (3), 114–35.

Grant, Robert M. (1995/1998/2002) *Contemporary Strategy Analysis: Concepts, Techniques, Applications*, 2nd/3rd/4th edn, Oxford: Blackwell.

Greenwood, R. and C.R. Hinings (1996) 'Understanding radical organizational change: Bringing together the old and the new institutionalism', *Academy of Management Review*, **21** (4), 1022–54.

Grönroos, C. (1995) 'Relationship marketing: The strategy continuum', *Journal of the Academy of Marketing Science*, **23** (4), 252–4.

Grönroos, C. (2000) 'Relationship marketing: The Nordic School perspective', in Jagdish N. Sheth and Atui Parvatiyar (eds), *Handbook of Relationship Marketing*, Thousand Oaks, CA: Sage, pp. 95–117.

Gulati, R., Nohria, N. and A. Zaheer (2000) 'Strategic networks', *Strategic Management Journal*, **21** (3), 203–15.

Gummesson, Evert (1995) *Relationship Marketing: From 4Ps to 30Rs*. Malmö: Liber-Hermods.

Håkansson, Håkan (1982) *International Marketing and Purchasing of Industrial Goods: An Interaction Approach*, Chichester: John Wiley & Sons.

Håkansson, Håkan and Jan Johanson (1992) 'A model of industrial networks', in Björn Axelsson and Geoff Easton (eds), *Industrial Networks: A New Reality*, London: Routledge, pp. 28–34.

Håkansson, H. and C. Östberg (1975) 'Industrial marketing: An organizational problem?' *Industrial Marketing Management*, **4** (1/2), 113–23.

Håkansson, Håkan and Ivan Snehota (1995) *Developing Relationships in Business Networks*, London: Routledge.

Håkansson, Håkan and Ivan Snehota (2000) 'The IMP perspective: Assets and liabilities of business relationships', in Jagdish N. Sheth and Atai Parvatiyar (eds), *Handbook of Relationship Marketing*, Thousand Oaks, CA: Sage, pp. 69–93.

Haley, G.T. (1997) 'A strategic perspective on overseas Chinese networks' decision making', *Management Decision*, **35** (8), 587–94.

Haley, George T., Tan, ChinHwee and Usha C.V. Haley (1999) *New Asian Emperors: The Overseas Chinese, Their Strategies and Competitive Advantages*, Oxford: Butterworth Heinemann.

Hallén, Lars and Jan Johanson (1989) *Advances in International Marketing*, Greenwich, CT: JAI Press.

Hallén, L. and M. Johanson (2004a) 'Sudden death: Dissolution of relationships in the Russian transition market', *Journal of Marketing Management*, **20** (9–10), 941–57.

Hallén, L. and M. Johanson (2004b) 'Integration of relationships and business network development in the Russian transition economy', *International Marketing Review*, **21** (2), 158–71.

Hamilton, Gary G. (1996) *Asian Business Networks*, de Gruyter Studies in Organization, vol. 64, Berlin: Walter de Gruyter.

Hamilton, G.C. and N.W. Biggart (1988) 'Market, cultures, and authority: A comparative analysis of management and organization in the Far East', *American Journal of Sociology*, **94**, 52–94.

Hammarkvist, Karl-Olov, Håkansson, Håkan and Lars-Gunnar Mattsson (1982) *Marknadsföring för Konkurrenskraft* [Marketing for Competitiveness], Liber: Stockholm.

Hampden-Turner, Charles M. and Frans Trompenaars (2000) *Building Cross-Cultural Competence: How to Create Wealth from Conflicting Values*, Chichester: John Wiley & Sons.

Hardin, Russell (2002) *Trust and Trustworthiness*, New York: Russell Sage Foundation.

Hedlund, G. (1986) 'The hypermodern MNC – A heterarchy?' *Human Resource Management*, **25** (1), 9–35.

Heenan, David A. and Howard V. Perlmutter (1979) *Multinational Organization Development*, Reading, MA: Addison-Wesley.

Heide, J.B. and G. John (1992) 'Do norms matter in marketing relationships?' *Journal of Marketing*, **56** (2), pp. 32–44.

Hennart, Jean Francois (1982) *A Theory of Multinational Enterprise*, Ann Arbor, MI: University of Michigan Press.

Hilmersson, M. and H. Jansson (2012a) 'International network extension processes to institutionally different markets: Entry nodes and processes of exporting SMEs', *International Business Review*, **21** (4), 682–93.

Hilmersson, M. and H. Jansson (2012b) 'Reducing uncertainty in the emerging market entry process: On the relationship among international experiential knowledge, institutional distance, and uncertainty', *Journal of International Marketing*, **20** (4), 96–110.

Ho, D.Y.F. (1976) 'On the concept of face', *American Journal of Sociology*, **81** (4), 867–84.

Hodgson, Geoffrey M. (1988) *Economics and Institutions: A Manifesto for a Modern Institutional Economics*, Cambridge: Polity Press.

Hodgson, G.M. (2013) 'Understanding organizational evolution: Towards a research agenda using generalized Darwinism', *Organization Studies*, **34** (7), 973–92.

Hofstede, Geert (1980) *Culture's Consequences: International Differences in Work-Related Values*, Thousand Oaks, CA: Sage.

Hofstede, G. (1983) 'The cultural relativity of organizational practices and theories', *Journal of International Business Studies*, **14** (2), 75–89.

Hofstede, Geert (1994) *Cultures and Organizations: Software of the Mind: Intercultural Cooperation and Its Importance for Survival*, London: HarperCollins.

Hofstede, Geert (2001) *Culture's Consequences: Comparing Values, Behaviours, Institutions, and Organizations across Nations*, 2nd edn, Thousand Oaks, CA: Sage.

Hofstede, G. and M.H. Bond (1988) 'The Confucian connection: From cultural roots to economic growth', *Organizational Dynamics*, **16** (4), 4–21.

Hohenthal, J. (2001) *The Creation of International Business Relationships: Experience and Performance in the Internationalization Process of SMEs*, Department of Business Studies, Uppsala University (dissertation).

Holst, T. and C. Winzell (1999) *Developing Scenarios for MNCs Acting on Emerging Markets: The Volvo Construction Equipment Korea Case*, International Business Master's Thesis, No. 1999:13, Graduate Business School, School of Economics and Commercial Law, Göteborg University (Master's thesis).

Hymer, Stephen (1976) *The International Operations of National Firms*, Lexington, MA: Lexington Books.

IPBES (2019) *Global Assessment Report on Biodiversity and Ecosystem Services*, Intergovernmental Science-Policy Platform on Biodiversity and Ecosystem Services, Bonn.

IPCC (2019) *Global Warming of 1.5°C*, Intergovernmental Panel on Climate Change, Geneva.

ISO (2016) 'ISO 14040:2006. Environmental management – Life-cycle assessment – Principles and framework', ISO.

ISO (2017) 'ISO 26000:2010. Guidance on social responsibility', ISO.

Iyer, G.R. (1997) 'Comparative marketing: An interdisciplinary framework for institutional analysis', *Journal of International Business Studies*, **28** (3), 531–61.

Jackson, Barbara B. (1985) *Winning and Keeping Industrial Customers*, Boston, MA: D.C. Heath and Company.

Jalkala, A., Cova, B., Salle, R. and T. Salminen (2010) 'Changing project business orientations: Towards a new logic of project marketing', *European Management Journal*, **28** (2), 124–38.

Jansson, Hans (1987) *Affärskulturer och Relationer i Sydöstasien* [Business Cultures and Relationships in Southeast Asia], Stockholm: MTC.

Jansson, Hans (1989a) 'Internationalization processes in South-East Asia: An extension or another process?' in Erdener Kaynak and Kam Hoon Lee (eds), *Global Business: Asia-Pacific Dimensions*, London: Routledge, pp. 78–102.

Jansson, Hans (1989b) 'Marketing to projects in South East Asia', in Lars Hallén and Jan Johanson (eds), *Advances in International Marketing*, vol. 3. Greenwich, CT: JAI Press, pp. 259–76.

Jansson, Hans (1994a) *Industrial Products: A Guide to the International Marketing Economics Model*, New York: International Business Press.

Jansson, Hans (1994b) *Transnational Corporations in Southeast Asia: An Institutional Approach to Industrial Organization*, Aldershot, UK and Brookfield, VT, USA: Edward Elgar Publishing.

Jansson, Hans (2002) 'Changing government strategy of multinational corporations in transition countries: The case of Volvo Truck Corporation in India', in Virpi Havila, Mats Forsgren and Håkan Håkansson (eds), *Critical Perspectives on Internationalisation*, Amsterdam: Pergamon, pp. 387–413.

Jansson, Hans (2006a) 'Gaining societal advantages in emerging markets: International stakeholder management in Malaysia', in Sten Söderman (ed.), *Emerging Multiplicity: Integration and Responsiveness in Asian Business Development*, Basingstoke: Palgrave Macmillan, pp. 132–50.

Jansson, Hans (2006b) 'From industrial marketing to business-to-business marketing and relationship marketing', in Stefan Lagrosen and Göran Svensson (eds), *Marketing: Broadening the Horizons*, Lund: Studentlitteratur, pp. 115–36.

Jansson, Hans (2007a) *International Business Strategy in Emerging Country Markets: The Institutional Network Approach*, Cheltenham, UK and Northampton, MA, USA: Edward Elgar Publishing.

Jansson, Hans (2007b) *International Business Marketing in Emerging Country Markets: The Third Way of Internationalization of Firms*, Cheltenham, UK and Northampton, MA, USA: Edward Elgar Publishing.

Jansson, H., Johanson, M. and J. Ramström (2007) 'Institutions and business networks: A comparative analysis of the Chinese, Russian, and West European markets', *Industrial Marketing Management*, **36** (7), 955–67.

Jansson, H. and S. Sandberg (2008) 'Internationalization of small and medium-sized enterprises in the Baltic Sea Region', *Journal of International Management*, **14** (1), 65–77.

Jansson, H. and S. Sandberg (2014) 'Local adaptation of international business-to-business marketing in emerging markets: The case of Swedish firms in China', in *Proceedings of the 56th Annual Meeting of the Academy of International Business*, Vancouver, Canada, June 23–26.

Jansson, Hans, Saqib, Mohd and D. Deo Sharma (1995) *The State and Transnational Corporations: A Network Approach to Industrial Policy in India*, Aldershot, UK and Brookfield, VT, USA: Edward Elgar Publishing.

Jansson, H. and S. Söderman (2012) 'Initial internationalization of Chinese privately-owned enterprises – The take-off process', *Thunderbird International Business Review*, **54** (2), 183–94.

Jansson, H. and S. Söderman (2013) 'How large Chinese companies establish international competitiveness in other BRICS: The case of Brazil', *Asian Business and Management*, **12** (5), 539–63.

Jansson, H. and S. Söderman (2015) 'International strategic management hybrids in China', *International Journal of Emerging Markets*, **10** (2), 209–23.

Jansson, H. and S. Söderman (2019) 'A typology of market-seeking investments: Swedish firms in China', *International Journal of Emerging Markets*, **14** (1), 254–62.

Jepperson, Ronald L. (1991) 'Institutions, institutional effects, and institutionalism', in Paul J. DiMaggio and William W. Powell (eds), *The New Institutionalism in Organizational Analysis*, Chicago: University of Chicago Press, pp. 143–63.

Johanson, J. and L-G. Mattsson (1987) 'Interorganizational relations in industrial systems: A network approach compared with the transaction-cost approach', *International Studies of Management and Organization*, **17** (1), 33–48.

Johanson, Jan and Lars-Gunnar Mattsson (1988) 'Interorganizational relations in industrial systems – A network approach', in Neil Hood and Jan-Erik Vahlne (eds), *Strategies in Global Competition*, New York: Croom Helm, pp. 287–314.

Johanson, Jan and Lars-Gunnar Mattsson (1991) 'Strategic adaptation of firms to the European single market – A network approach', in Lars-Gunnar Mattsson and Bengt Stymne (eds), *Corporate and Industry Strategies for Europe*, Amsterdam: Elsevier, pp. 263–81.

Johanson, J. and L-G. Mattsson (2006) 'Discovering market networks', *European Journal of Marketing*, **40** (3/4), 259–74.

Johanson, J. and J.E. Vahlne (1977) 'The internationalization process of the firm – A model of knowledge development and increasing foreign market commitments', *Journal of International Business Studies*, **8** (1), 23–32.

Johanson, J. and J.E. Vahlne (2003) 'Business relationship learning and commitment in the internationalization process', *Journal of International Entrepreneurship*, **1** (1), 83–101.

Johanson, J. and J.E. Vahlne (2009) 'The Uppsala internationalization process model revisited: From liability of foreignness to liability of outsidership', *Journal of International Business Studies*, **40** (9), 1411–31.

Johanson, J. and F. Wiedersheim-Paul (1975) 'The internationalization of the firm – Four Swedish cases', *Journal of Management Studies*, **12** (3), 305–22.

Johanson, Martin (2004) *Managing Networks in Transition Economies*, Amsterdam: Elsevier.

Johansson, E. and P. Larsson (2001) *Pole Position with Corporate Social Responsibility*, School of Economics and Commercial Law, Göteborg University (Master's thesis).

Johnson, Gerry and Kevan Scholes (1999) *Exploring Corporate Strategy: Text and Cases*, London: Prentice Hall.

Jones, M.V., Coviello, N.E. and Y.W. Tang (2011) 'International entrepreneurship research (1989–2009): A domain ontology and thematic analysis', *Journal of Business Venturing*, **26** (6), 632–59.

Karlsson, Agneta (1991) *Om Strategi och Legitimitet* [On Strategy and Legitimacy], Lund: Lund University Press (dissertation).

Keesing, Roger M. and Andrew J. Strathern (1998) *Cultural Anthropology: A Contemporary Perspective*, 3rd edn, New York: Harcourt Brace.

Khin, M.K. (1988) 'APJM and comparative management in Asia', *Asia Pacific Journal of Management*, **5** (3), 207–24.

Kingston, C. and G. Caballero (2009) 'Comparing theories of institutional change', *Journal of Institutional Economics*, **5** (2), 151–80.

Knickerbocker, Frederick T. (1973) *Oligopolistic Reaction and the Multinational Enterprise*, Cambridge, MA: Harvard University Press.

Knight, G.A. and S.T. Cavusgil (1996) 'The born global firm: A challenge to traditional internationalization theory', *Advances in International Marketing*, **8**, 11–26.

Knoke, David and James H. Kuklinski (1982) *Network Analysis*, Quantitative Applications in the Social Sciences, Beverly Hills, CA: Sage.

Kogut, B. and U. Zander (1995) 'Knowledge, market failure and the multinational enterprise: A reply', *Journal of International Business Studies*, **26** (2), 417–26.

Kostova, T. (1997) 'Country institutional profiles: Concept and measurement', *Academy of Management Proceedings*, **97**, 180–84.

Kostova, T. (1999) 'Transnational transfer of strategic organizational practice by subsidiaries of multinational corporations: Institutional and relational effects', *Academy of Management Review*, **24** (2), 308–25.

Kostova, T. and G.T.M. Hult (2016) 'Meyer and Peng's 2005 article as a foundation for an expanded and refined international business research agenda: Context, organizations, and theories', *Journal of International Business Studies*, **47** (1), 23–32.

Kostova, T. and K. Roth (2002) 'Adoption of an organizational practice by subsidiaries of multinational corporations: Institutional and relational effects', *Academy of Management Journal*, **45** (1), 215–33.

Kostova, T., Roth, K. and M.T. Dacin (2008) 'Institutional theory on the study of multinational corporations: A critique and new directions', *Academy of Management Review*, **33** (4), 994–1006.

Kostova, T. and S. Zaheer (1999) 'Organizational legitimacy under conditions of complexity: The case of the multinational enterprise', *Academy of Management Review*, **24** (1), 64–81.

Kotabe, Masaaki (2001) 'Contemporary research trends in international marketing: The 1990s', in Alan M. Rugman and Thomas L. Brewer (eds), *The Oxford Handbook of International Business*, Oxford: Oxford University Press, pp. 457–502.

Ledeneva, Alena (1998) *Russia's Economy of Favours: Blat, Networking and Informal Exchange*, Cambridge: Cambridge University Press.

Leonard-Barton, D. (1992) 'Core capabilities and core rigidities: A paradox in managing new product development', *Strategic Management Journal*, **13**, 111–25.

Leonidou, L.C. and C.S. Katsikeas (1996) 'The export development process: An integrative review of empirical models', *Journal of International Business Studies*, **27**, 517–51.

Li, P.P. (2007) 'Guanxi as the Chinese norm for personalized social capital: Toward an integrated duality framework of informal exchange', in Henry W-C. Yeung (ed.), *Handbook of Research on Asian Business*, Cheltenham, UK and Northampton, MA, USA: Edward Elgar Publishing, pp. 62–83.

Lu, J. and P. Beamish (2001) 'The internationalization and performance of SMEs', *Strategic Management Journal*, **22**, 565–86.

Luo, Y. (1997) 'Guanxi: Principles, philosophies, and implications', *Human Systems Management*, **16** (1), 43–51.

Luo, Yadong (2002) *Multinational Enterprises in Emerging Markets*, Copenhagen: Copenhagen Business School Press.

Madsen, T. and P. Servais (1997) 'The internationalization of born globals: An evolutionary process?' *International Business Review*, **6** (6), 561–83.

Majkgård, Anders (1998) *Experimental Knowledge in the Internationalization Process of Service Firms*, Department of Business Studies, Uppsala University (dissertation).

Majkgård, A. and D.D. Sharma (1998) 'Client-following and market-seeking strategies in the internationalization of service firms', *Journal of Business-to-Business Marketing*, **4** (3), 1–41.

March, James G. (1976) 'The technology of foolishness', in James March and Johan P. Olsen (eds), *Ambiguity and Choice in Organizations*, Bergen: Universitetsförlaget, pp. 253–65.

March, J.G. (1991) 'Exploration and exploitation in organizational learning', *Organizational Science*, **2** (1), 71–87.

March, James G. and Johan P. Olsen (1989) *Rediscovering Institutions: The Organizational Basis of Politics*, New York: Free Press.

March, James G. and Herbert A. Simon (1958) *Organizations*, New York: Wiley.

Martin, Joanne (1992) *Cultures in Organizations: Three Perspectives*, Oxford: Oxford University Press.

Mattsson, L.G. (1973) 'Systems selling as a strategy on industrial markets', *Industrial Marketing Management*, **3** (2), 107–19.

Mattsson, L.G. (1997) '"Relationship marketing" and the "markets-as-networks approach" – A comparative analysis of two evolving streams of research', *Journal of Marketing Management*, **13** (5), 447–61.

McDougall, P.P. and B.M. Oviatt (2000) 'International entrepreneurship: The intersection of two research paths', *Academy of Management Journal*, **43** (5), 902–6.

Meyer, J.W. and B. Rowan (1977) 'Institutionalized organizations: Formal structure as myth and ceremony', *American Journal of Sociology*, **83** (2), 340–63.

Meyer, John W. and Richard W. Scott (1983) *Organizational Environments: Ritual and Rationality*, Beverly Hills, CA: Sage.

Meyer, K. and M. Gelbuda (2006) 'Process perspectives in international business research in CEE', *Management International Review*, **46** (2), 143–64.

Meyer, K. and M.W. Peng (2016) 'Theoretical foundations of emerging economy business research', *Journal of International Business Studies*, **47** (1), 3–22.

Meyer, K. and A. Skak (2002) 'Networks, serendipity and SME entry into Eastern Europe', *European Management Journal*, **20** (2), 179–88.

Miller, Gary J. (1992) *Managerial Dilemmas: The Political Economy of Hierarchy*, Cambridge: Cambridge University Press.

Mintzberg, H. (1978) 'Patterns in strategy formation', *Management Science*, **24** (9), 934–48.

Mintzberg, H. (1987a) 'The strategy concept I: Five Ps for strategy', *California Management Review*, **30** (1), 11–24.

Mintzberg, H. (1987b) 'The strategy concept II: Another look at why organizations need strategies', *California Management Review*, **30** (1), 25–32.

Mintzberg, Henry (1994) *The Rise and Fall of Strategic Planning*, New York: Free Press.

Mintzberg, Henry, Quinn, James B. and Sumantra Ghoshal (1995) *The Strategy Process*, London: Prentice Hall.

Mintzberg, H. and J.A. Waters (1985) 'Of strategies, deliberate and emergent', *Strategic Management Journal*, **6** (3), 257–72.

Mitchell, Clyde (1973) 'Networks, norms and institutions', in Jeremy Boissevain and Clyde Mitchell (eds), *Network Analysis: Studies in Human Interaction*, The Hague: Mouton, pp. 15–35.

Monroe, Kent B. (1991) *Pricing: Making Profitable Decisions*, New York: McGraw-Hill.

Morgan, Robert M. (2000) 'Relationship marketing and marketing strategy: The evolution of relationship marketing strategy', in Jagdish N. Sheth and Atul Parvatiyar (eds), *Handbook of Relationship Marketing*, London: Sage, pp. 481–504.

Morgan, R.M. and S.D. Hunt (1994) 'The commitment-trust theory of relationship marketing', *Journal of Marketing*, **58** (3), 20–38.

Myrdal, Gunnar (1968) *Asian Drama: An Inquiry into the Poverty of Nations*, vols I–III, New York: Twentieth Century Fund.

Nabli, M.K. and J.B. Nugent (1989) 'The new institutional economics and its applicability to development', *World Development*, **17** (9), 1333–47.

Nakos, G. and K.D. Brouthers (2002) 'Entry mode choice of SMEs in Central and Eastern Europe', *Entrepreneurship Theory and Practice*, **27** (1), 47–63.

Nelson, Richard and Sydney Winter (1982) *An Evolutionary Theory of Economic Change*, Cambridge, MA: Harvard University Press.

Normann, R. and R. Ramirez (1993) 'From value chain to value constellation: Designing interactive strategy', *Harvard Business Review*, **71** (5), 66–77.

North, Douglass C. (1990) *Institutions, Institutional Change and Economic Performance*, Cambridge: Cambridge University Press.

North, Douglass C. (2005) *Understanding the Process of Economic Change*, Princeton, NJ: Princeton University Press.

North, Douglass C., Wallis, John J. and Barry R. Weingast (2009) *Violence and Social Orders: A Conceptual Framework for Interpreting Recorded Human History*, New York: Cambridge University Press.

Oliver, C. (1991) 'Strategic responses to institutional processes', *Academy of Management Review*, **16** (1), 145–79.

Oliver, C. (1997) 'Sustainable competitive advantage: Combining institutional and resource-based views', *Strategic Management Journal*, **18** (9), 697–713.

Orton, J.D. and K.E. Weick (1990) 'Loosely coupled systems: A reconceptualization', *Academy of Management Review*, **15** (2), 203–23.

Ostrom, Elinor (2005) *Understanding Institutional Diversity*, Princeton, NJ: Princeton University Press.

Oviatt, B.M. and P.P. McDougall (1994) 'Toward a theory of international new ventures', *Journal of International Business Studies*, **25** (1), 45–64.

Owusu, R.A., Sandhu, M. and S. Kock (2007) 'Project business: A distinct mode of internationalization', *International Marketing Review*, **24** (6), 695–714.

Owusu, R.A. and C. Welch (2007) 'The buying network in international project business: A comparative study of development projects', *Industrial Marketing Management*, **36** (2), 147–57.

Park, S.H. and Y. Luo (2001) 'Guanxi and organisational dynamics: Organisational networking in Chinese firms', *Strategic Management Journal*, **22**, 455–77.

Parvatiyar, Atul and Jagdish N. Sheth (2000) 'The domain and conceptual foundations of relationship marketing', in Jagdish N. Sheth and Atul Parvatiyar (eds), *Handbook of Relationship Marketing*, Thousand Oaks, CA: Sage, pp. 3–38.

Pava, M.L. and J. Krausz (1997) 'Criteria for evaluating the legitimacy of corporate social responsibility', *Journal of Business Ethics*, **16** (3), 337–47.

Peck, Helen, Martin, Christopher and Moira Clark (1999) *Relationship Marketing: Strategy and Implementation*, Oxford: Butterworth-Heineman.

Peng, Mike W. (2000) *Business Strategies in Transition Economies*, Thousand Oaks, CA: Sage.

Peng, M.W. (2003) 'Institutional transitions and strategic choices', *Academy of Management Review*, **28** (2), 275–96.

Peng, Mike W. (2009) *Global Strategy*, 2nd edn, Cincinnati, OH: South-Western Cengage Learning.

Peng, M.W., Sun, S.L., Pinkham, B. and H. Chen (2009) 'An institution-based view as a third leg for a strategy tripod', *Academy of Management Perspectives*, **23** (3), 63–81.

Peng, M.W., Wang, D. and Y. Jiang (2008) 'An institution-based view of international business strategy: A focus on emerging economies', *Journal of International Business Studies*, **39** (5), 920–36.

Penrose, Edith T. (1959) *The Theory of the Growth of the Firm*, Oxford: Basil Blackwell.

Peralta-Álvarez, M-E., Aguayo-González, F., Lama-Ruiz, J-R. and M.J. Ávila-Gutiérrez (2015) 'MGE2: A framework for cradle-to-cradle design', *Dyna rev.fac.nac.minas*, **82** (191), 137–46.

Peterson, M.F. (2016) 'A culture theory commentary on Meyer and Peng's theoretical probe into Central and Eastern Europe', *Journal of International Business Studies*, **47** (1), 33–43.

Pfeffer, Jeffrey and Gerald R. Salancik (1978) *The External Control of Organizations*, New York: Harper and Row.

Porter, Michael E. (1980) *Competitive Strategy: Techniques for Analysing Industries and Firms*, New York: Free Press.

Porter, Michael E. (1985) *Competitive Advantage: Creating and Sustaining Superior Performance*, New York: Free Press.

Porter, Michael E. (1986) 'Competition in global industries: A conceptual framework', in Michael E. Porter, (ed.), *Competition in Global Industries*, Boston, MA: Harvard Business School Press, pp. 15–60.

Porter, Michael E. (1990) *The Competitive Advantage of Nations*, New York: Free Press.

Porter, M.E. (1991) 'Towards a dynamic theory of strategy', *Strategic Management Journal*, **12**, 95–117.

Porter, M.E. (1996) 'What is strategy?' *Harvard Business Review*, November–December, pp. 61–78.

Porter, M.E. (2000) 'Location, competition and economic development: Local networks in a global economy', *Economic Development Quarterly*, **14** (1), 15–34.

Post, J.E., Preston, L.E. and S. Sachs (2002) 'Managing the extended enterprise: The new stakeholder view', *California Management Review*, **45** (1), 6–28.

Powell, W.W. (1990) 'Neither market nor hierarchy: Network forms of organization', *Research in Organizational Behaviour*, **12**, 295–336.

Powell, Walter W. and Paul J. DiMaggio (eds) (1991) *The New Institutionalism in Organizational Analysis*, Chicago: University of Chicago Press.

Prahalad, C.K. and Yves L. Doz (1987) *The Multinational Mission: Balancing Local Demands and Global Vision*, New York: Free Press.

Prahalad, C.K. and G. Hamel (1990) 'The core competence of the corporation', *Harvard Business Review*, **68** (3), 79–91.

Prahalad, C.K. and G. Hamel (1994) 'Strategy as a field of study: Why search for a new paradigm?' *Strategic Management Journal*, **15**, 5–16.

Putnam, R.D. (1995) 'Bowling alone: America's declining social capital', *Journal of Democracy*, **6** (1), 65–78.

Pye, Lucian W. (1985) *Asian Power and Politics: The Cultural Dimensions of Authority*, Cambridge, MA: Belknap Press.

Quinn, James B. (1980) *Strategies for Change: Logical Incrementalism*, Homewood, IL: Richard D. Irwin.

Redding, S.G. (1980) 'Cognition as an aspect of culture and its relation to management processes: An exploratory view of the Chinese case', *Journal of Management Studies*, **17** (2), 127–48.

Redding, S. Gordon (1990) *The Spirit of Chinese Capitalism*, New York: De Gruyter Studies in Organization.

Redding, G. (2005) 'The thick description and comparison of societal systems of capitalism', *Journal of International Business Studies*, **36** (3), 123–55.

Redding, Gordon (2008), 'Separating culture from institutions: The use of semantic spaces as a conceptual domain and the case of China', *Management and Organization Review*, 4 (2), 257–89.

Regnér, P. and J. Edman (2014) 'MNE institutional advantage: How subunits shape, transpose and evade host country institutions', *Journal of International Business Studies*, **45** (3), 275–302.

Reid, S.D. (1981) 'The decision-maker and export entry and expansion', *Journal of International Business Studies*, **12** (2), 101–12.

Ring, P.S. and A.H. Van de Ven (1994) 'Development processes of cooperative interorganizational relationships', *Journal of Management Review*, **19** (1), 90–118.

Rugman, A.M. (1980) 'Internalization as a general theory of foreign direct investment: A re-appraisal of the literature', *Weltwirtschaftliches Archiv*, **116** (2), 365–79.

Rugman, Alan M. (1981) *Inside the Multinationals: The Economics of Internal Markets*, New York: Columbia University Press.

Rugman, A. (1986) 'New theories of the multinational enterprise: An assessment of internalization theory', *Bulletin of Economic Research*, **38** (2), 101–18.

Rugman, Alan M. and Joseph R. D'Cruz (2000) *Multinationals as Flagship Firms: Regional Business Networks*, New York: Oxford University Press.

Saka-Helmhout, A. and M. Geppert (2011) 'Different forms of agency and institutional influences within multinational enterprises', *Management International Review*, **51** (5), 567–92.

Sandberg, S. and H. Jansson (2014) 'Collective internationalization: A new take off route for SMEs from China', *Journal of Asia Business Studies*, **8** (1), 29–42.

Scherer, Frederic M. (1971) *Industrial Market Structure and Economic Performance*, Chicago: Rand-McNally.

Scott, W. Richard (1983) 'The organization of environments: Network, cultural, and historical elements', in John W. Meyer and W. Richard Scott (eds), *Organizational Environments: Ritual and Rationality*, Beverly Hills, CA: Sage, pp. 155–75.

Scott, W.R. (1987) 'The adolescence of institutional theory', *Administrative Science Quarterly*, **32** (4), 493–511.

Scott, W. Richard (1994) 'Institutions and organizations: Toward a theoretical synthesis', in W. Richard Scott and John W. Meyer and Associates, *Institutional Environments and Organizations: Structural Complexity and Individualism*, Thousand Oaks, CA: Sage, pp. 55–80.

Scott, W. Richard (1995/2008) *Institutions and Organisations*, 1st/3rd edn, London: Sage.

Selznick, Philip (1957) *Leadership in Administration*, Evanston, IL: Pow, Peterson.

Seo, M.G. and W.E.D. Creed (2002) 'Institutional contradictions, praxis, and institutional change: A dialectical perspective', *Academy of Management Review*, **27** (2), 222–47.

Sharma, D.D. and A. Blomstermo (2003a) 'A critical review of time in the internationalization process of firms', *Journal of Global Marketing*, **16** (4), 53–71.

Sharma, D.D. and A. Blomstermo (2003b) 'The internationalization process of born globals: A network view', *International Business Review*, **12** (6), 739–53.

Shenkar, O. (2001) 'Cultural distance revisited: Towards a more rigorous conceptualization and measurement of cultural differences', *Journal of International Business Studies*, **32** (3), 519–35.

Sheth, Jagdish N., Gardner, David M. and Dennis E. Garrett (1988) *Marketing Theory: Evolution and Evaluation*, New York: John Wiley & Sons.

Sheth, J.N. and A. Parvatiyar (1995) 'The evolution of relationship marketing', *International Business Review*, **4** (4), 397–418.

Sheth, Jagdish N. and Atul Parvatiyar (2000) *Handbook of Relationship Marketing*, Thousand Oaks, CA: Sage.

Shi, W. (Stone), Sun, S.L., Yan, D. and Z. Zhu (2017) 'Institutional fragility and outward foreign direct investment from China', *Journal of International Business Studies*, **48** (4), 452–76.

Sjöstrand, Sven-Eric (1985) *Samhällsorganisation. En Ansats till en Institutionell Ekonomisk Mikroteori* [Organization of Society. Towards an Institutional Micro-economic Theory], Lund: Doxa.

Sjöstrand, Sven-Eric (1997) *The Two Faces of Management: The Janus Factor*, London: International Thomson Business Press.

Snehota, Ivan (1990) *Notes on a Theory of Business Enterprise*, Department of Business Administration, Uppsala University (dissertation).

Soda, G., Usai, A. and A. Zaheer (2004) 'Network memory: The influence of past and current networks on performance', *Academy of Management Journal*, **47** (6), 893–906.

Stoffels, John D. (1994) *Strategic Issues Management: A Comprehensive Guide to Environmental Scanning*, Oxford: Pergamon.

Stopford, John M. and Louis T. Wells Jr (1972) *Managing the Multinational Enterprise*, New York: Basic Books.

Suchman, M.C. (1995) 'Managing legitimacy: Strategic and institutional approaches', *Academy of Management Review*, **20** (3), 571–610.

Tallman, Stephen B. and George S. Yip (2001) 'Strategy and the multinational enterprise', in Alan M. Rugman and Thomas L. Brewer (eds), *The Oxford Handbook of International Business*, Oxford: Oxford University Press, pp. 317–48.

Teece, D.J., Pinsano, G. and A. Shuen (1997) 'Dynamic capabilities and strategic management', *Strategic Management Journal*, **18**, 509–33.

Terjesen, S., Hessels, J. and D. Li, (2013) 'Comparative international entrepreneurship: A review and research agenda', *Journal of Management*, **42** (1), 299–344.

Terpstra, Vern and Kenneth David (1985) *The Cultural Environment of International Business*, Cincinnati, OH: Southwestern.

The Economist (1998) 'Emerging country market indicators', The Prince of Wales Business Leaders Forum, Responsible Business in the Global Economy, Financial Times Guide Number One.

Treviño, Linda K. and Kate A. Nelson (1999) *Managing Business Ethics*, New York: John Wiley & Sons.

Tsai, T.S.H. and J. Child (1997) 'Strategic responses of multinational corporations to environmental demands', *Journal of General Management*, **23** (1), 1–22.

UNCTAD (2005) *Trade and Development Report*, New York: United Nations.

UNCTAD (2018) *World Investment Report: Investment and New Industrial Policies*, Geneva: United Nations.

United Nations (1987) *Our Common Future*. Report of the World Commission on Environment and Development.

United Nations (2015) *Transforming Our World: The 2030 Agenda for Sustainable Development*, A/RES/70/1, United Nations.

Uzzi, B. (1996) 'The sources and consequences of embeddedness for the economic performance of organizations', *American Sociological Review*, **61** (4), 674–98.

Van der Heijden, Kees (1996) *Scenarios: The Art of Strategic Conversation*, Chichester: John Wiley & Sons.

Van Wijk, Raymond, Van Den Bosch, Frans A.J. and Henk W. Volberda (2004) 'Knowledge and networks', in Mark Easterby-Smith and Majorie A. Lyles (eds), *Handbook of Organizational Learning and Knowledge Management*, Oxford: Blackwell, pp. 428–53.

Vargo, S.L. and R.F. Lusch (2004) 'Evolving to a new dominant logic for marketing', *Journal of Marketing*, **68** (1), 1–17.

Vernon, R. (1966) 'International investment and international trade in the product cycle', *Quarterly Journal of Economics*, **80** (2), 190–207.

Visser, M. (2003) 'Gregory Bateson on deutero-learning and double bind: A brief conceptual history', *Journal of History of the Behavioral Sciences*, **39** (3), 269–78.

Visser, M. (2007) 'Deutero-learning in organizations: A review and a reformulation', *Academy of Management Review*, **32** (2), 659–67.

Wernerfelt, B. (1984) 'The resource based view of the firm', *Strategic Management Journal*, **5**, 171–80.

Westney, Eleanor D. (1993) 'Institutionalization theory and the multinational enterprise', in Sumantra Ghoshal and Eleanor D. Westney (eds), *Organization Theory and the Multinational Corporation*, New York: St. Martin's Press, pp. 53–76.

Whitley, R. (1990) 'Eastern Asian enterprise structures and the comparative analysis of forms of business organization', *Organization Studies*, **11** (1), 47–74.

Whitley, Richard (1992a) *European Business Systems: Firms and Markets in Their National Contexts*, London: Sage.

Whitley, Richard (1992b) *Business Systems in East Asia: Firms, Markets and Societies*, London: Sage.

Whitley, R. (1994) 'Dominant forms of economic organization in market economies', *Organization Studies*, **15** (2), 153–82.

Whitley, Richard (1999a) *Divergent Capitalisms: The Social Structuring and Change of Business Systems*, Oxford: Oxford University Press.

Whitley, R.D. (1999b) 'Competing logics and units of analysis in the comparative study of economic organization', *International Studies of Management and Organization*, **29** (2), 113–26.

Whitley, R. (2003) 'The institutional structuring of organizational capabilities: The role of authority sharing and organizational careers', *Organizational Studies*, **24** (5), 667–95.

Whittington, Richard (2001) *What Is Strategy – and Does It Matter?* London: Thomson Learning.

Wilkinson, I. and L.C. Young (1994) 'Business dancing – The nature and role of interfirm relations in business strategy', *Asia-Australia Marketing Journal*, **2** (1), 67–79.

Williamson, Oliver E. (1975) *Markets and Hierarchies: Analysis and Antitrust Implications*, New York: Free Press.

Williamson, O.E. (1979) 'Transaction-cost economics: The governance of contractual relations', *Journal of Law and Economics*, **22** (2), 3–61.

Williamson, O.E. (1981) 'The modern corporation: Origins, evolution, attributes', *Journal of Economic Literature*, **19** (4), 1537–68.

Williamson, Oliver E. (1985) *The Economic Institutions of Capitalism: Firms, Markets, Relational Contracting*, New York: Free Press.

Williamson, O.E. (1991) 'Strategizing, economizing and economic organization', *Strategic Management Journal*, **12**, 75–94.

Williamson, O.E. (2000) 'The new institutional economics: Taking stock, looking ahead', *Journal of Economic Literature*, **38** (3), 595–613.

Wilson, D. and R. Purushothaman (2003) 'Dreaming with BRICs: The path to 2050', Global Economics Paper, no. 99, Goldman Sachs (https://www.gs.com).

Wong, Y.H. and Thomas K.P. Leung (2001) *Guanxi: Relationship Marketing in a Chinese Context*, New York: International Business Press.

Wong, Y.H. and J.L.M. Tam (2000) 'Mapping relationships in China: Guanxi dynamic approach', *Journal of Business and Industrial Marketing*, **15** (1), 57–70.

World Bank (2002a) *Transition: The First Ten Years: Analysis and Lessons for Eastern Europe and the Former Soviet Union*, Washington, DC: World Bank.

World Bank (2002b) *World Development Report: Building Institutions for Markets*, Oxford: Oxford University Press.

Wright, R.W. and A.R. David (1994) 'Trends in international business research: Twenty-five years later', *Journal of International Business Studies*, **25** (4), 687–701.

Yip, George S. (1992) *Total Global Strategy: Managing for Worldwide Competitive Advantage*, Englewood Cliffs, NJ: Prentice Hall.

Zadek, Simon (2001) *The Civil Corporation*, London: Earthscan.

Zahra, S.A. (2005) 'A theory of international new ventures: A decade of research', *Journal of International Business Studies*, **36** (1), 20–28.

Zou, S. and T.S. Cavusgil (1996) 'Global strategy: A review and an integrated conceptual framework', *European Journal of Marketing*, **30** (1), 52–69.

Zou, S. and T.S. Cavusgil (2002) 'The GMS: A broad conceptualization of global marketing strategy and its effect on firm performance', *Journal of Marketing*, **66** (4), 40–56.

Index

action network 125, 133, 159–60, 162, 172–5, 177, 198, 277, 280
    business development group 126
    capture team 159–60, 167–9, 174–5, 220
    project management team 159, 173, 175
    tracking team 159–60, 166, 173–4, 220
actors–resources–activities (ARA) model 93, 129, 132
acquiesce (IMS) 251–2, 257, 268–70, 273–5
    comply 93, 251–2, 257, 269–73, 275, 288–9
    habit 251–2, 257, 269–70
    imitate 251, 257
aftermarket 152
after-sale services 112, 139, 168, 172, 183, 197
agency problem 93–4, 218, 302, 322, 325–6
agency theory 214, 323
agent 73, 75, 81, 143, 152, 179, 181, 185–6, 191, 193–7, 203, 208
aid organization 143–4, 163–4, 166
Alfa Laval 182
American institutional economist 312
analysis mode (external institutional context)
    inside-out 223, 239–40
    outside-in 223–4, 239
analysis stage (external institutional context)
    explanation 224, 231, 238, 243
    identification 224–6, 243
    prediction 224–6, 238–9

Angola 59–60
anthropology theory 11, 312
Argentina 34–5, 49
arm's length network 121, 124, 139
Asia Pacific Economic Cooperation (APEC) 29
Asian financial crisis 29–30, 33–4, 48
Association of South East Asian Nations (ASEAN) 29, 33, 48
Atlas Copco 182
audit 268, 271, 273–4
Australia 26, 40–41, 52, 64, 129
authority
    formal 124
    patriarchical 307
    political 235
    relation 235
    role 234–6
avoid (IMS) 251–2, 257, 271, 273–4, 286–8, 307
    buffer 251–2, 287
    conceal 251–2, 271, 274, 287
    escape 251

Bangladesh 58–9
bargaining power 66, 263, 287
basic institutions model 13, 21, 106, 202, 206, 208, 210–11, 218, 221, 223–5, 235, 244, 248, 260, 310
basic networks model 13, 20, 106, 120, 126–7, 135–6, 202